The author lives in a cabin in the hills of Northern California surrounded by meadows and forest. It is very much like what she had imagined as a little girl growing up in Manhattan. She lives with her husband and her adult son, who suffers from schizophrenia, and works locally in a small community clinic.

This book is dedicated to all who suffer from mental illness and their loved ones, who also feel the burden and the heartache.

Indigo

DANCING WITH CHAOS

AUSTIN MACAULEY PUBLISHERS™

LONDON • CAMBRIDGE • NEW YORK • SHARJAH

A CIP catalogue record for this title is available from the British Library.

ISBN 9781528926904 (Paperback)
ISBN 9781528964876 (ePub e-book)

www.austinmacauley.com

First Published (2019)
Austin Macauley Publishers Ltd
25 Canada Square
Canary Wharf
London
E14 5LQ

Heartfelt thanks to all who helped me along the way.

Bread

This is about my son who went crazy. He was talking to magazine covers, but refused to talk to me.

He was living in a group home for severely disturbed children.

We could not talk; we could not share. We could not plan.

Home passes were like having a small, wild animal in the house.

Would he throw a chair, jump out of the car, break the fence?

And what exactly is the proper etiquette to respond to fence breaking?

a) Ask him to fix it? b) Fix it oneself? c) Let the broken fence lie there to remind you of your broken heart? or d) Wash the broken fence away with your river of tears?

Thus, I went to the library like any good academic.

But there was no book on responding to violence in your own home. Searches revealed nothing.

No parenting text explained how to avoid being hit with a stick: Dodge the stick? Take the stick? Remove all sticks from the house?

Stick, fence, chair, window—I missed my child.

The chasm between us had grown so deep.

One day after enduring his rage, I went to bake some bread. My old son, the well one, had always liked my cooking.

I handed him a piece of fresh warm bread.

He looked up at me, suddenly completely back in his body, with soul attached. "Thanks, Mom," he said and took the bread.

A poem by my nursing instructor Anita, about her son.

Prologue
Making Sense of Madness

Recently, I received an email from a NAMI representative in Seattle Washington. It read, "At this point you are an advocate for your son. Don't give up; you must stay the course."

I found these words to be extremely helpful. So often these days, I find myself feeling discouraged and confused. But this was a simple enough concept to embrace. Naturally, I must 'stay the course'. I must persist and do what I can to see that this nightmare has as positive a resolution as is possible.

If you're not familiar with NAMI, and if your life has not been touched—or shall I say ripped apart—by mental illness, you might not be; NAMI stands for National Association for the Mentally Ill. This is the second time they have offered me assistance, reassurance and emotional support at a time of crisis with my son. The first time was several years ago on New Year's Day. At that time, my son was 23 years old. He was still living at home and working for a friend, doing a variety of handy things that paid fairly well. Shannon was usually easy going, usually cheerful, and he had a good sense of humor. If it weren't for the fact that he raced around the country roads at break neck speeds getting numerous speeding tickets and citations, as well as complaints from neighbors, I would have considered him an easy child. In general, I was glad for his company—glad that he was still living at home with me. I had heard it said that in Italy, boys lived with their mothers until they were married, whatever the age. It seemed like a good and natural arrangement, especially with the economy these days. As for me, I had just gotten accepted into a master's program and was planning to do a combination of long distance learning over the internet along with an intermittent commute to class – four hours' drive from my home. In addition, a good friend, at a local rural clinic, had agreed to be my preceptor for my two years in the Family Nurse Practitioner Program. I was very excited, kind of scared, not daring to believe that I would actually reach my goal. It had taken a little planning to set things up to get ready for the classes. I had to have a satellite dish installed so that I could get the internet classes when they were broadcast. I purchased a good laptop computer and a printer. Then I set my bedroom up to second as a study, with the desk set at just the right angle to the window, to allow for good light but not too much glare and a view of the forested hillside that wrapped around the canyon, interspersed with patches of open meadow and a vast amount of sky beyond.

The first few months of the program, I had to be in class a couple of days almost every week. I was starting to precept in clinic as well, a couple of days per week. In addition, I was trying to keep up with my 12-hour shifts as a registered nurse at the local hospital because I simply could not support myself for the next two years without working. Life was pretty hectic. The days were full. I wasn't home very much and when I was at home, I was up in my room doing pages and pages of homework, reading medical books and writing case studies on the patients that I was seeing at the clinic.

Even now, several years later, I can work myself up into a state of despair remembering in vivid detail the moment when I realized that something was very wrong. I had recently come to the conclusion that Shannon was not ever going to be a mainstream type of guy. He was probably not going to go to college. He wasn't going to have that 9–5 job, Monday through Friday, with a good retirement plan. He wasn't going to fit my expectations in these ways, but he was going to be okay. He was going to be Shannon; a very good guy who marches to the beat of his own drum and is perfectly content with his life. I imagined him having a family and a little home in the country. Having a sweet and simple life surrounded by people who loved him. I still try and visualize this life for him, although more and more it seems like an unattainable dream. I remembered back to the time when he was 19. He had just graduated H.S. One summer's day, he asked me for gas money so that he could drive out to the coast—a 40-minute-drive on winding, narrow roads. I thought about it for a moment and then said, "You can have $5.00 for gas if you take out the garbage."

"No," he had simply replied. "I don't feel like it." Of course I refused to give him the money and still he got in his car and drove away. A couple of hours later, he had hitch hiked home and was calling around until he found a friend who would bring a gas can, drive him to town, buy him gas and then take him back to his car where he had run out of gas on his way to the coast. This worried me. *Defiance disorder*, I thought. Later, when he got his third speeding ticket in two weeks, it worried me. 'Obsessive compulsive' was the diagnosis that I contemplated this time. But mostly he was just a regular, good-natured guy who acted like a teenager and was, in fact, a teenager. Several times I had tried to get him into counseling, but always he had refused to go. By the time he was 23, however, I had decided that, whatever path he decided to take, he was a good guy and he would be okay.

My feeling of alarm was of the visceral kind where you feel like you are about to be very ill. You feel like any minute you will start sobbing but you can't let that happen because once you begin, you will never stop. Shannon had been spending more and more time in his small 8x8 room in his loft bed, basically isolated from the world except for the little skylight that let in a triangular patch of the sky, a small rectangular window by his bed with a view of the driveway so he could see who was coming or going, and a transistor radio/CD player that he had rigged to run off of the big house batteries so he could listen to music in bed. He was eating very little and had stopped bathing. I was not home that much and it took me a while to realize that he had not left his room or changed his cloths in several days. I feared that he was on drugs. How I hoped that it was that simple. The little window by his loft bed was just below my bedroom window. On those warm, early autumn days, we both kept our windows open. That morning the sound of Shannon's voice engaged in a long, rambling conversation drifted in through my open window. I wondered if one of his friends had come in without my hearing or if he was on the phone. I couldn't quite get the words but he would pause every once in a while as if listening for a response and then start laughing hysterically as if he were talking to someone who was very, very funny. I went down stairs and saw that the phone was still on the receiver. Hᵉ did not have a phone in his room. I knocked on the door. "Who are you talking t

I asked, although deep down inside I knew the answer. No one else was in the room. There was no one there; no one but the voices in his head. Voices that for some sense of self-preservation he would not admit to until almost three years later when he could finally admit to me that the voices were 'killing him'.

Not that I was in any manner new or naive to the chaotic and painful world of the mentally ill. Not that I hadn't, all my life, made concessions and come to some sort of grudging terms with the driving force of mental illness. I had even managed to come to terms with the uncompromising, irrational and inescapable chaos that mental illness in a loved one forces upon one's life as if you were repeatedly tossed into wildly churning rapids without a life jacket and told to swim for your life or, as another parent put it, "as if you were repeatedly being knocked down and run over by a Mack truck." I remembered back to the time when I first realized that the often irrational and sometimes bizarre behavior of my mother as well as our erratic life, that I had always taken for granted, was a consequence of severe mental illness. Again, I remembered the alarm bells going off in my head, at 27 years old, when my father, whom I hardly knew, told me that someone was planting radioactive plutonium in the dashboard of his car. I remembered the shock and grief I felt the night I was on duty at the hospital and answered the phone at the nurses' station to be told that my father had just committed suicide. And then, there it was again. I remembered the terror I felt one night when I was seven months pregnant and the father of my children had a psychotic break. I got so scared that I started to go into labor and had to be driven down the hill, late at night, to the local hospital where I worked as a nurse. In the urgency of the moment, John had managed to clear enough to get me and our sleepy four-year daughter into the car and down out of the hills, but as we got close town, he started laughing uncontrollably again; the loud evil laugh of the demons that, he claimed, had taken over his soul. Once at the hospital, surrounded by the safety of my night shift buddies, my labor stopped and I was able to carry the pregnancy to the relative safety of 37 weeks gestation, but I could never again return to my home. Somehow, with the passage of time, I had managed to make peace with the past and move on. But this was the worst, more painful than I could ever have imagined. The next day as I had stood at the window, helplessly watching my handsome, sweet, young son in the prime of his youth, griping his head in his hands as he paced back and forth in front of the house like a caged animal, ripping his hair out of his head, trying to silence the demons in his mind, I had understood all too well what was happening to him. The world had suddenly turned, for him, into a frightening and incomprehensible place. "Stay the course," that is what the NAMI president had said. "Stay the course," and I totally agreed. "Stay the course," but where, for the love of God, was my compass!

As I lay in bed that night, unable to sleep, a despairing sadness had swept over me. At the age of 16, I had walked away, leaving my mother to navigate her madness alone. Fourteen years later, seven months pregnant and as big as an elephant seal, I had walked out on my baby's father, grateful to be able to separate myself from his psychotic delusions that had turned our life into a waking nightmare. Now, here was my son, so young and still so innocent, his illness ripping both of our lives apart, but this time there was no leaving. I wanted to hold him in my arms like I did when he was a baby and comfort him, stop the madness, quiet the voices in his head with the shear strength of my love, but that was not possible. In his delusional mind, he viewed me as a threat. I had become the enemy. He would not let me near, but neither could I leave. I could not comfort him, but I could not walk away. I could only stand by watching, and the pain of it was almost more than I could bear. I understood what I must do. I must maintain a vigil and steer the ship to safety, but the waters were turbulent and treacherous, the boat had lost its rudder, we were lost in the storm, and I had no compass.

My mind struggled to comprehend, to make sense of a life once again being ravaged by the effects of mental illness. Many times, I had wondered what was wrong with me that my life was so often in a state of turmoil. What was I doing to create so much chaos? Like someone suffering from Post-Traumatic Stress Disorder, flashbacks from the past began to surface with their attendant emotions of fear, despair, confusion, and pain. Suddenly, it dawned on me that this was the very nature of mental illness. Like a tornado, mental illness, out of control, tore apart everything in its path, and like a tornado, mental illness was unpredictable and an act of nature. It was not something which its victims could choose or not choose. As I lay there in the dark, wondering if I had lost my son forever, wondering how I could possibly survive this, I began to see that in a way my life had always been a struggle for equilibrium, a journey that had at its very core a quest for harmony amidst disorder. I had recently read somewhere that often people go into medicine to heal themselves. Although it had not been something I had consciously thought about, it made sense. I realized that my work, my home, spiritual endeavors, and even my travels had, in one way or another, all been part of a search to find beauty and harmony in a life so often set off-balance by mental illness. As I watched the full moon rise up over the hills, its light spilling over the trees and into the room, memories began unraveling before me in a crooked, tangled path, like a ball of twine gone wild.

Part One
Troubled Times with Blanche

Chapter 1
Good Night, Irene

Blanche was born in New York City, in 1923, just three years after the 19th amendment was enacted, which gave women the right to vote. My mother had very little contact with her family after she left home. As a result, I only knew the bits and pieces of her background that I had managed to gather over the years, that Blanche's father was from Greece, that her mother was from Austria and that my grandmother, in order to please her new husband, had learned to cook the Greek dishes that my grandfather had enjoyed in his homeland. Her parents had come, separately, to America from Europe, landing at Ellis Island in the early 1900s. It intrigued me to learn that I was only 2nd generation American born. Gary Gerstle wrote of the immigrants arriving at Ellis Island: "Understand that America is God's crucible, the great melting-pot where all the races of Europe are melting and re-forming. Here you stand, good folk, think I, when I see them at Ellis Island, here you stand in your fifty groups, your fifty languages, and histories, and your fifty blood hatreds and rivalries. But you won't be long like that, brothers, for these are the fires of God you've come to, these are fires of God. A fig for your feuds and vendettas! Germans and Frenchmen, Irishmen and Englishmen, Jews and Russians, into the Crucible with you all! God is making the American."[1]

Blanche's parents married and had four children; a boy and three girls. Settling down to raise their family, they had continued many of their own special customs and practices that they had brought with them from the 'old world' while also learning and assimilating the customs of their new country. By the time I arrived on the scene, however, no traces of the old word culture could be found in Blanche. My mother was not interested in any of the old world customs or religious practices. She had melted in and what emerged was a modern American woman. In fact, much of her cultural preferences had been assimilated from what she had learned from watching the great American cinema. Greta Garbo, Ingrid Bergman, and Lauren Bacall, and not her immigrant parents, were her cultural mentors.

My mother was six years old when the stock market crashed, on the day known as 'Black Tuesday' in October of 1929. Her immigrant family was poor and struggled, like so many others during the Great Depression, to keep a roof over their head and food on the table. Then, in 1939, World War II began, which marked the end of the 'Great Depression' but brought a threat to world order and peace like no other previously experienced. I have no doubt that growing up in such turbulent times could have had an adverse effect on Blanche's mental stability, but her brother

---

[1] Gary Gerstle, American Crucible; Race and Nation in the Twentieth Century, Princeton University Press, 2001, p. 51.

and sisters had all ended up doing well with stable jobs, stable marriages, and stable home lives. There didn't seem to be any serious mental illness among them. I learned, years later, that when my mother was in high school, her family had been very worried about her. She had gone through a period of time, they said, where she had kept to herself in her room for days on end and would not speak to anyone or leave the house. It was, I believe, the onset of her illness. Shannon's onset was like a *déjà vu* of my mother's.

When she left home, Blanche moved to Manhattan, hoping to get a start in theater while her sisters and her brother moved to the suburbs in nearby boroughs to start families. They could have lived on the other side of the planet for how often she saw them. I don't think they even knew where to find my mother most of the time, but every once and a great while, she would resurface. Once, when she had made contact after 20 years of silence, they told me how happy and surprised they had been to see her. They had thought for sure that she was either dead or somewhere locked up in a mental hospital.

My mother once told me that when she was a young girl, something very bad and frightening had happened to her in the basement where she went to school. She could never quite recall what it was that happened, but nothing had ever seemed quite right to her after that. In 1949, she met my father, Joe. She was 26 years old.

Joe was a young man with some frightening memories of his own. He had been stationed at Pearl Harbor during Japan's attack. According to my mother, on that fateful day, my father had been manning radio communications and had stayed at his post while bombs exploded all around him. Later, he had endured the tortures of the Bataan Death March. As a prisoner of war, he had been taken to Japan to the Kamioka POW Camp where he survived against impossible odds and under unbearable conditions. It had an unsettling effect on me, years later, to find his name on a POW camp roster. There was so much that I would never understand about my father. I remembered how, a couple of weeks after I had been notified that my father had just died from taking a large overdose of aspirin, too many to have been an accident, a man had walked into the ER where I was working the late night shift. He was having a heart attack. Working as I did, late at night with very little staff and no doc in the house, I had always, in the back of my mind, dreaded the possibility that someone would walk into the ER about to die. I helped Mr. M., who was having severe chest pain, shortness of breath and was sweating profusely, into a wheel chair and then on to a gurney. I notified the doc and immediately began instituting standing orders. I took vital signs, put him on oxygen at four liters by mask and gave him sublingual nitroglycerine. To my great relief, the IV went in easily. It was always a good idea to start an IV early because it was so much harder to start one when the patient had gone into shock and all the veins were collapsed and everyone was frantic. Next I ran an EKG, which verified that he was having an acute event by the hugely elevated ST segment. Since Mr. M. was still having some chest pain, I pushed IV morphine, but just a touch, because I didn't want to run the risk of bottoming out his blood pressure. It was all he needed. By the time the doctor arrived, Mr. M. was comfortable and the color that had drained from of his face was slowly returning. Over the next few nights, as Mr. M. recuperated, we became friends. We talked about my father. Mr. M. had also been a survivor of the Bataan Death March. "Don't be too hard on your father," Mr. M had said as I straightened his blankets one night. "Those of us who managed to survive the Death March and then the prison camps were never the same. The torture and brutality we experienced changed us all. There was no one among us who could go back home and lead a normal life after what we had been through."

My father had told me that during the 'Death March' he was so weak from starvation and sickness and from the heat that he could hardly stand, but somehow, he had managed to keep moving along. "Anyone who stopped on the side of the road to rest was shot or stabbed to death," he had said. "Both sides of the road were flowing with blood and the bodies of dead soldiers were everywhere."

When the war ended, Joe had returned home to his folks to try and recover what he could of a normal life. My father told me years later, when I had traveled to Texas to introduce him to his little granddaughter, that when he came back from the war, his mother had cried out in despair, "Why couldn't it have been your brother returning from the war? Why couldn't it have been you who died instead?" This alone had almost killed him.

Once Joe had recovered somewhat, he had come to Manhattan 'to take singing lessons' my mother had told me. "Your father had wanted to be a singer when he was a young man, and he wanted to experience the culture and excitement of New York City." When he met Blanche, he courted her and she fell completely in love with this good looking, guitar playing southern man who serenaded her nightly with love songs. My mother liked to tell me about how he would sing *"Good Night, Irene"* to her when they would part at night. That song held special meaning for her. Two decades later, she would still sometimes sing it, in a sweet voice, with a faraway wistful expression on her face, lost in thought about what had been, as well as what might have been. He was the only man that Blanche had ever slept with and the unplanned result was me. When my father found out that she was pregnant, he went back home to a little town on the Texas panhandle called Borger. "Blanche, don't you worry. I'm just goin' home to pick up some papers," he had told her. "When I get back, I'm going to marry you." He never did 'get back'. And nothing ever was quite right for my pretty mother who had these episodic moods and dark thoughts that kept her life in a state of upheaval.

Chapter 2
First Memories

Steadily and persistently, the rain ran down the windowpane in narrow little rivulets that gathered in pools on the sill, like so many teardrops. Without warning, two policemen had come to our door and taken us out into the cold and moonless night. My mother went to jail, I later understood. And me they took to a jail of another sort. I remember being led into a dimly lit room with eight or ten cots all in a line against one wall and being told to take off my cloths and get into bed. Obediently, I climbed in at the foot of the bed, understanding nothing of what was happening, naked, turning away from the stranger child asleep at the other end of the bed. I lay there in the darkness very still, not daring to move, listening to fitful breathing and whimpers in the night. To my three-year-old mind, this prison-like place for motherless children was a heartless and despairing place, with just the insistent patter of rain for comfort.

Looking back, it seems to me that, at that early an age, there was no evaluation, no judging, just a helpless feeling of being blown about like a leaf in the wind, and a certain innocence that protected one from being broken by the fall. The days that followed were a blur. I remember standing in the yard shivering with the cold, watching the other kids running around playing. It reminded me a little of the nursery school I went to, which I also hated. I was always so unhappy being separated from my mother, and I didn't make friends easily. Instead, I stood off to the side, alone, feeling isolated and abandoned. There, at nursery school, I could at least go home at the end of the day. Here, there was no consolation.

By my fourth birthday, my mother was out of jail, and Jim had moved in with us. When we first met Jim, he was living in the same building as we were. The pay phone, on the second floor landing, was next to Jim's room. In the evening, when the phone would ring, Jim would come out of his room, with his cat following close behind, to answer the phone. I too started going out when the phone would ring because he was a very nice man and I liked his kitty. Pretty soon my mother started meeting with us on the second floor landing, and we would all sit together on the stairs talking, the kitty purring contentedly in my lap. This was a very sweet time for all of us, sitting on the carpeted steps in the dim light, enjoying one another's company. My mother was worried because she was having a difficult time coming up with the rent so one evening, Jim suggested, "Blanche, why don't I give up my room and move in with you and Julie and I'll pay the rent?" It seemed like a good idea, and so before long we were living with Jim who, with all his good natured, drunken charm, had won my young heart.

It was wonderful having Jim in our life. I wanted to go with him everywhere he went. Usually, he would let me go along as I raced down the street after him, my coat still in my hand, too much in a hurry to put it on, yelling "Jim, Jim, wait for me." More often than not, he was headed to the corner bar, to the 'White Rose'. It was a dark and rowdy place that reeked of beer and urine, but it was a home of sorts for many a drinking man. It was definitely Jims' home away from home. I too was happy there. His friends were always so jovial and friendly – drinking ale, buying me coke with a cherry in it, telling me amazing stories and giving me pointers on life's little, important lessons. "Sometimes a man doesn't want a beautiful woman," Mickey, Jims' best friend at the 'White Rose', was saying one Saturday afternoon when we were discussing beauty standards. "Sometimes, a man just wants a woman that he can feel comfortable with, sit around in his shorts, and watch the ball game on T.V. with. That's going to be easier to do with a woman who isn't so good looking."

"Hmm, I'm going to remember that," I had replied thoughtfully, noisily sucking the last of the soda up through the straw and into my mouth.

When we were at the 'White Rose', Jim liked to talk politics with his buddies. Our Jim was a working class rebel. He hated the government, and politicians, and he raved, at times, about the all mighty dollar and how everyone was so corrupted by it. "This is their god," he would say, sounding disgusted and rubbing his fingers together to indicate money. Communism was a big threat at the time, and Jim talked a lot about the communists. I don't think that Jim approved of them either. I remember seeing people carrying signs saying, 'Better Dead than Red', and it frightened me a little, although I didn't really understand it. I didn't like it when Jim talked politics. Jim was very good natured and I loved that about him, but when he was talking about politics, he became loud and angry. At times, he would go on and on for hours, in a bitter monolog, screwing his face up into a sneer, and shaking his fist in the air at some invisible politician. Blanche was politically much more conservative, and I wonder, looking back, if politics wasn't fodder for some of the bitter arguments that happened later.

The months that followed were precious for their harmony and simplicity. The kitty had a litter of kittens and then there were six or seven furry darlings stumbling around the house. My mother and I both stayed at home now, and so I no longer had to put up with separation anxiety on a daily basis or the bullies at Nursery School who liked to tease me and sometimes pinched me to make me cry.

On Sundays, we tried to get out and do something together. Jim washed windows for a living. During the weekdays, he worked long, hard hours hanging out of high story windows by a leather belt with his squeegee and bucket of hot soapy water nearby. Saturdays he spent drinking with his buddies at the 'White Rose'. But on Sundays, he liked to get dressed up in his one and only suit with the tie rakishly loose and the top buttons of his shirt undone. Over this he put on his long, chocolate brown, woolen overcoat, topping it all off with a stylish hat right out of a Humphrey Bogart Movie. Jim was 29 years old then and very handsome. He was lean and muscular with a strong build, and he had flaming red hair and sky blue eyes. Blanche also liked to get dressed up. When she was in a good mood, she could be exceedingly gracious and charming. As a young woman, in her early 20s, she had wanted to be an actress. To demonstrate her talent for acting, she liked to repeat a line from a Katherine Hepburn movie. She would say, holding her head high and with a bit of British accent, "The cala-lilies are in bloom again, such a beautiful flower." Barefoot, Blanche stood 5 ft. 1 in. tall. She always wore classy spike heels to make her look taller and bright red lipstick to accentuate her full, sensual lips. With those two accessories, she looked good in anything that she chose to wear. I thought that my mother was beautiful. If you were to look really critically, you might say that her one flaw was her longish nose and sometimes she made jokes about it. But she had a fine, shapely figure, large brown, almond-shaped eyes, and curly brown hair that sprung naturally in tight ringlets all around her pretty face. As for me, on one of his paydays, Jim had taken me downtown to Macy's department store where he bought me a beautiful red wool coat with a double row of shiny buttons and this I wore, with pride, on our outings. Together we would go, all dressed up, for long walks in Central Park, a crisp frost on the ground and our breath making wisps of fog in the air as we spoke. As winter gave way to the gentler breezes of spring, we would sometimes go down to the Statin Island Ferry. Then, for only a nickel, we would ride across the rough grey waters holding hands with the salty spray in our faces, watching the N.Y.C. skyline receding into the twilight sky. Such times were touched, blessed one might say, with amber glows and tender companionship.

Then, one day, the fighting began. I didn't know what it was all about, but then I didn't listen. I shut out the yelling and the angry words, in any way I could. I pressed my hands tightly over my ears, and ran the faucet on full force while reciting, out loud, the nursery rhymes I had learned, *"All the kings' horses and all the kings' men couldn't put Humpty Dumpty together again."* When all this didn't work, I would go out of our one-room flat, closing the door behind me, and sit on the steps with a kitty in my lap, waiting for the fighting to end and peace to be restored. Such were my first early attempts at creating peace and harmony where there was discord. One day the fighting ended because Jim had moved out.

From the very beginning, my mother set the pace of our erratic existence as Urban Nomads. In rapid succession, we moved around the city from one tenement or cheap hotel to the next. Sometimes we moved by choice, but many times we were chased out into the street by an irate landlord who hadn't received the rent in weeks. Looking back, I can see how this pattern was a symptom of my mother's illness but at the time it seemed normal. It was all I had ever known. When I started first grade, we were on welfare, living in a large, drafty tenement building. Each section of the building had its own bathroom and kitchen for ten or more apartments to share. Our bathroom had a jagged broken window above the tub. The winter wind whipped in through that broken window, making us shiver as we stood there under the tepid little stream of water. To make matters worse, from some of the tenement windows, anyone bothering to look could see us there, naked in the shower. It made me uneasy to think that someone might be watching. We got in and out as fast as we could. The kitchen too was awful. It was filthy and it smelled of rotting food. The only window was blackened from years of cooking grease and the kitchen was poorly lit, making it easier for the roaches and rodents that lived there to hide. It was a scary place, especially at night. We avoided using these facilities, storing our rationed block of surplus American cheese on the windowsill in the winter. The surplus powdered milk that tasted so much like cardboard in a glass, at least needed no refrigeration. I was afraid to go out to the bathroom alone so if I had to pee, my mother would have me use the tiny sink that was in our room. At night, she too was afraid to go out to the bathroom in the hall so she also would use the sink, hoping that her weight would not break it loose from the wall.

It seems odd to me that while some of these early memories are still so vivid in my mind, I remember very little about my mother in those early years. I think it's because she kept to herself so much of the time. She never had any friends except for Jim, and she was turned inward a lot, spending most of her waking hours living somewhere inside of her head. Consequently, I was allowed a lot of freedom. I spent most of my waking hours running about the neighborhood with my friends, in this way escaping some of the day-to-day drudgery of the tenement and learning, at an early age, to be independent and self-reliant.

Although we didn't live with Jim, he was still in our life, and sometimes on the weekend, he would visit and take us out to the movies. How I looked forward to those times when we were all together!

Chapter 3
The Neighborhood

When my mother could stand the tenement no longer, she managed to break free of her apathy and, in a burst of resourcefulness, changed our circumstances in a very positive manner. She found us an inexpensive but very pleasant room that was spacious and clean, in an old brownstone, a block from Central Park. It was a bright and cheery room. The windows, starting close to the floor and going almost to the ceiling, let in streams of light that rested crosswise on the wooden slats of floorboard. Our only furniture was a table, a couple of chairs and a double bed that my mother and I slept in together. That was normal for us. We always had just one bed which we shared. It was a comfort to snuggle up to my mother in the night. She always slept with her back towards me and so I would press my cheek and chest against her back and wrap my arm around her petite waist. We would sleep that way, like a couple of puppies, the warmth and closeness adding a sense of security to an otherwise unpredictable existence. The block too was clean and tidy, lined with a neat row of brownstone houses and with splashes of greenery every so many feet, where a tree had been planted to break up the monotony of grey concrete. I think my mom was pretty content there, for a while anyway. We were on welfare so she didn't have to worry about where the next meal was coming from or about being evicted.

There was a sweet little private school across the street with a homey atmosphere and somehow, in a stroke of genius, my mother talked them into letting me attend on kind of a scholarship. So there I was, starting 2nd grade, going to school with rich kids and child models and even Patty Duke was going there, I was told, although I never saw her. I always imagined that she was too busy to attend school, off somewhere instead making movies. Everyone was very nice to me at that private school. For one thing, I was very well behaved. I was quiet and shy and pretty much kept to myself. I learned quickly too and seemed to fit in at school even if after school my life was very different from that of my peers.

The neighborhood was a very colorful place. Downstairs on the ground floor lived a guy—at least I thought he was a guy—but then he told me that he was really a girl. His, or her, boyfriend was Mr. Clean. Yes, I didn't believe it either, until I met him. But then, there he was muscles, bald head, earring and all, Mr. Clean. Next door to us lived a very ancient, tiny, wrinkled, old woman named Floe. I thought she was kind of scary. Although I'm sure she was perfectly harmless, she reminded me of the wicked old witches in the fairy tales that I loved so much. There was one other tenant on our floor and she was very different from any one that I had ever known. I really liked her. She was friendly, very pretty, and decidedly sexy. Jim loved Brigitte Bardot movies, and he had taken us to see a few so I knew what sexy looked like. One day, our neighbor had run out into the hallway dressed only in a man's white button down shirt that came to the top of her shapely thighs. As she excitedly bent over the stair railing to see who was coming up to visit her, I could see that she wasn't wearing any under panties. The picture of her shapely behind bursting out from under the white shirt reminded me, exactly, of Brigitte Bardot. When she got a job as a salesgirl in a department store, she celebrated by buying me a lovely school outfit. It was a stylish schoolgirl, red plaid, pleated skirt and my very own white, button down shirt.

There were lots of other kids on the block too. I became good friends with a couple of Puerto Rican girls. One girl, Yolanda, was my age. She lived across the street from me and we often played together on the sidewalk outside of her house. She had an older brother who always seemed to be keeping an eye out for her. Sometimes, a group of us kids from the block would get together and we would play catch or double-dutch jump rope or hide and seek or some other fun game that I had never heard of before. Everyone was always sure to include me and I thrived on the feeling of belonging. Then there was the pretty teenage girl who lived down the street. She kind of took me under her wing. She had a large Puerto Rican family with brothers and sisters, a mom and a dad and even aunts and uncles. Whenever I had dinner with them, I always loved the way they would all sit down together to eat, everyone chattering and teasing each other and having a good time. "Con mucho gusto," they would say. It was such a welcome contrast from my silent, introverted life with my mother.

One Sunday afternoon when it was too cold to play outside, Yolanda came over to visit. "Why don't you go to the movies?" my mother suggested. "I have enough money. The Sunday matinee is only a dollar." I think that my mother wanted to be alone with her thoughts so she handed us the money and sent us off. She seemed relieved that we were leaving. There was a new Brigitte Bardot movie playing in a theater about eight blocks from our house. It was kind of an adventure all by itself just making our way across the huge, busy intersections to get to the movie theater. Every time we came to a big street crossing, we would wait, anxiously, for the light to turn green. Then, holding hands, we would run as fast as we could, giggling the entire way, until we were safely across and back on the sidewalk. The movie theater was almost empty. I liked having the theater to ourselves and watching Bardot. I was such a fan. When she came, half-naked, out of the bedroom and hungrily devoured her breakfast because her busy active night had left her famished, I totally understood the implications. But in the end, it turned out to be a poor choice on my part. I don't think Yolanda really enjoyed the movie and she got into big trouble over it. My mother didn't seem to think that anything was out of the ordinary but Yolanda's mother was furious and it was quite some time before she was allowed to play with me again.

Graduation from 2nd grade was a memorable event. Unfortunately, I was sick with a sore throat and a hacking cough but nothing short of being in a coma was going to stop me from participating. The event took place in downtown Manhattan in a fancy hotel. The other kids arrived in limos and private cars that were parked by valets in grey uniforms with red trim, just waiting to serve. My mother and I took the subway. The entire school was there (maybe a hundred kids) and their families, all dressed up. Each grade had their moment on stage. Our 2nd grade class had a little skit in which I stood up and sang C…A…T: cat. It was a wonderful moment, the thrill of which could not even be diminished by the high fever I was developing.

After I said my little part, my mother took me home. "You're really sick," she scolded as I started coughing so violently that I threw up in the street. "We shouldn't have come out." I was now officially in 3rd grade, but as it turned out, it was the last that I would be attending school for quite some time.

As the early summer days grew hot and muggy, my mother grew more distant and moody. She became frightened easily, and she didn't trust anyone. She started saying things that didn't make any sense to me. One day my mother told me that our pretty neighbor, who I liked so much, was stealing all her money. "That's why we're so poor that we can hardly afford to eat," she told me. Her face was hard and set and her arms were folded across her chest. She was fuming over the injustice. I was certain that it wasn't true, and it made me uneasy to think that she could believe such a thing. I had seen her this way before, but I had never understood what was happening. Not that I really understood anything now either, but now I at least understood that something was not right. When my mother stopped leaving the house to go to the store, our food supply began to dwindle. Still it was summer, and I carried on, business as usual, hanging out in the hood with my friends. I was accustomed to doing whatever I pleased, whenever I wanted, so it surprised me one morning when I had announced that I was going to visit Yolanda and my mother burst out with, "No, you can't go."

"Why can't I go?" I asked, thinking that she looked scared. I began fidgeting with my hands. I didn't want to look at her.

Her reply startled me, "They are going to try and poison you when you go over there."

I could tell that this was a very real fear for her, but I just couldn't take it that seriously. It was a ridiculous idea. "Of course they won't poison me," I stammered. "They're nice people. I'm not worried. I'll be back in a while." I started towards the door.

My mother put out a hand to stop me; she pressed harder. "No, Julie, you mustn't go. I won't let you. It's not safe."

We stayed locked together in the room all that day. There was no telephone and not really anyone to call. We were alone together, in our own private nightmare. There wasn't any food, and by nightfall I was really hungry and beginning to feel scared. I fell asleep that night curled up in a fetal position, watching my mother who had a haunted, withdrawn look about her. I'm sure she didn't sleep at all that night. By the next morning, she was crazy scared, so scared in fact that I caught her fear. I could feel it taking hold of me with an iron grip, seeping under my skin, quickening my breathing, and setting my nerves on edge. My heart was racing. My mouth was parched and dry but I wasn't thirsty. Our friendly, familiar neighborhood now seemed like a threatening and dangerous place. The weather too conspired to create an atmosphere of doom. The sky was grey and overcast, and thunderclouds rumbled ominously in the distance. It must have been a Sunday because the streets were deserted except for the occasional lone passerby to whom my mother would assign some dark, sinister significance. "Do you see that man in the black suit?" she demanded. "He's been stealing my checks, and now he is going to kill us."

I didn't reply. It didn't make that much sense to me but, nevertheless, I felt frightened. My mother dragged the big table over to the door and pushed it tightly under the door handle as a barricade. She put one of the chairs on top of the table for added security. Then she got out our biggest, deadliest looking kitchen knife and put it on the chair. It sat there, the blade gleaming under the florescent light, a constant reminder of the violence that lay in waiting for us. The very sight of it made me feel more afraid. The day wore on, the seconds ticking slowly by, in painful suspense. We took up our post by the window watching the street, anxiously, for signs of danger. By late afternoon, my mother saw a man that she knew, and she yelled out the window asking him to please come up and get us. We were terrified to open the door but we simply couldn't stay locked together in that room forever. With a friendly face on the other side of the door, at least we would have a chance.

Once out on the street, we were momentarily relieved to be out of the room, but we quickly discovered that we didn't feel any safer. There was nowhere to go that felt safe. We walked and walked aimlessly through the city, afraid of every shadow. Late into the night, we walked the streets, frightened by every passerby and every dark entranceway, glancing furtively behind us every few steps, certain that we were being followed. Every noise made us jump and cry out in fear. At one point, my mother got way ahead of me. The night was dark with clouds obscuring the moon, the city was silent. I felt alone and very vulnerable. I quickened my steps to catch up. Frightened, not watching where I was walking, I suddenly tripped and landed on top of a man who was lying unconscious on the sidewalk in a puddle. I couldn't tell if he was drunk or dead. In that instant, when I was down sprawled out on top of this stranger, I had a flashback to when I was really young, two or three. Then too, I had been struggling to catch up with my mother who had gotten way ahead of me on a deserted subway platform when I tripped and fell on some man that was passed out in a puddle. My mother, hearing my screams, had walked back to pull me up off of the body. That night we were just returning home from the Emergency Room because I had managed to spill a cup of scorching, hot coffee down my arm. I remembered how my arm was freshly bandaged and how I was frantically trying to keep my burnt arm, with its crisp white bandages, out of the dark puddle that was spreading out from under the man who lay motionless beneath me. Now too I was screaming, and the very sound of my screams frightened us. I struggled to get myself up and backed away, horrified from the body that I had just been laying on top of. My clothes were damp now, and I shivered in the early morning coolness. I couldn't tell if I was shaking from fright or from being cold. We walked on in tense silence. We were walking on the razor edge of panic, ready to flee, screaming at the slightest provocation. Then, as the sky began to almost imperceptibly lighten, a strange thing happened. The lighter it got, the less frightened we became until at dawn we had enough courage to go home to bed where we collapsed gratefully into oblivion.

To this day I still have an irrational fear of the night, and I must admit that some other traumatic incidents have happened to me over the years to solidify that fear. I mean I actually like the night. I find it soothing. I love the night sky, and the quiet of the night, but only if I am not feeling vulnerable. If I am alone, I seldom feel comfortable in the darkness. I know it's ridiculous but that knowledge does not change the feeling that I am in eminent danger. Of course the media doesn't help, and I certainly can't understand people's fascination with violence. There is so much cruelty in the world, and that is no delusion. I'm not sure what exactly all of my mother's fears were; they were very real for her, but there is certainly enough cruelty in the world to create a culture of fear if we let it. But then again, it seems like a terrible waste to live in fear of the dark when one could instead be blissfully entranced by the solitude and stillness of the night.

Chapter 4
، A Fact of Life

We slept like the dead for almost 24 hours, and when we awoke, my mother was refreshed and in good spirits as if nothing had happened. "We can't live in this neighborhood any longer," she informed me. "We're not safe here. We have to move as soon as possible." She immediately got busy finding us a new place to live. Within days, we were closing the door on yet another chapter of our life and walking away from the hood. I was enthusiastic about this move though, not only because my mother seemed to be feeling so much better but because I was going to have my very own bedroom for the first time in my life. In addition, Blanche had quit welfare; she had gotten a job as a waitress, and Jim was going to move in with us. We were going to be a family again.

Much to my disappointment, Jim didn't move in with us, and the joy of having my own room was definitely tempered by the fact that I was now spending long hours every day sitting in the nice apartment all alone. The rent on our lovely little apartment was high. Blanche couldn't afford the rent by herself unless she worked 40 plus hours a week. I don't think she liked leaving me alone that much and it was a strain for her to work those long hours on her feet every day. The kitchen was in the basement and so she spent the entire day walking up and down steep, narrow steps, carrying heavy plates, wearing her high-heeled shoes. One afternoon, a large group of people came in for lunch. It was an office party. They took up two tables and they all had complicated orders that they wanted just so. They were loud and cheerful and demanding. To listen to my mother tell it, I can't say which was harder on her; the fact that her feet hurt and that she was overwhelmed by so many complicated orders being yelled at her at once, or the fact that these people seemed to be so happy and were having so much fun. Either way, demurely and without further ado, my mother removed her apron and walked out smack in the middle of the order.

After a couple of weeks without paying the rent, we were forced to leave. We had no choice but to try and get a hold of Jim. There was no one else to turn to. It was a Saturday, so not even the Welfare offices were open. We tried calling the White Rose, and to our great relief, Jim was there. It was probably a good thing that Jim was a little intoxicated because otherwise he might have been angry with us. As it was, he came in a good mood, picked us up in a taxi, and took us to his place which was to be our new home.

We had never been to this place where Jim was living, and we didn't know quite what to expect. I was curious and even a little excited. He lived in an old Brownstone, and I imagined that it might be a little bit like our cute little room in the hood. As we walked up the four flights of steps to our new home, I felt happy. Nothing could have prepared me for the site before me when I finally peered over the threshold. The room was so tiny. Against the left wall there was a sink and a dresser, a small cot, and a big, filthy, stuffed chair, in that order. They were all shoved up together against the far wall, an arm of the chair resting just under the windowsill on one side and pressed up against the cot on the other. Against the right wall was a small table with a two-burner hot plate on it that was shoved up against a straight-backed chair that was shoved up against a desk that was next to the window. There was less than a two-foot isle between the furniture on the left side of the room and the furniture on the right side of the room. It was so small and so crowded that I wasn't even sure that we could, all three of us, fit in the room at the same time. However that was, by far, not the worst of it. As my eyes took everything in, all I could think of was how I would never step even a foot in that room, for every inch of the four walls was covered with the brown spattered entrails of thousands upon thousands of cockroaches. I looked over at Jim. He smiled a kind of blurry smile. How could he know or would he even care about the tempest that the site of all those dead roaches set off in my soul. I was terrified of cockroaches and now I was being asked to live in the middle of, what appeared to be, their breeding grounds. Without entering the room, I went back to the staircase and sat down, buried my head in my hands and began to cry. No one offered me much sympathy. It was a fact of life that I was just going to have to deal with. There was nothing that could be done about it now.

All through the hot and humid New York City summer, the three of us slept on that cot, my mother and I with our heads next to the chair and Jim at the other end with his feet in our faces. The big stuffed chair was where the cockroaches seemed to live. I got somewhat used to them, though, and would turn on a flashlight at night and watch them pour out from under the cushion after the lights were off. I didn't sleep very well, however, because I could not stop dwelling on the story that Jim had told me about how they liked to eat the skin at the base of your eyelashes once you were asleep. He had read it in a science magazine and he even cut the article out to show me. Finally, Jim took pity on me though. He couldn't get the chair out of the doorway without taking the door off, and so early one morning, he just broke the chair into pieces and threw them out of the window. I slept much better after that.

For a time, my mother tried her hand at home-schooling me and so I made great advances in learning to read. After that, many pleasant hours were spent lost in a book, forgetting completely about my surroundings. However, during the heat of the day, it was often unbearable to be in that room. On those days we spent a lot of time in Central Park. Sometimes, when the city held its heat all night, the three of us would go to the automat at 4 a.m. and sit there enjoying the air-conditioning until it was light. Then Jim would go off to wash windows and my mother and I would go spend the day in the Park.

Every Friday, Jim got paid. Usually, by mid-week he was broke, and by Wednesday or Thursday we were out of food so there would be no food for a day or so until Friday afternoon when Jim came home with his paycheck. "What do you want to eat?" he would ask. "We can get whatever you want!" It was always like a little celebration, getting something especially good to eat when we were so hungry. Things were not so bad after all. There were books and Central Park, the chair was gone and really, we were all together and there was no fighting.

October brought welcome relief from the heat of the summer. The leaves in the park were turning a myriad of shades of brown and gold and purple. The autumn leaves fluttered down from the trees and spread out on the ground in a kaleidoscope of color. The kids had all gone back to school. The busy paths were now deserted. We had the playground to ourselves now, and it seemed a little lonely, the swings all hanging limp and the jungle gyms abandoned, the sprinklers gone dry. I missed the sound of kids laughing and mothers yelling at their children to be careful. As the days got cooler and then cold, it became less and less appealing to spend our days in the park. But it was so crowded in the room. Another problem was that there was no refrigerator and cooking was almost impossible on the little hot plate except to heat up a can of soup or boil water to make Jim his instant coffee which he drank black. Without being able to escape to the park all day long or cook a decent meal, it became clear that, once again, it was time to move.

This time we got a bigger room that had a kitchenette and its own bathroom in a hotel that had weekly rates. To help with the increase in rent, my mother decided to give it a try as a sales girl at the downtown Macy's department store. It was a classy store, and Blanche looked like a classy lady, with her high heels and red lipstick, so they hired her right away. It wasn't long before the three of us fell into a routine of sorts. You'd think that with Blanche and Jim both working, we'd have plenty of money, but we were as poor as ever because all the money that they earned went to feed our separate addictions. Every evening, after working all day hanging out of windows, Jim would come home and settle in with his bottles of ale. As he grew sloppy with his drunkenness, there would be the inevitable puddle of sticky ail drip dripping from the table drawing flies. There would be Jim, sweating profusely, mumbling half asleep, head heavy on his arms, arms weighted on the table, sticky with sweat and ail. My mother's new love, and what proved to be a lifelong addiction for her, was clothes. Every few days there would be a pathetic scene where she would come home from work and wait for Jim to fall into a drunken stupor. Then she would carefully sneak in the bags of new cloths she had bought that day at Macys and had stashed in the hallway so that no one would know. "Don't say anything to Jim," she would caution if she caught me watching her. For my part, I blocked out the world by watching T.V. from the minute I woke up in the morning until I closed my burning, weary eyes at night. The T.V. cost three dollars a day to rent and I begged, pleaded and cried if necessary, on a daily bases, for them to let me have my drug.

Chapter 5
Homeless

It was getting late in the day. We knew that we would have to get going soon or it would be too late. The Welfare office would be closed in a few hours, and then we would have no shelter for the night. It was the dead of winter with below-freezing temperatures. We couldn't be without shelter in such weather. As I hungrily wolfed down a piece of toast, I tried not to think about where we were going to spend the night. Now that we were out of our hotel room, there was no going back. We had stayed there in the room as long as we could but finally we had to leave, and when we walked out the door, we understood that we were leaving everything behind. In those days if you didn't pay your hotel bill, when you left the room, they would alter the lock so that you couldn't get back in and they would keep everything you owned. We knew this but there was nothing we could do about it.

My mother hadn't been able to hold on to her job for very long. It seemed like there was a recurring pattern. She would have short periods of time where she seemed to keep things together, to be fairly normal and even high functioning, but then some stressor would come along and everything would fall apart. After my mother lost her job, she started going out alone at night. She was being very secretive and evading our questions. We had no idea where she was going. One evening Jim followed her and found her on a park bench with some guy. He was furious. To his credit, he didn't get violent but he wasted no time. He stormed back to the room, packed up his few possessions and left. We had no money so we just hung out in the room until we were starving, and then we too walked out leaving everything we owned behind including all those pretty new clothes that my mother had stockpiled.

We sat there in the cafeteria knowing we should leave but it was so cold outside. The place was very drafty, and the stained, discolored table tops and tiled floor held no warmth, but we had some hot tea and we were reluctant to set out on what we knew was going to be a long weary ordeal. Just then, a man in rags, sitting a few tables away fell to the floor unconscious. His whole body was convulsing. A crowd gathered around him. "Call an ambulance," someone shouted.

A bystander tried to protect him from cracking his head open on the hard tile floor. He must have bit down on his tongue because blood was spilling out from the corner of his mouth. It was a frightening scene. I didn't understand what was happening.

"He's having a seizure," I heard someone say.

By the time the ambulance arrived, his seizure had subsided. A few of the people who had been looking on helped him, dazed, back up to his chair. We couldn't wait any longer; we had to go. Out in street, we pushed our way against a chilling wind to the downtown subway line. It felt like it was going to snow. Neither of us spoke.

We were miserable, cold, hungry, tired, scared. Things seemed to be as bad as they could get, and then they got a little bit worse.

The welfare office was packed with the city's poor and indigent. On one side of the room, a baby, wrapped in a thin blanket and cradled in its mother's arms, was screaming inconsolably while the little boy with snot dribbling out of his nose and down to his chin was sucking his thumb and whining as he tugged anxiously on her skirt. There was a row of chairs in the center of the room that were occupied by group of woman. The women were dressed like hookers in short, tight dresses and sheer stockings through which you could see their dark hairy legs. They sat together talking rapidly in some other language. I wondered what they were saying. Sitting across from them was a man with wild eyes and a long matted beard having a loud, animated conversation with himself. His speech was like 'word salad'. Although he was speaking English, nothing he was saying made any sense. Several young children chased each other around the room. One of them tripped and fell and started crying. A young mother rushed over and grabbed her child by one arm, scolding him as she dragged him away screaming. The other kids kept running in and out of the chairs. They bumped into a slow moving little old lady, almost knocking her over. The kids just kept on running and yelling at the top of their lungs. It was a cacophony of sound. The stark neon lights illuminated every stain on the shabby green walls, every sign of poverty and human suffering in that overcrowded room. The red nose and swollen belly of the alcoholic, the dark sunken eyes and glassy stare of the drug addict, the pale, sunken cheeks of the starving and of the old, and a dozen other miseries in bandages, on crutches and in wheel chairs, all cried out, as if with outstretched arms, pleading for someone, anyone, to help. Under such searing lights, there was no hiding; every one's misery was apparent. There were so many before us to be seen and it was so late in the day. Probably many of these people had a place to stay for the night. We did not. Then, just as we had feared, the announcement came over the loudspeaker that they were closing up shop for the day. Desperate, my mother went up to talk with one of the workers who was about to leave. The intake worker looked tired. She was a little cross at being delayed from heading home to her family after a long day surrounded by so much noise, bright lights and suffering. She looked at my mother and then at me. Wearily, she put down her satchel, pulled out a piece of paper, and wrote an address on it. "There is an office about 30 minutes from here by subway that stays open for another hour. If you hurry, you can catch them before they close, and they will give you a voucher for some food and a room for the night." Gratefully, we took the piece of paper and rushed out into the cold.

We hurried along the dark street down to the subway. It was rush hour. There were people everywhere, heading home at the end of the day. How I envied them. I imagined that each one of them was making haste to get home to a warm, cheery house and a hot dinner. I imagined that there were people waiting for them, who loved them and would be happy that they were finally home, safe and sound. There was a long line of people making their way through the turn style. There was just no way to hurry things up. We felt impatient as we heard a train stop and then pull away from the station and we hoped that it was not the train that we needed to take.

When we finally made it to the office where they had the vouchers, it was late and they were just closing up. There were three other people; a woman and two men, who had just arrived also and we were, all of us, desperate not to be sent out into the night with nowhere to go. Outside, a storm was developing. I think that at least one of the five of us would have perished that night if we had been left to sleep on the street. Instead of putting us out, they agreed to let us spend the night locked in the little foyer that was separated from the main offices by a series of doors. They shut off the heat and the lights, locked everything up and left us there sitting on the wooden benches that lined either side of the small room. The wooden benches were too hard and narrow for the adults to lie down on but I was able to curl up with my coat wrapped tightly around me and my head resting on my mother's lap. It was a huge comfort under the circumstances. Outside, the wind howled and wined. Great gusts of wind would hit without warning, sending debris flying down the sidewalk and rattling the heavy metal sign that hung from chains above the door. We were grateful for the shelter. The streetlights shone in dimly through the plate glass window, casting long, eerie shadows across the room and illuminating the faces of the five of us enough to show that we were a group of unkempt, hungry, and harmless misfits. None of us slept much that night. Besides my mother and I, there was an old man, dressed in a long tattered overcoat, who seemed a little slow in his thinking, like he was really not capable of caring for himself. He didn't say much; he just kept nodding, without a pause, as if his head were attached to his body by a spring. The other man, who looked to be in his late 50s, was an alcoholic whose life had been completely taken over and ruined by his addiction. Perhaps, like the ghost of Christmas future, this was a preview of where Jim was headed. The young woman in our group told us that she suffered from a severe seizure disorder and it kept her from being able to hold a job. I thought about the old man in the cafeteria who had lain shaking on the ground with the blood pouring out of the side of his mouth and my heart went out to her. The clock struck 2 a.m. as she told us about how her mother had been an alcoholic and because of this she had been born having seizures. "I grew up in foster care," she explained. "No one could deal with my seizures so I was shuffled from one foster home to another. Some were okay, some were terrible. I never belonged anywhere. No one ever loved me. No one ever even wanted me. I still don't belong anywhere. I have no one." When she was finished speaking, she looked away as if there was nothing more that could be said. The man with the drinking problem had a cheap bottle of ripple wine which he now passed to her in a gesture of friendship. Hungrily, she gulped down the bitter liquid. It was, after all, a way to forget. As each of them shared a little of their story, a common thread of loneliness and an absence of love could be found weaving through their sad tales. I glanced up at my mother who seemed to be in her own world; she was lost in thought. She was like that a lot of the time, distant, not really present, but every once in a while, she would say something that would make me feel like she really did love me. I remembered the time when she finally came to pick me up from the group home where I stayed after her arrest. One night, she just showed up to get me. "Your mother is here," the caretaker had told me. "Put on your clothes; she's taking you home." I couldn't believe it. My heart was about to burst. When I saw my mother, I started sobbing. I ran to where she stood, throwing my arms around her in a tight grip and holding on for dear life. I never again wanted to be separated from her.

"Oh, darling," she had exclaimed as she lifted me up. I held on to that one little "Oh, darling" because from those two words, uttered so spontaneously, I could tell that she cared.

My attention was drawn back to the man with the bottle of wine who was talking again. He too had a sad story to tell about how twenty years ago his wife, whom he had been very much in love with, had left him for another man. When he told the story though, he tried to make it seem funny and he succeeded in making us all laugh a little. As the night progressed, a feeling of camaraderie spread between us that was like a benediction and so the light of morning found us weary and disheveled but with the trace of a smile.

I rarely pass a homeless person now without thinking of that night. It's a known fact that many hard-working, minimum wage families live on the edge, just one paycheck away from living on the street. Anything, an illness, a lay-off, an injury, and they can become homeless overnight. In addition, a major portion of the homeless suffer from mental illness. That good old ethic that if you haven't got it together, it's because you are not working hard enough just doesn't apply to the mentally ill who often can't even get motivated enough to fix a meal when they are starving, let alone hold to a job. So many of the homeless are good-intentioned people who, for reasons beyond their control, find themselves on the fringe of society, wondering where their next meal will come from. There is a 2010 initiative, adopted by many of the states, to provide affordable housing to all who need it, but as I look around me and see the numbers of homeless growing, I doubt that we will ever reach that goal. With the inequalities as our society continues to foster, so many of us are vulnerable.

It must have been a time of heavy volume for the welfare office because they still didn't get to us the next day. It was Friday evening and everyone was packing up and rushing out, anxious to begin their weekend. This time we didn't make it to the voucher office in time. We were stuck. It would be two days, three nights, before the welfare office would open again and it had just started snowing lightly. There were so many people on the street that the snow, which was a little damp, did not have a chance to collect on the sidewalk and instead made kind of a muddy slush that soaked your feet if you weren't lucky enough to be wearing boots. The beautiful white flakes drifting down from the sky landed on our coats and then proceeded to melt and sink in. I loved the snow. I would have thought it a welcome sight had I not been so cold and damp. For some reason, my mother chose to sit, as if on display, at the top of the subway steps, fully exposed to the wind and snow and in the path of the people who were hurrying in and out of the subway. Perhaps she thought that some rich person would take pity on us and rescue us like in the play Pygmalion, where, on a bet, Professor Henry Higgins turns the poor flower girl Eliza Doolittle into a lady who could pass for a Duchess and in the process falls in love with her. It was a pretty fantasy. In fact, no one paid any attention to us at all. They just walked around us as if we were an inconvenience that they had to circumnavigate, a stonewall or some other inanimate object. It was really foolish for us to be sitting there, where we were so exposed to the elements. If we couldn't manage to stay dry, I didn't know what would happen. I thought of the story of 'The Little Match Girl'. If I froze to death here on the subway steps, would anyone care or even notice? It was a hard lesson in the indifference of strangers. The message I got that night was; "Look out for yourself because no one else really cares."

My mother and I were both shaking from the cold. We needed to get up and start moving and get somewhere where at least we could stay dry. I guess my mother finally got it that no one was going to rescue us. She surprised me by announcing, "I'm going to call the White Rose and see if Jim is there." After what had happened, I didn't think that Jim would ever talk to us again, let alone take us in. It is a tribute

34

to Jims' good heart that he could not leave us out there in the snow and perhaps, too, he missed us. He gave us his address and met us at the subway station. There are no words adequate to convey the great relief and happiness I felt at being warm and cozy and safe and once again with Jim. It was as if I had been holding my breath for an entire month and, finally, I could breathe again. For the remainder of the winter, we hunkered down, not interested in going anywhere. Jim had bought a cheap record player and a few opera records. We listened to Caruso and the operas La Traviata and Carmen. The powerful music echoed off of the high ceilings, enveloping the sparsely furnished room in crashing waves of melody and song. In the evenings, my mother and I read poetry out loud to each other and I spent much of the time contentedly lost in my books. It was a time of recovery and healing, but of course it didn't last.

Eventually and inevitably, the fights started again. One day, unexpectedly, my mother packed up our few belongings and we walked out on Jim. We went straight to the Paris hotel and checked in. We stayed there all week long, eating all of our meals in their fancy restaurant and swimming daily in their indoor, heated pool. There was a T.V. in the room and so we watched movies all day and all night. In spite of all of the luxury and entertainment, I was very depressed. I felt completely empty and desolate. My mother felt that way too, I think. We didn't talk much going about the days, more or less, in our own separate worlds. Finally, they realized that we weren't planning on paying and they threw us out. We retraced our steps back to Jim, and he let us in but then, the very next day, he packed up and left.

For the next couple of weeks, my mother and I hung out, trying to ration the little bit of food that Jim had left in the refrigerator, sleeping a lot and reading to pass the time. Every evening, we would get out the poetry book and over a hardboiled egg, a piece of toast and a cup of tea, our one big meal of the day, we would read poetry aloud to each other. The beautiful poetry certainly helped to sweeten the bitter memory of those days. *The Raven* by Edgar Allen Poe was a very favorite of mine and one that I almost invariably chose to read out loud.

"And the raven, never flitting, still is sitting, still is sitting.
On the pallid bust of Pallas, just above my chamber door;
And his eyes have all the seeming of a demon that is dreaming,
And the lamplight o'er him streaming throws his shadow on the floor;
And my soul from out that shadow that lies floating on the floor shall be lifted,
nevermore!"

It was the last stanza of the poem, and it blew me away. It was so sad and melancholy and so beautiful, all at the same time. It made my own misery seem as if there was perhaps a sad and melancholy beauty to it as well.

Falling right in step with the repetitive cyclic pattern that Blanche had established years ago, we were soon evicted. Without any apparent sympathy, a couple of policemen came and escorted us out into the street. I wondered what they were thinking, those two protectors of the people, as they walked away, leaving us standing there in the cold with nothing and nowhere to go. Once again we managed to get a hold of Jim at the White Rose and we followed him to the sanctity of his latest room on the top floor of an old brownstone building. Jim let us stay with him for that night and then he told us, emphatically, that we had to leave. Blanche couldn't believe it but, obediently, we left the room and went out onto the street. Without so much as a glance in our direction, Jim locked his door and went off to work. Then my mother completely lost it. I had never seen her so distraught. I stood there watching helplessly as she ran into the middle of the street screaming incoherently and flailing her arms wildly about. Traffic slowed. The cars had to come to a complete stop and then edge their way around her. A passerby stopped and asked me in a kindly voice, "What's wrong with your mother, little girl?"

I shrugged "We're homeless." I said sadly. I didn't cry though; it had become so familiar. Just then a taxi cab driver pulled over to the side of the road and got out to find out what was going on. Somehow between the Good Samaritan passerby and the Good Samaritan taxi driver, they managed to pack me and my mother, who was now sobbing uncontrollably, into the taxi and deliver us to the welfare office. That simple act of kindness brought wonderful results.

The last couple of years had been troubled years and lonely ones. We had moved so often that I had never managed to make any friends or get established at any school. Now the welfare office insisted that if they were going to help us, then Blanche had to enroll me in school immediately. Since I had been accustomed to reading to myself, as an escape with which to fill the empty hours, I read very well so they put me in a grade with other kids my own age. There was just two months left of fourth grade before the summer vacation. Enthusiastically, I threw myself into my schoolwork. With a new focus of a routine and study, I felt much happier. To be sure life still had its dramas but I didn't feel so isolated or alone anymore and slowly, over the next few years, I began to understand that the way of life that I knew was not necessarily the way one would want to, or had to, live.

Chapter 6
A Turning Point

I attended about six weeks of 4th grade, and then I had to stop going. My mother and I had found a very nice apartment in a good neighborhood about ten blocks from the school. It had a nice little kitchen, a good size studio and a bathroom. We couldn't pass it up even if it didn't have any furniture. It was the perfect place to live. We moved in with nothing but the cloths on our backs. We would be starting from scratch again. Our first night at our new apartment, we took the curtains off the windows for bedding and slept wrapped up in them on the floor. Oh, my, God! Those curtains were made from fiberglass. Over the next two days, every inch of our bodies became a bright red, burning, rash. I didn't leave the house for over two weeks and when I did, school was out.

That summer, Blanche decided that she wanted to be a poet. Little by little we fixed up our small apartment and made it comfortable. As we settled into our new home, my mother threw herself into writing poetry day and night. She took over the big table in the kitchen for her workspace. Head bent, she would pour over her papers and books for hours on end, totally consumed by the process. I think that it brought her a degree of peace to have her mind focused like that, on creating something beautiful.

When school started again in the fall, I automatically went back to the 4th grade class that I had been in the year before, figuring that since I had only gone for six weeks, I would have to repeat the year. That first day, I was a little late and the class was all settled in by the time I arrived. At lunch break, the teacher consulted her roster and said she couldn't find my name on it. "You'd better go check in the office and see what class you're supposed to be in," she advised. I had made a mistake. To my surprise and delight, I had been put on to the 5th grade and to the most advanced of the 5th grade classes at that. After getting everything straightened out at the office, I went up to my new classroom.

Hesitantly, I stood at the entrance of the class. The teacher, noticing me standing there, walked over to see what I wanted. "Can I help you?" she asked in a stern voice. I explained my mistake to her, feeling a little embarrassed. She looked me up and down and then she said to me, irritated, "If you're so stupid that you can't even figure out what class you're supposed to be in, then I doubt that you belong in my class."

Normally, I would have felt crushed by criticism so harshly delivered but, just then, I was feeling so happy that I was no longer in 4th grade and so incredibly pleased to be in an advanced class that I didn't pay it that much attention. I walked to the back of the classroom, sat down, folded my hands in my lap and waited for the lesson to begin. It was the one and only time that my teacher ever talked to me in that way.

One Saturday afternoon, I was home alone, doing my schoolwork when my mother burst into our apartment and slammed the door behind her. She looked about her wildly, her pupils black and dilated from fear. "I'm being followed," she whispered. She sounded scared. After double locking the bolt, she rushed over to the closet, threw open the door and flung aside the clothes. There was no one there. Next, she got down on her hands and knees and examined the space underneath the bed. "There's no one under there," she announced, this time sounding a little relieved. Once she had finished checking the kitchen and behind the shower curtain, she seemed to feel safer. I could see her tense posture and facial muscles relax a little. After a minute of staring off into space, she looked suspiciously around the room with her arms folded over her chest and her mouth set tightly. I knew this look. Her eyes settled on me. I had been standing there apprehensively, watching, wondering what would happen next. "You're not my daughter," she said accusingly, out of the blue. "Who are you?" she demanded to know.

The question caught me off guard. "What are you talking about, Mother? Of course I'm your daughter. Who else would I be?"

"You're a communist plant," she said, after a pause, like she was just now figuring it out. "You're here to steal my money. My check came in the mail today. You stole it and gave it to the communists! You don't even look like my daughter; my daughter is pretty, you're not." She was being cruel now and she seemed to enjoy it. "My poetry is being published and you're stealing all of my royalty checks," she added, almost shouting.

It hurt me deeply to hear her talk like that. I felt like I didn't recognize my mother either. But for me it was different. I knew that she was my mother. I just couldn't understand what was going on in her head. I doubted whether she had ever really known or loved me at all. Although I felt totally devastated, it was, in a way, a turning point for me, a moment of clarity. Suddenly, I knew beyond a shadow of a doubt that all of my mother's fears were and had always been, imaginary. I knew for certain now that there was no one following her, no one stealing her money, no one trying to kill her and I knew, for certain, that I was Julie, her daughter. It was an epiphany for me really. I suddenly understood how a person could create their own living hell simply by how they chose to view and interact with the world around them. The wisdom of Helen Keller came to mind. "Keep your face to the sunshine and you will not see the shadows."

"I choose the sunshine," I said to myself. It wasn't until years later when I was battling with the process of forgiveness and compassion that I began to understand that part of the tragedy of mental illness lies in the fact that those with severe mental illness are deprived of that freedom of choice. Because the very brain chemistry itself goes haywire, they become helplessly swept up in a current that leaves them no option for choosing. Vincent Van Gogh wrote in a letter to his brother, "As for me, you must know that I shouldn't precisely have chosen madness if there had been any choice."

Like all the other times, this episode too passed and things settled down once again. We didn't have to move this time and that, in itself, was a blessing. My mother seemed depressed though. She was unusually gloomy and withdrawn and hadn't worked on her poetry in weeks. She wouldn't talk about what was bothering her. I worried that I had, perhaps, done something to upset her. Then one evening, when Jim came over, Blanche started to cry. She cried and cried and she couldn't stop. My

38

mother actually didn't cry that often. If she did cry, it was because we were being evicted or didn't have any food or something like that. Neither of us had ever seen her crying her heart out for no apparent reason. I could tell that it disturbed Jim very much to see her like that. She looked so frail and vulnerable. Her thin shoulders were hunched over and shaking as she sobbed into her hands. "Blanche," Jim cried out. "Blanche, what's wrong?"

She just cried harder so Jim reached out and pulled her onto his lap. Cradling her in his arms, he rocked her gently like she was his baby. "Blanche, please don't cry," he pleaded. I was touched by the tenderness with which Jim held my mother. I had rarely seen a display of affection between them. It occurred to me now, for the first time I think, that Jim really loved my mother. Gradually, her sobbing subsided. Once she was able to calm down, she rested there, quietly, in Jim's arms for a while. Finally, Blanche smiled and it was the small, shy smile of a girl. She sat up and straightened her clothes. Suddenly, Jim pulled her face to his and their lips met. They began to kiss passionately. They stayed locked together in their embrace for several hours, sometimes kissing, sometimes stopping to talk to one another in a hushed whisper. I was relieved that my mother had stopped crying but I was also a little embarrassed at their new found intimacy. I retreated into my schoolwork in an awkward attempt to give them some privacy.

In the days that followed, Blanche seemed happy. She went around humming and rearranging the furniture in the apartment and she started writing her poetry again. As part of her furniture rearrangement project, she pushed our big double bed into the small kitchen. It looked kind of odd in there. If the sink and stove had been a little lower, you could have sat on the bed to cook and wash the dishes. But it did afford some privacy. The next time Jim came over, he spent the night and Jim and my mother slept together in the kitchen while I slept on the couch in the other room. The following morning, I saw Jim take a picture of Blanche with his Polaroid camera as she was naked, getting into the shower. He carried this picture in his wallet for years. My mother had, for Jim, replaced Brigitte Bardot.

With their new, budding romance, they tried going out on a couple of dates. Blanche decided to give it a go at the bar scene. She had never been much of a drinker and had never smoked cigarettes. Maybe she felt it would bring her closer to Jim if she tried these things. It was kind of a disaster. One night they came home late. Blanche was very ill. Jim and I were both very attentive to her as she curled up in fetal position with her arms around a bucket. She vomited repeatedly that night, and she looked so pale. "Oh, Julie, I'm so sick," she moaned.

In a way I was glad. I didn't want my mother smoking cigarettes and drinking the days away like Jim did.

Not long after that, Jim invested in an old 1949 Ford. On the day before Valentine's Day, unexpectedly, my mother and Jim picked me up after school. "Jim and I have decided that we are going to get married tomorrow," she announced. She was smiling her broadest, most sincere smile and her eyes were sparkling. I got into the car and just like that the three of us drove off to Maryland because, they said, they could get married there without any delay. They seemed very pleased because they had suddenly had this great idea to get married on Valentine's Day which, by the way, was also my birthday. I was happy for them but I wasn't having that much fun. The weather was stormy and it was a long, tedious drive. It was an odd wedding really, unromantic and the essence of poor planning. I stood there in the judges' chamber listening as they made their vows, a silent and invisible witness because my mother had declared that she had no children when she was filling out the marriage forms. Then we spent their honeymoon night freezing in the ford as we waited outside of a Western Union for one of Jims' White Rose buddies to wire us some money so we could put enough gas in the car to get back home to New York City. Surprisingly, the hours we spent freezing in the car, while it snowed outside, did not seem to put a significant chill on the pleasure the two of them derived from being newlywed.

Part Two
Coming of Age

Chapter 7
A Future Calling

It had been almost a year since that cold, snowy Valentine's Day when Jim and my mother had gotten married. I was in my first year of Junior High School. Jim still wasn't living with us, and Blanche had recently started working again. She had found a good job as a bookkeeper that was in walking distance from our apartment. That time when I was little, she had ended up in jail because she was a bookkeeper and she had been caught embezzling money from the company. The way my mother told it, they were really stealing her money and she was trying to outsmart them by stealing it back. However, somehow the judge had not seen it that way and it had taken her almost 10 years before she had the nerve to apply for a bookkeeping job again. She liked her job and her boss and the pay was decent. She seemed pretty happy, and Jim and my mother were busy making plans to find a place where the three of us could live together.

My focus in life had totally changed because now I had a best friend! It was an incredible experience, this sisterhood. Limping into the classroom on my first day of Junior High School, I had felt very nervous and awkward. Classes had actually started a week earlier but I was starting late because I had ended up in Children's Hospital for minor surgery on my foot after developing a planter wart that had grown down to the bone. Normally, we didn't go to doctors but I was in so much pain that I couldn't walk. I was in the hospital for several days. The things that I saw there made a deep impression on me. Limping around the crowded wards, I saw troubles and miseries that I had not even considered before. I saw kids, lying in bed lethargic and pale, with water dripping into their veins from glass bottles that hung above their heads. I saw one unhappy little boy, who was encased from his neck to his toes in a body cast, and there was a shy little girl who was terribly thin and frail and had lost all of her hair. But the saddest and most disturbing of all was the little girl lying helplessly in the bed next to mine. She was very sweet and surprisingly cheerful but she was unable to sit up because her little body was not strong enough to support her giant head. Hospital life was the only life that she had ever known. On the night after my surgery, a man in a bright red and yellow clown costume had, unexpectedly, bounded into our midst doing tricks, juggling colorful balls and telling funny stories. Looking around me, I could see the faces of the kids, all lit up and glowing. *These kids are suffering and yet look at them; they're all smiling. They are so stoic and so brave. I will never forget them,* I promised myself. When Jim came to pick me up, two days after my surgery, I was so very glad to be going back out into the world relatively intact. It had been a humbling experience and perhaps a seed had been planted, for after that I became fascinated with medicine but, as yet, I did not know that it was to be my calling.

That first day, as I entered the classroom still limping slightly, wearing the same red eyeglasses I'd gotten when I was in the 5th grade, I had felt acutely aware of the awkwardness of my adolescent body. I was so thin but in a sudden, upward, growth spurt I had outgrown all of my clothes and my blonde hair frizzed and jumped out in all directions despite the pins that I used to try and hold down the wayward locks. Not everyone seemed so adversely affected by the age. I didn't know any of the kids. A couple of the girls stared at me. They actually looked hostile, and they whispered and laughed as I walked by. Self-consciously, I limped to the back of the room, trying to reassure myself that I would feel better once I got into the swing of things. As I took my assigned seat next to Diane, she smiled at me, an unconditional, open, welcoming smile. I felt the warmth and color rush back to my cheeks as I realized with relief that I was going to have a friend after all.

At the time when I was in Jr. High, the threat of nuclear war cast a dark shadow over the world. Nakita Khrushchev's statement, "We will bury you," lurked ominously in the back of every one's mind. Later, he amended this statement by announcing, "I once said, 'we will bury you,' and I got into trouble with it. Of course we will not bury you with a shovel. Your own working class will bury you." It made me think of Jim, our working class rebel, when I heard that. Then I worried even more.

It was a great consolation to me to have Diane in my life. Her friendship made the world seem like a less scary place and, with Diane to cheer me on, the dramas in my home life faded into the background as well. We had become inseparable. We were always either at her house or mine or at school. There was never a situation where we didn't fully support, encourage, and stand up for one another. We had become, each for the other, friend, sister, parent, and confidant.

New Year's Eve arrived. It was our first New Year's Eve as friends. I went with Diane to her babysitting job so that we could bring in the New Year together. We were feeling silly, even a little giddy. The kids were already in bed and asleep when we arrived. "We should have a toast at midnight," Diane was saying. "I know where there's some wine!"

"Good idea, and let's put some makeup on and fix our hair," I added.

We stood in front of the mirror, studying each other's hair, trying different styles. We both had frizzy, dirty blonde hair, but the similarities ended there. I was as skinny as a rail. Diane was taller, with a bigger build and a little overweight. I wore glasses, she didn't. "Let's sing some songs," I suggested when we were finished primping in the mirror. "We could take turns choosing the song. Let's start with *the Beatles*!"

"Okay," Diane agreed. "You start." Diane was always so agreeable and easy going. She could be tough too, when she wanted, but mostly she was easy going and cheerful. It wasn't hard to please her. I was kind of like that myself, so we always managed to have fun and we never ever argued. I stated singing a Beatles tune but had to stop because I started to laugh when I caught a glimpse of myself in the mirror. I had just put on some of my mother's red lipstick and it looked ridiculous on me.

Diane finished up with the song *When I'm 64*. I think we'll still be the best of friends when we're 64, don't you?" she added.

"Of course, we will," I said, giving her a big hug.

"Do you think Mr. Mollahan is handsome?" I asked, while searching for the phone book.

"Absolutely, don't you?" Diane was amazed that I had even bothered to ask. There was no question about it.

"He's really a sweetheart too," I added, feeling like maybe he was the man of my dreams. I had a serious crush on him. Just a few days before, as we were leaving class for the holiday break, I had given him a big hug. When I went to give him a little kiss on the cheek, our lips had accidentally touched at the corners. I was so embarrassed that I wanted to fall right through the floor. I could feel my face turning bright red and that embarrassed me even more. But, I had to admit, it was also kind of a thrill. We found his phone number listed in the book and then hesitated. "I don't know if we should really do this," I said, starting to get cold feet. "I mean, if he finds out it was us, we will be so embarrassed; we'll never live it down."

"It'll be fine." Diane assured me. "We have to wish him a happy New Year. We'll just disguise our voices. He won't know who called."

"All right," I said with a nervous laugh. "Let's do it."

We called the number and Mr. Mollahan's voice that we knew so well from homeroom, English and History, answered. "Hello."

Right away we started giggling, "Happy New Year," we yelled, in unison, into the receiver, laughing so hard now that we were falling to the floor. Immediately after we had said it, we slammed down the phone. We were rolling around on the carpet in hysterics. He probably figured out who called him but he never said anything. He just smiled that gorgeous Mr. Mollahan smile.

We were still so young and innocent in those days. When we finally managed to pull ourselves together, we poured a small glass of wine for each of us. As the clock struck midnight, we raised our glasses and drank a toast to our incredible friendship and to life which seemed to stretch ahead of us, so full of promise, far into the unforeseeable future.

Chapter 8
Changes

In the middle of the second year of Junior High life took another one of those sharp left-hand turns that you just don't see coming. My mother and Jim had, unexpectedly, decided to move to Los Angeles, California. That's where Jim had grown up. His mother was still alive, and he had a brother out there, somewhere, in a mental institution. I must admit that the idea of California was kind of exciting but I didn't want to leave Diane. She was the best friend I ever had, and now that I had found her, I couldn't imagine my life without her. Diane took the morning off from school to hang out with me while Jim and Blanche finished packing the U-Haul trailer. Finally, everything was loaded and we were just waiting in the back of the car for Jim and my mother to come down from the room. "I'll write to you every day." I promised. "As soon as we get settled, we'll figure out a way for you to visit. We can go to the beach together!" Any other destination and I would have been completely miserable, but in truth I really liked the idea of living in the California sunshine with surfers and bikinis and beach parties. It sounded like a fabulous place to be a teenager. We were trying to find positive things to say about the move, in order to bolster each other's spirits, when Jim came down. Some man I didn't recognize was with him. It took me by surprise when Jim said to him, "Do you want to drive or shall I?"

"What is going on? Where's my mother?" I wanted to know. Everything happened so quickly after that. It was like a bad dream. Jim actually seemed relaxed. I looked over at Diane; she was smiling. I felt uneasy without really knowing why. A car pulled up and double-parked right next to us, blocking our way from pulling out. I looked over and in the back seat I saw my mother. She was staring, sightless, straight ahead. The look of despair on her face said it all. I had seen that look once before and I knew what it meant. "Get out of the car, Diane," I said, in barely a whisper. My heart was pounding and I could feel that I was about to be overwhelmed with a flood of emotion. Tears welled up in my eyes and I could feel them spilling down, hot and salty, over my cheeks and into my open mouth. It was hard to breathe. I pushed out of the car, past Diane and began to run as if all the demons of hell were hot on my tracks. I didn't stop or look back for a very long time. I was afraid that they were following me, planning to lock me up in some detention place for motherless children again and I couldn't bear the thought of it. It had been 10 years, but the memory of it was still fresh in my mind. I would live under a bridge before I went back there. Besides, I was 13 years old now. I could take care of myself. I ran down to the subway. Once on the train, I knew that I had escaped. Breathing became easier, and I started considering what I should do. I took the subway down to Penn. Station. I had in mind that I would still go to California and make a fresh start. I would take the train. It was a foolish idea, of course, but it helped me to calm down. For a while, I had been suspecting that something was up. We seemed to suddenly have quite a bit of money. We ate out in good restaurants and took in the theater. We bought beautiful new clothes. It was fun, but I knew that something wasn't right. I had suspected that my mother was embezzling again but I didn't say anything. I pushed the thought to the back of my mind and had kind of forgotten about it until I saw that look on my mother's face and then I knew. So there I was at Penn Station, I had stopped running, and I didn't know where to turn to next. I found a pay phone and dialed Diane's number. The phone picked up immediately. "Julie, where are you? I've been so worried," the concerned voice on the other end answered. She was throwing me a lifeline. Diane was so solid and stable. I had never known anyone like her. Although she was only13 years old herself, in a way she was like a mother to me. She was always so protective and caring. She was amazing really. "You've got to come to my house," she was saying. "My mom and dad know what happened. We want you to be here with us. Julie, don't worry; everything is going to be alright. I'll be here waiting for you." My dime was up. The phone clicked off and although it was still early in the afternoon, I suddenly felt very tired. I got on the train and gratefully went back to Diane's.

I'll never understand why, but Jim and Blanche were not in prison for very long, only about a month. But the 'apple cart had been overturned' as they say and the pieces of our life had gone spilling in all directions. As it turned out though, life was about to change anyway, just as the natural progression of things. A big disappointment for me was the fact that Diane had been accepted to the High School of Music and Art, and I had not. Following Diane's lead, I had tried to get in for drawing. Diane really had talent but I didn't, so Diane went to a hip and progressive art school in a beautiful gothic setting, and I went to a hostile and dreary, all-girls school far on the other side of town. Slowly, life fell haphazardly back into place in a new and different arrangement. There was a different school and different friends. There was a different apartment in a different part of town and if that weren't enough, I had a different body and a different set of aspirations and emotions to contend with.

Chapter 9
A Summer Job

After Jim and Blanche had been released from jail, we got a one-bedroom apartment downtown and my mother started working back at Macy's. Now it was a long bus ride to anywhere that I wanted or needed to be. My High School actually took three buses to get to. It was so miserable standing on the corner in the freezing wind waiting for the bus, with my teeth chattering and my knees knocking together from the cold, in my little mini-skirts. Since starting High School, I had become very style conscious. I babysat to make enough money to buy the latest fashions. My breasts had pushed their way up and out of my flat chest. I had learned new and interesting ways to control my hair, and boys had actually begun to give me a second look. I had made a couple of new friends at school but no one even came close to the powerful and easy friendship that I shared with Diane, so every weekend I took the bus ride uptown to her house. Diane had made a couple of new friends also, at Music and Art. Gloria was adopted and lived in the building right next door to Diane with her younger sister, Mari, and their artist dad who they called Poppie. Celia lived a few blocks further uptown in a fancy apartment building overlooking Central Park. We all got along amazingly well. When the weekend came around, at the end of each interminable week, the only place on earth that I cared to be was uptown with my girlfriends.

Then summer vacation arrived and my friends all left to different destinations with their families. Once again, I found myself alone, and I started to get depressed. The weather was hot and humid, and our little apartment cooked during the heat of the day. If you left the window open, hoping to get some airflow, the place filled up with flies. After moping about for a week or so, it occurred to me that perhaps I too could get out of the city for the summer. I bought a newspaper and looked up ads for 'mothers' helper'. There was an ad for a family that was looking for someone to spend the summer in Connecticut with them, helping with their kids. I circled it and then gave them a call. After my interview, I was hired. It was that simple. It was my first real venture in creating my own destiny, and I liked it.

The day I left, Jim and my mother took me out for an early morning breakfast while the city was still cool and relatively quiet. Afterwards, I caught a train at Penn Station bound for Connecticut. I felt really good about this independent venture, and as the train raced past rolling hills and green forests, it seemed to me that a whole new world of possibilities was opening up.

The family that hired me had two children; a six-year-old boy and a four-year-old girl. I liked the kids better than I liked the mother, who actually seemed to me, to be a little bit spoiled. They were good kids, fairly well behaved, and sweet. They made me a little nervous sometimes though, like the time the parents had friends visiting and they sent me down to the dock with a bunch of kids. While I was busy trying to get a fish hook out of the pants leg of a little boy who was screaming bloody murder, one of the younger ones fell off of the dock into water over her head. One minute the little one was standing there next to me, holding on to my skirt in order to steady her chubby little legs, and watching the commotion with interest. The next instant she was floating, face up in the water, with her eyes closed and her baby fine hair floating in a halo around her baby face, looking like a sweet little cherub. That vision will be etched into my mind for eternity. Panicked, I snatched her out of the water. She grinned at me like something fun and tricky had just happened. Right then and there, I marched everyone back up to the house, but after that I was terribly nervous around the water with the kids.

The family kept me busy each day looking after the children, washing dishes, and helping with the housework. By the time the kids had to go to bed, I was ready for bed too. I would lie awake in the dark, listening to the rhythmic symphony of crickets and frogs. I was entranced by the sounds, which were so totally new to me, of a summer night in the country. To my delight, sometimes a firefly or two would drift into the room flashing its mysterious signal into the darkness. It seemed like magic. And the stars were amazing. You didn't see stars like that in the city. Here the stars were so bright and clear, and sharp and infinite in their numbers, a myriad of twinkling crystals, sparkling in the dark indigo of sky. I was discovering a peace and harmony in the sights and sounds of nature that seemed to be more enduring, more meaningful, than the constant chatter of the city.

One afternoon, one of the local boys took me for a ride in his father's car which was kind of a thrill since none of my friends had ever driven a car. We were driving along the little two-lane dirt road when, suddenly, a thick fog descended upon us out of nowhere. We were unable to see more than a few feet ahead of us and had to slow down, almost to a halt. All that was familiar disappeared, and I had the eerie feeling that we had been transported to some other planet or dimension. I was thrilled with this new sensation of being suspended in space and time. When a mob of frogs appeared out of the mist, hopping around playfully and making croaking music, I could no longer contain my delight. I felt at that moment that if my world consisted only of this thick, moist shrouding of grey and these frolicking green creatures that I would always be happy. It was my first indication that perhaps I was really a country girl at heart and not a city girl at all.

Chapter 10
A Life Come Apart

The summer job had come to an end, and I returned home a few weeks before school started. Diane was still in Michigan with her family, and New York City was in the grip of a stifling heat wave. It was a depressing scene that I returned to. Jim was drinking heavily. When he got up each morning, he looked pale and sick. His hands would shake so, that it was difficult for him to get a cup of morning coffee (instant with hot water straight from the tap) to his lips without it spilling. If he had a little wine left from the night before, he would drink it down hungrily and after that he would seem to be a little better. Without that early morning drink, his insides would revolt, and I could hear him retching painfully before he would emerge from the bathroom, pale and shaken, to hurriedly leave for work. One miserably hot day, I was sitting around the apartment in my bathing suit reading an Agatha Christie mystery story. Flies buzzed annoyingly around me, landing, here and there, on my bare skin. They were very persistent, and I had almost given up trying to swat at them, but it was distracting and I was having a hard time concentrating on the murder that was about to be committed in the pages before me. Suddenly, the door opened and in staggered Jim. He was nursing a hurt leg. "What's up?" I asked, looking up, reluctantly, from my book. "How come you're home so early?"

He grinned, exposing an even row of tobacco-stained teeth. "I was doing some high ladder work and lost my footing." As he said this, he stumbled and a look of pain flitted across his flushed and sweaty face. Jim collapsed into a chair. He was in a good mood, his senses dulled by much alcohol. As the drink wore off, he began to look like he was in pain. "I think I'd better go to the hospital," he announced, rousing himself from a momentary stupor. His words kind of slurred together as he got up and limped painfully towards the door.

"Do you want me to go with you?" I asked, starting to feel concerned.

"No, I'll be fine. I'll be back in a little while."

I thought that perhaps he was just going to the bar, but several hours later he reappeared, aided up the four narrow flights of stairs by two policemen. "Guess I'll be out of commission for a while," he muttered half to himself, his leg looking cumbersome in white plaster.

We had always been a good friend to our neighborhood pawnshop. Through the years, we had lost countless appliances to those loan sharks. Now that Jim was out of work, he certainly did not intend to be without his drink. One by one, he brought our household possessions to be pawned. These he replaced with quickly emptied bottles of cheap wine. "Wine will kill you quicker than whiskey," Jim announced, cavalierly punctuating this statement by unscrewing the cap from his wine bottle and taking a drink. "It's 'cause there's no nutrition in wine," he added after he had swallowed. In the days that followed, the house was divested of anything of value. First the iron, then the toaster went. Soon my radio was gone and the little guitar that my mother had given me for my birthday. After the T.V. went, there was nothing left to pawn.

One afternoon when Jim had hobbled off to the bar and I was home alone, a mood of intense gloom overtook me. The apartment felt stark and unfamiliar. My mood darkened. That desolate hollow feeling that I experienced from time to time washed over me like a tidal wave, suffocating and crushing me. Hunched in a corner, back against the wall, I sank to the grey linoleum. Tears came with wrenching sobs. Hours passed. Darkness fell. The room seemed to revolve slowly through the dim blur of tears. I felt as if the world had come to an end, and by some cruel twist of fate I was the only one left alive, a solitary figure amongst the debris. I had read somewhere that there was a high rate of suicide among teenagers, and this fact kept echoing ominously in my mind.

As the days wore on, we all became extremely depressed and irritable. It was a bad situation with Jim injured and out of work and school not yet started. The intense August heat which made everything, even breathing, a chore, acted like a catalyst to intensify every one's misery and dissatisfaction. As bad as all this was, it was made much worse by the fact that Jim was drinking so heavily. It seemed like he was on some sort of downhill slide. The vision from the welfare office that night, of the homeless drunk who had entertained us with his stories of a life come apart, looked like it might indeed be coming close to fruition for Jim. This time it seemed like a good idea when Jim decided to move. He was collecting unemployment and he wanted to save money by moving to a cheaper place that was uptown on the West Side, closer to the White Rose and to his buddies. He seemed to no longer have any interest in anything other than where his next drink was coming from. I wanted to be closer to my High School which was on the Upper East Side. My mother was in agreement with me and so we all moved. Jim moved in with his friend Mickey in the West 70s, and my mother and I moved to the East 70s, within walking distance of Julia Richmond High.

The next few years marked a time of transition from childhood to womanhood. It was a time of experimentation and of discovery and a time of many mistakes. In a lot of ways, it was a really hard time. It probably would have been easier if my mother hadn't been so unstable herself, but I certainly can't blame it all on her for each of us has to learn their lessons in their own way. I don't know if anybody could have saved me from myself and from my mistakes. I do know that a driving force for me was looking for love. It took me a while to understand that I was looking in the wrong places and that was, for me, the hardest, most painful part of 'coming of age'.

Chapter 11
Friends

It occurred to me, as we crossed the threshold of this new apartment, that before too long we would be exiting from this same door, hurriedly gathering what few possessions we could carry. That was the pattern we had, long ago, established as urban nomads.

Jim didn't completely drop out of our life but he lived way on the other side of town and he spent most of his free time at the bar so we didn't see him very often, but of course we always knew where we could find him. My mother was working five days a week now and didn't get home until the evening. With this new schedule, she had very little free time to herself, and I saw very little of her. She was holding up pretty well though and so, for a time, things were fairly stable. I had become completely absorbed with my friendships, chattering on the phone for hours each evening about anything and everything. I was learning about a variety of new and interesting and grownup things and I was learning about boys.

There were two new girls at school with whom I struck up a friendship. The three of us got along quite well, but I was mostly a sounding board for them, an interested observer, someone they could impress with their escapades. One day after school, we walked over to Daisy's house. "We went down to the village the other night," Tina was telling me, "and we met these two cute guys, one for each of us."

"I had some Darvons and we all took one." Daisy added, raising her eyebrows slightly. "Then we bought some wine and went to their pad. It was this one little room, almost empty except for two beds with a curtain hanging in between them."

"So then we get drunk see," Tina had picked up the tale again, "and we all go to bed, Daisy on one side of the curtain with her guy and me and my guy on the other side. Well, my guy gets up in the middle of the night to go to the bathroom. Before I know it, the other guy gets into bed with me and my guy gets in to bed with Daisy. Then we just kept switching all night. It was great fun but, boy, was I sore the next day." Tina threw her head back and started laughing as she rubbed the inside of her thighs.

Once at Daisy's house, we all settled down around the table. They were giving me this great little lecture on drugs. From her years in psychotherapy, Daisy had a large repertoire of drugs that she was personally familiar with. "I can't believe that you've never smoked grass, Julie. It won't be long before you do," Daisy predicted, "and you won't stay a virgin for too long either, I'll bet," she added with a wink.

I liked them both a lot and admired their self-confidence, but it really wasn't my style and I knew that. Recreational sex was not something that resonated with me. I wanted a more romantic, loving relationship. It was the '60s, though, and casual sex was beginning to be the cool thing among young people. I felt that I should be more open, but I just couldn't take sex that lightly. It is an issue that has, in fact, caused me a lot of inner turmoil and pain over the years. Mostly, I hung out with Daisy and Tina on weekdays but on weekends I would walk or take the bus across the park to Diane's. There I would happily spend my weekend with my dearest and best friends of all time, Diane, Gloria, and Celia.

"What's it supposed to feel like?" I wanted to know.

"Sometimes it's hard to tell. I think you're supposed to feel kind of happy and a little silly and have kind of this pleasant, relaxed feeling." Celia giggled as she passed the joint.

I'd never been able to inhale cigarette smoke so I was surprised when the smoke from this little white reefer we were passing around went so smoothly into my lungs. We were lounging in comfortable, old-stuffed chairs in a dark corner of Diane's basement. We were laughing because we all thought that we felt a little different, maybe a little silly, as Celia had said, but we weren't quite sure. "I do know that it makes you real hungry, so if you get the munchies, then you know you're high!" Gloria exclaimed.

Instantly, we were all famished. We had moved from the secrecy of the dark corner and were fidgeting around by the washer and dryer underneath an unshaded 100-watt light bulb. We began peering into each other's eyes with a tremendous amount of enthusiasm.

"Can you tell?"

"Do I look stoned?"

"How do I look?" We all wanted to know.

Everything was so vague that it was hard to make any definitive statement. Finally, however, we decided that we were all really starving so that meant that we must be high whereupon we immediately took off skipping and twirling, laughing and playing leapfrog down the street, jackets open and hair blowing free in the wind. At the little pizzeria on the corner, we ordered a large pizza and watched with expectation as the middle-aged Italian man flipped the round, flat white dough high into the air. He was flirting with us and we loved it. We played 'Help Me, Girl' on the jukebox all singing the words together in unison, dancing around the little shop as we waited, blissfully, for our pizza.

"I knew it wouldn't be long before you were smoking," Daisy said, with satisfaction, as she passed the roach that she had just found in her pocket. She pulled on her boots, and we headed out to the park, trudging through the crisp white snow that had come early that year to the city. It had been snowing heavily for 24 hours. Schools were closed and the city was muted, blanketed in white. Things had more or less come to a standstill. The sharply defined New York City skyline appeared all blurry now as a never-ending procession of white flakes fluttered to the ground. In the park, the familiar paths had all but disappeared and mountains of fine, powdery crystals were emerging everywhere, rendering the landscape unfamiliar. "I can't believe it, lost in Central Park. I know this place like the back of my hand but everything looks so different now. I'm really not sure which way to the Boat House. Wait a minute." I could just make out enough of the skyline to orient myself in the storm. The snowfall was so thick that we could only see a dotted, grey and white world for a short ways, and then everything else was hidden. Using the indistinct skyline as a guiding landmark, we headed southwest to where we hoped to find the Boat House. We had been throwing snowballs and rolling around in the soft powder as we went so that when we finally arrived at the Boat House, we were cold and wet. We hadn't seen a soul in the hour or so it had taken us to get there so we were relieved and elated to find that they were open. The large cafeteria was stark and empty except for a solitary man standing stiffly behind the counter. There was an icy breeze blowing through the large, drafty room from a window left cracked open somewhere. We took a seat by the big plate glass window that looked out over the frozen lake and surveyed the winter scene before us with awe. The rowboats were all disguised as little mounds of snow outside the window, and here and there a grey branch rustled and sagged under its icy load. A few cheerful little brown sparrows, apparently not minding the cold, were hopping about chirping, leaving tiny bird prints in the snow. Aside from that, everything was very still. We managed to thaw our freezing hands by wrapping them around a cup of hot chocolate and we were grinning at one another across the cold expanse of plastic counter top. "Ever seen this place before?" Daisy asked in wonder.

"Doesn't look like anyplace I've ever been," I replied truthfully.

"Maybe we've stumbled into a faraway land where everything is pure and innocent, maybe another dimension!" Daisy grinned as she said this, her stocking cap perched crookedly on top of her head.

"It reminds me of the fairy tales that my mother used to read to me when I was little. I used to have this fantasy that I lived in a little cabin in a clearing in the woods beside a frozen lake and that the birds and squirrels would come and visit me every day. Anyone else wanting to visit would have to first skate across the frozen lake and they could only get across if their hearts were pure. That's what this reminds me of; a fairy tale." I looked at Daisy. In this setting, she looked like a big kid, not so jaded and worldly any more. I felt that this moment, surrounded as we were by the beauty and grace of nature, had changed us somehow and that somehow we were better for it.

"I kind of have a boyfriend," I was telling Daisy when we had gotten back to her house and were changing into dry cloths. "He's a sweet guy, I really like him."

"What's he like?" Daisy wanted to know. "Have you slept with him yet?"

"No, really, we just met. He's a friend of Gloria's boyfriend, Darwin. They go to the Bronx High School of Science together. Gloria and Darwin brought him by my house not that long ago, and we hit it off. We ended up spending the whole day together. Now he comes almost every day to see me, over an hour on the subway, each way."

"What's his name?" Daisy was drying her hair with a towel and putting on water for more hot chocolate.

"Harry; he's sixteen and he's very smart. He's kind of stocky but not fat, his hair is brown and silky and straight and he has this big, broad smile that looks just like the Cheshire cat. That's Harry. He's fun, not pushy but very confident and reliable. We've kissed a couple of times, that's all. The other evening, he went to the grocery store with me to pick some things up for my mom. She always cooks canned stuff and T.V. dinners, if we have extra money. Harry was reading the labels on all the things I was getting. He asked me why I didn't read the ingredients and compare prices. I had never heard of such a thing. I told him about how I used to think that vegetables were manufactured products because we only ate them out of the can. We laughed so hard. We were just doing something really boring, going to the grocery store, but it was really fun with him."

Daisy smiled, "Well, just like I was saying, it won't be long."

Of course I knew what she meant.

The elevator clanked and banged as it settled on the basement floor. I was trying not to be nervous, whistling cheerfully and acting all nonchalant. It was no use. I never could stand doing the laundry down in the basement of our apartment building. After all, anyone could come down here. I might never hear a thing above the noise of the washer and dryer until it was too late. Scenes of terror from Alfred Hitchcock movies persistently needled my consciousness in spite of my cheerful whistling. Then there were the stories that Jim used to tell about giant rats living in dark basements, in boiler rooms and water pipes. Rats that, if cornered, would lunge at your throat. Ugh! Once when I was little, my mother and I had walked to the lake in Central Park during a rainstorm. The cheerful paths where starlings and sparrows once fluttered were now covered with huge water rats scuttling in all directions because we had startled them. I had shrieked as, in their haste to get back to the water, a couple of rats had scurried over my feet. Just at that moment, my thoughts were interrupted by the sound of the elevator door clanging open. Nervously, I looked around. *I should have some sort of a weapon*, I was thinking. Diane, Gloria and Celia appeared in a cluster at the door.

"I'm so happy to see you. I was nervous down here all by myself." Gloria's new puppy scuttled joyfully around my legs, "What's up?" I asked as my gaze fell on the white bandages in neat figure eights around Gloria's small wrists.

Following my gaze, Gloria sighed, "It's my mother. I miss her so much. Don't worry, Julie. I'm seeing a psychiatrist now. It'll get figured out. Everything is going to be alright."

I knew that Gloria was adopted and I knew that her mother had died, but she hadn't ever told me the whole story and this didn't seem like the right time to ask. But I believed her when she said that she was going to be alright. Gloria was smart and gorgeous and fun to be around. Poppie was a good man who loved his daughters very much. Her sister Mari was a sweetheart, and they all had each other.

When the clothes were dry, we brought the folded laundry upstairs to the apartment and then took off for the park. We were, all of us young teenage girls, experiencing hard times just then. Diane's father and mother were arguing more than ever and Diane suspected that her mother had a lover. The idea really tore her up. Her father, whom she loved dearly, was starting to drink heavily. She felt like her family was falling apart, and she was miserable over it. Celia too was unhappy. Her parents were wealthy. Their apartment was an entire floor of a large apartment building over-looking the park. But Celia's parents weren't around very much, and she felt neglected. She felt as if they were trying to replace their time and love with money and a maid to look after her. She too was pining away for the love of a mother. My mother had just quit her job, and I knew that, soon, we'd be on the street again. That's how it was for us four unhappy girls that day. We sang folk songs and tried to console each other with our love and understanding. We walked, arm in arm, to the swings behind the mall. The playground was deserted. Up and up and up into the clouds we went, swinging higher and higher while singing the saddest songs we knew. The sweet notes of the songs and the harmonious blend of our voices was soothing. As up and up into the sky we went, the cares of the world seemed to fall away. Higher and higher we ascended singing through all the pain and sadness in our young lives. We stayed there on the swings until dusk. When it was time to go, we parted reluctantly with long lingering hugs and deep sighs. We were the best of friends and we were all hurting but because we had each other, things didn't seem quite so bad.

Chapter 12
A Diagnosis

"When I first met you, Julie, I thought you were a dizzy blonde. I was so wrong." Harry and I were sitting on the steps in the hallway of my apartment building while two policemen were busy escorting my mother down to the lobby with the few possessions that she had been allowed to hurriedly gather up. I had grabbed two shopping bags full of school books, clothes and of course my portable hair dryer which I considered a necessity. We were in the throes of an eviction.

"Why, what do you mean, Harry?" I was so glad that he was there with me.

"Well, look at you. You have no food or money and you don't know where you'll sleep or where your next meal is coming from. On top of that, your mother is so depressed and saying all those crazy things. I've never been through anything like this, Julie. I couldn't take it. You're so strong!"

I smiled and squeezed Harry's hand. It made me feel good to hear him say that. I had become so acculturated to this way of life that it didn't seem that unusual. Harry's statement was like a little reality check. "I didn't used to have friends like you to see me through. This is so much easier, you know. Just because you're here with me and holding my hand, it doesn't seem so bad."

As I said this, my mother had carried the last of her things that she could salvage down to the street; the policemen were leaving and Jim had arrived in a taxi to pick us up. Good old Jim. Once again he had come through for us. I had no idea where we were going or what was going to happen next. "I've got to go now, Harry. I'll call you when I know what's going on. Thank you for being here."

Harry gave me the best hug of my life, and then he was gone. Without his presence, it was hard to be so cavalier. We drove through the park in depressed silence to a hotel on 72nd street on the west side of town where, I learned, Jim had paid a week's rent for us. We weren't going to be living with Jim this time. He helped bring our stuff up to the room and then he left to go join his buddies at the bar. Once Jim had left and it was just my mother and I and a few of our things scattered haphazardly about the small, dingy room, I began to feel really down. I could feel that reoccurring, empty, desolate feeling that I hated so much, beginning to take hold again. I couldn't take it another minute. But now, I had somewhere to go. "I'm going to Diane's for a while, Mom. It's just a short walk to her house from here."

"No, you can't go. You're staying here with me!" My mother sounded so desperate.

"Why, I won't stay long. I need to get out for a while, Mom." I too was desperate.

"It's not safe. Someone is trying to get us. It's too dangerous for you to leave." After she said this, she stared off dismally into space, her arms folded across her chest and her mouth set tightly.

It was more than I could stand. "I'll be back in a couple of hours."

"Juliet, you can't go!" my mother yelled as I headed towards the door.

The next instant I was out the door and down the steps. As usual, Diane welcomed me with open arms. There were a bunch of kids at her house. Everyone was sympathetic and supportive and my mood quickly lifted. Once I had started feeling better, I started to feel guilty about leaving my mother alone when she was so depressed. I felt that I should return in a couple of hours like I had promised, but it was such a disheartening prospect. Really what I wanted was to get away forever. I wanted to make a different kind of life for myself, one that was more harmonious and stable. I didn't know quite what that meant or how to get there but I knew that life with my mother was always going to be chaotic and depressing, and I didn't want any more of it. I'd had enough!

"My mom has some sleeping pills. You could take one and just go home and go to sleep," Diane offered.

"Yes! I could sleep through; my mom's being angry that I left. I could sleep through her craziness. I could sleep right through all that depression. Wow, Diane, you're so wonderful!"

I took the pill before I left and then started back to the room. Jeff, Gloria's new boyfriend, offered to walk me back to the hotel and that made it easier too. As we got close to the hotel, I began to yawn and feel overwhelmingly sleepy. "It's starting to work already! Gee, this is great!" I was feeling almost happy. Back at the room, Blanche was already in bed, although it was still light out. She had her back turned towards me, and I wasn't sure if she was asleep or not, but it was perfect. I didn't have to explain anything or apologize for my behavior. I climbed into the little twin bed that was next to my mother's bed and settled in for a blissful night's sleep. Perhaps everything would look better in the morning.

I couldn't have slept for more than 20 minutes but when I woke up, I was full of energy and raring to go. "This is all wrong," I muttered to myself, "I should be sleepy." I lay there for another half an hour, all sorts of thoughts rushing busily through my head. "At least, I'm not depressed," I told myself, "I've got an idea; I'll go to school tomorrow!" Since the whole eviction thing had started, I had stopped going to school. Working up to an eviction was always so stressful. To ease the stress, I had started playing hooky and hanging out with anyone who wasn't going to school that day. Then, because I had missed so many classes, I had been called before the principle. "You're suspended from school for the next week," she told me coldly. "And when you come back, you're out of all your college prep classes and you'll take typing and shorthand. With a little luck, you just might be able to get a job as an office girl." One good thing that had come out of it was that they had sent me to Youth Consultation Services and so now I had a counselor. I hadn't really taken advantage of it yet, but I was thinking that I should. I rummaged through my shopping bag looking for old homework and schoolbooks. I worked quietly by a dim lamp that was next to my bed. My mother seemed to be asleep. I was alone with my thoughts and this tremendous well of energy. The clocked ticked away the hours as I did page after page of neglected schoolwork. When a ray of light slid under the window shade, I sprung out of bed in complete surprise. "It's morning!" I exclaimed to no one in particular. *Wouldn't it be fun to have breakfast with Diane before school starts,* I was thinking out loud as I hurriedly got dressed. Weeks later, I found out that the pill I had taken was actually a diet pill with Dexedrine, a type of speed, in it.

Celia had stayed later in the evening than usual. She was unhappy at home these days and she was rebelling. Her mother had called every one's parents so often, trying to track Celia down and coral her in, that now I was the only one who was even allowed to hang out with her. We were spending a lot of time together, and it was good for both of us I think. I needed Celia's sweet companionship at this time more than ever and without me, she would have been very isolated. We had become very close. It had grown dark outside and we were hanging out in the hotel lobby, talking about maybe cutting school together the next day and spending the day in the park. "I could take the Central Park West bus uptown, and you could take the Central Park West bus downtown, and we could meet where the cross town bus stops to take us to the East Side of the park. We could go to the zoo!"

Celia liked the idea. It was a plan.

"It's getting late. I've got to call Harry. I promised that I would. We talk on the phone almost every day. I hope you don't mind, Celia, I won't be long."

"No, that's fine. You go ahead. I'll look at these magazines."

I had a handful of change and walked over to the lobby payphone. I could see Celia from where I was standing. She was sitting in a comfortable chair, and she was shuffling through a stack of magazines. She looked content.

"Julie, I've been reading about paranoid schizophrenia. The symptoms sound just like your mother. Hold on a minute. I'll get the book and read it to you." Harry sounded worried. I waited on the line feeling a little nervous. I was so accustomed to my mother being kind of crazy that I had never actually even considered the idea that maybe she did suffer from mental illness. I associated mental illness with the things I had seen in the movies, insane asylums and shock treatments—people who were catatonic or wildly dangerous. I didn't associate these things with my mother but as I waited nervously on the phone, I started to realize that my mother was mentally ill. The idea really upset me. I didn't want my mother to be crazy, and she seemed so normal at times that it didn't really make sense. Harry came back on the line. He started reading to me out of the book, but I was getting so upset that I was having a difficult time concentrating on what he was saying. He tried to simplify it by reading just the parts that would make sense to me. "The essential feature of the Paranoid Type of Schizophrenia is the presence of prominent delusions or auditory hallucinations in the presence of a relative preservation of cognitive functioning," Harry was reading. I thought of how, lately, my mother had been making me taste her food before she'd eat it to make certain that I had not poisoned it. She certainly suffered from delusions; there was no question about that. "Associated features include anxiety, anger, aloofness and argumentativeness." Aloofness epitomized my mother's personality, and as I listened to these words, I began to wonder if all those destructive arguments that I had blamed on Jim and his drinking were not, in fact, perpetuated by Blanche. "Some evidence suggests that the prognosis for the Paranoid Type of Schizophrenia may be considerably better than for the other types of Schizophrenia, particularly with regard to occupational functioning and capacity for independent living." That would explain why my mother seemed so high functioning at times in spite of having Schizophrenia. "The persecutory themes may dispose the individual to suicidal behavior and the combination of persecutory and grandiose delusions with anger may predispose the individual to violence." (Taken from DSM-IV 4th edition, Published by The American Psychiatric Association Washington, DC, Page 287.) "If delusions are directed against specific persons, violence may ensue and confinement becomes necessary," Harry added. I could hear the dull thud of the book closing. My head and my heart were reeling from these words. At this very moment, my mother was slipping into a world of darkness where I could not reach her. Was this what the future held for her, to commit suicide or murder or both or to be locked away in some insane asylum? I dropped the phone. I was overwhelmed by a tidal wave of emotion, fear, pain, shock. My heart started racing, pumping adrenalin through my veins. The fight or flight response took over and I responded to its dictum by running. I ran through the lobby, out of the door, and into the night.

Celia was right beside me. "Julie, what's wrong? What did Harry say?"

When we finally stopped running, we found that we were on the steps of a very ornate, gothic style, Catholic Church. We sat there on the steps in the darkness, for a long time, talking in whispers. Once I had managed to calm down, we started walking again, aimlessly. We ended up at a housing project, wandering around the tall buildings in the dark. No one was around. It was very quiet. Normally, I would have been afraid because the projects had a reputation for being dangerous at night, but that night, such thoughts were far from my mind. Finally we got on the elevator and for some reason that felt like a good place to be. We sat down on the dirty floor and rode up to the 15th floor and then back down to the 1st floor and up again, up and down, up and down we went over and over again. Somehow it was soothing. After a while, we realized how silly we must look, sitting on the floor of the elevator, riding up and down in the middle of the night. We both started smiling at the thought.

"Your face is all tear smudged," Celia said in her sweet way. "Let's go home now. It's late."

Chapter 13
Making the Break

Two weeks had passed and our rent was long overdue. Jim wasn't offering any further assistance, and Blanche was just sitting in the room, helplessly, waiting for the ax to fall. Time was running out. I was trying to work out a plan but in the end, it was Harry's mother who came to the rescue. She lent me the money to get my mother a room at the YWCA, and it was simply arranged that I would stay with Diane until my mother had things worked out. I helped Blanche spirit a few things down the back stairs to where a taxicab was waiting. Without much emotion or even a farewell, she got in the cab and left. I couldn't tell if she was upset or happy that I wasn't going with her but someone was taking responsibility for the next move and that was good enough for now. After she left, I stood there in the empty street and wondered dimly, what next. Then I went back upstairs to see what I could gather of my own things but a broken key had already been placed in the lock and there was no entering. Luckily, I had stashed a few things in the hallway utility closet so that I had most of what was needed. As I made my way down the steps, my mood began to lighten in degrees. At first I was relieved that the waiting was over. There was always so much tension leading up to an eviction. Then I started feeling almost happy that the move had been made without an exhausting emotional scene. Finally, out on the street, my mood became elated. Free! I was free! I could have jumped up in the air and clicked my heels together the way they do in the movies, except for this awkward assortment of books and clothes and my precious portable hairdryer that I was carrying. I needed my shopping bags.

Diane was happy to share her small room with me. She gave me a shelf to put my stuff on, and we decided that we would sleep with our heads at opposite ends of her tiny bed. It was fun. It was like having a sister or like an extended pajama party. Even though we were living under such close conditions, we still got along incredibly well and we never fought about anything. To this day, I can't stand arguing and you'll have your work cut out for you if you want to try and pick a fight with me, but Diane was a good friend and she never even came close to instigating a fight or hurting my feelings in any way.

I worried about my mother after I packed her off in the taxi. She had a diagnosis now and now it was clear that her erratic behavior was outside of her control. She wasn't in such good shape, mentally, when we separated, and I wasn't sure how she would manage on her own; however, she did well. I think being sent off on her own like that kind of jolted her back into reality. By the time her two weeks' rent at the Y was up, she was collecting her first paycheck. She was a single woman on her own now and it seemed to agree with her. Sometimes, I wonder if Blanche would have had a better life if she had been in treatment and on medications but she was always very suspicious of pills and the older antipsychotic medications had a lot of unpleasant and even dangerous side effects. I'm almost positive that she would not have taken them even if she'd had the opportunity.

When the school year ended, everyone immediately took off, in different directions, for the summer again. I probably could have stayed with Diane and her family in Michigan for the entire summer but they didn't directly invite me and I felt a little self-conscious. I didn't want to be a burden to anyone. I was 16 now and felt that I should contribute to my upkeep at least somewhat so I decided to get a job. I did drive to Michigan with them though and stayed for a couple of weeks, but then I took the bus back to New York City, stayed for a couple of days with my mother at the hotel she had recently relocated to and then took the train to Connecticut where I was met at the station by my new employer.

Adam, a little bit naughty, a lot nice. He was six years old, my charge for the rest of the summer. We slept in twin beds, side by side in the old country house. He awoke promptly at 6:30 every morning, and it required no small amount of ingenuity and quick action on my part to intercept him before he darted out the door and down the steps to awaken his mother. That, she told me unconditionally, was totally unacceptable. She wanted to sleep, undisturbed, until 9 a.m. or I was fired. So there I was, every morning suddenly and sleepily standing in the doorway, barring the little guys' way to his mother, coaxing, bribing and pleading, "Don't wake your mother up this early, Adam. You and I can do something fun."

If we hung out around the house, it was constant coaxing and intercepting on my part. We needed to get away from the house, so we began to take early morning walks. At first we would not get far before Adam would drop to the ground and throw a fit if I refused to carry him (and refuse I did). Each day, we would walk a little farther and explore a little deeper until our walks became adventures that we both anticipated eagerly. Then the mornings ceased to be a struggle. We would awaken at dawn while the household slept peacefully, throw on our clothes, and rush out into the early morning sunshine. Our explorations took us skirting along the lakeshore with its inviting clear waters in which the blue of the sky was reflected, through the cool, dappled shade of the forest and further and further up into the hills that were dotted, here and there, with a perfusion of pink and yellow wildflowers. "Where do you go so early and for so long?" his mother asked one day.

"Come with us and see," I replied. And so, one day, we all went together.

There was a cute little beach nearby that had a lifeguard. We went there a lot. It was fun playing in the sand and splashing around in the cool, shallow water with Adam. One day, the lifeguard, who was quite good looking, started flirting with me. I was very flattered, and I flirted back.

"How about if you and I go out tonight, I'll pick you up around 7?" my lifeguard said with a big, friendly grin on his handsome face.

"Sounds great, I'll be ready." I was so excited. Back in the privacy of my room, I threw my towel up in the air, "Yes!" I shouted.

"What are you so happy about?" Adam asked.

"I've got a date, Adam!"

"Oh," he said.

I really didn't know what to expect from this date. I'd never been out with an older guy before. In fact, I'd never been out on a date with anyone other than Harry and besides, there wasn't really anywhere to go. "Where shall we go?" I asked, feeling animated, as we drove off into the night.

"I thought we'd just cruise around down by the lake. I'd like to show you this quiet little place that I'll bet you've never seen before."

I tried to make conversation but it didn't seem like we were on the same wavelength, maybe not even on the same planet. "Do you spend much time in Manhattan?" I asked, trying to establish a common ground. He shook his head, no, and the car came to an abrupt halt. We were on an isolated little cove of the lake.

"Let's take a swim," he suggested.

The evening was lovely, clear, and warm. In a flash, my lifeguard had his clothes off, and he stood there before me, naked, in the moonlight. He looked down at me from his tremendous height of over 6 feet with an expectant expression in his grey-blue eyes. Embarrassed, I laughed a small, self-conscious laugh. "So lucky I thought to wear my bathing suit," I said as I took off my pants and shirt and jumped into the water. We swam around in the moonlight for a bit but the evening was not developing well. I was chatting away cheerfully about how beautiful the night was and how much I liked Adam and what a great summer it was turning out to be.

My lifeguard was silent until finally he said, "You don't need a bathing suit. Why don't you just take it off?"

I was getting chilly and starting to shiver a little and my date was starting to sound annoyed so it seemed like a good time to get out of the water and back into my clothes. My attempts at lively conversation were going stale.

"Let's sit in the back seat," he suggested, once we were both back in the car with our clothes on. "We can get more comfortable there."

I looked at him across the safe expanse of bucket seat and emergency break. Conflicting needs for approval and for self-preservation assailed me.

"Okay," I said hesitantly, feeling like I must do something to retrieve the evening. As we settled into the back seat, my thoughts were rudely interrupted by a tongue being shoved deeply into my mouth. I sputtered a little, thinking that maybe that's what you have to expect when you go out with a lifeguard who is in college and who is majoring in biology. My mind was working to understand the situation I had gotten myself into and how I could gracefully get myself out of it. He was unzipping his pants now. I wasn't feeling into a 'hand job' just at the moment but this joker had something else in mind.

"Put it in your mouth," he ordered.

I recoiled in disgust but he grabbed me by the hair and tried to shove my face down on his penis. I could not believe that a seemingly nice, responsible guy would act like this. I was as amazed as I was outraged. The harder, he pushed the more amazed and outraged I became until, finally, I was kicking and screaming and fighting my way out of the car.

"Alright, alright, I'll take you home," he said coldly as if I had done something wrong.

On the way home, I tried to make polite conversation. I guess in some weird way I felt like I had failed.

The next weekend was my weekend off for the month. Friday night I took the train back to Manhattan and walked barefoot through the streets to my mother's hotel room.

"Want to be in an off Broadway play?" A nice looking young man asked me as we approached the hotel.

"Sure," I said, sneezing loudly. "What do I have to do?" I asked, blowing my nose and sounding kind of nasal.

"Meet me in the hotel lobby tomorrow evening. I'll bring you the part to read."

"Sure thing," I said with a big smile and another sneeze. But my recent experience with the lifeguard had made me really suspicious and although I thought it might be a cool thing, I wasn't entirely certain that I would keep the date.

The next day, Saturday, Blanche went off to work and Harry came into Manhattan for the day to hang out with me. We kissed and found delight and comfort in each other's company. Softly, we spoke of our recent time apart. I told Harry about my lifeguard experience. He made it seem funny, and we laughed. I was starting to feel feverish. My throat was sore and I had no energy so we lay down together, getting all snug and cozy. We talked quietly for a while and then we made love. It was the first time for me, not for Harry though.

"That was so sweet and gentle. I'm surprised that we didn't do it sooner," I said, feeling all relaxed and glowing.

"I wanted to wait until you knew that I really cared for you, Julie." It was the sweetest thing that he could have said.

Even though we had just taken things to the next level, Harry and I were sort of drifting apart. We were still the best of friends and now we were also lovers, but we didn't see each other that often anymore and I had heard rumors that he chased other girls at school. I wasn't jealous. I never even really understood what jealousy meant until I met John, the father of my kids, but it made our relationship ambiguous. We never really talked about our relationship or tried to define it. Perhaps if we had been clearer with each other and more committed, it could have saved me a lot of heartache. They say that everything happens for a reason and what's done is done. By now it's all just 'water under the bridge'.

Sunday I felt awful. It took a tremendous amount of energy just to dial the phone. I was calling Jeffrey Pond, the news broadcaster and my employer. "I'm really sick," I was telling him. "It's my weekend off. I'm supposed to return today but I don't think I can make it."

"You have to," a stern voice replied on the other end of the receiver. "My wife is expecting you. She will be very upset if you don't show."

I liked his wife, Adam's mother. I understood that she was delicate. I think she had some issues around depression. She listened to me talk about my mother and she understood things that others didn't. She helped me gain insight and compassion for Blanche and for myself also. I didn't want to disappoint her or make her feel stressed.

He finished by adding a little more gently, "Why don't you go back this afternoon, and if you still feel sick, I'm sure that you can rest up tomorrow."

Never let it be said that I turned away from responsibility out of weakness. I made my weary way down to the station. The summer sun didn't touch the icy chill that rattled my aching body. Once on the train, I sank gratefully into my seat. Distantly, I wondered if I would ever rise again. For the first part of the trip, the train was crowded. People came and went beside me but it was hard for me to tell if they minded my scrunched up fetal position which took up 2/3rd of the double seat. Nor did it really matter. It only mattered that I stop this violent shaking of my body and preserve whatever warmth I could manage. "Did you say something? I wasn't quite sure," I mumbled my apologies and sunk back into a delirious sleep. Nothing mattered anyway. I was really quite comfortable if only I could get a little warmer. My throat was on fire, and I was continually being roused by the ticklish sensation of spit drooling out the side of my mouth and down to my chin. How embarrassing, of course, so I mumbled more apologies. "Glad to meet you. I'm going north... I'm fine, just a little chilly."

The fog parted briefly and I saw a middle-aged man looking at me with concern. I smiled wanly. When I opened my eyes again, the train was almost empty. With a feeling of relief, I lay my head down on the empty seat beside me. "Of course it's just a little further. Yes, where am I going, I forget just now."

Someone was shaking me. "This is the last stop. You'll have to get off the train." I gave what must have been a glassy eyed nod.

"Are you all right?" The owner of the voice sounded impatient.

Slowly, the world revolved back into focus. "Last stop," I exclaimed, with a feeling of alarm. "I've missed my stop." Heavily and with great effort, I got up and the porter showed me what I must do to get back to my stop where Mrs. Pond was no doubt waiting for me, greatly annoyed. This time I stayed awake, taking a certain amount of pleasure in the distant and uncaring feeling that went with my weak and fevered body.

Mrs. Pond's annoyance at having to wait changed to annoyance at her husband for sending her an invalid nanny. She took me home and put me to bed.

"Well, you're here now. I suppose we'll have to take care of you."

She took my temperature, 104.2

"Adam will have to sleep downstairs with me until you're better."

It was Sunday again. The last couple of days I had managed to be of some service, but I still felt very weak. Harry called to say that he'd been to the doctor and he was ill with strep throat. He thought that maybe he had gotten it from me. "So that's what I had," was my reply. Mr. Pond was up from Manhattan for the weekend. I think he felt bad for insisting that I return to work. He was being very kind and considerate, and he told us that he had a special treat for us all. He took us to nearby Massachusetts to 'Tanglewood' where the Boston Symphony Orchestra played in an open-air theater that was cloistered in the Berkshire Mountains. It was a magnificent setting. I lay listlessly but content in the warm sunshine while the music of Beethoven floated around and above me, the melodic strains echoing off of the hills that surrounded us. I was feeling very open, like a vessel, trying to fill myself up with the beauty of the surroundings, the mountains, the sunshine, the music, the very air when, unexpectedly, my soul was lifted to one of those inexplicable moments of pure ecstasy.

Chapter 14
Trial by Fire

My job had ended a few weeks before school was to start back up and so I was faced with the predicament of where to live. Diane and her family wouldn't even be back for a couple of weeks yet, and they hadn't actually invited me to come and live with them when school started. The original agreement for me to live at Diane's had just been a temporary one. The most obvious answer was to, once again, share a bed with my mother in her little hotel room. She was up for it and it seemed like the right and comfortable thing to do. Things were working out and so when school started, I just stayed on.

One evening I was sitting in the room by the open window, smoking a joint while my mother was in the shower. I was thinking about this very cute older guy who lived upstairs in the hotel. He wanted to be a model, and he had a portfolio full of 8x10 glossy photographs of himself in different outfits and poses. It seemed unbearably vain to me. Still, he seemed like a nice guy. When I had refused to sleep with him the other day, he had asked in amazement, "But then why did you kiss me like that?"

One evening, while waiting for the crosstown bus to come, we had stood pressed together in a narrow doorway to get out of the freezing wind. As I had looked up, he reached over to brush a wisp of hair from my cheek. Somehow our lips met. The warmth of his lips, so unexpected, drew me deeper and deeper until I had momentarily lost myself. The bus came. It was nothing really, just a moment in time.

"Your mother wants me to teach you about love. You shouldn't learn it from the wrong person. I will be so very gentle with you."

He said this to me as if it made perfect sense and should be very convincing. However, it had the opposite effect. I knew that my mother really liked him, and I wouldn't put it past her to make just such an arrangement, but I didn't intend to have any part of it. The spattering of shower water on hard tile abruptly stopped, interrupting my reflections. Hurriedly, I crushed the roach out and swallowed it, ashes and all.

"What's that funny smell?" my mother asked, sniffing the air as she emerged from the bathroom, a smallish towel wrapped around her shapely torso and a clear plastic shower cap drip, dripping water down her longish nose. She tilted her head and her pretty brown eyes looked at me inquiringly.

"I don't smell it," I said shrugging.

Just then the phone rang, saving me from further inquiry. It was a man I had met in the park the day before. He was about 28. We had casually talked about radio stations and hit songs. He wanted to be a DJ. When we parted, he had bent and kissed my forehead with such a caring gentleness that it had left me feeling mesmerized.

"Hi, Sweetheart, what-cha doin'?" His open friendliness swept me off of my feet. Without knowing why I felt that he wanted to care for me. He made me feel really good.

"Can I take you out to dinner tomorrow night? I know this little café in china town that has great food. All the Mafiosos eat there. You like Chinese food, don't-cha?"

Of course I do and of course he could and so it was arranged.

The little café in china town looked like a likely hangout for the mafia. It was quite small. The room was too bright with a bare light bulb glaring down on a white tile floor and stained beige tabletops. The few people eating there looked like tough guys. But the food was really good and I managed to convince myself that the atmosphere was worldly and exciting. After dinner, he said he was taking me to visit some of his friends. That sounded like fun. It turned out that no one was home but he just happened to have the key. The apartment was plush with nice furniture and thick, wall-to-wall carpeting. He showed me a large dresser drawer that was filled with marijuana. *They must be dealers*, I thought to myself. He started rolling a joint all the while chatting in a friendly, lighthearted way that put me at ease. I wanted this to work out.

"Let me give you a massage. Take your clothes off," he said in an offhand manner.

I had known it was coming and he said it so nicely, what would be the harm. He rubbed my back and legs tenderly it seemed, with scented oil. It felt luxurious. When he started taking his own clothes off, I found myself feeling confused again. I was not an innocent little girl. I knew what was happening but I was not quite comfortable with it. Again, I was having conflicting feelings of wanting to be cool, to be accepted and at the same time, wanting to follow my gut which was telling me to get out of the situation as fast as possible. As he took the last of his clothes off and pressed his hairy body on top of mine, suddenly I knew that I didn't want to be there. I didn't want to be intimate with this man, more than ten years older than myself, whom I hardly knew. Finally, out of all my confusion, emerged the clear realization that this wasn't what I wanted. Too late it seemed, for a moment he wouldn't let me go. Then he did.

"I can't do this. I want to go home," he seemed so nice and I was young. I was sure that he would understand.

He regarded me coolly as I regained my underwear.

"No, you don't," was his unexpected reply.

He tackled my legs and I fell to the floor. *He must be playing*, I thought in disbelief. I struggled to get up but then he was on top of me with the tremendous weight of his body pushing me down into the scratchy fibers of carpet. *This is a game*, I thought. I almost laughed. I struggled with every ounce of strength to push him off of me. I could not even budge him. He only explored with more persistence between my legs. I locked my ankles with rock determination. Only now did I fully realize that he intended to force me. I became frightened. I began to scream and scream a prolonged piercing scream of fear and anguish.

"Stop," I pleaded. "Please stop, I'm only 16. Let me go. Help, somebody help me," I appealed to the world outside as my assailant proceeded with immutable intent. Beyond the door was empty silence. I remembered hearing a story of a woman being murdered in the street while onlookers watched out of their windows. Some even cheered, they said. Fear seeped into every fiber of my body, leaving me sick and weak.

"Spread your legs," he growled between clenched teeth. "Spread your legs," he yelled. He was angry now. How could I know what this man would do to me, what he was capable of? Out of fear I submitted.

When the act was completed, his anger abated and I was allowed to dress. Once again he picked up that same casual banter. "Look at this electric tooth brush. Ever use one?"

I shrugged. The little motor whirred as he meticulously brushed his teeth. Outside, it had grown dark. He had not turned on any lights, there was just this one little candle that was lit and I found the darkness comforting.

He drove me home. Once we were out of the apartment, I felt less frightened. Actually, I was relieved to be more or less unharmed and somehow I couldn't even quite blame him. Hadn't I undressed voluntarily? "You know I can't continue to see you if you don't like to fuck," were his parting words.

I ran upstairs to an empty room and sobbed for half the night, without thought, blind, despairing sobs.

Days of depression ensued in which it became impossible to distinguish my internal mood from the cold, grey weather that had come on the fringes of winter. I didn't talk about my experience to anyone until later. For the moment, all I wanted to do was forget about it and get on with my life. Then, one afternoon, my mother approached me with a worried expression on her face. "Julie dear," I wondered what was coming. "I don't know what to do. The hotel management has told me that you can't stay here. The room is only coded for one occupant. You're going to have to leave but as soon as I have enough money, I'll get a place for the two of us." She tried to console me with the offer that, for now, I could stay with the model guy that she liked so much. She had already talked to him about it. "He thinks it's a good idea too and it's just until I can raise some money."

It didn't add up. He had the same size room as we did. "It's alright, Mom, I'll figure something out."

The next day was Friday. I went to see my councilor at Youth Consultation Services. "Well, Juliet," she used my full name and she smiled at me warmly, "I think what we'll do is get you a room at the YWCA downtown for the weekend. No men are allowed in the building. You should feel safe there."

I had explained to her that something very traumatic had happened to me recently although I didn't give any details. "That sounds good to me," I said, breathing a sigh of relief.

"It will only be for a couple of days, but by then I hope to have something else worked out for you, Julie; would you consider going back to live with Diane and her family?"

"That would be great but I hate to impose on them and they haven't asked me."

"I'm going to arrange a meeting with them. We'll see what we can work out."

I left her office feeling relieved that someone was taking the burden of responsibility out of my hands, at least for the moment.

When I got to the Y, they were expecting me. Everything had been arranged by phone. I took the rickety elevator up to my room on the 4th floor. The elevator man, who was so ancient that he seemed to be part of the very fabric of the old stone building, was the only man allowed in the place and that did make me feel safer. As

I walked down the narrow hallway with the drab green walls and faded, fraying carpet, I found myself wondering why I hadn't just gone to Diane's. But they hadn't invited me and I took it as a sign that they didn't want me. I was a displaced person and the loneliness of it was hard to take. The room consisted of just the bare essentials; a small bed, a little dresser and a sink. Really, I didn't need anything else, but I found myself wishing for something familiar and pretty with which to warm the room. There was absolutely nothing to do and nowhere to go now that it was getting dark. I resigned myself to a quiet, lonely evening. I hadn't had dinner yet, but this was the business district where everything closed down after dark so it was to be a hungry evening also. It was just as well. My stomach was in a knot, and I probably wouldn't have been able to eat anything anyway. I decided to get out my books and do some homework. Schoolwork was actually kind of comforting at those times when I was feeling lost or abandoned. I remembered running down the steps at nursery school, calling after my mother and crying. Well, this was a little different. I wanted this independence as much as it frightened me.

It was hard to sleep that night. I had gone to bed too early for one thing, and then there were all the strange noises in the night; the room felt so alien. It was a relief, in the morning, to escape into the street and hunt down a little café for breakfast. Things looked brighter in the day, cloudy though it was. After scrambled eggs and hot coffee with lots of cream and sugar, I decided to give Harry a ring. It was Saturday, and I could not stand the thought of spending the day in that room all by myself. Harry said that he and his mom would drive down to Manhattan and take me back to his house for dinner. When I hung up the phone, I felt a little surge of happiness. I was singing as I did a little jig down the deserted street.

It was dark when Harry and his mother drove me home. I'd had a delightful evening and I was feeling recharged by the love and kindness shown to me by Harry and his family. When I got back to my little room, its bleakness seemed somehow inviting, like an adventure. Harry had given me a good book by Salinger to read. I had a box of chocolate chip cookies and a soda, and Harry's mom had given me a pretty green comforter to throw over the bed. I plumped up the pillows and got all cozy and warm. My favorite thing in the world was a good book to read.

The next day was Sunday and if things were quiet in the business district the day before, now it seemed like a ghost town. I wasn't in too bad a mood though, considering everything but I was restless for something to do. I went out in search of breakfast. The towering skyscraper buildings that crowded together, pushing upwards in the only direction that afforded space for them, all but blotted out the grey sky. There was a chill in the air. The streets were empty except for this lone guy standing on the street corner, by himself. "Have you got a match?" this tall mulatto guy of about 25 asked me.

"No, I'm sorry, I don't," I replied.

"Do you live around here?" He sounded lonely.

I pointed to the 'Y' across the street. "How about you?" I asked, glad for a little conversation.

"Na, I'm from Brooklyn. I came down to visit some friends but they not at home. Not much happenin' around here, is there? Is there anything to do?" he added incredulously.

"Nothing except, maybe take a walk," I replied, not able to come up with any good ideas myself.

"Well, come on, girl, les do that. Will ya walk with me?"

"Sure," I replied, thinking that walking with this stranger would be better than sitting up in that room alone all day.

Aimlessly we headed east. The freeway and the East River were just a few blocks away. It was an area that I was not familiar with. I was more or less following him, although it didn't seem like he had any destination in mind either. He was asking me about school and my parents. I had a lot to say on both subjects and so it wasn't long before we had gone as far as we could go heading east and we now found ourselves walking on a narrow strip of pavement that went between the water and the freeway. On our right, a concrete wall, four or five feet high, separated us from the churning waters of the East River. On our left, cars zoomed by at high speeds. A giant truck raced by, causing a swirling surge of wind and debris that left me totally disheveled and mildly disoriented when it had passed.

"I've never been down here. I don't think I like it, being so close to the cars," I said while trying to get the dirt out of my eyes. They were stinging like mad.

"There's a platform here over the river. Let's just slip over the wall onto the platform and we'll be away from the traffic," my new friend suggested.

Adventurous, foolhardy soul that I am, it sounded like an interesting idea. We pulled ourselves up and over the wall dropping down on the other side onto an 8x8 square of concrete that was suspended inches above the swirling grey waters. The sky was blanketed with a thick covering of clouds that were reflected in the water and completely blocked out the sun so that everything, water, sky and buildings beyond, were all the same dull shade of concrete grey. You could still hear cars whizzing by on the other side of the wall but it was a relief to be protected from the clouds of debris that they created. Before I even had a moment to consider the thought that maybe it hadn't been such a good idea to come here, my companion had taken my hand and was pressing it against the hardness in his pants. *Oh no*, I thought in dismay. I truly hadn't expected this. I drew my hand away. He seemed to take no notice and started unzipping his pants. "I want you to make me come," he ordered. The tone of his voice, cold maybe even a little cruel, struck me as an ominous sign. I looked around me, assessing the situation I had gotten myself into. The wall was pretty high. It was hard for me to get over it without help and couldn't be done quickly. The traffic beyond was deafening. No one would hear. I felt sick. Why had I let myself be led here to this isolated place? The waters rushed by in vast undulating waves, carrying aggregates of garbage with it. It was really upsetting how much garbage there was, reflecting people's wanton violation of that in nature which should be sacred. He took my hand again forcing open my stiff fingers and closing them around his penis. He held my wrist tightly, moving my hand up and down. "Like that," he ordered.

There was a tension in his voice that frightened me. Looking down at the water I thought again of trying to escape. I wasn't a very strong swimmer. I was actually afraid of deep water. I envisioned jumping into the icy water and being buried under one of the packs of garbage floating by. My hand moved up and down obediently at the thought of being left to drift among the garbage in the churning murky waters. A feeling of numbness stole over me as I swallowed back the fear. He came quickly. I heard him groan as the thick grey substance poured out onto my hand and over onto my skirt in a pulsating stream. The front of my skirt oozed and dripped as the sperm ran down its innocent little purple flowers with buttercup yellow centers. I felt repulsed but said pleasantly enough, "I really should change this skirt. Maybe we could go to my place." He knew that I lived alone. To my intense relief, he replied, "Alright, let's go." I was too engrossed in survival to feel much emotion at this point, but as we climbed back over the wall and drew away from the threat of deep waters and rushing traffic, the knot in my stomach began to release. I felt like I was going to have a bad case of the runs. I kept up a flow of pleasant chatter as we neared the 'Y'.

"You'll have to wait here," I said as we stood safely in the doorway. "There's no men allowed in the building and there's an elevator operator so I won't be able to sneak you in." I tried to hide from him the fact that I knew that I was a free bird now and the rising feeling of elation as I said this.

"Well, you come right back down here after you change your skirt," he demanded. "I'll be waiting for you. Don't be long."

He certainly talks as if he owns me, I thought, too relieved to have escaped to feel resentment. There wasn't any pretense of friendliness in his voice now either. Maybe he knew that I had got away.

As I walked down the hall, a few of the doors stood open a crack and strange ancient faces peered out at me with curiosity. *I could become a water worshiper*, I thought, once under the shower, as an avalanche of hot water cascaded down over my face and body, washing away the crusted on layers of hurt, fear and self-recrimination. The bathroom filled with steam and somehow, in that dripping, foggy warmth, things didn't seem so bad. I felt safe and out of harm's reach. Back in my room, I went over to the little sink and began to wash the sperm out of my skirt. I felt exhausted and withdrawn, but at least I wasn't back there, floating in the East River. At least he hadn't entered me. It could have been so much worse.

Grateful for this safe space and so very weary, I settled into bed with my school books and '*Catcher in the Rye*' by Salinger. It was still morning. That whole ordeal had taken less than two hours of my life but it had seemed like an eternity. *Would this qualify as trial by fire?* I wondered. I felt sure that it did. Morning passed and afternoon came and went. Evening arrived and darkness settled outside of my window. Still I didn't move from my bed, content for the moment to be safely out of the rapids.

In the morning my rent was up. I wondered if the guy was still standing outside waiting for me, probably not. No need to worry anyway. It was Monday and there'd be crowds of people on their way to work. I packed up my few belongings and brought them to a locker in nearby Penn Station. School was already in session when I got there and since late notes were a requirement, I sat down on the steps to compose my own. "Please excuse my lateness. I had to give up my room at the 'Y' because I have no more money and then I brought my things to a locker at Penn Station, because I have nowhere to live. That's why I'm late." Feeling very self-righteous and more than a little neglected, I handed in my note.

Chapter 15
Kaleidoscope

You'd think that with all the traumatic experiences I was exposing myself to I'd be wising up, taking a little bit better care of myself, but the search for love and acceptance can be a very pressing and confusing ordeal, especially when you are a teenager. Unbeknownst to me, I still had yet another hoop of fire to jump through and it was to be one that would change the course of my life forever.

Like a kaleidoscope, the pieces of our young lives were constantly changing, falling into new and different patterns. Everything and everyone was changing so fast that there was little time to wonder why. Daisy had ended up in a mental institution almost catatonic with depression. I didn't see her after that. She never came back to school. Tina had also dropped out of sight. Poppy moved Gloria and Mari to Hawaii. I think he saw the handwriting on the wall. That we were, all of us, at a vulnerable age and headed for trouble with the lightening pace of the city. Celia was sent to finish out her schooling in Israel, and we quickly lost contact with each other. Diane too had drifted away from me. She was caught up in a new social circle of young artists in which I was not included. My councilor had kindly arranged for me to stay with Diane and her family, and I had lived with them for a few months but I felt estranged because I wasn't as close with Diane anymore and so when my mother got an apartment nearby and asked me to please come live with her, I agreed. Blanche had moved a few times and even changed jobs a couple of times in the past year but ever since that day, almost a year ago, that I had put her in the taxi and she had taken off on her own, she had been holding her life together as best she could. She really deserved some credit. She was keeping it all together, working with a tremendous handicap that caused her to suffer greatly and that, for the most part, only she was aware of. During this time, with everyone drifting apart, Harry called me and announced that he had joined ALANON and that they had insisted he stop seeing me. He was calling to say goodbye. I was very saddened and confused by this. I couldn't imagine what Harry might be addicted too. I never did understand what really happened. Perhaps it was me and my crazy life that was his addiction that he wanted to escape from. Jim was continuing, rapidly, down his path of self-destruction. I don't think he even worked anymore because now, any time, day or night you could reach him at the bar. We rarely saw him, and he didn't look well when we did. He had what I now recognize as the hallmarks of severe liver disease with cirrhosis. His belly was huge, swollen from the ascites that results from a complex derangement of physical processes as liver function becomes increasingly compromised. His skin had a sallow yellow tinge to it as did the whites of his eyes and he had the wasted appearance of someone who is suffering from a chronic illness. It pained me to see him this way. As for my mother and I, we were, once again, living alone together. She was working full time as a secretary, and I was a junior in High School. After school, every day and on Saturday, I worked at Woolworths and so we were both busy and didn't see that much of one another. I had absolutely no social life, no friends. It was a lonely time for me.

It was during this time of feeling somewhat isolated and depressed that I met Ray. He was about ten years older than me, and once again I had that compelling feeling that here was someone who wanted to befriend and care for me. He gave me his sunshine yellow sunglasses as a token of our new friendship and promised to turn me on to something magical and completely wonderful. There was, indeed, no denying the magic of LSD but as to the completely wonderful, I was not convinced. As I stood there in the middle of the street swaying to the rhythmically flashing neon lights in rainbow colors, my chemically challenged psychedelic mind pondering all the possible reasons for existence, my newfound friend abruptly walked away. He said, casually, as he glanced back over his shoulder, "I can't continue to see you if you don't like to fuck." Hadn't I heard that before, somewhere?

After a full day of medical tests, I sat wearily in the clinic waiting room at N.Y. Hospital, waiting for the doctor to see me and tell me what was wrong. For the last few months, I had not been feeling well. I was ridiculously tired all of the time. I'd been having a hard time eating because I was always nauseous and sometimes I would vomit for no reason. I talked to my counselor about the way I was feeling and she had sent me to this clinic that was part of the large N.Y.C. Hospital complex for a checkup. Probably, deep down inside, I knew exactly what was wrong but when my name was called, I entered the doctor's office in deep denial and totally unsuspecting.

"You're pregnant," he told me bluntly and with a hostility that he did not bother to conceal. I received the news with a confusing mixture of joy and wonder and crazy, desperate sorrow. Instinctively, my hand went to my belly and a feeling of tenderness washed over me that was as painful as it was sweet. I did, at precisely that moment, turn a corner and I knew that I would not be looking back.

Chapter 16
Dana House

Suitcase in hand, I rang the bell at the locked entrance to the weathered old brownstone that was to be my home for the next few months. A kindly woman, sixtyish with graying hair, greeted me at the door and ushered me silently upstairs and along the dimly lit, carpeted hallway to the dormitory style bedroom that I would be sharing with three other pregnant girls. "Get settled, dear, and then I'll show you where everything is," the woman had said reassuringly after introductions had been made. I sat down on the bed and looked around. The room was painted a drab institutional green. Each one of us had a twin-sized bed, a dresser and a little nightstand. There wasn't much else in the already crowded room. The girl in the bed next to mine looked to be about 15 or 16. She seemed in good spirits. "When I give my baby up for adoption, my dad is going to buy me a portable radio," she told me with enthusiasm.

It all seemed so sad to me, so sad and lonely and kind of hopeless. I lay back on the hard, thin mattress and closed my eyes, trying to imagine how a portable radio could ever, even remotely, compensate for this immense heartache of birthing a child that was to be given away and never heard of again.

When I had first found out that I was pregnant, there was no doubt in my mind that I would keep my baby and I would make a life for us, somehow, whatever it took. When I told my counselor this, she immediately sent me to a psychiatrist in a fancy office on Park Avenue. The moment I walked in the door, he said to me, "I'm going to be honest and straight forward with you. I'm not going to candy coat it. You must give this baby up for adoption. It is foolish for you to think that you could take care of it, and it would be a disaster for you to try. I am telling you this for your own good. You have to give this baby up." That was it. Visit over, and he showed me to the door. It only served to strengthen my resolve to make a new and happy life for myself and my child. After that, I was sent to a different psychiatrist at N.Y. Hospital. He was young and very handsome and he did not come off as arrogant or judgmental. He listened to me and, like the skilled practitioner that he was, he led me to draw my own picture of my life with my mother, a life that had been so filled with heartache. Then he showed me how I was headed down that same path as a single, lonely girl who had nothing and no one and had not even finished 11th grade. It had taken time and patience and many visits to finally bring me to this conclusion but when I saw it, I had cried a river of tears for my unborn child whom, I now understood, would be better off without me.

That first evening at Dana House, as we all filed into the dining room for supper, I was introduced to the other ten or so resident girls who were in various stages of confinement. When I met Maryanne, I felt suddenly as if, once again, I had been thrown a lifeline. Maryanne was a shining star in our group of seemingly clueless young, pregnant girls. When she introduced herself, I was instantly won over by her charm and brightness. Lately, I had begun to suspect that there were Guardian Angels in action, sending me assistance in one way or another whenever the going got too tough. I had begun to realize that if I really paid close attention, I could see their work; the Angel's blessing touch, at almost every difficult crossing. Often the signs were subtle like an unexpected smile of encouragement, a kind word at just the right moment, a fortuitous coincidence or chance meeting or even something so natural as a grove of trees carpeted in pink velvet blossoms or a beautiful sunset just when it felt like nothing in the world mattered anymore. Now it occurred to me that perhaps my guardian angels had arranged this crossing of paths with Maryanne. She was pretty and funny and unpretentious, unselfconscious and confident, sincere, hard-working, and fun to be around. In short she was, to me, a shining light in a time of darkness. As she laughed and talked about her home in California, her nine sisters and one brother and her plans for the future, her pretty blue eyes dancing and sparkling all the while, I experienced that blessed lifting of spirit that is a reaffirmation of light and life, and I suddenly felt that everything was going to be alright.

The days turned into weeks and the weeks to months. Girls gossiped and took turns at kitchen duty. We read books and knitted baby blankets, and we swallowed down our prenatal vitamins, dutifully, every morning. Sometimes a friend would come to visit and we would take our guest into the little guest room and sit and talk. I only had a couple of visitors the whole time I was there but on Christmas Eve, my mother and Jim came to visit me. Jim didn't say much. Perhaps he felt uncomfortable seeing me so big with child. I didn't know it at the time but it was the last time that I would ever see Jim. If I had known, what would I have done? Would I have thrown my arms around him and told him that I loved him very much; that it had grieved me so to watch him ruin his life, day by day, with his drinking. I had kept a picture of Jim in my wallet for years. He was smiling and he looked happy and handsome in the picture. The first time I ever rode on the San Francisco Trolley, I was pick-pocketed and lost that picture. After that I had nothing but my memories. I found out later that he had died within the year of my seeing him at Dana House. He had died homeless and penniless in the Bowery from severe liver disease. It was about the time period that I myself was living down in the Bowery and sometimes I imagine that maybe he was one of the many drunken bums that I had taken a little detour around in order to avoid contact. But that night I had no idea, and when he left, I had politely thanked him for coming and wished him a Merry Christmas. As for Blanche, I had spent what little cash I had managed to stash away on Christmas presents for her for the simple pleasure of seeing her smile. It wasn't anything fancy; a pretty necklace, a blouse and a winter scarf. But they didn't please her. She didn't even take them with her when she left. She was unhappy with me because I had decided to give the baby up for adoption. She had wanted it to be just her, myself and the baby, all living together in our little apartment. Once I had gained some perspective and could see the situation with more clarity, the very thought of it frightened me. It wasn't that I didn't love my mother; it was just that if I were going to survive, I needed a different way of life, and I was ready to find out what that meant.

Chapter 17
A Labor of Love

I was almost two weeks past my due date, and I felt impatient, gigantic, and anxious to be through with my confinement. I had been having mild, irregular contractions for a couple of days but nothing that progressed into true labor. Maryanne had another couple of weeks to go before her due date. Time was passing slowly for both of us. "I think we should go out for the day," Maryanne was saying. "It will help pass the time, and maybe the activity will get your labor going."

It seemed like a good idea so we decided to go visit the apartment. The two of us, huge and feeling like a couple of pregnant cows, stood packed together in a crowded subway car. No one bothered to offer us a seat. We headed downtown to where Kathy, Maryanne's friend from California, lived alone in a one-room apartment. Maryanne had lived there, with Kathy, before entering "Dana House" for the last few months of her pregnancy. Her empty bed stood awaiting her return after the birth of her baby. As if it had been predestined, the little apartment had come furnished with three beds. I had been invited to join them, and my little bed also stood waiting, patiently, against the wall.

When Maryanne had found out that she was pregnant, she and Kathy had decided to go back east where she could have the baby without her family knowing. Even though Maryanne didn't have some of the pressing social issues that I did and she was a couple of years older than I, she had felt strongly that she was too young to raise a child as a single mother and that her child would be better off in a two parent home like the one that she had been raised in. She was so sensible and clear headed about the whole matter that she had really helped me to accept my decision and to move forward with my life. I felt that there was a lot that I could learn from her and Kathy who were only a couple of years older but light years more grounded than myself. I was excited and grateful to Maryanne because she was, in essence, offering to have me join her on a path that was positive and worthy and lead in a direction that was away from my own troubled past.

When we arrived at the apartment, Kathy was still at the department store where she worked, in the photo studio, photographing customers. I sat down on what was to be my bed in my new future and listened as Maryanne told me about her sister. "My younger sister Sally," she was saying, "is really eccentric. She doesn't have any friends and she spends all of her time out in the yard crawling around on her hands and knees studying bugs and plants with a magnifying glass." We laughed because it did paint a funny picture. It was Sally though who, in the end, had the last laugh because she later grafted two kinds of cotton together and amazed the world with a hybrid that grew cotton in beautiful shades of green and yellow.

A couple of the girls at Dana House liked to refer to Maryanne as the 'folk singer' because she had such a pretty voice and she liked to sing. I too, loved to listen to her sing, but I hadn't realized that she also played the guitar. "Oh, play something for me, please," I implored.

Maryanne wasn't shy, and I didn't have to ask her twice. She got her guitar out of its case, sat down on a straight-backed chair and began finger picking. Even with her big belly in the way, she played beautifully while she sang a pretty folk tune that spoke to our predicament. *"See what careless love can do."* We weren't laughing quite so much now. After we made ourselves a little something to eat, we decided that it was time to head back to Dana House.

Spending the day out, walking around, had been a good idea. It had been fun to be out in the world, and when we got back to Dana House, my contractions seemed to be getting stronger and more regular. I went to bed along with everyone else that night but as I lay there in the dark feeling the rhythmic tightening of my belly, I knew that I would not be sleeping. Around midnight, I got out of bed, as quietly as possible so as not to wake anyone, and made my way upstairs to where Manny, our resident nurse, had her quarters. It was her job to help the girls through the early part of their labor and to know when it was time to take them to the hospital. Manny was good at what she did. We all trusted her judgment without reservation. As soon as any of us felt any unusual activity, it was always Manny who we looked to for advice. "I think this might be it, child," she told me cheerfully. "But it's early; now's the time to walk around the table to make sure that the contractions don't stop."

That was how Manny handled her laboring charges as one by one our time came up. She would insist that anyone in early labor had to walk around the long recreation table many, many times until the contractions were so strong that the laboring mother could no longer walk. Then and only then was it time to go to the hospital. Up one side and down the other I went over and over again, obeying the wisdom of one who had safely guided hundreds of young girls through this difficult and sometimes frightening process. Manny was taking up the hem on one of her huge dresses. There was so much material that it looked like she was hemming a sheet. Manny had immense, motherly breasts and she was as black as coal. She might have been a little intimidating if wasn't for the fact that she knew everything about pregnancy and labor, and she was so incredibly kind. She chatted reassuringly in a gentle, quiet voice as she sewed. I was glad for her company, and I was also glad that it was so quiet and that everyone else was asleep. Finally, around 3 a.m. when my contractions had grown quite strong and regular, Manny announced that it was time to go to the hospital. She called a taxi and we drove off into the night. In spite of my discomfort, I was feeling acutely aware of everything around me, the brisk chill of the early January morning, the tired boredom of the taxi driver, the dark, silent, empty streets and the lone grey kitty, sitting on a stoop, meticulously washing its paw. Everything seemed to be supercharged.

Manny stayed with me until she knew for sure that they were going to admit me. It was just starting to get light outside when she left. They must have been changing shifts or something like that because they left me completely alone in the little exam room for what seemed like a very long time. I could hear the clock ticking away the minutes. It sounded very loud in the otherwise silent room—tick, tick, tick, tick. The electric lights were turned off and the first rays of early morning light filtering in through the window softened the feeling of total indifference that radiated off of the sterile tile surfaces. My contractions were about five minutes apart, lasting less than a minute so I had a rest between them. Sometimes, I'd actually fall asleep for a few minutes. It felt a little weird to be laying on a gurney in that exam room, all by myself and having contractions but really, I didn't mind it. Things were moving along the way they were supposed to and I was thankful enough for that. At last someone showed up and brought me upstairs to a small labor room where, to my pleasant surprise, I had been assigned to a couple of young student nurses who were going to help me through labor. They were both very sweet and entertaining and things went exceedingly well, for a while. When a woman doctor came in and offered me something for pain, I declined, feeling confident that I could do this myself, no problem. Everything was going so well that I was caught completely off guard when all at once the pains got too strong and too close together to stay on top of. Then suddenly my body slipped into a kind of darkness. Back to back the contractions came with such unrelenting intensity that I could not catch my breath. I started to spiral out of control. My thoughts got fuzzy and I no longer understood, or cared to understand, what was happening to me. "Something for the pain," I managed to stammer in the brief interlude between contractions but everyone ignored me. They were busy hurriedly wheeling me into another room that had shockingly bright, glaring lights. Someone handed me a black rubber mask and told me to hold it over my nose. Then I fell into a sort of a trance where people were talking and bustling about and things were happening but I couldn't quite figure out what was going on. It felt as if my body was being torn asunder by stampeding horses and I could not focus nor comprehend nor run for safety. Everyone was too busy to pay any attention to my feeble appeals for help. My baby was making her entrance into the world. She was being drug out of her safe warm haven and into the sterile delivery room by a couple of steel forceps that were clamped firmly around her skull and I was too out of it to even appreciate the welcome sound of her first cry.

After the delivery, I stayed on in the hospital for a few days. I was so exhausted that a couple of the girls, who were due to deliver soon, came to visit and they got scared when they saw how pale and totally beaten up I looked. "You look terrible," they had commented. "We weren't scared before but we're scared now!"

During the few days that I was in the hospital, I got to know my baby a little. She was tiny, just around seven pounds, and she wasn't fussy at all. They brought her to me for all of her feedings. I gave her a bottle and she was satisfied to lay there in my arms, sucking down the formula and looking around demurely at a world that was so completely brand new to her. The nurses had put tiny gloves on her tiny little hands because she had been scratching at her face. They said that it was something that babies do but it worried me. I thought that perhaps it was a sign of her troubled beginnings. Could she sense that she was about to be sent off into the world banished forever from the womb that had carried her and cherished her for the last nine months? It seemed like we were content just sitting on the bed gazing at each other, but we were on a trajectory course and there was to be no changing of plans now.

On the day that we were discharged from the hospital, my councilor came to pick us up. I gazed at my baby, sleeping peacefully in my arms. In silence we took a cab to the adoption agency where I would be saying a last farewell to my little daughter. It was a cold January day, and I had swaddled her in a colorful blanket that I had knit for her. It was a complex repeating pattern of leaves that twisted and intertwined together throughout the blanket. I hoped that they would keep it for her and that someday she would be able to see, in its design, a labor of love. She was so very perfect and lovely and so content to be safe and warm, resting against my chest, that it really did seem like we belonged together. I had been told that her new family lived on a wooded lot outside of the city, that her mother was a retired school teacher and that she would have an older sister who was also adopted. It sounded like a perfect situation. I felt confident that I was doing the right thing and that everything was going to work out for the best. Still, it was hard to be letting go. All too soon I was handing my baby over to her new future and walking empty handed and heavy hearted, with shoulders bent, out of the door.

Chapter 18
A New Start

I had only 25 cents with which to start my new life, but my assets also included two wonderful new friends, a roof over my head, and a plan. When I awoke in the apartment that first morning, it had taken me a moment to remember where I was. I had collapsed into bed the night before tearful and exhausted but now a new day had dawned and I was determined to give it my very best. Kathy was already up and getting ready for work. She was so cheerful and friendly that I immediately felt at ease and welcomed. After a bite to eat, I set off on foot for 34th Street and Broadway. It was a bustling intersection of businesses about eight blocks from our apartment. I invested a nickel in a newspaper, a dime in a cup of coffee and I saved my last dime for the phone. Because of my limited finances, I had to get the first job that I applied for and it had to be in walking distance. The Angels were with me that day for within the hour I had landed a job as a personnel clerk, just across the street, on the 24th floor of a new skyscraper with an incredible view of the city.

It wasn't too long afterwards that Maryanne joined us and the three of us fell easily and naturally into step with one another. I have a couple of friends who, when I discuss mental illness with, always say to me "Yes, but what is normal. Everyone's a little crazy." For my example of what normal behavior is, I always think of Maryanne and Kathy. They were both holding jobs and they paid their bills. They didn't overspend. My friends were positive, even-tempered, young women and they didn't have any destructive habits. Except for the occasional glass or two of wine on the weekend, they didn't drink and they didn't do recreational drugs. They didn't overeat, they exercised, and they didn't fall prey to dysfunctional relationships with men. Their lives were steady and productive. That to me is 'normal' and normal was what I needed to learn. The months that followed were harmonious and for me a time of growth and enchantment. On the weekdays, we all worked 9–5 jobs, and in the evenings we just hung out and talked. Sometimes, Maryanne would play guitar and sing to us, and usually Kathy would do her yoga. She spent a lot of the time standing in the middle of the room, on her head, a trick which fascinated me. Maryanne worked at a fancy needlework boutique on the East Side, and one day she brought me home a needlepoint canvass. On it she had painted a jungle scene. To go with it she brought me some very high quality wool in beautiful jungle colors of greens and browns and parrot red. I spent many a pleasant hour working contentedly on that needlepoint on our evenings spent at home.

Not that long after leaving Dana House, Maryanne and I celebrated our birthdays. We were both born in February, within a couple of days of each other. I was turning 18 and she was turning 20. We each celebrated with a little cupcake with a single candle and then we all went out to ride the Staten Island Ferry which was still only a nickel and still the cheapest thrill around. "You'd love California," Maryanne was telling me. "The beaches are so beautiful, and where I'm from, just south of San Francisco, it's so much warmer than it is here. Sometimes, we just take our sleeping bags and go spend the night out on the beach. We make a big campfire and watch the sunset over the ocean. It's so much fun. Julie, we're probably going back in the beginning of June but you really should plan to visit us. I think you'd love it." Maryanne was feeling a little homesick and she was making California sound very inviting. She was also feeling bad about the prospect of leaving me alone and on my own in the big city. She was really a dear friend, and I felt lucky to have met her.

We pulled our coats around us tightly and went out onto the deck. It was windy and cold but we had a bottle of red wine and it warmed us from the inside out. After passing the bottle around a few times, we were getting a little silly and we decided to take turns saying or doing something entertaining. Maryanne sang us a little tune, *"I was dancing with my honey when my nose got kind of runny, everybody thought 'twas funny but it's snot."* It was so silly that it surprised us and we all had to laugh.

I did my imitation of Mae West saying, "Is that a banana in your pocket or are you happy to see me?" But when I said it, I sounded more like W.C. Fields so then I decided to repeat one of his famous lines. "Go away, boy, you bother me." I drawled, sounding very much like Mr. Fields himself.

"You've got a point there," Maryanne responded, taking her index finger and pointing it in the direction of my left nipple.

Kathy took our birthday picture with her wide-angle lens camera with flash and when we got home, she developed it in our bathroom which was, I thought, the best entertainment of all.

Back when I was living with Diane, her family had rented the two little attic rooms in their building out to a couple of college guys. They had long hair and always wore blue jeans and they smoked marijuana so I guess that made them hippies. Gary was such a sweet guy. He always had something positive to say. He was good looking, and he was funny. That day when Ray had walked away leaving me in the middle of the street flying high on acid, I had not known where to go. I didn't want to go home and have to talk with my mother in my condition, and I didn't want to run into Diane's parents either so I had gone to visit Gary. Luckily, he was home and he took me in and made me feel safe and welcome, keeping me there with him until I finally felt like I was back on planet earth. That wasn't until the next morning. He had been a perfect gentleman the entire time, and I was eternally grateful to him for that. When he moved down to the lower East Side to be closer to the Fillmore East where he was working, I had loosely kept contact with him. Now that I was a working girl myself, I decided to pay him a visit.

Gary was living in the Bowery on 3rd Street and 2nd Avenue on the third floor of an old brownstone walkup. A painted wooden sign on the door to their apartment announced '3rd Street Music School Settlement'. I knocked on the door, suddenly feeling a little shy, not entirely sure of what to expect. Someone yelled, "Come in." I opened the door and found myself standing in a little kitchen that had a big claw foot bathtub next to the sink. It was what they called a railroad apartment with the rooms all in a line like railroad cars and all of the fixtures that needed plumbing, all in the same room. It was a simple set up. To my left I could see a tiny room with a set of bunk beds and guys' clothing scattered all about. To my right was a set of double glass doors that opened into the small living room. There was a mattress on the floor that was covered with a bright, flowery Indian bedspread and a big wooden table which was loaded down with the record player and their huge stacks of records. There were a bunch of people sitting around on the floor, playing guitars and talking. Smoke, from the fat joint being passed around, filled the air and the smell of marijuana filtered into the kitchen/bathroom from the living room. When Gary saw me standing there hesitantly, at the door, the smile on his face widened. He got up and came over and gave me a big hug. "Julie, it's so good to see you, what have you been up to?"

He explained that he was sharing the apartment with his friend Rick and his younger brother Donny. I had met them both many times before when he lived at Diane's. All three of them were from a little town in upstate New York and perhaps that explained why they were so nice. They were country boys. They were all so surprised and happy to see me that I was really glad that I had decided to come. Their little apartment was full of people and life and good cheer. "How is Diane?" Gary wanted to know. I had to admit that I didn't know. I hadn't seen her in months.

"And how about you, how are you doing?" Gary asked with a sincere, friendly interest.

I filled him in about Dana House and the adoption and Maryanne and Kathy and my new job keeping files on all of the employees for this gigantic firm. "I'm really happy these days. I have no idea where I'm headed. It's just one-step at a time I guess, but right now things are good. And you, Gary, what are you doing these days?"

"I'm doing really well. I'm working at the Fillmore as a bookkeeper and I go to all the shows. I get to see all the great rock bands. I love it. Rick and Donny work at the Fillmore too, as ushers. We have lots of friends who are musicians. People are dropping by all the time. We usually get together in the evenings and play a little music. It's a blast. Our life is all about music. What could be better than that?"

"Nothing," I had to agree. "It sounds really cool. Music is the best!"

"Let me walk you to the subway," Gary suggested when it was time for me to go. It made me feel really good. I felt like he no longer saw me as the kid downstairs but as a young woman, and it also seemed like he wanted to have a few more minutes to be together. That felt really good as well.

In the spring, when the weather was getting warmer and the New England countryside was all in bloom, Maryanne and I decided to go to Woodstock for the weekend. Kathy was busy and didn't want to go so it was just the two of us. We took the train part way and hitch hiked the rest of the way. We got rides easily and it was fun talking to all the different people. When we got to Woodstock, we rented a room in a quaint little bed and breakfast for the night and then set out for a walk in the countryside that was so enticingly fragrant and bursting with color. That evening, pleasantly worn out from our busy workweek and our long exhilarating walk, we settled into our cozy room with a bottle of red wine, some cheese, a loaf of French bread, and green olives. We poured a glass of wine, and we were happily munching away on our little feast as Maryanne told stories. She had a gift for bringing out the humor in almost any situation. If you could have bottled her personality and sold it, you could have made millions. It was amazing really. She could talk about any ordinary and even boring event, and soon everyone in the room would be laughing.

I was laughing now as she talked about some guy named Reese that she had been crazy about in High School and about growing up with nine sisters. "Yea, one day my sister was angry with me and she told me 'you're not the only grain of sand on the beach.' I was so shocked! 'I'm not?' I had said to her in amazement."

"Maryanne, you're so funny. I wish I had a sister." Actually, she was really like a sister to me.

Our life experiences had been so very different. I talked a lot about my mother. "I'm so glad to be out of that crazy, depressing life. I'm never going back, no matter what. My mom's working right now, and that's really good, but she lost the apartment and now she's back living in a hotel room. I don't see her that much but when I do see her, she seems like she's okay. Lately though, she always has something really mean to say to me. She can make me feel so bad. It makes me feel like staying away."

"What are you going to do when Kathy and I leave?" Maryanne was looking at me with a worried expression on her pretty face.

"I've got a job. I'll find a little apartment that I can afford, other than that I'm not sure. I guess I should try and finish High School at some point."

"What are you going to do when you get back to California, Maryanne?" I asked, wanting to change the subject. The wine was making me feel sleepy and I had started putting on my pajamas.

"Well, first off I'll probably go stay with my family for a while. I really miss them, and my mother really misses me. You'd love her, Julie. She's really sweet and funny. I get my sense of humor from her. I have a very good friend, who's also named Cathy, but with a C instead of a K. I can't wait to see her. Let me see, I guess I'll get a job for a while. Maybe take some classes at the local junior college. Go hiking in the Sierras, go and watch the sunset over the ocean. There is so much to do, Julie."

As I was drifting off to sleep, I was thinking about that day back in Junior High when I had almost moved out to California with Jim and my mother but how, at the very last minute, things had changed. Perhaps I would be making it out to California one of these days after all.

Before leaving N.Y.C., my roommates wanted to do a little sightseeing so we decided to hit some tourist attractions over the next few weekends. We went to the top of the Empire State building, and we visited the Statue of Liberty, we took a ride in a horse drawn carriage around Central Park, and we went to see a show on Broadway. We were having a lot of fun but also, I knew that with every passing day our time together was coming to an end and it made me feel sad and anxious.

As June crept closer, I was half-heartedly looking for a place to live. On my salary, I couldn't afford to keep our apartment. Time was running out. We had to be out of the apartment by June 1st. Maryanne was flying out on that day, and Kathy would be staying with a friend of hers for a couple of days and then flying back to California as well. It was really hard to find decent housing at an affordable price in N.Y.C. but I had made incredible progress in forging a new and better way of life, and I was determined not to lose ground by going backwards into my old life. One evening, after work, I decided to go and visit Gary and talk the situation over with him to see if he had any suggestions. Once again Gary proved what a good friend and a good guy he really was. "Why don't you stay here with us until you can find a place?" he offered.

When he said this, a huge weight was so suddenly lifted off of my shoulders that I imagined I might float up to the ceiling. The plan was to stay just a short time until I could work something else out; however, this move, unexpectedly, opened up a whole new set of experiences and lessons that I was happily caught up in for quite some time. When our month's rent was out, we packed up our few belongings and amidst hugs and tears and promises to write, Maryanne and Kathy went home to California and I took the subway down to my new home at the Third Street Music School Settlement.

Chapter 19
The Fillmore Days

In the two months that I had been living at the 3rd Street Music School Settlement with Gary, Rick and Donny, we had gone to the show at the Fillmore every weekend. Rick and Donny worked the weekend shows but since Gary worked the weekdays, in the office, he was free to go to the weekend shows with me. So far we had seen The Grateful Dead, Joe Cocker, Ike and Tina Turner, Three Dog Night, Jefferson Airplane and Crosby Stills Nash and Young. The latter were definitely one of my favorites. They came on stage, settled down with their amplified acoustic guitars and proceeded to blow everyone's mind with their incredible music and good vibes. As they sang the song *Our House* I looked over at Gary. I had really lucked out this time. I was happier than I had ever been in my entire life. Since moving in with the guys, Gary and I had become inseparable. One evening, as we were sitting together having dinner in a hip, crowded little café in the West Village, Gary had put his arm around me and pulled me close to him. The place was buzzing with conversation and laughter and the clatter of dishes. Rick and Donny were sitting directly across from us talking about some show that was coming up, in a few weeks, that they were both really excited about. In spite of all this commotion, it felt like Gary and I were the only people in the room. As we sat together, acutely aware of the closeness and heat of our bodies touching, gazing at each other and talking in hushed tones about how much we were enjoying being together, everything and everyone else in the room, seemed to fade into the background. "Do you feel it?" Gary whispered, looking deeply into my eyes. "We're falling in love!"

Everything stood still for a moment as the words hung, heavy, in the air. We were falling in love. We had been having nonstop fun since I had moved in, and our friendship had just kept getting sweeter and sweeter. That was it. We were falling in love. Now as we listened to Crosby Stills Nash and Young singing *about how much easier life was now that he had found someone to love* those were the very words that I wanted to say to Gary.

I think of that time period in my life as 'the Fillmore days'. When I hear people say that they long for the carefree days of their youth, I always think of that time. Bill Grahams Fillmore East opened its doors in 1968 and closed them in 1971, just three years later. In its brief but glorious history, the Fillmore was known as the Church of Rock and Roll. It was a very special time and we, of the 3rd street music school settlement, were totally caught up in its magic. We were young and full of energy and grateful to be alive at, what we regarded as, a very special time in history. The theater had a capacity of 2700 and on show night the lines went well around the block. Young people poured in from all over, dressed, decoratively, in everything from rags to velvet and lace. Many were stoned on pot or acid or a variety of other drugs, but they were peaceful as they filed into the theater happily, anticipating what they knew was going to be a dynamite show. The famous 'Joshua Light Show' added to the surreal and stoned out atmosphere of the place with its flashing, pulsating colors and strobe lights that created the illusion that you were tripping on acid, even if you were stone sober. And when the music started playing, there really was no better place on earth to be. Everyone in the huge crowd was high on life, and out for a good time.

It was also a fabulous time to be living in the Village which was so alive with music and cool cafés and thriving with the hippy movement. It was, as well, a time of intense dissatisfaction as the Vietnam War claimed more and more of our youth who were being drafted and sent overseas to fight a war that they didn't support. Young people were searching for a new and better way to walk on the earth. We wanted peace and love and solidarity and freedom of expression. We didn't want to go overseas and kill innocent people and die for a cause that we did not believe in. Clandestine meetings were regularly occurring events in the Village where young men, whose number had come up in the draft lottery, would gather together to figure their way out of going to war. When Donny's number came up, we all held our breath but to our great relief, he was rejected for flat feet or something simple like that. But there were incredible and sometimes funny, stories of what some guys went through to escape the draft. It was also a time of marching and protests and of great solidarity. 'Love Ins' were happening events where young people would come together by the hundreds, sometimes by the thousands, declaring peace and love for all. We would all hold hands, strangers and friends alike, and sing peace songs and feel high because our hearts were all united in one love.

After I had been living with Gary and the guys for several months, I got word from Maryanne that she and the Cathy whom I hadn't met, were driving to Maine to pick up Cathy's older sister who was stranded there. They wanted to see some of the country on their way back to California and Maryanne thought that it would be a great idea if I were to go with them. They could pick me up on their way to Maine. What did I think? I was wild with excitement. I missed Maryanne, and the offer to explore the country with my good friend was one that I could not turn down. I hoped that it would not be a problem for Gary. Much to my relief, although Gary was not pleased with the idea, he saw how excited I was and he did not try and stop me. Within days I had given notice at my job and bought a cheap backpack and a sleeping bag. When my friends arrived in Maryanne's blue Volkswagen Bug with a bulging luggage rack, looking all beautiful and carefree and ready for adventure, I was ready to go with them.

Our first hour out of NYC, as we were racing down the freeway headed north, some of our stuff flew off of the roof rack because it was not tied down properly. It was our first lesson in road physics. Then we had to run down the side of the highway for a quarter mile gathering up what possessions we could manage to retrieve. In the next hour, a thunderous rain squall suddenly opened up upon us with such vigor that we could hardly see out the windshield even with the wipers on high and then they broke. Maryanne, using her good common sense, then rolled down her window and drove in a peculiar manner with her head stuck out the window while giant sheets of rain lashed through the car. We took the next exit and headed for the nearest gas station. Thanks to AAA, we were soon back on the road with new windshield wipers but, by then, it had stopped raining.

We found Maureen on a stretch of wild, windswept coastline, living communally with some other young folks in a big red barn that had, artfully, been turned into a living space. The area was very remote and hauntingly beautiful like a scene out of a gothic novel. I liked Maureen immediately. I was impressed with her poise and self-confidence. She was a blue-eyed Irish beauty, and she fit right in with the untamed magnificence of her surroundings. There seemed to be some hushed talk of a love affair gone wrong and a misunderstanding. Perhaps that explained why Maureen was so anxious to get going. That night we threw our sleeping bags out on the floor in the huge empty space beneath the gigantic wooden rafters which supported the lofty steeple ceiling that towered above our heads. We slept, fitfully, to the sound of the surf crashing against the rocks below. The next morning, we arose at dawn, added Maureen's things to our already weighted down little V.W. Bug until the shocks were creaking and sagging under the weight. Then we all piled in and hit the road.

We started off in high spirits, deciding to take a little detour north to see Quebec and Nova Scotia. In Nova Scotia, we camped out on a beach that was wild and lonely. Maureen and I shared one tent and Cathy and Maryanne the other. We spent a day exploring, walking along the rocky shoreline following a curving path that meandered in and out of secluded coves. The surf, pounding against vertical cliff walls, sent dancing sprays of foam high into the air in a rhythmic cycle of advance and then retreat. The sound of the crashing waves was so powerful and so loud that it seemed to drown out most thoughts and unless we were standing right next to each other, it was hard to hear what the others were saying. There wasn't much talking that day. We were too entranced by our surroundings to say much. Except for the four of us, the beach was deserted. We cooked over a campfire and made steaming hot camp coffee which tasted delicious in the chill of the early morning. When the afternoon sun was high in the sky and silky warm and the wind had died down, we spread out a blanket and lay resting in the warm sunshine, planning our next destination.

Quebec, with its old world stone buildings and narrow, winding cobblestone streets reminded me a little of the West village but on a much larger scale and older. It felt like we had stepped back in time a century or two. We sat drinking espresso in a crowded little sidewalk café. The weather was perfect, warm, and balmy. People bustled about their day, around us, talking to each other in French. I tried to remember some of the French that I had taken in High School, while I had still been allowed to take college prep classes. "Le pain, fromage y le vin, S'il vous plait," I said, trying to order us some lunch in French. I was pleased with the attempt in spite of its very minimal success.

"I don't think they like Americans very much here," Maureen was saying. "There's a left wing nationalist group known as the Front de Liberation du Quebec that wants Quebec's independence from Canada and they want to establish a French speaking workers society. In February, they bombed the Montreal Stock Exchange, and there's been rioting. People are getting killed. There's a lot of unrest right now, I think we should be careful."

We had to decide where we were going to spend the night. We didn't have money for hotels so, every evening, we had to find a safe camping spot. "Well, there's no place to camp around here anyway so we're going to have to head back down south and we should do it before it gets dark." That was Cathy's very sensible input and we all had to agree so we paid our bill then we walked around for a bit and then left that lovely city while we still had time to find a place to camp before nightfall. On our second night out, we hadn't timed things well and we had ended up sleeping on the side of the road. We had spent a miserable night and we didn't want to do it again.

Somewhere around the Great Lakes, we dropped back into the United States. Maryanne and Cathy had been on the road for almost a month and they were getting tired of traveling. Maureen too was feeling anxious to be home. We were driving to make time now, stopping midafternoon in some scenic spot to have a picnic lunch and then getting back on the road until it was time to look for a place to stay for the night. The scenery raced by, changing constantly like a slide show in three dimension. We passed through cities, noisy and grey with smog and through farm country with miles and miles of level plowed fields in checkerboard patches of greens and yellows and browns. There were mountain roads, so steep and narrow and twisting that they seemed to go on forever and misty mountains that were covered with evergreen forests that looked so inviting and beckoned to us to explore deeper into their mysteries. Then there were the bare rock mountains of a thousand hues of red and sienna. I looked on, awe struck, when the sun suddenly shone on them and a thousand hues of pinks and reds and purples sprang to life. We passed through deserts and around lakeshores and over spectacular, rocky passes. It was an incredible variety of landscapes that we were seeing and at a certain point I began to realize that I would not be happy spending the rest of my life living in the city surrounded by concrete. I also began to suspect that I had a little touch of road fever in my blood and that, in fact, was to define much of my life that still lay ahead of me.

We stopped for a day or so at some of the more spectacular places and then moved on always on the lookout for a safe place to sleep. Every few days I called Gary at the Fillmore from a payphone. As the days passed, he grew more and more impatient with me. "Aren't you there yet?" he would say, sounding annoyed. "What's taking you so long? Why don't you just fly back now from wherever you are?"

"But you can't go back without seeing California," Maryanne would say, equally annoyed.

"Of course I can't." No matter what, I was on the trip until its completion.

We stopped for a couple of days outside of Boulder Colorado, camping in the Rocky Mountains. The air was thin and crisp and pure. Just breathing the air made me feel high. We stayed in a campground with a shower! It was a glorious feeling to roll out of the sleeping bag in the early morning sunshine and then go stand, naked, with the hot water pelting down washing away all of the road grime and the stiffness that comes from sitting in a car for hours at a time. When I stepped from the steamy wooden shower stall into the fresh mountain morning, feeling all clean and sturdy and as free as the mountains that towered above and all around us, I felt that life had reached a new pinnacle. "Could life ever get any better than this?" I asked Maureen who was drying her hair in the sun.

She nodded, smiling. "It's incredible."

It took us a month to get to California. My friends were happy to be home. I was thrilled as we drove across the famous Golden Gate Bridge and into San Francisco. I watched with delight as the sailboats that looked like so many colorful little toys, glided into and away from the blue horizon. We went, right away, to Maryanne's house that was south of San Francisco, and I met some of her family. They were all very friendly and gracious, and they made me feel welcome. Over the next couple of days, Maryanne took me on a whirlwind tour of the local sights. We went to the beach, of course, and I watched, for the first time, as the sun set over the ocean, dropping down behind the horizon and leaving in its place a riot of colors, pinks, purples and yellows, all mixing together and spreading out, like a water color, across the darkening sky. We also spent a day touring around San Francisco. I was struck by the beauty and cleanliness of the city. When I had left N.Y.C., there had been a garbage strike and Manhattan, which had already seemed to me like a dirty city, was overflowing with garbage. In comparison, San Francisco looked like everyone came out of their houses in the morning to scrub the streets. The San Francisco trolley was fun to ride as it struggled up the steep streets, clanking its cheerful presence to those passing by, but it's where I lost my only picture of Jim and I will always regret that.

There was so much to see in the city, the beaches, Golden Gate Park, the very streets that climbed up and up at such steep angles only to drop steeply down and out of view on the other side. I couldn't see everything but I knew that one day I would return. For the time being, I had to get back to N.Y.C. and to Gary. When the plane landed in N.Y., Gary was there to meet me in a loving welcome that made it the sweetest homecoming that I had ever known.

It was Christmas Eve. I had put a few colorful decorations up in the living room to get us into the spirit of the season and we had all bought each other a present to open. In the past, I had seldom received Christmas presents because we never had any money. We considered ourselves lucky if we had food. This Christmas was a special time with my friends in many ways. There was so much to be thankful for. The thought and care that each of my roommates put into their gift to me was a gift in itself. I wanted to learn to play the flute so Rick bought me a beautiful old, weathered silver flute. I also liked to paint pictures so Donny bought me a set of oil paints and Gary bought me a classic, white silk, cowboy shirt with rows of tassels that looked kind of sexy and turned a few heads when I wore it. After opening presents, the four of us walked across town looking for the coolest, sweetest little café we could find to have dinner. We were all jolly and singing Christmas carols as we walked along in the frosty night air. Life was good.

After dinner, Gary and I went uptown to visit my mother. Blanche was living in the same hotel that we had been evicted from when I was in High School. We found her, sitting on the bed, in a dingy little room all alone. The dim light from the bedside lamp illuminated a small area of stained carpet and tattered bedspread. I could tell that she was writing again from the chaos of typing paper scattered around the room. The pages were covered with her elegant handwriting in a format that looked like poetry. She seemed glad to see us so we sat and talked for a while.

"Mom, I'd like you to meet Gary. We live together now and we are so very happy."

She liked him I think although with my mother it was always so hard to tell because one minute she could be acting as if she really liked someone and the next she could be accusing them of trying to steal her fortune.

"It's a pleasure to meet you, Blanche," Gary said with his sweet smile, extending his hand to my mother in a gesture of friendship.

"What have you been doing, Mom?" I wanted to know. "Are you working?"

"No. I'm collecting unemployment right now. Money's kind of tight. I've just been out of work for a short time though. I'll get another job soon."

"Do you ever see Jim?"

"No never. I haven't any idea where to find him. I think he's working for the CIA and they have him on a special mission. He's not allowed to contact me right now. I thought I saw him the other day but he wouldn't talk to me. It was probably too dangerous."

Her answer didn't surprise me. It just reminded me of why it had been so important that I move on with my life.

"Well, Mom, do you get out much?" I was starting to feel depressed, knowing all too well what her life must be like.

"Oh, Julie, I'm fine. Don't bother me. You ask too many questions!" She was starting to get annoyed.

I felt like we should probably get going, but we left her with some money and that, more than anything, cheered her up.

Once back home in our cozy little railroad apartment, with music playing and friends dropping by for the evening, the gloom that had descended upon me began to lift. I looked around me with pride and gratitude. I was happy again. Gary put his arm around me and we sat there together with our heads touching, feeling content just to be close. I knew that my mother's life was miserable and it wasn't something that she brought upon herself. It was the curse of mental illness. But I couldn't go there with her. I had to save myself.

Right around my birthday, the Grateful Dead were scheduled to appear at the Fillmore. We were all excited to see their show. Their soundman, Stanley Owsley, was going to be there with them. He was known for manufacturing very pure LSD and there was much discussion about whether or not it would be available at the show. I rarely did drugs anymore and the one and only acid trip that I had ever taken had been a little overwhelming. I wasn't really interested in repeating the experience. However, everyone else was really up for it and I started feeling that if it was available, I should not pass up a chance to try the famous Owsley Acid.

A couple of days before the show, I had come home from work about 30 minutes later than usual. As I had walked across town from the West Village, where I worked as a cashier in a shoe store, to the East Village where we lived, I had stopped in a little shop that was still open to look at some earrings. When I got home, Gary was angry with me and demanded to know where I had been and what I had been doing. When I told him, he didn't believe me. These little episodes had been happening more and more frequently of late. They were the one dark shadow on our otherwise happy relationship. I didn't understand it. It seemed like he was insecure about our relationship and jealous of some imaginary indiscretion. He didn't trust me. Looking back, I wonder if it wasn't the start of some restlessness on both of our parts. We had been living together for nine months and having a great time but where was it going. I had been talking to Gary about the possibility of us getting our own place. We had looked around a bit but we hadn't come up with anything. I was also bored with my job. I wanted something more interesting, more fulfilling. Maybe that was bothering him, or maybe he also was brewing some desire for change, something that he wasn't, as yet, aware of.

The night of the Dead show, when we arrived at the Fillmore, Owsley Acid was being passed around in sodas. It was flowing freely like it was wine. I wouldn't doubt if there were at least several hundred young people in the theater tripping on acid that night, maybe many more. I drank some of the spiked soda and settled into my seat to watch the show. The Dead were taking a long time to come on stage. When another round of LSD soda came my way, I had a bit more. Finally, they came on stage. As soon as they started playing, the place came alive. The music was fantastic and the audience was buzzing like a beehive. It was as if we were one organism, the band and the audience. The beat of the music was our common heartbeat. I was coming on to the acid strong now. The infectious rhythms got everyone on their feet, moving and murmuring and sighing and shuffling and laughing and coughing, clearing their throats until the roar of the audience got so loud that it completely drowned out the sound of the music. The vibrations of all those people in one spot, just breathing, became overwhelming. Suddenly, I jumped to my feet, pushed my way through to the isle and rushed out of the theater. It was such a relief to be away from that immense chasm of pounding sound and energy. The street was completely silent. No cars, no people, and it was snowing! It was so incredibly beautiful. The snowflakes fell in slow motion, softly, through the air. Each individual snowflake was a perfect filigree of crystal. I looked around in awe. Gary was there standing beside me. "Don't be afraid," he whispered. But I was afraid, afraid of my restlessness and what it might do to us. It was as if the acid was some sort of catalyst that served to define feelings and desires that I myself had not been aware of. California was calling me.

Chapter 20
A Change of Heart

Recently, on my birthday, I got an email from Gary. He said that there was a song that, whenever he heard it, he thought of me. He went on to say that it was serendipitous the way it had come on a radio station, which never plays that sort of music, the day before my birthday. He was sending me the link so I could hear it. The song was 'Hearts' by Marty Balin *and it told the story of how our love just seemed to fade away.*

I sat and cried for a while after I read the words to the song. I was happy with my life. No big regrets but I was lonely sometimes and relationships had always been difficult for me. Gary on the other hand was happily married and had been so for years. *What would my life have been like*, I wondered, *if we had not split up? Could we have held it together all these years? Would it have saved me a lot of pain?* I realized, in retrospect, that Gary and I had been good together. We were very compatible. There is that possibility that it could have been the match made in heaven, so to speak, if only we had been able to see it at the time. But we were very young and the path not traveled will always be a mystery.

After the Owsley acid experience, I had begun to realize that I had to get out of the city and I really wanted to get back to California. One day, I just up and left N.Y. Gary came after me, which I think is the most romantic thing that has ever happened to me in my entire life. I was very happy that he did. Then we decided to do some traveling together so we bought an old station wagon and we went to Mexico. It was a fantastic adventure. We lived for a month in a lovely little hacienda in the hills of Puerto Vallarta, overlooking the ocean. It was an idyllic and romantic setting, and I will always treasure the memory of the time we spent there, together. After leaving Puerto Vallarta, we went back to California. Gary got a job at the post office and I started going to Junior College. At that time, Junior College was free in California and for some reason they didn't ask me for my H.S. transcripts. It was great. I was enjoying going to school and happy to be learning new things. I had a student job that brought in a little money and life was good. One day, after my classes, I went to the house of a fellow student to look at the bamboo flutes that he made. I was interested in buying one. I got home about an hour late to find Gary in a rage. He met me at the door and told me that I couldn't live there anymore. I had to leave immediately. I guess I could have just said no. I had done nothing wrong, but leaving was something that I did well. From a very young age, I had been conditioned to leave at a moment's notice. Without protest, I gathered a few of my things and went back to the house of my flute maker.

I never really talked with Gary about the details of that time. We just kind of said that we let each other slip away and we left it at that. I do believe that he had met another girl at the post office where he was working because right after that it was hard to get a hold of him in the evenings by phone and shortly after that he left for Mexico. Also he was in a good mood and not upset, at all, about the turn of events. As for me, after Gary got on the plane for Mexico, I tried to move back into the little apartment that we had shared. I was ready to try living alone but it was as if the forces of the universe were herding me, with purpose, in a certain direction. On my very first night alone, two guys came to the door asking for Gary. I told them that he wasn't home. The top half of the door was a window and I could see them through the glass standing there in the rain, shivering. Then one of them asked to use the bathroom so I let them in. One fellow seemed like a nice guy but he was very stoned. We stood by the door talking about my cat and my very cute doggie, who were lying curled up together, while the other fellow went into the bathroom. When he came out of the bathroom, however, he pulled a knife on me and he told me to get into the bedroom. Somehow, I managed to throw open the door and run screaming, to a neighbors but that was it. The damage had been done. Now I was terrified to go back there and I was terrified to be alone at night.

Part Three
It Might Just Be a Lunatic You're Looking For

Chapter 21
The Four Noble Truths

When I had run screaming to the neighbors, my intruders had run in the opposite direction carrying with them our record player. The neighbors called the sheriff and I made a full report, then they kindly drove me and my dog, Sammy, to John's where I wouldn't have to be alone. John was happy to have me stay and Sammy too. As the days passed, it became clear that I wouldn't be leaving any time soon. It was the beginning of a fourteen-year odyssey.

"Now play the open 'E' string," John instructed me. We were sitting in his cute and cheery little kitchen. John was heating a small iron rod on the stove and using it to burn the note holes in the flute he was making. He would start with a small hole and keep enlarging it until it came into tune with the note on the guitar. He also spent many hours sanding the inside of the flute smooth as glass and then coating it several times with a clear epoxy base paint. It was a process that took a lot of patience, but the end result was a beautiful sounding flute that was a work of art. I was learning to weave. We liked to sit together in the kitchen, John working on his flutes and me, surrounded by a colorful assortment of wool, weaving pleasing tapestries on the frame loom that I had made. I plucked the 'E' string. It wasn't in tune yet. The hole needed to be bigger. A thin stream of smoke rose up from the flute as the little hole sizzled and enlarged, turning a rich shade of charcoal and coffee brown. The smell of the burning bamboo was pleasant and earthy.

Sammy lay there watching us with his head resting on his outstretched paws. He was such a shaggy dog that you could hardly see his eyes. Was he awake or not? Sammy looked just like a Sheepdog but only about $1/3^{rd}$ the size. He had such a wild mane of hair in multicolored shades of grays and browns that he appeared to be a chunky, medium-sized dog. However, when he was soaking wet, you could see that he was surprisingly scrawny. Sammy was a little dog with a big heart and he was the smartest dog that I have ever known. His tail started to wag when he saw that I was watching him. "You must be awake, Sammy. You're such a good dog," I said this knowing full well that he was the best dog that a girl ever had. Just to prove what a good dog he really was and how eager he was to please, he jumped up and ran over to give me a big kiss on the cheek. It tickled and I was delighted. "Sammy, you are the best!" It was getting late so we decided to stop what we were doing and go to bed. All of a sudden, there was a racket in the street, noise-makers, fire crackers, people yelling. We could just make out the celebratory cry of "Happy New Year." We'd been so caught up in the day that we had totally forgotten.

John was 6ft 4in, tall and lanky. His upper back was slightly rounded which added to the impression that he was an old soul. Looking at John, one's first impression might be that he looked like a mad man for he had long black hair and a wild bushy beard that he did not try to tame. His gaze was very intense. When you looked beyond that, however, you saw that he had incredibly beautiful, large hazel eyes that were lined with thick dark lashes and a wide, full, sensual mouth. Many women thought that he was beautiful, although others thought that he strongly resembled a Neanderthal man. I was 19 years old and John was 24, but he was serious and reflective and it made him seem older than his years. While most other guys his age were talking about sex, drugs, and rock and roll, John talked eloquently for hours about Zen Buddhism, the crusades and the dark ages, politics, and the Theory of Relativity. I thought that he was brilliant, maybe even a genius. He seemed to know everything about anything anyone could think of to talk about.

John was teaching me about Buddhism, and I was fascinated. I drank in every word he said about Buddha and meditation, the Eight Fold Path, and the Four Nobel Truths. "The story goes," John was telling me, "that Buddha was born a prince. He lived surrounded by all the luxury and material possessions that a man could desire. His parents would not allow him to go beyond the walls of the castle because they did not want him to know about all the suffering in the world. One day he went into the village, where he was forbidden to go, disguised as a commoner. What he saw that day was that life was filled with pain, illness, and suffering. He was so troubled by all the human misery that he saw; everywhere he looked that he left the castle to forever wander as an esthetic. He was trying to discover a path that would lead to the cessation of suffering. Buddha's message was simple, that life is suffering. Birth is suffering, aging is suffering, illness is suffering and craving is suffering. Freedom from desire brings release from suffering when it is practiced along with the eight fold path which is: right view, right intention, right speech, right action, right livelihood, right effort, right mindfulness, and right concentration."

We were both quiet for a minute. I was thinking about all the suffering I had already seen in my 19 years. I felt that I had been witness to an incredible amount of suffering in the two people that had been dearest to me, my mother and Jim. Mental illness was certainly suffering and so was alcoholism. Much of the time, I had suffered along with them. I was very interested in this path that spoke of a way to attain freedom from suffering. "That is so beautiful. I want to learn more. I want to learn to meditate," I told John excitedly.

He nodded looking like a young, old sage. "Follow the breath," he told me. "Sit very still with your back straight. Forget about everything else and pay close attention to your breathing. That is the basics of meditation."

Chapter 22
A Surprise Guest

Early one morning, we were lying in bed talking about going to Port Angeles and visiting John's family over spring break which was only a little over a week away. I was really looking forward to it. There was a knock at the door. "Who could that be this early?" John said lazily as he stretched and yawned.

"I'll go see," I said, bouncing out of bed. When I opened the door, there was a stranger standing there. "Hi, can I help you?" I asked, thinking that he was probably lost.

He sounded grumpy and somewhat annoyed when he answered. "There's a lady in my cab that says she's your mother and that you'll pay the fair. It's $25.00."

I was so surprised that I just stared at him for a moment. My mother probably hadn't told him that she didn't have any money until she had arrived at her destination. It was a good thing that we were home. I knew that Blanche was having a hard time, all by herself, in New York, and I had suspected that one day she would be evicted again. She had come with just the clothes on her back. She was distraught and close to starvation from five days and nights on a bus across the country with no money and hardly anything to eat. My mother had put all her faith in the desperate hope that when she got to the other side of the continent, there would be shelter and a safe port. And so there was!

I brought her in and sat her down. She was frazzled. She was on the verge of tears and she looked like she might jump up and bolt, out the door, at any moment like a frightened deer. I introduced her to the surprised but cordial John and made her some breakfast and some hot tea. After a while, she was able to relax a little. "So what happened, Mom? How did you end up coming out to California? I can't believe you're really here. You'll be glad you came once you get settled." It had been almost a year since I last saw her but I called her every few weeks. The last time we talked, she had sounded troubled saying that she had been walking in the snow, barefoot, so that people would understand how hard her life was. At that time, I had suggested that she come out to California because life was so much easier. The weather was warmer for one thing and people were nicer. Also, I had been surprised at how easy it was to find work and a place to live. I never really expected to see her though. I guess she had nowhere else to turn to for help so she had left everything she owned behind and traveled 3000 miles by bus, not really sure of what she would find when she arrived. Just a week later and we would have been gone. After a couple of days of rest and good food, she started to come around, not seeming so frightened or depressed. But when I informed her that we were going up to Washington for a week, she fell apart again. "No, don't go. Don't leave me," she pleaded.

Blanche was crying when we left. She went and lay down on the little bed we had set up for her in the living room and she turned her back to us. She would not say goodbye. I felt bad but we had left her some money and food and of course the key, and we had talked about her looking for a job while we were gone. "We'll be back in a week, Mother, before you know it. I love you." She didn't answer.

It was a long drive up to Port Angeles, a small town on the Olympic Peninsula. We drove for 18 hours, basically all through the night. When we got there, we were exhausted. We decided to lie down for just a minute but then we were out for hours. When we finally emerged from the bedroom, rested, everyone was anxious to visit with John and to get to know me. John's family was very sweet. His mother was of Italian heritage and she made us a fantastic Italian dinner, with homemade raviolis and sauce that she had been simmering over the stove for two days. John's younger brother Darwin seemed kind of shy. He was still living at home, and they had three older sisters who lived in Seattle. With so little time and so much to see, we weren't sure we would make it out to Seattle this trip to meet them.

The first place that John took me to see was the Olympic National Park. It was a spectacular sight with the tall mountain peaks still covered with snow, the glaciers and the wild mountain goats that stood proudly on the hilltops, surveying their territory. "You are so lucky to have grown up surrounded by all this beauty. It's so different from where I grew up in Manhattan where everything is concrete," I told him.

"I can see these mountains from my bedroom window," John replied, with an appreciative nod.

The next day we drove out to the Hoe Rain Forest where we were dwarfed by the immensity of the trees that surrounded us. John had described it well when he wrote to me in a letter, "Green is everywhere, chlorophyll running and gushing in wild patterns." We spent a magical day wandering around in a world that was self-contained, blocking out even the sky and completely engulfed in opulent, dripping greenery.

There was so much environmental diversity in this one little area of the world that I was blown away. The beaches were endless, wild, and windy. A chill fog hung low over the Peninsula most of the day, every day. We drove around seeing the sights and visiting his friends from childhood. We were having a fantastic trip. I was captivated by all these extreme and wildly beautiful expressions of nature. All too soon it was time to head back to the more tame and temperate Bay Area. When we parted, John's parents gave me a hug and welcomed me into the family. "We hope to see you at Christmas," they said as they stood on the sidewalk, waving goodbye.

When we got back home, Blanche met us at the door and she was smiling. She seemed comfortable now and confident. She had some good news for us. In one short week my mother had not only found a job but also a place to live. Blanche was quickly becoming a California woman. It has been written of schizophrenia that, for reasons not clearly understood, often times when a person reaches their 40s, their illness will stabilize. Blanche was 48 years old when she showed up at our door. I've always thought that if she had stayed by herself in N.Y.C, she would have died young. But life actually was a bit easier out in California, and I'm happy to say that the next 15 years marked a time of peace and stability for my mother such as she had never experienced before. When I think back on her life, I am grateful for her years spent in Berkeley where she worked for JC Penny, had an apartment literally stuffed full of pretty cloths and a steady boyfriend who took her out to fancy places where she could wear them.

Chapter 23
San Cristobal

At the end of the spring semester, we invested in an old VW Bus. We set it up like a colorful little gypsy wagon on wheels with a bed, some storage and a tidy little cooking area. Once all the preparations were complete, John, Sammy and I took off for Mexico. We had no particular plans other than trying to live as frugally as possible, traveling until the money ran out.

After an endless monotony of grey top highway and bland, desolate looking desert, we arrived at the charming coastal town of Guymas. On the outskirts of town, we parked the car and hiked over the cliffs for a mile or so until we dropped down to a secluded sandy cove where we set up camp. As dusk approached, we settled down to watch the splendor of the sunset over the ocean. It felt good to be there and present in the moment. We were free from all ties and free to wander where we pleased. Life, for us, was an open-ended adventure.

Underneath a star filled sky, I fixed a simple meal of cheese and bread and tea. The ocean was calm and the rhythmic swishing of the waves on the sand, as they advanced and retreated, was comforting. In my Buddhist readings, I had read that we should have a personal connection with the divine spirit at every moment. In this setting with the sound of the surf, the millions of bright stars overhead and the tender kiss of the warm, gentle breeze, it required no leap of faith to feel connected with the divine forces at work in the universe.

I awoke early to a brilliant morning and sat quietly for a time following the breath. When I finally got up, I felt cheerful and content. John had wandered down the beach with Sam, and I was enjoying spending the morning without talking. The sand felt warm and pleasantly course between my toes. As part of the morning meditation, I tried to stay aware of each and every sensation and to be totally present in each and every moment. I didn't want to miss a thing! A group of pelicans glided gracefully by in V formation. The smell of the fresh, salty ocean air was invigorating, and I felt young and strong. The surf was up now. The tide pounded in with a loud booming crescendo followed by a swishing, crunching sound as it withdrew dragging with it pebbles and sand. The steep, jagged grey rocks surrounding the cove were silhouetted in sharp contrast against the brilliantly blue sky. I felt mesmerized, moving about slowly as if in a trance. I put the sleeping bags away in their stuff sacks and then knelt in the warm sand to get out the little Coleman stove and make some tea. I gazed, undistracted, as the little flame came to life and danced and flickered in the light breeze. When the water boiled, I placed a spoonful of loose tea in it and watched as the dark and fragrant particles dispersed in the simmering fluid. Gradually, the clear water turned a dark amber color and I mixed in honey and spices. Perhaps it was the setting, perhaps the clear attention, probably a little of both but it was the most delicious cup of tea that I had ever tasted. I wanted to savor each precious mouthful and each precious moment of this beautiful morning.

We camped for a few days and then continued south. Everywhere we went, we had our compact little home and each other's sweet companionship. Sammy was a wonderful traveling companion. Every new situation he met, head on, with a wagging tail and a cold wet nose. His love and enthusiasm in all situations made him an indispensable part of our daily life. John had become outspoken and gregarious since traveling, and he was a virtual encyclopedia of information. We made a nice family, the three of us, traveling around in our little home. Everywhere we went, we made friends. Our Spanish too was improving, and so we were soon able to have simple and entertaining conversations with the many people that we met along the way who didn't speak any English. I even learned some car repair terminology when we parked for a few days next to a family who fixed cars. "Liquido en los frenos," I could proudly say (brake fluid) and the charming older man who wanted a kiss taught me, "Un beso, mi amor." Inevitably, however, spending so much time together, John and I began to discover things about one another that we would struggle with for years to come. I was fairly independent and accustomed to leaving whenever I didn't like what was going on. It was a pattern that, for better or for worse, influenced my life for many years. John, I began to notice, exaggerated stories quite a bit. He even changed them somewhat to make them seem more interesting. It wasn't that unusual a trait. What alarmed me was when I began to realize that he actually believed his fabrications. At first, when I would point out the exaggeration or twisting of the truth in the telling, he would belittle me and treat me as if I were dumb and didn't know what I was talking about. After that, I strained to pay close attention to details so that I could be sure of what was really happening. Before long, it became clear to me that, in many cases, John's perception of reality was somehow distorted. Still I didn't, as yet, recognize this as a sign of his mental illness. The other personality trait that caused us much grief over the years was that John was what I would call a 'womanizer'. He loved beautiful women and could not resist seeing how far he could take it when a beautiful woman crossed his path. John's mind was so astoundingly full of interesting information that most people, including gorgeous women, could not resist getting to know him a bit better just to see what he was all about. It was with John that I finally learned the painful lesson of jealously. Any time a beautiful woman would enter our space, I would suddenly feel insecure, devalued and on the periphery looking in. John on the other hand would flourish, turning on the charm and acting as if I were of no consequence. I had seen other wives and girlfriends in that position before, and I had always felt sorry for them. I didn't like finding myself in that situation.

We took our time traveling down the coast, stopping here and there to meet the people, experience the local culture and work on our Spanish. Another difference between John and I, that we were discovering as we traveled, was that I was a restless soul. I liked to keep moving where as John liked to settle in and stay in one place. However, finally both of us agreed that it was getting too hot and humid on the coast. It was time to go inland, up into the mountains, where it would be cooler. We headed inland around Mexico City.

The crisp, cool mountain air was a welcome change. You could tell that Sammy liked it. He was more his perky self. We had gotten off onto a dirt road that led up to an abandoned observation tower. The views were spectacular. Mountains beyond mountains beyond mountains as far as the eye could see. Sammy chased some stray, skinny cows up hill in a delighted frenzy, more energetic than we had seen him in weeks. The fog blew about the mountain tops like a capricious, friendly visitor gracing now here, now there with a transforming presence. One minute we could see forever in undulating, verdant ridgelines and mountain peaks. The next moment we would be wandering in a mist so thick that one had to be careful not to step off of the road and over a cliff. The world would suddenly seem close and hidden. We found a safe place to park the bus and walked up to the top of the ridge. Sammy raced all around us with enthusiasm and renewed energy. John had brought along a Shakuhachi flute that he had made. It was a special flute. He had inlaid the mouthpiece with abalone shell and tuned it in an East Indian scale. Sitting on the top of the world as we were, John now removed it from the case that I had woven for him and he began to play a slow, meditative piece. The rich, clear notes glided through the mountain air like a fleet of melodic angels, swirling around us until we were totally engulfed in the harmony of the moment and could but sit on the ridge top and smile in wonderment and unwavering rapture.

We camped on the mountain in solitary bliss for a few days, and then we again headed south, deeper into the heart of Mexico. It was in Oaxaca that we got a cruel and painful sampling of the impermanence of life. One fine moment we were sitting in the town square, writing postcards while enjoying the shelter of a giant shade tree in the lazy afternoon. The next we were driving wildly around town looking for a vet while I tried, helpless and sobbing, to support our violently convulsing and foaming-at-the-mouth Sammy, who had just eaten poison. Our frenzied efforts were to no avail. He did not last ten minutes. He was gone so suddenly and there was no one, nothing that could bring our dear friend back to us. In stunned silence, we buried him beneath a weeping willow tree beside a bubbling stream. It was a setting in which I could see him wandering, happily forever, in the after world.

In the days that followed, nothing felt quite right without the cheery, loving presence of Sam. Silences were slightly strained, laughter a little forced. I felt kind of lonely and not-so-confident or adventurous any more. As the days passed, gradually, we began to adjust to being with one another without our funny, furry companion. When we came upon the enchanting town of San Cristobal De Las Cases, nestled in the Jovel Valley at an altitude of almost 7000 feet, we both agreed that it was a place that we should spend some time. We hoped that a break from living in the van might help us to get beyond our grieving. On the outskirts of town in a small adobe building, we rented a room for just pesos per week. The place was captivating in a rustic sort of way. The huge and heavy wooden double doors opened out to an overgrown field that was strewn with purple and yellow wild flowers. The room had adobe walls, a stone floor and a small stone fireplace. It was furnished with just the basics; a large wooden bed, a couple of wooden chairs, and a big table. The simplicity and earthy atmosphere was inviting. We brightened the room up a bit with the colorful weavings we had bought at the market, and before long it felt like home. The first morning in our new home I woke up to the sound of roosters, crowing a raucous welcome to the new day. I threw open the wooden shutters to let in the morning light. Mist filled the meadow, giving the impression that we were adrift in a sea of fog. It was chilly so I made a small fire using the pitch wood that I had bought at the market. It flooded the room with warmth and the fresh scent of pine. As the flames crackled and danced on the hearth and we ate our delicious breakfast of sweetbread and tea, I felt a sweet and simple appreciation for the dawn of another day.

We spent the next few days exploring in the hills and visiting the markets. There was a large indigenous Indian population that mostly lived in the surrounding hills but came into town to shop and sell their wares. Their mellow presence and colorful hand woven dress added to the impression of having stumbled into another world.

Since Sammy had died, John and I had not been relating as well to each other and I had been getting to see a different side of him since we had started traveling. John no longer bore any resemblance, at all, to the hermit-like wise man that I had been so drawn to in the beginning. The John that I now saw was a gregarious, knowledgeable, and opinionated young man who loved to engage in passionate and lengthily disputes over politics and religion or any other controversial subject. He was a radical thinker and a philosopher who took the greatest pleasure in a hearty debate and never, ever admitted defeat. With his long, black beard and piercing eyes John looked the part of a radical philosopher. In fact, he had an uncanny resemblance, in both appearance and lifestyle, to Rasputin the Mad Monk as he was sometimes called. If I believed in such things, I would have thought that he was Rasputin come back as John. I was quite taken aback when, years later, I read that Rasputin felt that his alcohol abuse and sexual escapades were beneficial to his spirituality for they kept him humble. As the years went by, that became John's persona as well.

Now that we were hanging out in one spot for a while, John seemed to have grown bored with my company and as we edged into the café scene, I found myself more and more alone while John had long, intimate, and absorbing talks with other travelers and hip locals. One day, he brought Maria home. She was a gorgeous, independent young woman who had traveled extensively all over the world. She impressed us both with stories of her opium smoking adventures in Afghanistan. On a scale of 1–10, Maria was at least a 10. She was as smart as she was beautiful and very seductive. John was, understandably, infatuated. It seemed like they were entering into some sort of dance in which I was in the way, and I couldn't deal with it. I told John that I had to get away for a while but that I would return in a couple of weeks and we would see where to go from there. John offered no resistance and so early one misty morning, I shouldered my backpack and boarded a bus headed south across the border and into Guatemala, destination, Lake Atitlan. As soon as the bus pulled away, I knew that it was the right move. For weeks now I had been feeling muted and repressed in the shadow of this man who, I was discovering, had a dominant and headstrong personality. Now as I set off on my own adventure, I felt my dampened little spirit light spring into brightness.

Chapter 24
Lake Atitlan and the Discovery

The bus wound along steep, narrow roads, twisting through verdant and wild mountains. Occasionally, we would stop at a wide spot in the road or a small village to let off people and chickens. Small children would crawl out the window and swing, with agility, up to the roof of the bus to throw down household wares and market purchases. Sometimes, entire families would set off into the mountains on foot, laden down with their goods, set intently on some mysterious destination. I was intrigued. These people of the land, where were they headed, and what was it like where they were going?

It was two days travel by bus to Lake Atitlan and the town of Panajachel. As I stepped off the bus and into the bright afternoon sunshine, stretching the stiffness out of my body, I felt somewhat disoriented. I hadn't made any plans. I stood there wondering what I should do next. Looking around me, I could see groups of Indians wearing the hand woven dress of their particular village and selling their crafts. The many shades of reds, purples, blues, and greens in beautiful patterns were pleasing to the eye and lifted my spirits. A young American man, who was standing on the side watching everything, stepped up and introduced himself as Ed. After we had spoken for a few minutes, he offered his assistance in helping me find a place to stay. "I live in the little Indian village called Jucanya, which literally means 'across the river'. It's just over the foot bridge about a ten minute walk from here," Ed explained. "I've lived here for almost six months with my girlfriend Ejidia. We love it. I know all the places that are for rent. I could show you around if you like."

It sounded like a great idea. "Thank you, I would like that. I don't have very much money," I told him a little bit about John and the circumstances under which I left. "We pooled all our money and put it in the bank in San Cristobal. I only took a little out for this trip. The less I spend the longer I can stay."

"Then you should, for sure, stay in one of the little huts for rent across the river," my new friend advised. "They cost just pesos per week and there aren't so many tourists there. There's no electricity but candles are cheap. In fact, I know of a place for rent just down the street from me and Ejidia. Come on I'll show you, and I'll introduce you to a few folks as we go."

I couldn't believe my good luck. I'd run across the perfect guide within minutes of getting off of the bus. I must have looked young and lost or something like that for Ed was definitely taking me under his wing. We set off for Jucanya in high spirits. The main street of Panajachel was lined with little shops and several quaint cafés. Ed pointed out a couple of small hotels with colorful courtyards. Bogenvilias and brilliant tropical flowers poured over the stonewalls, spilling onto the streets. The tangle of colors dazzled the eye and enticed the passerby with the promise of a paradise within. It was most definitely a 'visual feast'. We walked together through Panajachel, stopping for greetings and introductions until we came to a slender, winding river traversed by a wooden footbridge. Once across the river, the hustle and bustle of Panajachel fell away and it was quiet and peaceful. A dirt path ran along the top end of the village lined on our right by simple earthen huts with fenced yards and bright flowers everywhere. A small stream ran along, following the fence line. Ducks clucked about from yard to yard looking for morsels to eat. On our left, orchards ran, as far as the eye could see, planted in coffee beans and avocado trees. Ed stopped to talk with a friend that we were passing on the path. "Lenny, this is Juliet. She's planning to stay here for a couple of weeks. I think she's going to rent the place down the road from us."

His friend looked Guatemalan but he spoke perfect English with a light Spanish accent.

"I've lived in N.Y. all my life but I was actually born here," Lenny explained. "It feels like I've come home. I love it here. I could show you around tomorrow if you like," he added. "What if I pick you up around 9 o'clock? I'll take you to the best café in town for breakfast. Maybe Ed and Ejidia will come with us."

"Thanks so much; that would be fun. Do you think Ejidia will go?" I looked at Ed.

"Yes, I'm sure. She loves to go to El Sol for breakfast."

By the end of the day, I was all settled in. My new home was just one small room with mud walls and a dirt floor. There was not a single item in the room other than what I was carrying with me in my backpack. As I lit a candle, shadows flickered across the bare walls. I rolled out the reed mat that I had bought at the market and laid my sleeping bag over it. It had been a long day and I was tired but I felt content and happy. Everything had fallen together extremely well. I had only just arrived at Lake Atitlan and already I had a place to call home and the promise of breakfast in the morning, with my new friends. I was looking forward to using this time away from all obligations and distractions to develop a meditation practice. My hope was that meditation would help me to become more centered and more confident. I was also hoping to get some sense of direction and purpose; a vision of where I wanted to go with my life. It had been a very long journey from that first night in a N.Y.C. children's shelter to this hut in a Mayan Village in Guatemala. I was finding out that life was more varied and colorful than one could ever even imagine. I sat for a time following the breath, letting the busyness of my mind settle and relaxing into a feeling of spaciousness and wellbeing. Before going to sleep, I repeated an ancient Tibetan mantra I had learned. I am filled with loving kindness. I am well. I am peaceful and at ease. I am happy. That was pretty much how I wanted to walk in the world. I slept peacefully that night.

Breakfast started out a festive affair with lots of hip locals hanging out at el Sol Café drinking delicious locally grown Guatemalan coffee and discussing the local news. At one point, the conversation turned to politics. Apparently, the indigenous Indians were being persecuted in many parts of the country. In some instances, they were being tortured and murdered in attempt to gain control of their lands. If John had been there, I realized, he would have jumped right in to dominate the conversation with lots of information and strong opinions. I said nothing. It made me sad to think about how, once again, a beautiful native culture was being exploited and destroyed. History was repeating itself, over and over again. As a species, we seemed to be slow learners and very aggressive.

After breakfast, Lenny offered to show me the local swimming spot. "This time of day, it's perfect for swimming," he was telling me. "Later on in the day, the afternoon the winds called the Xocomil come up. The lake can get really rough." As we walked along the narrow dirt path that led to the lake, Lenny was telling me about an American girl he had met in Panajachel. "I was very much in love with her but she wanted to travel alone for a while. She promised to return. I never saw her again. It's been a year. I know she's not coming back but I still find that I'm waiting for her. I really miss her."

We turned down a narrow, steep path that was dark and overgrown with trees and shrubs and then, abruptly, we popped out into the open. We were standing on the shore of Lake Atitlan. I was enchanted by the scene before me. The lake was ringed in a semicircle by three volcanoes. A fine mist was rising off of the calm, glassy water. In the distance, a Cakchiquel man in native dress stood erect in his wooden canoe. His paddle strokes were smooth and graceful. We watched as the boat glided silently through the mist.

"This volcano," Lenny said pointing to the left and across the lake, "is Toliman. The one directly across is Vulcan Atitlan and over there is San Pedro."

A little ways back from the lake, close to where we were standing, there was a small natural hot pool. Some Cakchiquel women were washing their clothes and laying them out in the sun to dry. They laughed and chatted with each other as they worked. They seemed happy. Looking around me, I felt as if I had stepped back in time a few hundred years. "It's beautiful here," I told Lenny. "It's very magical."

"This is a magical spot," he replied. "There is said to be a lot of power here."

"I can feel it," I responded and, in fact, remembering back to that day, I can still feel the magic.

Lenny was a sweet young man. He admitted to me that he was lonely and truth be told, so was I. We quickly became good friends. He introduced me to locals, took me to the colorful markets, and even took me to hang out at the cemetery late one night, on the full moon. "In the beginning of November," Lenny was telling me, "we have a holiday we call *Dia de los Muertos.* The holiday dates back to indigenous culture thousands of years. On this day, people go to the cemeteries to communicate with the souls of the dead."

We brought some fruit and some flowers with us as an offering. "The flowers are thought to attract souls of the dead to the offerings," Lenny explained. "I hope you are not frightened," he added.

"No, not at all," I assured him. "I like it here. It's peaceful."

The light from the full moon filled the small cemetery with a warm glow, giving the impression that there were spirits present, and that they were glad for our company. We sat together on the ground, quietly, leaning against one of the gravestones. We were trying to open up our psychic channels to see if we could tune into any spirits that might be sending us a message but we couldn't pick up anything, and we started getting really sleepy. We ended up walking back to my little hut, pulling my sleeping bag over us like a blanket and falling into a deep and dreamless sleep.

A few days later, we were hanging out at Lenny's house, and he told me about a narcotic pain reliever that could be purchased, over the counter, in Guatemala. "You don't need prescriptions here. You just go to the pharmacy and buy what you need," he explained. "So I like to buy Prodalina; it's like Demerol. It makes you feel really good. I like to mainline it in both arms at the same time. If you do it just right, it goes up your arms to the left side of your head and the right side of your head at the same time and it meets in the middle with a huge bang. You get such a rush! It's fantastic!" Lenny was very animated and enthusiastic as he talked about his drug experience.

My ears perked up when he said this. It was actually very useful information because John suffered from kidney stones. Back in California, I had been with him when he had his first attack. He had been in excruciating pain. We spent an entire day in the Emergency Room where they did a full work up and concluded that there was nothing to be done other than give him pain medication and lots of fluids to drink until the stone passed. Perhaps because of some dehydration or a different diet, John had another bout with a kidney stone while we were traveling in Mexico. Suddenly, he was incapacitated, writhing in pain. We had to ask someone, whom we hardly knew, to drive our car from the isolated beach where we were camping to town where we could find a doctor (I didn't know how to drive). When we found a doctor, he had given John an intravenous injection of some kind of painkiller and not long after that, the small stone had passed. Listening to Lenny talk, I got the idea that having some Prodalina on hand and knowing how to give an IV injection might come in handy before this trip was over. "Will you teach me how to give an intravenous injection?" I asked, excited about the idea.

"Si, como no, of course," Lenny said after I had explained the situation to him. As he rolled up his sleeves, he explained how to set the tourniquet and how to pump up the vein so that it was easier to access. Once everything was in place, he explained how to hold the vein steady by putting traction on the skin and then how to insert the needle, gently, bevel up into the vein. Once in the vein, he instructed me to pull back on the plunger, just a tad, until I saw a blood return letting me know that I was indeed in the vein. Then, holding the needle steady, inject, not too slow, not too fast. I pushed in the plunger and almost immediately Lenny looked ecstatic, like he had found his own private nirvana. I guess that was part of the appeal of drugs. That they could make you feel so happy for no reason. The trouble was that it wasn't real. It didn't last long and there was usually a tremendous price to pay. However, when someone was in a lot of physical pain, narcotics could be a blessing. I bought some Prodalina that day and tucked it away in my pack for a time when it might prove beneficial.

John had promised to write to me at general delivery Panajachel but it had been a month and no word had arrived. I was almost out of money. Really, I had let my funds go down a little too low. I had just enough for a bus ticket back to San Cristobal and a little food on the way. "Lenny, I've got to go back to San Cristobal. I'm out of money and I need to find out what's happening with John." Lenny looked at me sadly. "I'm going to miss you. You know I have a friend who is a teacher in a mountain town called Nebaj, on the way to the Mexican border. I've been meaning to visit her. I could travel with you part way and then you could continue on to Mexico or you could come with me to meet my friend. The bus doesn't go right to the town. We'd have to walk a few miles to get there. It's very remote. I'll pay your way if you want to go with me," he offered. "I would like to have your company."

"I'd really like to go with you, Lenny, but I need to get some of my own money and I need to find out what's happening with John. We didn't actually split up. We were just taking a break. I haven't heard from him and I don't know where we stand. I need to find that out." I was really feeling torn. It sounded like an incredible adventure that was way off the tourist track. I was afraid that I would regret my decision not to go but under the circumstances, it just didn't seem like a sensible thing to do. I felt like it was time I got back to San Cristobal.

A few days later, I said my goodbyes to Ed and Ejidia and to my little hut where I had felt safe and content. I boarded the bus with Lenny that was headed north, towards the Mexican border, glad that he was going with me at least part of way. As much as I wanted to be an independent adventurous woman like Maria, I didn't actually like traveling alone. Lenny was a great traveling companion. He was relaxed, adventurous, considerate, and fairly together. Another big plus was that his Spanish was fluent. At the end of the first day, we had to stop for the night in a small town. Alone, I would not have known what to do. I didn't have enough money for a hotel but Lenny had his two-man tent with him and so we walked to the outskirts of town, put up the tent, crawled in and went to sleep. I've always loved that feeling of being totally at home and comfortable just roaming around, out in the world, with few possessions. That night was one of those times. Next day, we traveled north together for a few hours. Then Lenny had to change buses to head northeast to Nebaj. It was hard for me to see him go. I really wanted to go with him but I felt that it was not the right thing to do so I continued on alone, on my journey north. At the next stop, a young, attractive woman from France got on the bus and sat down next to me. She was headed to a large town north of San Cristobal where she was attending medical school. Her English was very good and we struck up a fine conversation. I was nervous about what I would find when I got back to San Cristobal and I was very nervous about not having any money. I did most of the talking, and she listened with interest as I told her my long saga about my travels with John and Lake Atitlan. When we got to the border, everyone had to disembark and go through the Mexican customs. It had never occurred to me that there might be a problem with getting back into Mexico but as I stood in line, waiting my turn to get my entrance visa, I began to worry. The Mexican Customs Officer was asking everyone to prove that they had at least one hundred American dollars before he would grant them an entry visa. What would happen when he found out that I only had a couple of dollars on me? When it was my turn, I stepped up to the counter. I stood there for a moment, wide eyed, not knowing what to say. Anything I said could get me into trouble. I was in a precarious position. I didn't have the money to go forward into Mexico or the money to go backwards into Guatemala. I was in no man's land. How had I allowed this to happen? As I stood there, tongue tied, I became aware that something was being slipped into my pocket. Instinctively, I reached down, into my pocket, and pulled out one hundred dollars in ten-dollar bills. The French girl had slipped them to me. I'm sure I looked incredulous when I handed over the money. The guard counted it out and gave me my visa. He handed me ninety dollars back. He had seen, but for a mere ten dollars, he was going to let it slide.

That had been a very close call, and I was indebted to the French woman for her assistance. Now I learned that the bus was not going to continue on to San Cristobal but that we were forced to lay over until the next morning, spending the night, in the one and only hotel at the border. I looked around me, frustrated, trying to decide how to proceed. I thought of Lenny with his cozy little tent, and I wished that he was there with me. Then I noticed a car, with a young Mexican couple, parked nearby. Without stopping to think things out, I ran over to them and asked if they were going to San Cristobal and would they give me a ride. They were a sweet young couple, just married, on their honeymoon and headed to the north of San Cristobal. They readily agreed to take me. I hopped into the back seat, and we were on our way. Another close call!

When we arrived, it was late. Between my broken Spanish and their broken English, we had gotten to know each other a bit, and they were happy to take me to the hacienda where John and I had been staying. It was on the outskirts of town and not very far out of their way. They left me off at the stone entranceway and, waving goodbye, wished me good luck.

"Gracias, Via con dios," I called after them. I think they hadn't actually planned to travel so far that night but they were very kind and had wanted to help me.

It was late and quite dark. I hoped that John would be home and I hoped that he was not with Maria. When I knocked expectantly on the door, there was no answer. I tried the latch. It was locked. I stood there in the darkness, alone, considering the possibilities. I was thinking that I would just wait there on the doorstep and see what happened. I was contemplating taking out my sleeping bag and getting some rest when the owner of the hacienda showed up. He was very drunk. We were a little isolated where we were, off of the beaten track, and I found myself feeling a bit uneasy. "John no vive aqui," he told me. "He left," he added in English to be sure that I understood.

"I don't believe it," I said, suddenly feeling lost and confused.

The boracho landlord opened the door so that I could see for myself. The room was empty. It was obvious that no one was living there. Before I could think of what this might mean, the landlord was grabbing at me and trying to press his wet, sticky, alcohol soaked lips to mine while pushing me clumsily towards the bed. I shoved him away, suddenly frightened, and started running. I knew of a house nearby where some young hippy Guatemalan guys lived, and that's where I headed.

When I arrived, minutes later out of breath and crying, on their doorstep, I was welcomed in by a young man whom I had met before. "Yes, your John has left," he told me. "He went north with Maria. He won't be back. You'll never see him again. You can stay here but you should sleep with me because your John is gone."

I took this news with a mixture of disbelief and at the same time I was thinking that it made perfect sense. "I'd like to spend the night if I could please, but I want to sleep alone."

We talked for a while, about Guatemala, and then he showed me to a room where I could stay for the night. Even though he was very flirtatious, I felt safe with him and I was grateful for his assistance.

"What are you going to do?" my friend asked me the next morning.

In truth, I didn't have a clue but I felt like I should go off by myself for a while and try and think things through. "Do you mind if I leave my things here?" I asked. "I'm going out for a while but I'll be back."

"Si, como no, of course, bueno suerte," he said as he looked me up and down. I felt relieved to have found an ally even if it was for the wrong reasons.

I walked over to the house where I had last seen John. The landlord did not actually live there and no one was around. The building was deserted. I sat down on the stone steps and took out the little drop spindle I was learning to spin on and a bit of freshly shorn gray wool that I had recently purchased at the market. It was soothing and meditative to wind the wool around the spindle, then drop it and spin, feeding more and more of the wool onto the yarn as it slowly lengthened. I watched with satisfaction as the rich fibers twisted into threads of varying thickness. Hand spun wool, with its irregularities of color and texture, was so much more beautiful than the uniform acrylic yarn I had always bought in the states. As I worked, I started to think things through. I had somewhere to stay for a few days. That was hugely helpful. There might still be some money in the bank. The account had been in both of our names. If worse came to worse, I could always go to the American Consulate, wherever that might be. I still couldn't believe that John had left. I missed him but I didn't like the feeling of being jealous so I had managed to convince myself that I didn't really care. I was staying nonattached.

As I was assessing the situation and keeping my mind calm and unruffled with the repetitive process of drop and spin, I became aware of a familiar sound in the distance. I listened more intently. Yes, definitely, the noise was growing louder. It was coming my way. I looked up, in the distance I could see what looked like a large vehicle coming in my direction. As it got closer, I could see that it was a Volkswagen Van. The very next minute there was John, all smiling and happy to see me, looking very handsome with a new haircut and clean shaven. He was on his way to Panajachel to find me but he thought that he would check this spot where we had last been together, just one more time, before leaving town. That was the closest call of all. Was it merely a fortuitous coincidence that we hadn't just missed each other like two ships passing in the dark or was there some greater force at play?

"Why didn't you write?" we both asked, almost in unison. "I did," was both of our replies. The postal service was just that bad!

"Everyone said you had left. I didn't know what I was going to do." I was relieved and happy to see John but I also wanted to know what was happening with Maria.

"I did leave to go to Oaxaca with Maria and her girlfriend but it was just for a few days. I've been back for a couple of weeks now. Maria and her friend went north. I was so worried when you didn't answer my letters." John was so glad to see me and I so glad to see him that we didn't trouble each other with too many questions. We just thanked our lucky stars that we hadn't missed one another and that we were both safe and both together again. For the rest of the trip, he was much more considerate and he went out of his way to include me in all situations.

We wanted to be back in Washington for Christmas but we still had a little time and a little money left so we headed back down to Lake Atitlan. We stayed there for a few weeks in Jucanya, taking up residence in one of the mud huts that was a bit bigger than the one that I had rented. John put together a few rustic pieces of furniture and it was really very comfortable and cheery with a perfusion of morning glories falling in the window every time I would open the wooden shutters and our very own avocado tree in the back yard. I loved going to the outdoor market in the morning and then walking home along the narrow country road, in the early morning sunshine, with my straw bag laden down with fresh fruits and just-baked sweetbreads. Then we would sit together and enjoy the most delicious breakfast feast while making our plans for the day. One morning, I returned from the market to find John in a lot of pain. He was having another kidney stone. He was in too much pain to sit or stand so he just lay there in bed clutching is right flank and moaning miserably. I had almost forgotten about my Prodelina. Now I pulled it out of my backpack and drew it up in the syringe. After explaining to John what I was about to do, I repeated the steps that I had learned from Lenny and injected into John's giant antecubital vein. We waited expectantly. Minutes later, John was sitting up and smiling. The pain had gone. Within the hour, he had passed the tiny stone that was causing him so much trouble. John was really grateful and he was very impressed. I was elated. It was a life altering moment for me for I realized that, in some small but very practical way, I could help to ease suffering.

"When we get back to California, I am going to go to Nursing School," I declared emphatically. "I am going to be a nurse!" I had discovered my calling.

Just before John and I left to go back to the States, Lenny showed back in town with a couple of teenage Guatemalan girls who followed him everywhere. He seemed very happy. Years later, I ran into Ejidia at the San Francisco airport. She and Ed had split up and she was living in San Francisco. She told me that, shortly after John and I left, Lenny had been canoeing out on the lake when the Xochomil came up. Lenny had some sort of a seizure they said and he fell out of the boat and drowned. I thought that it was probably the Prodalina that had got him. When I learned that he had died, I did regret not spending that time with my friend in Nebaja but I also knew that I had made the right decision not to go.

John and I did a little more exploring and we had a couple more adventures before heading home to the States. We got together with some friends and climbed a volcano outside of Antigua called Pacaya. It was very exciting. We camped overnight at the bottom of the volcano where it was rich with vegetation. Early in the morning, we set off hoping to summit by the afternoon. As we got closer to the top, the vegetation ended and the ground beneath us turned to a fine, black, sand-like substance. When we got close to the top, the sand turned to a fine ash and it became so steep that I had to dig my fingers deeply into the ash and hang on just to keep from slipping back down. As I dug my fingers in, I was surprised to find that it was hot, almost too hot to handle. Once at the top, we peered over the rim of the caldera. We could see, through the steam, a ribbon of red-hot lava far below. "If you hang over the side naked, it would make a fantastic picture," Howard, John's friend, said to me. It struck me as a poetic image, naked and vulnerable, hanging on for dear life suspended above a river of glowing, molten lava, surrounded by the awe inspiring, exquisite forces of nature. I was reminded of a Buddhist parable in which a man is chased to the edge of a cliff by a tiger. As he hangs over the side of the cliff faced with the impossible choice of either falling from a great height to his certain death or climbing up to be eaten by the tiger, he sees a beautiful flower growing near him and pauses to appreciate its wonderful fragrance.

We were getting down to the wire now with our time and money but before heading for home, we decided that we could not go without first visiting Tikal, the site of the Ancient Mayan ruins. It was a long, difficult drive on rutted out jungle roads. When we finally arrived, we were exhausted and shaken from the constant vibration of continuous washboard for mile after jittery mile. In those days, Tikal was not as well restored as it is now. We spent a day wandering through the jungle and we climbed, using vines and cables, up a temple that rose far above the jungle canopy. Then we ate some mildly psychedelic mushrooms that John had picked and sat watching, captivated, as a little black beetle pushed around a piece of bread from our lunch. One minute, the little fellow would be on top of it. The next minute, he would be pushing it, victoriously, along. Then, suddenly, he would be underneath and struggling with all of his might. It seemed like hours passed while we sat, far above the lush green canopy, watching with fascination as the little beetle worked heroically to bring the prized food home to his family. Meanwhile, we tried to imagine what life had been like for the ancient civilization that had flourished there in the Peten Jungle from about 700 BC when it was first settled by the Mayans until their collapse around 900 AD. We imagined that we could feel the presence of ancient spirits in the richness of the living, breathing jungle that surrounded us. That afternoon, we were so in tune with each other's thoughts that it was as if we were sharing one soul. When I want to remind myself of the special times that John and I shared together, I often think of that magical day, on top of the ancient Mayan temple, when our spirits and minds were truly in union.

Chapter 25
One Track Mind

My mother used to complain that I had a one-track mind because, although I was usually easy going, if I really wanted something badly, I was persistent and pushy to a fault. This trait proved useful now that I had a goal that was meaningful but was not easily attained. Every step I took, when we got home, revolved around my plan to become a nurse.

We returned to the States just in time to spend a cheerful holiday with John's' family, then we returned to Berkeley in plenty of time to get settled and start the spring semester. We went to see my mother right away. She was doing well but we were still living in our bus and she wouldn't let me take a shower at her house. It was irritating and it hurt my feelings but what could I do? I just had to accept that this was my mother and try to love her. I was glad that she was, at least, taking care of herself. She had been in contact with my father, Joe, and I actually spoke with him on the phone for the first time in many years. He wanted to know if I had nice breasts. It seemed really odd to me that he would ask such a question, especially since I barely knew him. He said it was because his mother had beautiful breasts and he wondered if I had inherited them. I looked down at my chest, curious myself, after this new piece of information. I used the expression that I had heard John use for women that he was attracted to. "Not bad," was my reply.

Joe was pleased with my plan to go to Nursing School and he told me that I could probably get financial assistance for education through the Veterans' Administration since he was a disabled war veteran. Now here was a very useful piece of information, and I thanked him kindly. I followed through on that tip, and for the next four years I received a small stipend while attending school which definitely helped to make ends meet.

We returned to Grove Street Junior College. John continued taking classes in math and history and I took what I needed to finish up my general education in preparation for Nursing School. After doing a little research, I decided to go for an Associate in Science degree as a Registered Nurse. A Bachelor in Science would take more time and more money and it looked like the outcome was basically the same. Either way, I would be a Registered Nurse. I decided on the Santa Rosa Junior College Nursing Program because it had a good reputation and it seemed like an area where we would enjoy living. I actually applied for the coming fall and was accepted into the school but not into the program. I wasn't discouraged though because I still had lots of classes to take like Anatomy and Physiology and Nutrition, to name a few. I was satisfied for the time being. The foundation was being laid.

I felt that it would be easier to get into the program if I was already going to that school so, when the spring semester ended, we moved to a small coastal town outside of Santa Rosa called Jenner by the Sea. We really lucked out in finding a charming little one room studio that had an unobstructed view of the Russian River flowing by, about 15 feet away from our big picture window. Not far beyond that, we could see where the river emptied into the ocean. It was incredibly beautiful and entertaining just to sit and watch the river where a variety of sea birds such as egrets and pelicans and sea gulls could always be seen. I pushed the bed up to the window so that we could lie in bed at night and look at the stars while listening to the sounds of the river and the surf beyond. It was an idyllic spot. John and I were both very happy.

September arrived and with it, the first day of school. I was learning to drive but I didn't have my license as yet. My classes were of the Monday, Wednesday. Friday variety and John's were of the Tuesday, Thursday variety. That was actually a bit of poor planning because not only did I not have my license yet but it was extra money in gas and other expenses for us to be going on separated days. However, my classes were non-negotiable because of my very specific goal. John offered to drive me that morning but it didn't make sense for him to go all that way and hang out with nothing to do. I was almost ready to take the driving test. At that point, it was but a mere formality. "I'll go for my driving test next week," I promised him. "Don't worry about today. I'll be alright." I set off in the best of spirits. Little by little I was getting closer to my goal. The last thing I remember of that day was letting off a hitchhiker who was in a hurry. He told me that I was driving too slowly. Then I got on the entrance ramp that led on to the freeway south that was to take me to SRJC. That particular entrance ramp, from River Road onto 101, has a very sharp curve right at the end just when you are supposed to speed up to enter in with the flow of traffic. Volkswagen Buses are not known to be the most stable of vehicles. According to the police report, the van entered the freeway out of control, swerving across the three lanes of traffic before rolling, several times, on the grassy median that separated north bound traffic from south bound traffic. Not wearing my seat belt, I was thrown out of the car, landing in the grass just inches away from the concrete and north bound traffic. The way I figure it, those couple of inches of grass saved my life or at least my brain. As it was, I was unconscious, in the Intensive Care Unit of Santa Rosa Community Hospital, for several days with an ID band that read Jane Doe. John told me later that when I didn't come home that night, he was frantic. He called the police and they had told him not to worry. "She's probably off somewhere partying," they had said, trying to reassure him, I guess. When he finally located me, I was still lying unconscious in the ICU. Once I regained consciousness, they moved me to the general unit but I was very 'out of it' for a while. I'd get confused easily and had trouble remembering even simple things. My doctor's name was Dr. Rosa. I really liked him but I could only remember his name by going through this complex process of remembering that I had moved to Santa Rosa and then dropping off the Santa and then calling him Doctor Rosa. One day I saw him out in the hall. I was anxious to talk to him about letting me go home; I got so excited that I became confused and started yelling Santa, Santa, Santa! Sad but kind of funny. My balance was off as well because of the closed head injury and I had shattered my right ankle. I ended up having one surgery to pin my ankle and later another surgery to take the pins out because they bothered me. John visited me every day for the three weeks that I was in the hospital, driving back and forth from Jenner without a front windshield and with the wind pounding in his face. When he took me home to Jenner,

I was still kind of out of it for several months and it was hard for me to get around with my balance off the way it was. However, I spent the next few months sitting in bed watching, captivated, as the river raged with the winter storms. At times when the river would swell to flood stage, after days of torrential rain, it would rise almost to the front door. Then there would be alerts and evacuation warnings, bells, whistles, and sirens. I loved being so close to the drama and wild forces of nature while at the same time feeling safe and cozy in my little home. I watched the river as it carried with it trees and stumps and other debris that it had grabbed along the way. Sometimes, birds could be seen riding driftwood in the current which was bound rapidly and with immutable determination, for the open ocean. In the distance, I could see and hear the surf raging away at the beach in its frenzy. It was like a wild dangerous party that only those initiated dare attend. I sat on the outskirts where the surf and spray could be seen from a mile away, flying high into the air, content just to watch as the wild forces of wind, air and water whirled and tumbled together in a wild chaotic dance.

By spring semester, I was ready to pick up the trail again in my quest to become a nurse. I had missed the date for the entrance exam that you needed to take in order to apply for the fall semester but, because of my circumstances, they agreed to set up a special testing date for me. John drove me to St. Helena were the test was being held and I hobbled in, still on crutches, to spend the entire day in testing. I did everything they asked me to do as part of the application process. I did some volunteer work at the hospital. I wrote a paper on 'Why I Want to be a Nurse'. I took the anatomy physiology class and, of course, I went for my interview. The competition was fierce that year. I was told that they had 500 applications and could only accept 40. Once again, I was not one of the chosen. Then I got a letter explaining that sometimes some of the people they choose go to a different program or cancel for one reason or another so they always make up an alternate list of 10 people. I was on that list. That was welcome news. That summer as I waited, with baited breath for word, I got busy taking care of loose ends. We moved to Forestville and that cut about 45 minutes off of the drive. I went ahead with minor surgery to have the pins removed from my ankle because they were really causing me a lot of discomfort. Also I took the required nutrition class. That was a good move because I met some of the people that had been accepted into the program. One very nice young woman named Jerry lived close by. She agreed that if things were to work out, we could commute together. She would do the driving and I could help pay for gas. All summer long, I kept calling the administrator of the program. "No news," he would always tell me.

One day I asked him, "What number am I on the list?"

He replied, "It's just a list. I don't know."

I persisted. "One's place on the list makes a really big difference. For instance, if I'm number 10 on the list, then the chances of my being called are slim. But if I'm first on the list, I have a pretty good chance of getting in. Do you see what I mean?"

There was a momentary pause. Perhaps he was tired of my calling him so much or perhaps he was impressed with my perseverance for he said to me, "Okay, if someone cancels, you'll be the first one we call."

"Thank you so much!" I was ecstatic. I now felt that there was a very good chance that I would be starting the program that very fall. Every day I went down to the little country mailbox and checked the mail. Time passed. It was almost

September. Classes would be starting soon. One day there was a letter for me from the school. I opened it, trying to stay calm. It read: "You have been accepted into the nursing program. Please be there next Friday for the fitting of uniforms."

Chapter 26
Nursing School

"How long do you think it's going to be? Do you think it's going to happen today?" Ms. M. looked up at me expectantly. She wanted an answer.

"I have no way of knowing. I don't think it's going to happen for a while. You seem so healthy." It was our first rotation in patient care. The program was divided into six rotations, and geriatrics was our first. Here we learned how to make a hospital bed and give a bath. We learned how to take vital signs and how to assist someone to dress and eat and we learned the five checks that must be done before giving a medication to a patient. Ms. M., who was to be my assignment for the entire six weeks, was an exceptional woman. She seemed like the sharpest patient there. In a setting where so many of the residents suffered from varying degrees of dementia, she was totally alert and oriented times three (a medical assessment that means oriented to person, place and time). According to the patient roster, she was 98 years old. That meant that she had been born in 1876, a figure that astounded me. She was from Norway. "Girls were raised to marry in those days," she told me. "I didn't want to get married. Instead, I took up sewing so that I could make enough money to come to America."

"When was that?" I asked, thinking that she must have stood out as an unusually strong and independent woman for her day, a true adventuress.

"That was about 1899. Eventually, I made it out to California where I lived in the Sierras for many years. I never married," she had told me when I had asked.

She talked about the first wind up car that she had owned and about her little cabin in the hills outside of Guerneville on the Russian River where she had lived alone until that September. "I believe in God," she had said to me. "I'm not afraid to die, and I'm very tired. I'm ready to go." That was when she had asked me if I thought that it might happen today. After I said that I didn't think so, she looked a little disappointed and then meandered off to visit with one of the other residents who were still capable of holding a conversation. I heard them laugh about something but I couldn't catch what they were saying. I was too busy trying, with all my powers of concentration, to make the perfect hospital corner with the sheet that hung loose at the bottom of her bed.

The two-year nursing program is a misnomer. I mean the program itself is two years but there is two years' worth of classes that must be taken before you begin most programs. I was glad that I had managed to get all of the classes I needed out of the way because the program, all by itself, was very demanding. Clinical was two full days per week and then there were all the nursing concepts plus pharmacology, pathology, microbiology, and terminology, papers to write and tests to be studied for. I was constantly on the go. John and I were living in Lucy's house over the winter for free rent with the agreement that we would act as caretakers, keeping the property in ship shape condition for her enjoyment over the summer. She was a sweet older woman who was originally from Russia. Her husband had died long ago and she appreciated our help with keeping everything in working order. I had my Veterans' dependent stipend for food and other expenses, and John worked on peoples cars when he needed money for his personal needs. Things were tight but we managed to get by. We didn't see that much of each other. John didn't go to school anymore, and he cultivated a group of friends that I hardly knew. He had several women friends that lived in the neighborhood, and he spent most of his time with them. I was too busy to worry much about his affairs and we slipped into what I would loosely call 'an open relationship'. I hear guys mention it every once and a while when they are trying to convince a woman to sleep with them even though they already have a girlfriend. "Oh yes, we have an open relationship," they will say. "We give each other complete freedom."

We didn't discuss it in those terms but John did his thing and I did mine and for the most part, we didn't ask any questions. Once I caught some girl on the block wearing an item of clothing that belonged to me; "John, let me borrow this," she had said innocently when I asked where she got it. Another woman on the block that John hung out with described something very personal that I was sure was unique to John and John alone. But she talked about it with me as if she were talking about a man that she had just met. I felt like she was trying to get a rise out of me but I didn't take the bait. "I've got to go now," I said. "I've got a test that I have to study for." These things bothered me but I didn't have the time to dwell on them. I continued on about my very busy life because I had a goal and nothing was more important to me than reaching it. These little injuries, however, were not without an effect. They contributed, I believe, to all the crazy times that happened later when we tortured each other until one of us broke. Because of an underlying mental instability that I didn't as yet appreciate it was John who, in the end, suffered the most.

By the end of the first year of the program, I was feeling a little more confident. I was still intimidated by my instructors, and I lived in fear of doing the wrong thing to the wrong patient or something like that; but I was getting good grades and I was enjoying the work. I liked the intimacy of being of service to someone who was feeling vulnerable and frightened. I got tremendous satisfaction in being part of a professional team that was helping to heal the sick and ease their suffering and I was discovering that often times the best medicine could be something as simple as a soothing presence or listening, without judgment, to some ones fears. In short, I thrived on the patient-nurse relationship.

The summer between year one and year two of the Nursing Program was an incredible time for John and I. We were off on another adventure together and away from all the things and people in our daily life that caused us grief. Traveling around British Columbia we experienced a taste of what, I imagine, explorers and adventurers all through history must have felt. That is, the irresistible attraction of the wild and the unknown. When classes ended, we did some work for Lucy. After we had painted the inside of her house and did a few other little things, she moved in for the summer. We stored our things in her downstairs room and set off on our adventure. Our first stop was Washington where we visited with John's' family and did some more house painting so that we could earn enough money to disappear into the wilderness for a month. John had managed to get hold of a canoe. We planned to take it up to Canada to explore a couple of wilderness lakes called Chuchi and Tchentlo. They were separate lakes that were connected by a few mile stretch of river. The only point accessible by road was at the beginning of Lake Chuchi and it was a long, bumpy drive on an isolated dirt road to get to it. After that there were no roads, no towns, and no people. We were truly in the wild.

The weather turned stormy when we first arrived at the lake. Chuchi was a tempest of crashing, seething water. It looked like the ocean with huge cresting waves and the opposite bank out of site in the dense fog. We settled in, contentedly, to life in the van for a few days of reading and napping, playing guitar and taking walks during breaks in the rain. It was enjoyable but we soon became restless to get on our way. After several days, the rain stopped and the wind died down. Although it was still a little churned up, the lake looked fairly calm. There didn't seem to be any point in waiting any longer. This was British Columbia. We weren't expecting a lot of fair weather or a walk in the park. "You take the front," John directed. "I'll sit in the back and do the steering. Let's not get too far away from the shore. This water is cold and deep. If we capsize we could lose all of our equipment and die of hypothermia before we even get close to shore. Things can get serious out here. Quickly," he added, raising his eyebrows and nodding his head to punctuate this statement.

I knew that he was right and I did take it seriously but I didn't feel afraid. Things in nature didn't frighten me the way that people did. Nature could be dangerous and out of control, but it was not malicious. What frightened me most was the intentional cruelty that was unleashed when man turned against man. I would gladly take my chances with the forces of nature.

We started off in good spirits in spite of the grey overcast sky but before long the waters got rough and the wind started blowing hard, it started to rain. The waves were cresting over the gun wall of the boat now and slapping against my face. The water was freezing. Our precious shore, that we were clinging to, provided no shelter, only sheer cliffs. There was no place to beach the boat. "We're going to have to keep the boat facing into the waves," John yelled above the roar of the wind. "If we go sideways, we'll capsize and if we let them push us to shore, we'll be dashed against the rocks."

Much to our dismay, we got further and further from shore but we went at a slight angle and so we managed to move further up the lake, little by little. We were both totally focused on keeping the boat stable in the water and we were paddling furiously with all of our might. In spite of the cold weather, we were sweating inside of our rain gear. Finally, we spotted a beach. "Let's head into shore. We can land there and set up camp in the trees," John sounded relieved.

He didn't have to ask me twice. I was wet and cold and a bit scared after all.

The next day, the weather continued to be stormy. We started to feel a little discouraged. It was just not possible to be out in the boat when the water was so rough. We contemplated making a run for the car during the next break in the weather. "Maybe we should just go home. If we do continue on, there's a good chance that we could get stuck. The weather could continue like this for the rest of the summer." I was up for an adventure but I also wanted to get back home in time for school.

"Let's see what tomorrow brings. We'll make that decision tomorrow." John sounded sensible and I agreed. We had come a long ways. We had to give it a chance.

Next day it was drizzling but it was calm. We had good rain gear and the glassy water looked inviting for the first time since we had arrived almost a week before. Some nuthatches were walking upside down on nearby tree branches making friendly little clicking sounds. Just then the sun broke through the clouds and it cast a rainbow across the sky. "Let's keep going," was John's' vote. I had to agree. We had stuck it out through a week of bad weather and now we were being given a personal invitation. The rainbow was like a good omen, pointing us deeper into the wilderness.

It took us three days to make it up the first lake, approximately 20 miles from where the van was parked. The weather continued to be wet, and we had to stop every so often when the water got too rough. It was slow going and less than ideal conditions, but the untouched beauty that surrounded us more than made up for any minor discomforts that we were experiencing. As we went along, we got tougher too. The cold and damp bothered us less and less and as our arms got stronger, the rowing became fun. It was like a meditation, focusing on the bough of the boat, keeping it on course and using long smooth strokes to move the boat gracefully through the water. Now stroke right then left, right left, rest, glide, stroke, and so the day went as hour after mesmerizing hour we moved through the crystal waters, drawing further and further away from the world we knew.

When we got to the ribbon of river that connected Chuchi to Tchentlo, it was immediately apparent that we were not going to be able to row upstream. John seemed disappointed but to me, it looked like an opportunity for fun. I began to line the boat, containing John and all our gear, up the little rapids. It reminded me of the Adventures of Tom Sawyer that I had loved so much as a kid. I pulled the boat through the water up a narrow, tree-lined channel. Crows cawed overhead announcing the approach of strangers. Brilliant displays of green, iridescent moss and colorful wildflowers delighted the eye. The water was crystal clear and we could see the bottom strewn with colorful rocks and fish darting about in abundance. I waded along in the river where it was shallow enough. When we would come upon a snag that extended out into deeper waters, I would scramble up the steep banks and over fallen trees, catching the bowline and pulling the boat around until we were once again back in clear unobstructed waters. That night we camped on the river bar and the next day we started off again, in the early morning mist, quietly plodding through the water while the canoe glided silently along. Looking up we saw a bald eagle, great and powerful and very close, checking us out or maybe he was just looking for breakfast. We arrived at the outlet of Tchentlo in the early afternoon. The sun was shining and we made good time canoeing ten miles up the lake before stopping to make camp. The next day was also sunny and warm so we decided to enjoy a day at camp and dry our equipment out in the sun. Everything was becoming damp, our cloths, sleeping bags, books. A lazy day in the sun was just what we needed. That afternoon, we saw a giant bear across the lake on the opposite bank. "It looks like a grizzly bear," John was saying as he watched it through the binoculars.

"I'm glad it's on the other side of the lake. I like Grizzlies at a distance!" We were both in agreement there.

We also saw what we thought were giant cat tracks very close to camp but we weren't too worried. We made sure that there was no food anywhere near the tent. Most of the food was hung high up in a tree. That night we lay awake in the tent, listening, as the howling wolves and the arctic loons, with their eerie cry, seemed to be sending some mysterious message to one another, back and forth, beneath a star-filled sky.

At the far end of Tchentlo, there was another body of water that was separated by a mound of earth which was about four feet high and six feet wide. We took everything out of the boat and then dragged the boat over the hill to the other side, then we carried all our gear down over the little hill and reloaded the canoe. It was beautiful in an eerie sort of way. We decided that we must be in a bog. All around us were tall reeds. We felt tiny and dwarfed in a forest of reeds that towered above and all around us as far as we could see. The water was no longer clear but murky and the shallow bottom looked like thick muck. When we tried to touch the bottom with a paddle, it disappeared into the soft mud like it was quick sand. We looked at each other. If we were to fall in here, there would be no return. Birds and ducks swam around us almost tame from lack of exposure to humans then, without warning, a thunderstorm hit in the bog. Great and mighty thunderclaps resounded off of the mountains. Rain pelted down hitting the water like flying darts until our very bones felt damp and cold and yet we were enraptured by the wild beauty. We headed back to the little hill that we had come over and repeated the process in reverse to get us back to Tchentlo. It was getting late. We made for the nearest place to beach the boat and made camp for the night.

The next day was spent in the tent while the weather raged outside. We read books and drew pictures and entertained ourselves as best we could in a space that was too tiny to even sit up fully. Our equipment was cheap and we found that everything was getting uncomfortably damp again. If the weather had been even slightly colder, it might have been dangerous. "We need to find a place that's a little more sheltered from the rain," John was saying, "Someplace with more trees. We should pack up really early in the morning and go because the water is always calmer just before dawn."

"That's a really good idea and hopefully we'll have another sunny day sometime soon." I was getting a little tired of all the rain.

The next morning, we packed up in the early dawn and set off, across the lake, for the north shore. The water was as smooth as glass and a fine mist rose from the surface of the lake, silent and mystical as in a dream. A family of ducks swam nearby in V formation with the largest in the front and the little babies trailing along in the back. By the time we made it to the opposite shore, it was getting light. There in the clearing stood a small trappers cabin. It was unoccupied. The unwritten law of such isolated areas is that if you need a place to stay, you can use it but you must leave everything the way you found it or better, so we moved in. We made a hot fire in the barrel stove and hung all of our things, including our soaking wet tent, out to dry. Because there was a lot of storage area in our canoe, we had brought lots of things with us. Now we brought everything into our new little home. We made hot coffee and delicious freeze-dried apple pie. We got out our two guitars and played music together and sang folk songs. We scanned the bird books to identify species that we had seen along the way and we talked, for hours, about our adventure, then we made love, late into the night.

Just before dawn, I woke up. As I opened my eyes, I became aware of two little bright, beady eyes staring down at me from the rafters above the bed. It was a large wood rat. Although it was much cuter than any city rat I had ever seen, it still startled me, and I could not rest until John had chased it out of the cabin and stuffed the whole, where it had entered, with paper. He must have been accustomed to coming in to the house whenever he pleased because that night he kept throwing his rather large body against the door, trying to get it to open. Each time he would rush at the door and hit it with such an impact as to cause the door to shutter and shake with a loud banging noise. Finally, John got up and chased him away. I was relieved when he didn't come back the following night.

After a couple of luxurious days, everything was dry and so we packed up and began our journey back to where the van was parked. The wind was behind us now and John got this great idea that we could rig up a sail using thin tree limbs and our huge rain tarp. It worked like a champ. We sped down the lake with the wind in our sail and although I didn't really know what I was doing, I managed to maneuver the sail with a rope so as to always be catching the wind while John worked his paddle like a rudder to keep us on course. Effortlessly, we sped down the lake. It was amazing. We stopped for lunch at a place where we had camped on the way up the lake and where I had lost my little red knife. The knife had been given to me by a woman in Guatemala. When she gave it to me, she had said, "This knife is magic; if you are ever in trouble, this knife will come to your rescue." I was sorry to have lost it and I wanted to look for it at the campsite where I had seen it last. I searched all around the camp while we had lunch, sifting through small rocks and digging in the dirt. Just before leaving, I went to check one other place and there it lay, sparkling in the sand. Happily, I slipped it into my pocket and off we went. We set up the sails again and were cruising along when, suddenly, a strong wind came up. This part of the shore was all cliffs and the wind in the sail was driving us steadily and rapidly, towards them. In an instant, we were out of control and our canoe was listing, dangerously close to capsizing. It all happened so fast. I didn't know what to do. "Cut the ropes to the sail!" John yelled. "Cut the ropes now!" I grabbed the knife out of my pocket and cut the ropes to the sail just seconds, it seemed, before we overturned into the icy, churning water. The sail, no longer attached to its mast, fell slack and the little boat righted, itself, in the crashing waves. We made for shore as soon as we possibly could. "That was a close call," John said as he pulled the boat up on to the shore.

"It sure was. I'm really glad I had my magic knife!"

A couple more days with the wind at our backs and we were back at the van, safe and sound. It had been a fine adventure.

Soon we were back at Lucy's, and I was starting my second and final year of the Nursing Program. It was an incredible time really. I called those days my own personal Renaissance because I was learning so much about life, responsibility and the work of fulfilling one's dreams. We were young adventurers. With schooling, I was working towards creating order and purpose out of a life that had been filled with chaos. With our travels, I was learning to love and cherish the incredible and varied world that we live in. John and I were still having problems though and I probably should have taken the warning signs and gotten out before the real craziness began but then I wouldn't have my three beautiful children whom I love and adore. As some friends pointed out, "You must have had karma with him that you needed to work out." As it was pointed out in the book '*Women Who Love Too Much*' that Maureen had given me, if a woman grows up in a family that is severely dysfunctional, then she will be comfortable in a relationship that is unhealthy and dysfunctional and will tend to continue the pattern that she learned as a child. When things are going well, she will tend to get bored and will, subconsciously, want to stir things up. Really crazy relationships were all that I had ever known as a child. We did have some wonderful adventures together though, John and I, and John was clever and never boring. He could *MacGyver* anything. For instance, if we were stuck in the middle of nowhere with our car broke down, John could rig it with a coat hanger or whatever was around to make it work. Also, he would never have left me. He wanted us to be together forever even if he did torture me with his arrogance and his infidelities.

As I got further along in the second year of the Nursing Program, I did become a little discouraged and I experienced feelings of disillusionment. Rotating through obstetrics, as a student, we weren't allowed to do much and the nurses made us feel like we were inferior and in the way. We looked on dispassionately as mothers labored, flat on their backs in bed, attached to a fetal heart monitor and full of drugs. Psych I thought I would love but instead I began to hate it. The patients seemed to be able to manipulate my feelings. All my buried neuroses and insecurities began to resurface during that time period. I began to feel like I was a mental case myself. During the Med/Surg. Rotation, the instructors hovered so closely and were so critical that I was always nervous and I usually felt like a complete idiot. The rigor and stress of the nursing program and of my life with John began to get to me. There were times when I felt like giving it all up and running away. I had to keep reminding myself that it had been a lot of work and a struggle to get to this point and that I would regret it if I threw it all away so close to fruition. I made a deal with myself and I would remind myself of it when things got too miserable. All I had to do was to graduate. If I did not like nursing, I could do some other kind of work, but I must see this schooling through until completion. I gave myself little pep talks and it helped to get me by. In June of 1976, I graduated with Honors from the Santa Rosa Junior College Nursing Program. John did not come to my graduation but my mother took the bus up from Berkeley and I felt proud as I stood with my classmates waiting my turn to be pinned as a Registered Nurse.

Chapter 27
Home Birth

I spent the summer preparing to sit for the Nursing Boards and then, when I got my license, I worked for a short time in the Nursing Pool at Santa Rosa Community Hospital. It was difficult going from the relatively sheltered experience of nursing school to being out there on my own with as many as twenty, very sick, patients. I often felt overwhelmed and over my head, and usually I was working the night shift when all I really wanted was to be in bed sleeping. I didn't have any scheduled shifts but if they were short staffed, they would call, expecting me to come in with little, or no, advance notice. Shortly after I got the job, I began to feel extremely tired all of the time and I was feeling sick to my stomach a lot. Several times in a row, when they called me to come in, I didn't feel well enough to go and so they stopped calling and they dropped me from the pool. Soon after that, I discovered that I was pregnant. Less than 10 years had passed since I was a lost, pregnant, young teenage girl entering Dana House to have a baby and yet it seemed like lifetimes ago. So much had happened since Dana House. Things were not perfect in my life but I felt sure that I was ready to have this child.

I had been having light contractions for several days. We were planning to have a home birth and I hoped that everything would work out as far as getting hold of my midwife when I needed her and my friend Susan who planned to be at the birth also. Most importantly, I wanted John to be there. He still stayed out late a lot and the idea that he might miss the birth of our child scared me. John had been so resistant to having this baby. I felt that if he was at the birth, it would be a huge step in creating a loving bond between him and his child. It was just past midnight on September 8 when I went into labor. Fortunately, John was home with me that evening. He was so tired of the days of false labor that I had been experiencing that he didn't take me seriously when I said, after a particularly strong contraction, "John, I think you should call the midwife now."

"You call her," was his reply as he studied me from where he was lying, comfortably, in bed.

We didn't have a phone so it meant that one of us was going to have to go next door and wake up the neighbors. Just then another strong contraction hit and I had to lean against the wall and concentrate to keep on top of it. Instantly, John was out of bed.

"I'm going to call the midwife," he said, looking nervous.

"Don't forget to call Susan. I think this is it," I added when I had recovered.

The contractions were strong and regular but there was a nice rest between them. By 1:00 a.m., Susan and Alexis had arrived. "Do you want to check me to see if I'm dilating?" I asked Alexis. I knew from my rotation in Obstetrics that my cervix had to open to ten centimeters and that it was usually a slow process.

"No, it's still early. You have hours to go. Why don't you get out of bed and come and sit in the living room with us. You can rest later."

I liked Alexis. She was sweet and gentle, and I felt comfortable with her. I followed her advice and came out to sit on the couch in the living room where John, Susan and Alexis sat talking. I didn't join in their conversation but I was very happy to have them there with me. I felt confident that everything was going just as it should. The contractions were very strong now and I found myself tensing up through them. I tried to relax. John washed the dishes and Alexis put on water to make some tea. Susan put soft, airy, meditative flute music on the record player and adjusted the lights down low so that it was all very cozy and restful. Just after 2 a.m., my contractions started coming very close together. I thought about what I had learned in school. "Transition, the time between eight centimeters and fully dilated when contractions get very close together. Dilation often speeds up at this point." Things were so intense now there was no way that I could relax. Alexis got behind me and talked me through the next contraction while gently rubbing my shoulders. "Try to stay loose," she gently instructed. "Let everything go."

I gave it a try at letting everything go and I suddenly felt the baby move down.

"Alexis, I felt the baby drop. A lot," I added.

"Maybe we should check you," she said as she helped me back to bed.

Eight pushes later, Emily was born all sticky and wet and laid upon my bare chest. Everyone was very emotional, laughing with tears in their eyes. I held my baby close to my heart. She was so precious and tiny and perfect in every way. Already, she looked like her dad only much more beautiful. The placenta was taking a little while to deliver so John took his little daughter and gave her a warm bath, loving her and examining her, with pride and reverence, in the dim light. For the next couple of days, I rested up with Emily lying next to me in bed. I wrote in my journal, "I am completely hooked, in love, charmed and totally content to spend my days in her magical presence."

After I had my daughter, my priorities changed a bit, as well they should. I realized that I had to get serious about my nursing career if I was going to be able to support my family. John had never held a job and I seriously doubted that he ever would. Supporting the family was going to rest squarely on my shoulders but I had a good, steady occupation that paid well. Now it was time to cultivate it. Another big issue was that I wanted my daughter to grow up in a peaceful and loving home. That meant having a committed and monogamous relationship with the father of my child. I talked to John about this and, to my surprise, he agreed and without protest. We were, solidly, on the path to 'the good life'.

Everything didn't fall apart at once. It was a slow process that, with greater maturity and insight, could perhaps have been arrested and things mended at any point along the way were it not for the brutal and uncompromising force of mental illness that inevitably changed our lives.

Chapter 28
The Nursing Pool

Not only was I a new graduate with very little experience, but it had been over a year since I had graduated from nursing school. No one wanted to hire me. I went to interview after interview and always got the same answer. "We'll call you if something opens up."

No one ever called. Finally a friend's mother, who worked in Central Supply at Santa Rosa Community Hospital, suggested that I go to them and offer to orient for a couple of weeks without salary. I could offer to then work at an LVN's wages so that they could afford to always have an RN scheduled with me until they felt comfortable putting me out on my own. The hospital was always short on staff and on money and she thought that they would be enticed by such an arrangement. It was worth a try. I was incredibly happy and relieved because they liked my offer and agreed to hire me back as a float nurse in the pool. That meant, again, no scheduled shifts but knowing that I had a new baby they said that they would try and schedule me in advance as much as possible. Most of my shifts alternated between the three medical/surgical floors but sometimes they would float me to ICU or Post-Partum. I enjoyed and benefited from the varied experience. Usually, I worked night shifts and John would stay at home with Emily. On my break, I would go up to post-partum and pump my breasts because if I didn't, they would become painful and engorged with milk. It also served to keep my milk supply plentiful for my baby. At first I found the work and the hours very stressful but I was grateful to have been given a second chance. Little by little, I got familiar with the routine of getting report, doing rounds, giving medications and treatments, checking orders, doing rounds again, giving more meds and then charting. As I got more comfortable and less anxious, I began to love the work. We did team leading a lot in those days and I enjoyed the challenge of organizing the work for each night, assigning duties and then keeping everything running smoothly, completing my duties in time for the morning report. I liked many of the tasks as well. Successfully starting intravenous lines and drawing blood gases at 6 a.m. for the morning labs gave me a tremendous amount of satisfaction. Changing dressings, irrigating wounds and making sure that my patients were comfortable and not in pain were just a few of the nursing duties that gave me a sense of order and purpose in my work. Most of all, I derived satisfaction from sitting with a sick or lonely person in the early morning hours before dawn and finding a way to give them comfort. That was a big part of why I had been attracted to the profession in the first place and now all that schooling and dedication was finally beginning to bear fruit.

My favorite place to work was Med/Surg I. It was separated from the other wards by a long corridor and it had just nine beds. Because the patients were very sick, they always gave me a nursing assistant to work with. I liked the boundaries there, away from the bustle of the rest of the hospital and knowing that I would not be responsible for more than nine patients. It was like being captain of my own little space ship. We kept the lights down low and hurried quietly from room to room putting things in order and seeing to it that everyone was safe and out of pain. One night, on my first set of rounds, I was dismayed to find an older woman lying in bed, groaning and in pain. Report had not prepared me for the sight of this poor woman whose body was swollen and covered with little purple hemorrhages into the tissue called petechiae. She was a 'no code' and not expected to survive the week. She was in the hospital basically for comfort care but we were failing miserably in this regard. Normally, you didn't wake the patients' doctor up in the middle of the night unless you had a damn good reason. Actually, I had never done it before. Always, when a problem had come up, I had felt that I could handle it until morning. This was different. Someone was suffering needlessly. It wasn't right. I looked up her doctor's number and called him. A sleepy, stern voice answered the phone. "Doctor M.," I began. "I'm so sorry to wake you but Ms. D. is in a lot of pain. She's laying there moaning, with her eyes open. She looks frightened. I asked her if she wanted something for pain and she nodded but all she has ordered is Tylanol and Codeine. I'm sure she wouldn't even be able to swallow it."

There was a momentary pause and then he answered. "Give her two milligrams of morphine IV; push every two hours as needed to control pain." He had hung up before I could thank him.

I gave her the morphine and watched as her features relaxed and the look of consternation was replaced by a look of relief, then I left to check on the other patients. I was falling a bit behind. After about twenty minutes, I returned to check on Ms. D. The minute I opened the door, I became aware of a palpable change. There was a new calmness and serenity that I could feel even before I set foot in the room. Ms. D. had died. It was my first experience with the death of a patient. It seemed to me that she had not been able to relax enough to let go while she had been in so much pain. She was now released from her suffering. I learned, that night, that there are times when death can be a welcome visitor.

One of the great benefits of being in the nursing pool is that if you want some time off, it's not a problem. Although it wasn't a benefited position, the freedom it provided was benefit enough for wanderers like John and I. Summer was here; it was time to move out of Lucy's house again and we planned to go to Canada for another canoe trip. We had friends who lived outside of Price Rupert and we had visited them over Christmas to see their new baby and have them meet Emily. At that time, we had concocted this crazy idea to take two canoes around the semi-protected waterways that ran a jagged course in and around the Queen Charlotte Islands. At first, the idea of taking our babies, who would not yet be a year old, in wilderness ocean waters seemed dangerous and in fact, insane. I wanted no part of it. But as John and our friend Al worked over the details of the trip and Al's partner Leslie assured me of the safe nature of the adventure, I began to warm to the idea. We would be traveling through protected channels with islands on either side. We would not be in direct line of the open ocean. The water would be much calmer and more predictable and we would never be far from shore. The plan was to travel for three weeks, camping each night in a sheltered cove and we would be about as far from civilization as one can get. We would truly be in the wilderness. It was the call of the wild and I could not resist.

Emily was a beautiful child, sweet and with a good temperament. She rarely fussed. The long and tedious drive up to Prince Rupert was amazingly easy with Emily who would sit contentedly for hours either napping or gazing, with interest, out of the window. The four of us and our two little ones, Rose and Emily, flew from Prince Rupert over to Queen Charlotte Island while our canoes were ferried over with our cars. One gloriously sunny day, our two little families put the two canoes in the water and took off. I was in the front of the canoe as was our habit. Just in front of me, face to face, sat Emily buckled into a seat fashioned out of the frame pack that I used to carry her around on my back. We had bought the best life jacket for her that money could buy and it had a large collar that would keep her head above water no matter what. Still, she was tiny and the water was cold. We could not afford to capsize. Safety was everyone's first priority. I was pretty confident though. We were a good crew. John had more than once proven his quick and excellent judgment in a tight situation. Al had been a professor of paleontology at UC Berkeley, and he had spent a lifetime out in the wilderness. He was careful and organized and he knew what he was doing. Leslie had been one of Allen's prize students at UC Berkeley. She was a strong and capable woman. I had medical skills. We were going to be just fine.

We tried to travel at least a little ways each day which meant a lot of setting up and tearing down of camp but we developed a little routine and the process became stream lined. We could do it quickly. If the weather was good, we would travel long hours but if it was wet and stormy, we would rig up a couple of tarps which provided a makeshift shelter and we would hang out watching the rain and the waves while our babies crawled around under the tarp happily investigating each other and all the equipment. It felt very tribal. Emily and Rose were such good and easy-going babies. You could tell that they were enjoying the fresh air and having everyone so close together at all times. Our destination was 'Hot Springs Island'. We reached it in about seven days. By then, all of our gear was getting damp and we were more than ready for some hot water. To our delight, there was an abandoned hunting cabin on the island. It was just what we needed to take a break and dry everything out. There was a fishing vessel anchored nearby and they gave us all the fresh salmon we could eat. Several luxurious days were spent soaking in the hot springs, eating fresh salmon and sitting, contentedly, around the cabin, reading by fire light.

When we started on the turnaround journey home, we noticed a tiny island with a charming little house on it. We moored there for lunch and went up to the house to see who lived there. There was no one around. The place was a little messy with kids' toys and other household articles scattered about but it didn't look lived in and it looked like they had left in a hurry. I wondered what it would be like to live out there on a rock, in the middle of nowhere, surrounded by water. It had a certain wild and lonely, romantic appeal. I remembered a story that a doctor, who had once been a bush pilot, had told me. He had found a journal in a cabin by a lake in Northern B.C., far from civilization. The journal had begun, in neat and ornate handwriting writing, talking about how these two women had been dropped off by a bush pilot at the beginning of summer. They planned to stay through the winter and they were excited about experiencing the remote beauty of the wilderness. They had come with plenty of provisions and glowing expectations, hungering for solitude and for adventure. The first couple of months of their stay, they filled the pages of the journal to overflowing with eulogy and praise for the glory of nature and the beauty that surrounded them. They talked about how happy they were and how they never wanted to leave. As the months passed, however, the bright, cheerful writing turned to thoughts of depression and loneliness. Then as they became completely isolated and locked in by the harsh winter winds and snow and the prolonged, dark days and nights, the handwriting itself began to deteriorate. It became sloppy and hard to read, sentences were incomplete. The flowery language disappeared, completely replaced by a kind of madness that spoke of evil spirits and of death and destruction. "This place is hell." Those final words, scratched out across the page, were almost illegible. I wondered about the family who had lived in the house on this island. Had they too discovered the trick of how nature, in the blink of an eye, could become brutal and unforgiving? Had they too had romantic ideas that turned frightening with the reality of harsh winters and extended periods of extreme isolation and darkness? I too was drawn to the idea of living on this beautiful island away from the world but I knew that for me it was only a fantasy. I knew that I would be scared out of my wits on my very first beautiful, stormy, starless night alone.

We stopped one evening at De'labesh Inlet to make camp for the night. After dinner, we sat around the campfire talking while the babies slept peacefully in the tents. Sometimes, I felt a bit out of place with my companions because they were all fairly intellectual and would talk political and scientific jargon that I was not adept at or even interested in. That evening, the three of them were going on about the tidal plane and how you could figure out how high the tide would come up by calculations involving the moon and the stars and factoring in the type of vegetation, or something like that. They were very engrossed in their debate and they all sounded so knowledgeable. I wasn't really paying that much attention to what they were saying when I became aware of a strange, sizzling type sound. I looked down at the fire. The tide, that we were so busy discussing, had crept up unnoticed and was putting out the perimeter of our campfire. "Uh guys," I said laughing. "We're about to experience how high the tide can come." In an instant, we all jumped up and for about twenty minutes we ran about, like a bunch cartoon characters in high speed, moving all of our gear and our tents with our sleeping babies up to the safety of higher ground. We were grateful that it hadn't happened while we slept.

Day after day, Emily sat inches away, facing me in the boat. She never fussed. She gazed about her with a serene calm taking everything in, the water, the sky, ocean birds and the mountains in the distance. I like to think that, in some small way, she absorbed some of that beauty and it became part of who she is. When we got back to the main island and our cars, we spent the night in a little backwoods hotel with a bar attached. We had a fine dinner and drank wine and played pool with the locals. That night we celebrated. We were a happy, satisfied group.

When we got back home, I was able to jump right back into my job in the Nursing Pool. I had picked the profession of nursing because I had wanted to help people but it was also proving to be practical and flexible as well as rewarding. I couldn't have chosen anything more perfect.

Chapter 29
Maui

When September arrived we settled back into Lucy's and, for a time, things went well. Emily was a healthy and happy baby. I loved being a mother, and I liked my work but eventually I became dissatisfied with my relationship with John. I wanted a home of our own and I wanted something more. It was hard to define. I longed for affection and for sensitivity and for more of a partnership. John wasn't giving that to me. I once saw a cartoon of a group of female skeletons, all dressed up in fancy cloths, sitting in chairs in a waiting room. The caption read, 'Women, waiting for the perfect man!' Was I just creating more misery through craving something other than what was before me or was I in a relationship that I needed to get out of? I wasn't sure. One night John asked me with a sensitivity that was uncharacteristic of him in a voice that was both mystified and hurt. "Why can't you feel my love?" I didn't answer. It was complicated. Perhaps my crazy childhood was partly to blame, but I didn't think so at the time. How could I trust his love when he disregarded my feelings so completely? I felt like a prized meal ticket. I tried to be understanding about his carefree life hanging out with his friends, many of whom were women, but as I found myself more and more isolated in my life of work and household duties, without any appreciation, I began to feel resentful. Then I caught John in a couple of boldfaced lies about where he had spent the day and who he spent the day with. I was completely torn up by it. Then, one night he crawled into bed with me around 1 a.m. The strong scent of our neighbor's perfume permeated his beard. I almost couldn't believe my own senses. He made up some sort of excuse but it was the final straw. I could not take it any longer. The next day I notified the hospital that I would be out of town for a few weeks, and Emily and I got on an airplane bound for Hawaii.

We traveled around the balmy Islands for a couple of weeks like vagabonds, staying here and there. On Maui, we met two women who were camping at a hippy beach so we joined them. There were lots of other people there, as well, with tents and hammocks and huge campfires that everyone would gather at after dark. The water was clear and warm. It was a beautiful spot. One afternoon, I was sitting at the water's edge next to Emily who was playing happily in the sand. A couple of guys that I hadn't seen before walked down the beach past us throwing a Frisbee. "Hello!" one of them exclaimed when he saw us sitting there in the sand.

"Hello," I replied.

He immediately abandoned his friend and came and sat down with us. "Have you been here long?" he wanted to know. "Are there more places to camp?"

"I've been here a few days. It's lovely. It's really fun too. A couple of the people here juggle and there's a bunch of musicians, a couple of belly dancers. It's kind of like a big circus. You won't be bored." I was happy to have someone to talk to and apparently so was he because we sat there and talked for the next couple of hours. We got down and personal and before long we knew all about each other. His name was Alan. He had recently moved from Colorado to Washington, and he had recently broken up with his girlfriend. I told him my story with John and we talked for a while about how hard it was to make a relationship work and how both parties had to be invested and willing to change. We really hit it off. We liked each other immediately and we were both pleased to find that we would be camping on the same beach. "So what do you do in California?" my newfound friend asked me as he sifted the warm sand, slowly, through his fingers.

"I'm a registered nurse. I work at a Community Hospital." It had a nice ring to it. I was happy and proud to say that I was an RN. "What do you do?" It was polite to ask back.

"I'm a doctor," he told me. "I was working in an Emergency Room in Colorado. It could be brutal at times. I don't have a job lined up in Washington yet but I've decided to take a few months off from work and just enjoy life."

We smiled at each other as the surf lapped gently at the shore and the sun hung low in the brilliantly blue sky. It was a perfect plot for a romance novel. Brokenhearted nurse runs away from a bad relationship and meets brokenhearted doctor on a tropical beach. Do they fall in love? Read on and find out.

Alan pitched his tent close to where Emily and I were camping, and we traveled freely between the two tents sharing meals, stories and good vibes. It felt comfortable to spend time together and he was affectionate, something that I had been missing in my relationship with John. We had a couple of romantic evenings under the stars and Alan talked about my coming to visit him in Washington. My time to leave was drawing near and at first Alan talked about flying back to the mainland with me. I was excited by the idea but then he suddenly changed his mind. It was my first clue not to give my heart too freely to this lovely man with a big appetite for all the delicious treasures of the world.

When I got back home to the Russian River, I found a cute little cabin to rent close to Lucy's where I could drop Renee off with her dad on my way to the hospital. Things were working out alright, but still, I was restless and dissatisfied. I wanted a family and here I was living my mother's legacy after all, as a single mother. It wasn't completely fair to say that though. I was lucky in so many ways. I had a profession that I loved and friends, I earned a good salary and I lived in a beautiful setting but I felt that I still had more work to do.

As summer drew near and John's time to move out of Lucy's approached, he started courting me and pressuring me to go to Canada with him again for the summer. It was tempting. I was not happy living alone and we always had such a wonderful time exploring the wilderness together. Alan wrote me several lovely letters about how much he had enjoyed being with me in Maui. They were sweet letters and well written. He kept inviting me to come up and visit. I felt conflicted. I was afraid of falling back into the same patterns with John but also I had a feeling that Alan was not the monogamous marrying kind either. Nevertheless, he had sent me an invitation and I was curious to see more of his world. Once again I took a break from my work. I loaded my little Volkswagen Bug with a few things and drove, with my daughter, up to The Metthow Valley where Alan lived in a little cabin on the edge of the National Forest. Amidst the tangle of narrow, dusty, back country roads, I miraculously found the one he lived on and drove up to the cabin. He knew that I might come but didn't know for sure or when. He didn't have a phone. His cabin was very remote, a mile from his nearest neighbor, steeply up hill, on a bumpy gravel road. The road was lined with trees and thick, matted vegetation. Behind the cabin were hundreds of acres of uninhabited, national forest. As his little house came into view, my first impression was of the little log cabin in the middle of the woods that I had fantasized about as a kid. There was a large, cheerful porch and big picture windows that welcomed in the colors and sights of the outdoors. It was very quiet. Alan was home alone working in his big garden. He looked up as my little multicolored VW Bug approached and when he saw who was driving, a big grin spread across his face. "I'm so glad that you decided to come. Welcome to the Metthow! You must be tired. How long have you been traveling for? Was it hard to find me? Come see my garden. You can help me with it. It needs flowers. Are you hungry?" A dozen enthusiastic questions popped out at once. He dropped his shovel and gave me a big hug. He picked Emily up in his arms and they said their hellos as we walked slowly, holding hands, up to the house. It was completely charming and rustic. After Alan showed us around, we unloaded my things out of the car. Then, as a welcoming gesture and to help me to feel refreshed after the long trip, Alan led me down to a nearby stream and he washed my hair in the fresh, icy cold, mountain water. I did feel welcome and refreshed. I was glad that I had come.

That evening it was chilly so we made a small fire in the wood stove. Alan cooked up some rice and vegetables from the garden by the light of a lantern and we sat down together at the big wooden table that took up half of the little log kitchen. Emily was enjoying her new surroundings and we were, for the time being, a harmonious little family. After dinner, I read *Frog and Toad* aloud to Emily until she fell heavily asleep, tired from her busy day. Alan and I talked for a while but I too was tired from all the driving. He put his arm around me and I curled up next to him feeling safe and content. Before long, I was fast asleep.

The next day dawned bright and sunny. After a leisurely breakfast, we set off to meet the neighbors. Janie and Allen lived at the bottom of the road and they had a beautiful daughter, Emily's age, by the name of Tara. Allen was actually an old friend of Alan's from Colorado. To keep from getting the names confused, I decided to call my Alan by another name. I nicknamed him Lano. The name suited him and has stuck over the years. Janie and Allan had once been city folk but they had escaped to the country. They had a lovely log house and a big yard with a huge garden and some farm animals. They had chickens and a couple of goats. Emily was thrilled with her new friend Tara and with the animals. Allen was a little edgy and I wasn't all that comfortable with him but Janie was a wonderful, strong, independent, and sweet woman. We hit it off immediately. "Come and visit us any time," Janie said as we were leaving. She gave me a hug. "You don't need Lano to bring you. The girls can play together."

"I really like Janie," I said, after we had left.

"I really like Tara," Emily said sweetly.

What was that they said about the 'terrible two's. Emily was almost two and she was as fun and as sweet as any child could be. The marvelous two's, I would have to say.

We spent the days working in the garden and visiting friends. When it was really hot, we would go down to the river and swim in its refreshing, clear waters. One afternoon, down at the river, I crawled beneath a tangle of weeds and brush to get out of the bright sun. I lay there quietly in the shade snuggled up to Emily while she took a nap. Lano crawled under the brush and stretched out beside us. "I like having you here," he said. "What do you think about spending the winter? We could deliver babies together here in the valley for people who want to have their babies at home."

"That sounds wonderful," I said, surprised and happy that he wanted me to stay and intrigued by the idea of doing home deliveries with my friend and lover, the local doctor. "I still have to go back for a while though. I'd have to make a little money and pack things up, give up my cottage. There are a few things that I have to take care of."

"Well, just think about it." He took my hand and we lay there quietly for a while in our little wooded shelter while Emily slept.

"We have to go to Seattle for a week," Janie was saying. "I thought that you might like to stay here and watch the place for us. It would really be a help to us if you took care of the animals and it could be like a little get away for you."

"That would be great. It would give Lano a break too since I just kind of moved in on him and Emily would love to help with the animals. We'd love to stay here."

That first night I sat on the porch while my daughter slept and watched as an orange full moon rose, huge and bright, over the hills in the distance. All was quiet except for the chorus of crickets and frogs. It was very peaceful. After I went to bed, I lay awake for a long time. The moon was so bright that I almost felt like it was daytime and I should be up doing things. I missed snuggling with Lano and I wondered if he missed me. I half hoped that he would come down the mountain and lay next to me but he didn't show. Finally, I fell into a fitful sleep. The next day we didn't see anyone all day. We puttered about the farm and fed the animals and cleaned up some. I felt independent and adventurous but also, I was already starting to feel lonely. Emily picked up on my energy and she was a little fussy. After a couple of days and no Lano, I decided to go visit him but he wasn't around. His absence fueled the unsettling feeling I always had with him that he was withholding things from me. I cared about him deeply but I sensed that he was not open and forthright with me. My difficulty trusting others ran deep and so this trait that Lano had, of keeping part of his life hidden, made it hard for me to let down my own defenses and get really close to him and I felt that, on some level, that was exactly how he wanted it to be. It was all so very vague. I didn't really know. Was I making it up? Was it all in my head? Sometimes reality was so hard to pin down. When the week was up and Janie and Allen had returned, Lano was there to bring me back up the mountain. He was very evasive when I asked him where he had been. *Was it really any of my business anyway?* I wondered. I wasn't sure of anything.

Another month's rent was due on the cottage and so it was time for me to be heading home. As little as seven years ago, I would probably have just dropped everything and stayed on to see what would happen but things were more complex now that I was older. My life was not as flexible at 28 as it had been at 21. Now I had a child, a career and bills to pay. We left things open. We were both actually going to have to get back to work soon and the future just wasn't clear. What was clear was that we cared about each other. We got along well. The time we spent together had been a very special time and no amount of confusion or intrigue could diminish that. We had a friendship that could go the distance.

Chapter 30
Piercy

When Emily and I arrived back on the Russian River, we found John Laying in the sun, with his eyes closed, on the sandy river beach by Lucy's house. He was very tan and very thin. As we walked up to him, he looked up, "Juliet!" he exclaimed. "Oh, Juliet and little Emily, oh how I have missed you!"

The look on his face said it all. He looked drawn and sad and very anxious. My heart went out to him. To see this confident and arrogant man looking so fragile and dismayed was a shock. "What have you been doing, John? You don't look well," I wanted to know.

"I'm alright. I've been living in the van and doing some car work for money. I'm getting by but I miss my family so much. Please let's be together as a family. We can buy a little land and build a house together. I want to be monogamous. I want my family back!" We were both silent for a minute and then he added, "The highest achievement of our lives is a loving supportive family, spiritually growing together. Only this will give us peace of mind. I can get a job, buy you a house. I'll take care of you forever, anything you want. You are the most intelligent, independent, beautiful, sensual, and loving being I've ever known. Bring our family back together, Juliet. My heart pours out love to you!" He paused again before continuing on. My mind had suddenly become a churning turmoil of confused emotions.

"I've learned my lesson, Juliet. Leave your anger behind. Bring only love and compassion home," he pleaded.

I was weakening. Then he delivered the winning argument.

"Let's leave illusion behind and realize the beauty, harmony, love, and support that our family brings us. Illusion and Maya have been the winter of our relationship, yet our soul bonds remain strong, our closeness untouchable, our passion unmatched. Let's celebrate Emily's miracle, renew our spiritual bonds, and bring our family into full bloom. Trust in the honesty and strength that a relationship based on goodness and trust will bring us. Give our daughter her flesh and blood father!"

This last statement, more than anything else, moved me to tears. Still he continued on.

"Emily deserves the pure love and devotion pouring from my heart into her innocent soul, growing every day, growing on my love, growing on your love, growing on our love together as a family. Anything else is cosmetic. Emily will suffer. We have a responsibility to set a perfect example for Emily's innocent consciousness to grow on. Please don't break up our family, Juliet. Don't break my heart!"

My mind was reeling. I turned to walk away but he came after me, begging me to consider all that he had just said. Emily, sensing the drama, started to cry. It was more than I could bear. Wasn't a family the thing I wanted most in the world? John was the natural father. Everything he had said made sense. I had to give him an answer. I could not walk away and leave him like that. I did love him, I just couldn't live with him, but he said that he would change. I had to believe that change was possible. I had to give it a chance. Thoughts were racing through my head. "We can't stay here," was my answer. "There are too many bad memories. We have to move. Look to the north. Buy some land. Raise our family. Maybe it could work." I didn't know if I was speaking from my head or from my heart. I felt like I had no other options. I had to give our family another chance.

I sent Lano a note, letting him know my plans. He didn't seem fazed. "Good luck," he wrote back. "Let me know what happens. You always have a place to come to, here in the Methow, if things don't work out; all my love always, Lano."

Days later, we were heading north looking for a new home. We headed up the coast, stopping in small towns along the way. We spent a couple of days camping outside of Fort Bragg and looking at real estate. I liked the coast but it was foggy and damp and expensive. We headed further north and inland. In the little town of Garberville, we stopped to get Emily some ice cream. It seemed like a nice little town and for a town so small, it had a lot to offer. There was a movie house, a good restaurant, a nice dress shop and yes, there was a hospital. I stopped in just to check it out. A couple of nurses were rushing around looking very busy. One of them stood still long enough to ask me if I needed any help.

"Do you have any openings for an RN?" I asked, while looking around me. It was a cute little place, nothing like the 300-bed hospital that I worked in. As far as I could tell, there was only one floor and one long corridor.

"Can you start right now?" was her harried reply. "I'm very busy at the moment but here's an application to fill out. If you want to work, you have a job." Then she rushed off with an IV tray in one hand and a bottle of intravenous fluid in the other with a package of IV tubing tucked securely under her arm.

I went back out to the car and told John. "They're hiring. It looks like an interesting little place. Let's look around and see what real estate is like."

We looked in the window of one of the realty places that was on the main street going through town, all five blocks of it. A flyer for an acre in Piercy with a little cabin on it caught my eye. It was unbelievably priced at $15,000. Everything happened quickly after that. By Emily's 2nd birthday, we were living in our new little home in Piercy, and I was in Eureka taking an Advanced Cardiac Life Support class in preparation for working night shift when I would be the only licensed medical person on the hospital grounds. I would need to be prepared for anything, they informed me.

I threw myself into our new life with gusto. Our little piece of land was fairly remote. There were neighbors who lived on the same dirt road but we were well spread out and no one was within earshot. The house was small, very basic but had good potential. People referred to it as 'half a house' because the previous owner had meant to build on to it but had never gotten around to it. There was a large main living room/kitchen combined and a tiny 8x8 bedroom and tiny bathroom with a bathtub but no plumbing for a toilet. Instead, there was an outhouse. It was all we needed for the present, and it was ours. The monthly mortgage payments were low. The place was a little drab and I tried to fix it up some but our funds were very limited. Still, it was cozy. We spent our days preparing for the winter which would soon be upon us. Heating was by the wood stove that stood in the middle of the room. We spent a month cutting wood and stacking it outside the house to use when it got cold and the rains came. We closed up any holes in the walls and places where cold air leaked in. We stocked up on warm blankets for the bedroom and went to Good Will to pick up a couple of comfortable chairs for hanging out around the wood heat stove. I splurged and bought a bright red, Indian design throw rug for the living room floor and that worked wonders to cheer things up and keep Emily's little feet warm when she walked around barefoot. As the weather grew colder, we settled in. The rains hit in November with a vengeance. The weather had been much more temperate just a few hours south. We were thankful for the wood that we had cut because we were able to stay warm and cozy. Long hours were spent reading contentedly by the fire. I read Withering Heights out loud to John on stormy nights. The character of Heath Cliff reminded me of John with his dark intensity and his determination to come out on top at all costs.

✔ Night Shift was from 11 p.m. to 7 a.m. I worked four per week. Every evening before work, I would lay down around 7 p.m. and wake up around 10 p.m. to hurriedly throw on my uniform, slam down some coffee, and head down the road, about a half an hour drive to the hospital. The Garberville Hospital was like a bonsai of a larger hospital. It had 18 acute beds, two of them equipped with cardiac monitoring, a fully equipped delivery room, surgery complete with a full 'on call' surgery staff and a busy emergency room. At the end of the long corridor was X-ray. Around the corner from that, in the shape of an L, was the fully equipped lab and medical records and at the tip of the L was the Garberville Clinic. In those days, on the night shift, there was only one licensed nurse and a nursing assistant. The doctor on call lived 10–15 minutes away. It was a lot of responsibility but I loved it. When I arrived at work, I would get report and then hit the ground running. There were patients to check on, medications to be given, IV solutions and medications to be hung. On top of that, there was often a cardiac patient on the monitor that needed almost constant observation and then there was the ER, unpredictable as always. Some nights were quiet and you could make it through the shift feeling somewhat organized and in control. Other nights all hell would break loose as motor vehicle accident victims or some other catastrophe would come in by ambulance and throw the whole night into chaos. Some nights, the little ER waiting room would be full, and I would have to run back and forth between the ER and my acute patients keeping a detailed list in my pocket of when medications and treatments were due. At such times, an experienced Nursing Assistant was invaluable. When I had very sick patients on the floor and a trusted Nursing Assistant, I would sometimes send my assistant down to the ER to set up for a suture repair or take vital signs while I finished rounds making sure everyone was stable. I loved Labor and delivery but if a mom came in at night and delivered on my shift, I would be there until 10 or 11 a.m. finishing up on the preponderance of paper work that went along with bringing a new life into the world. It was a unique place and I was sure that there was no other place quite like it on the planet. I had stumbled into one of the most interesting and challenging hospital environments to work in. I couldn't have been more pleased.

Back in those days, all of our doctors lived in and were committed to the community. It was a wonderful group and I felt privileged to work alongside of them. There was a great team spirit and a mutual respect that made the work exciting and rewarding. As Dr. Bill would say, "I don't work to live; I live to work!" Dr. Bill was young and very good looking. He had good energy and a certain charisma to him. Dr. Bill was also very talented. I loved to hear him sing and he played guitar and fiddle like a pro. He could have been a star. He was our star, and everyone loved him. Dr. Jerry was the elder Dr. and everyone loved him as well. He was capable and experienced and could really do anything that a medical emergency called for. He was our chief surgeon as well. I remembered one night when a man came into the ER who had a tiny but deep cut on his wrist from a piece of glass. I called Dr. Jerry in and we prepared for a small suture repair. As it turned out, the man had cut a nerve, a tendon, and an artery. As he searched for the artery to repair, a thin stream of blood spurted in rhythmic pulsations across the room. "Why don't you glove up and assist," Dr. Jerry had said. "I want you to get in there and hold these retractors so I can see the artery." It was difficult keeping the wound clear of blood so that he could see what he was doing, but he was skilled. Before long, he had sutured the cut ends of the artery back together and stopped the bleeding while maintaining circulation. That was all that we could do for the man in our little ER though. He needed a hand specialist. We arranged for a transfer and Dr. J. thanked me for my help as gracious as any man could be. It was such a pleasure to work with him. I never saw him loose his temper or his composure. Sometimes, in the middle of the night, he would come whistling softly down the hall, and I would feel comforted just knowing that he was nearby. Dr. W. was a little less accessible but he was well liked and a valuable part of the crew. Dr. K. was young and new to the community. He didn't really fit in, and he didn't last long. When I had worked in a bigger hospital, I hardly ever saw any of the docs but here we were on a first name basis. We were friends.

Our little family made it through the first winter happy and healthy and excited about life but I think that the isolation was hard on John. I had plenty to keep me busy but John had a lot of free time on his hands and that is often a prescription for trouble. The spring arrived with the hills bursting with the vibrant colors of various wildflowers. White daisies, pink and purple lupines, foxglove, and wild mustard scattered along the roadside gave one the impression of having driven into a fairytale land. We flung open the doors and windows and welcomed the gentle breezes and bright sunlight into our little abode. We bought fresh cow milk that was from our neighbors' cow and skimmed the cream off of the top to put in our coffee and to make fresh whipping cream, and we made ice cream and picked blackberries off of the vine to make cobblers that were delicious topped with our homemade ice cream. We also began to explore the wild Northern California Beaches that were now only a short drive from our front door. We bought some baby chickens so we could have fresh eggs and we set up a little swing set in the yard for Emily to play on. This was the life that I had dreamed about, living in harmony and peace with my family surrounded by the beauty of nature.

With the better weather, John began to make trips every couple of weeks down to Sonoma County so that he could visit his old friends. I didn't mind, and it made sense. He was kind of isolated here. He hadn't made many friends, and he was very gregarious. He needed to get out. I didn't see any reason to worry, right at first, things were going so well but soon little warning signs began to appear. John had a friend in Cotati who I knew liked cocaine. John started hanging out with him and coming home from his trips all animated and jacked up. He started getting irritable and saying paranoid things like, "I think I'm being followed." It sounded so much like my mother that it almost seemed normal to me, and I was used to John's exaggerations and fabrications. Then John made a friend locally. It wasn't anyone I knew. John described him as an old recluse who lived in the hills. Apparently, together, they came up with a scheme to make some money off of trafficking drugs from the bay area up to Humboldt County. I figured it was probably John's' idea, and I didn't really take it that seriously. John was always coming up with grandiose outlaw schemes but he didn't follow through with them. Still, I needed to let him know that such ideas were not an option when raising a family in 'peace, harmony, and love,' a picture he had so eloquently painted not so very long ago. "Relax," John said when I protested. "It's between me and old so and so. You don't have anything to do with it." I knew better than to push. It was useless. There was nothing I could do unless I was prepared to leave and for now anyway, I was not going anywhere. I tried to put it out of my mind and concentrate on my home and work but as John became more animated and irrational, I did begin to worry and I started to have anxiety attacks in the night. I feared all sorts of things; nuclear war, pestilence and starvation, earthquakes. I began having tidal wave nightmares in which I was swallowed up by a wave of water too huge to escape from. Suddenly, things began to deteriorate. The next thing I knew, he brought home a baggie full of cocaine and he was snorting it constantly. Then things changed rapidly. Within a few days, I was living with a maniac whom I didn't know. He had a couple of gourds filled with beans and he would turn the radio on very loud and shake them in rhythm for hours with his body swaying and his eyes closed as if he were in some sort of a trance. Every once and a while he would laugh out loud for no apparent reason. He sounded diabolical, as if he were possessed by the devil. Soon he stopped leaving the house and taking showers, and he was very paranoid. One day he told me. "The FBI is after me. You didn't know this but they've been after me since High School because of my anti-war activities." He'd act weird for a while and then he'd seem more himself. I knew that the drugs were at least partly to blame but there was more going on than that. He seemed to be having a psychotic break. It all happened so quickly. One day I was joyously celebrating the glorious rebirth of spring, and just a few weeks later, I was grabbing my daughter and running for my life. One afternoon, he got really crazy. I felt uneasy as I went about my day cleaning up the kitchen and sweeping our pretty red rug. I always said that a house could be totally neat but if the floor was dirty, things looked messy. Putting the house in good order always helped to quiet my nerves and put me in a better mood. John had been shaking his shakers for an hour or more when he suddenly announced, "The voices are telling me to do bad things." I got really frightened with that bit of information. Then he walked over and turned the oven on and he said to me in an angry, demonic voice, "I'm going to have to burn you and Emily in the oven." In an instant, I had picked my daughter up, grabbed my purse and was running down the road. I wasn't thinking clearly. I was just running, terrified. I heard a car on the road behind me and I jumped into the bushes to hide, clutching Emily, tightly, in my arms. She wasn't crying. She just looked at me, confused not sure of what was going on, thinking that maybe it was some sort of a game that we were playing. The car belonged to a neighbor. They saw me jump into the bushes and stopped to see if anything was wrong. "Are you all right?" they asked in surprise as we emerged out of the tangle of vines. Gasping to catch my breath, I explained the situation. I needed to get away. They were very concerned for our safety and they drove us down the road to a phone so that I could call the sheriff. There was a protocol for this. Although no violence had actually transpired, it did fall under the category of domestic violence. They would take us to the women's shelter in Ukiah where we would be safe and I would have time to think things through. I couldn't fall apart. I needed to keep a sense of stability through all of this for Emily's sake. Besides, it wasn't all that different from anything I had been through many times before with my mother. History was repeating itself. I called the hospital. "You won't be seeing me for a while," I told them. "My life has come unraveled."

I can't sing praises of the Women's Safe Shelters enough. Many towns and cities across the country have them. They are a place that a woman, who is vulnerable and in danger and often has no resources, can go to at a moment's notice and get her life together in a supportive and safe environment. They were kind and respectful and gave me space and protection and asked nothing in return. I stayed there for a few days with Emily, trying to regain my equilibrium. What was I to do? I was now afraid to be in such an isolated area with John, and I felt vulnerable to his manipulations. I didn't want to see him, at least not until I felt stronger. There was no one that I could rely on other than myself. At least I could rely my own brain to give me somewhat accurate information. I had to be grateful for that. I had seen, close up, what happened when the brain chemistry scrambled and presented distorted and inaccurate information to itself to be evaluated. How was one ever supposed to make sensible decisions when you could not rely on or effectively translate incoming information? My brain was working. I could figure this out. I counted my blessings. I tried to analyze what had happened. Certainly the drugs had not been good for John but they were not the whole problem. All the dysfunctional behavior patterns that John had exhibited over the years, when taken separately, could perhaps be explained away but given this new information it was clear to me now that John suffered from schizophrenia. Why hadn't I recognized it earlier? Perhaps it was because it was so familiar to me, I couldn't see it. One could make an argument that the drugs caused the psychosis but I knew that all the scientific evidence pointed to the fact that drugs could not actually cause schizophrenia in a person who was not actually wired for it. It explained so much. The inability to hold a job, the overindulgence in sex and drugs, the fantastic stories that he made up and then believed, John suffered from severe mental illness. I had to forgive him just as I had forgiven my mother. Mental illness, although painful for the loved ones, was obviously most distressing for the one who suffered from the illness. Nevertheless, I had to go on with my life. I could not live that way.

Fortunately, my little VW Bug was in town at a repair shop and I had a little money in a bank where I deposited my paychecks. The account was only in my name. We took a bus up to Garberville and picked up my car and took some cash out of the bank. We headed north on hwy. 101. I didn't really have a plan. I thought that I would check things out along the way, possibly ending up in the Methow Valley where I would have friends. Emily seemed fine. I don't think she understood what was happening and I tried to keep things light so as not to alarm her. We were just out for a little road trip. This was another adventure. That's what I kept telling myself.

When we got to Arcata, a little over an hour north of Garberville, we stopped at the Natural Foods Co-op to get some food for the drive. I looked on the Notices Board and saw an advertisement for a room in a house for very little money. It was nearby. I checked it out more or less on a whim. Things kind of snowballed from there. One of the guys in the house was a nurse and he said that the local hospital, where he worked, was desperate for ICU Nurses. I had Advanced Cardiac Life Support certification so he thought that they would hire me. By that afternoon, I had a room, a job and a friend. Wow!

We stayed there through the summer and into the early fall. There was always someone in the house to look after Emily, for a small fee, on the nights that I worked and there was a delightful little daycare center nearby that Emily loved to go to. It was a good set up. I liked working ICU. I never had more than two patients and although they were very ill, it was a welcome change from the unpredictable nature of the rural hospital. I learned to adjust ventilator settings and draw blood from central lines and how to take central venous pressure readings. It was interesting, technical work. There was a young woman there, barely 21, who every one's heart went out to. She was dying of cancer, and she had recently become paralyzed as an unexpected side effect of her aggressive chemotherapy. We were taking care of her because she was on the ventilator. She was dying slowly but although her body and mind still lived, her spirit and the will to live had already left her. It made everyone so sad turning her and bathing her and caring for her as she lay there completely helpless and broken hearted. She had gotten married at a very young age when life was so open-ended and full of promise for her. Right after she got married, she got sick. At first, they thought that she had a virus or maybe just too much celebrating but after some simple blood tests, it became very clear that it was something much more serious. She got worse quickly after that. Her young husband couldn't handle it and never came to see her. I don't know if it was because it was too painful for him or if he was just that cruel. She couldn't even weep so we wept for her. We told her stories and brought her presents and tenderly rubbed her back and arms and legs with healing oils to soothe her and to stimulate circulation. But it was the sight of her young lover that she longed for and he didn't come. I remembered what Buddha had said, "Life is suffering."

I worked and spent my free time with Emily and tried to settle into my new life. I sent Lano my phone number and he called me frequently to say hello. "I'm coming to see you," he would say. "I'll be there Saturday."

Saturday would roll around and no Lano. He'd call again. "I'll be there Monday. I can't wait to see you."

All day Monday I would expectantly watch the driveway, but no Lano.

"I'll be there Thursday," he would say but he never showed.

This went on all summer, and I learned that here was yet another person in my life that I could not count on. I gathered a little set of friends, mostly nurses. We went out dancing sometimes and out to dinner. It was entertaining. The respiratory therapist had a little crush on me, and I had a little crush on someone else who had a little crush on someone else who I think had a crush on someone that we didn't know. Nothing worked out. I felt sad and the sadness turned to depression. I felt lost. What was I doing? What had become of my dream of a family? These thoughts were rattling around in my head one afternoon as I was sitting in the Arcata Square with Emily who had way more energy than I did at the moment. I was in a funk partly because I had just worked a couple of night shifts and had not gotten enough sleep and partly because I was dissatisfied and my analytical, trouble-shooting mind was failing me. I didn't know what to do. I was thinking about Emily's father and wondering if he missed her when I suddenly looked up and there was John getting out of the car and walking directly over to me as if he had known that I would be sitting there. He startled me. I felt like I was seeing a ghost. "I came to find you," he said. "I felt that you would be here."

It almost made sense and in fact I, kind of, did believe in telepathy. Had I subconsciously sent him a message? I was so very lonely. I had to admit it. Within a couple of weeks, I was back in Piercy and working nights again at my little rural hospital. I was happy to be home. John seemed to be alright and with any luck, there would never be a second episode. We would have to be vigilant.

Within a few months, I was pregnant. We hadn't actually planned it but we were happy. Emily had recently turned three and we felt that she needed a little sibling. Someone she could play with living so remotely, as we did, out in the hills. I wanted another baby. It never even once occurred to me to consider the genetics of mental illness. Would it have made any difference if I had? Probably not and I have no regrets.

Once in my second trimester, about four months pregnant, I went full throttle into the nesting mode. I bought a goat for milk, baby chicks for eggs, lumber to build an additional bedroom and I planted a big garden. It was spring and I wanted everything to be perfect for the new baby that was due at the end of October. I pushed on John to build a little bedroom for the kids and to finish some of the work that had been started by the original owner. He went along with my plans in an easygoing and cheerful manner, but he didn't do much. "Tomorrow," he would always say, or "Relax." It was frustrating but I had to let it go for my own sanity.

As time went by, it became harder to stay up all night so I cut back on my work to three nights a week. Consequently, I lost my medical benefits. We planned to have another home delivery. It was much cheaper than a hospital delivery but that wasn't the main motivation. We had loved Emily's home birth and we didn't want to go to the hospital. I didn't get that much pre-natal care either because I couldn't afford it. I was trying to be frugal with my earnings so that I could take a month off after the baby was born. I planned to work right up until I delivered. We laughed about it at work. "Maybe you'll deliver on your shift and then you can help with the paper work!" the other nurses teased.

The staffing at the hospital had changed quite a bit since I had first started working there. There was a group of us now, all around the same age, all starting a small homestead. We got along really well and we took turns hosting little get-togethers. I was excited because we were having a barbeque at our house, and I was looking forward to having my friends over. Judy, who was one of the day shift RN's, arrived first. She lived further out of town than I did and more towards the coast. She had a sweet boyfriend who was an artist. He usually didn't come to our get-togethers. Judy was gorgeous, and she seemed very dignified. She always reminded me of Greta Garbo. "Hi, Juliet, John, how are you. So nice to be here; is there anything I can do to help? Don couldn't come. He's painting." She had brought a couple of bottles of wine and a salad from her garden. We started setting up the table. Maryanne and Bruce arrived next. Maryanne was the PM charge nurse. Bruce often worked with me on night shift as an aid. They had met while working at a Psych hospital back east and they fell in love. After they got married, they moved out west and bought 40 acres. Now they were in the process of building a house. I thought that they made a good couple. They were both, intelligent, opinionated, and exceedingly headstrong, and they were both very good people. After a while, Polly drove up. She had worked before as a Psych Tech, as had Bruce, but now she too worked nights as an aid. We often worked together. It was fun working with my friends. It made for good team dynamics.

John and Bruce started talking politics. Maryanne looked at me. "How far along are you?" she wanted to know.

"Five months," I told her.

"Are you sure about your dates? You're huge for five months. How many you got in there anyway?"

We laughed. "I'm having a litter," I joked.

Emily liked having company even though there weren't any other kids. She went around proudly showing off our little chicks, and she gave everyone a tour to visit Annie the goat and the brightly colored flowers that she had planted in the garden. After dinner, we started discussing the community. We were all basically newcomers, transplants from other locations. We were drawn here by the beauty of the area and because it was a remote rural community with a hospital. We were, all of us, in healthcare. "There are so many families in this area with beautiful children and so many families have cute little homes way out in the hills. I love this 'back to the land' lifestyle. This area seems so 1960s. There really aren't that many jobs though. I wonder how everyone gets by. Do you think they make it just living off of the land like Thoreau?" I had wondered before about all the back to the land hippies in the area. None of them seemed to hold jobs but they all seemed so well off with nice cars and winter vacations. Maybe they all came from wealthy families.

"Don't you know what this area is known for?" Maryanne asked, surprised that I was apparently in the dark regarding a very well-known fact.

"Well I haven't really gotten to know anyone around here except nurses and we're kind of isolated. What is this area known for?" I wanted to know.

"Humboldt County Pot. All those people out in the hills are growing pot, and they're making a shit load of money doing it. Some of the best pot in the country is grown right here in Southern Humboldt!" Maryanne slapped her thigh emphatically. "There's a good economy in this little rural area, and it's because of the pot growers. It used to be logging but that died out a long time ago. Now it's pot."

"I don't smoke it anymore," I commented. "It makes me feel horrible, but I don't see anything wrong with it for people who like it. It has some really great medicinal properties. We've all seen it used, with great success, on cancer patients who can't eat. It settles their stomach and gives them an appetite and people who are agitated seem to calm down nicely after smoking it. I've also heard that it is good for glaucoma, although I'm not sure how that works." Everyone was quiet so I continued on. "I've seen so many people come into the ER with alcohol related problems, car accidents, domestic violence, and sometimes terminal liver failure. Alcohol killed my stepfather. I've never seen anyone in the hospital with a marijuana related problem except for once when this older woman ate a marijuana brownie by accident and thought that she was losing her mind. She cleared up pretty quickly though, and she was fine."

We had all been teenagers in the 1960s and had all smoked pot at one time or another. We were in agreement that it was definitely more benign a drug than alcohol.

After everyone left and the dishes had been cleared away, the goat milked and Emily had gotten into her pajamas, I snuggled up with my daughter to read her a bedtime story. It was a fairy tale about a man who could spin straw into gold. I liked to think that my life had been like that, taking adversities and troubles and making something beautiful of it. Creating harmony and order out of chaos. Emily fell asleep while I was reading, and I wrapped my arms around her, holding her warm little body close to mine. I gazed out the window, above our loft bed, at the stars that shone so brightly in the sky. Except for my child's soft breathing, the night was very still. "These are the good years," I whispered to the sleeping Emily. "I will never forget this moment. I am so at peace and so completely happy."

Chapter 31
God and I

This pregnancy seemed to be physically harder than my last. I was bigger, more out of breath, and had less energy and more aches and pains than I had remembered. I was of course a little older but I was only 30 years old. It was probably the night shifts and the heat of the summer that was taking its toll on me. I decided to pay a visit to the PA midwife that was going to deliver my baby at my home. I checked into the little clinic. "I'm glad you came for a prenatal visit," she told me. "You're almost seven months now. We should be seeing you more frequently. How is everything going?"

"This pregnancy is harder than I remember. I'm always so tired and out of breath and people stop me on the street. When I tell them my due date, they always ask me how many I'm having. I just want to make sure everything is alright."

She listened to fetal heart tones, checked the height of my uterus and felt for the position of the fetus. "Everything looks good," she told me. "Don't worry. Everything is going to be fine. I'll see you again in two weeks."

I left feeling reassured but I was beginning to doubt that I would really be able to work up until delivery. One night, I was talking to one of my patients who happened to be awake at 1 a.m. He looked at me and said, "I feel like I should get out of bed and you should get into bed. I should be taking care of you." We laughed. I have a relatively small build and my belly was gigantic.

The X-Ray tech at the hospital was a dynamic young woman who took matters into her own hands one day. "You are just too huge," she told me one night when I had called her in to do X-rays in order to clear the cervical spine of a motor vehicle accident patient. The X-rays were all good and we were able to send the patient home. Willamina stuck around to talk for a minute. "Are you sure of your due date?" she asked me.

"Yes, I'm sure. I went to the clinic the other day. They said not to worry. Everything is fine."

"Have you had an ultrasound?" she demanded.

"No, I haven't. I don't have medical insurance. I can't afford one. I don't think it's necessary, do you?"

"Yes, I do," she answered without hesitation. "What if there's something wrong with the baby? You could have polyhydramnios, too much amniotic fluid. It could be a sign of fetal problems. We are going to have to get you an ultrasound and I have an idea." It seemed like she had already been thinking this through. "We have a new ultrasound machine. We could bill it as a demonstration to show the staff our new machine and we could get a good look at your baby. What do you think?"

I know I had a big grin on my face. "I would love it," I had to admit.

Willamina made all the arrangements. The following Monday our little break room was jammed with people. People from the lab, X-ray, the clinic and the hospital all showed up for the event. It was an ultrasound party. They wheeled me in on an ER stretcher along with the new ultrasound machine and a large TV that the images of my baby would be projected on to. Everyone was chattering away, cheerfully. There was an air of excitement in the room. I was very excited to see my baby, and I was looking forward to finding out if it was a boy or a girl. I wasn't worried in the least. John had been acting a little strange lately, and he had grown more reclusive. He didn't come to the show. When the doctor arrived, sat down, and turned on the machine, everyone got very quiet. After making a few adjustments, he put the Doppler on my belly just above the pubic bone. Slowly the blurry image came into focus and you could see a round object resting down in the pelvis. "This is the head of the baby," Doctor Elliot explained. "It's down in the pelvis in the perfect position for delivery." He measured the diameter of the head. "Just perfect," he reported.

This was good news. One of the things Willamina had been worried about was a condition called hydrocephalis which is too much fluid on the brain. Hydrocephalic babies had big heads. My baby's head was normal. Next he scanned the Doppler upwards. You could see the tiny little vertebrae and the pulsing heart. He explained what we were seeing as he went along. It was incredible to be seeing my baby before it was even born. It was a boy! I felt a surge of love wash over me. "Everything is looking good so far," Doctor Elliott informed us. Finally, he brought the Doppler up towards the top of the uterus to look at the feet or hands as the case might be. We expected to see something that looked like a little foot but instead there was something round, a little bigger than a handball. The room was completely silent as everyone examined the image up on the screen. You could have heard a pin drop. Doctor Elliott said nothing for a moment. I held my breath, not sure of what I was seeing. Finally, Doctor Elliott spoke. "And here you see the head of twin B," he said in a very calm voice. Everyone started talking at once. It was exciting being there to see it firsthand. I could not believe my eyes or my ears. Twins; how could I be having two babies? It was not possible. I had been worrying about John's' mental stability the last couple of weeks. I didn't want to think about what the strain of having two babies might do to us. I had to fight back the tears. At the same time, I felt a surge of love for the two babies I was carrying who filled my womb to almost bursting. Dr. Bill was out in the hall and when he heard the news, he said to me, "That's it for you. No more shifts as of today. There is too much danger of prematurity carrying twins. You won't be able to have a home birth either, too dangerous." I couldn't work, and I was having two babies. This definitely presented some logistical problems. I wondered how John would take the news.

When I got home, John was waiting. "So how did it go?" he asked, looking up from the book that he was reading.

"There are two of them in there," I said, not knowing whether to laugh or cry. Feeling a little like both.

"What are you talking about?" John asked, not immediately comprehending.

When I explained that we were having twins, he received the news calmly and he seemed pleased, but later in the afternoon, he said something odd about superpowers and he started to laugh in a way that made me nervous. A few nights later, we went to the movies to see *Ishi*. It was a wonderful movie, but something in the movie set John off. As we drove along the dark and shadowy country backroads, he started laughing for no reason and babbling about spirits. Then he started talking about an alien superpower that lived under the ocean. It was planning to take over the earth and he had been chosen to be its spokesman. As part of his growing power, he had been given the twins.

It is a given fact that stress can precipitate psychosis in a person with schizophrenia. It made sense. When I was stressed in the ER, I had trouble doing math. I would have to take deep breaths to center myself and sometimes I'd have to go somewhere quiet before I could think straight enough to figure out a complicated drip rate. Multiply this effect hundreds of times, as it was with schizophrenia, and you could see how the neurotransmitters and other chemicals released with stress could cause the brain to go haywire and scramble the thoughts until everything was jumbled and all incoming information, nothing but a mosaic of impressions, partly true but mostly wrong. I felt like I could almost see the catecholamines squirting rapidly and chaotically into John's bloodstream and all his fine axons and dendrites that carried chemical messages to the brain firing erratically and out of sequence. I could see all of this in his expression, or so I imagined.

When we got home, I went to bed with Emily feeling exhausted, worried, and anxious. Where was all this leading and what was I to do? I desperately hoped that I would wake up in the morning to a bright and clear day to find that all this craziness had passed and that everything was going to be alright. Then John turned on the radio and started up with the shakers. When I asked him to please keep it down, he got mad. "You don't have to work now. Why are you going to bed so early? Get up and keep me company." He was insistent and he sounded agitated. I felt like he was escalating and I wasn't sure how to handle it. I decided to humor him so I got out of bed and went to sit in the living room. Before long, he was shaking the shakers in a frenzied rhythm and yelling something about the underwater aliens. Suddenly, he stopped and he walked over to where I was sitting, huddled up and apprehensive, on the small bed that we used as a couch. He had a very intense, angry look on his face and his voice sounded cruel as he said to me, "You're not going to like what I'm about to say to you but you won't be able to run because you're pregnant with twins."

I had been trying to stay calm and objective but now I became frightened. My own release of hormones and other chemicals brought with it a strong, hard and long uterine contraction followed quickly by another and then another. Regardless of how calm my mind was managing to stay, my body was responding honestly by pouring out catecholamines and oxytocin and sending me into preterm labor. I had to get to the hospital. It was a crazy, terrifying ride, tearing down the hill and into town with John throwing back his head and laughing his maniacal laugh but finally as the lights of town drew closer, I felt the fear begin to release its grip on me. I could breathe again and the contractions slowed down almost to a halt. I breathed a sigh of relief. My babies weren't going be born that night almost two months too early.

My night shift buddies put Emily and I in the little side ER and told John that he had to leave. They would be observing me overnight. For the next month, I stayed with another nurse and his wife who lived right next to the hospital. John left me alone. He had gone over the edge, and now he was keeping to himself up at the house. No one felt comfortable going to check on him. We were all relieved that he was staying away. Then one night I was asleep in bed when I awoke suddenly to find that I was lying in a puddle. My waters had broken. The babies weren't due for another month but this was good enough. They would be alright. I woke up my friends to tell them what had happened. "I'm just going to walk over to the hospital and have the nurses check for fetal heart tones," I said. "I just wanted you to know so that you could keep an ear out for Emily."

"Sure, of course," was the sleepy reply. "Let us know if you need anything at all."

I walked out into the night. We had recently been hit with a heat wave that had been very uncomfortable but now there was a welcome cool breeze. As I walked across the road to the hospital, I felt several contractions. Maybe it would be tonight. I started to feel excited. I was anxious to meet my babies and to be through with this confinement. I wanted to be free of my big belly that made it so difficult to be comfortable in any position.

The hospital nursing station was a welcome and familiar sight and both the nurse and the nurses' aid on that night were friends of mine. It was very comforting. After walking around for a while to stimulate contractions, I decided to get some rest. I crawled into bed in the little labor room where I had helped many other mothers get ready to deliver their baby. Now the roles were reversed. Cynthia, the night nurse pulled up a chair and sat down beside me. My contractions were getting stronger and I was having painful, back labor. "See if this helps." Cynthia pushed hard on my tailbone all through the next contraction and it was like a miracle.

"The pain almost totally went away," I said, feeling very relieved and surprised. I was unbelievably comfortable. I could do this. By 4 a.m., things were getting very active and Cynthia called in Doctor J. Because it was twins, he wanted two docs so he called in his son, Dr. Mark, who had recently started to work there at the hospital with his father. We all loved Mark as well. He was as warm and friendly and genuine a person as you will ever meet. He was a 'salt of the earth' type of guy, and he made everyone feel special. He gave me a big hug when he arrived, rubbing the sleep from his eyes. I was glad that he would be at my birthing. Around 5 a.m., they moved me to the delivery room and after just a few pushes, Boden was born, all wet and sticky and crying like a healthy newborn baby should. They gave me a few minutes with my first-born son but then they took him away to clean him up. I still had some work to do. "This will be easy," Dr. Mark was saying as way of encouragement. "You're already dilated. All you have to do is push him or her out." We hadn't been able to see the sex of the second twin so I had decided on the name Shannon because I loved the name and it was good for either a boy or a girl. We would know very soon. Finally, my contractions started up again. It felt like I had closed back up a little and the baby wasn't in the birth canal yet. I would give it all I had. It wouldn't take long. I pushed with all my might on the next contraction but it felt like nothing happened. This went on for maybe 20 or 30 minutes. I was getting tired and loosing track of time. Then Dr. Jerry did a vaginal check. He looked worried. "It's not the baby's head that I'm feeling," he reported more to his son than to me. It wasn't good news. "It feels like a shoulder," he said after checking things out some more. "I think we can turn the baby a little and get it going head first but I want to start an intravenous line before we do that." There followed a flurry of activity. Stacy, a nursing assistant that I had worked many a night with, stayed next to me holding my hand and talking soothingly. She was an angel. I had prided myself on being able to maintain control throughout my labor with Emily and with Boden even managing to carry on a little conversation at times to entertain my companions. Now as my physicians, whom I adored and trusted completely, reached up into my uterus and pressed down on my belly, trying to force Shannon into a position where he could be birthed, I came apart. I was already exhausted from Boden's birth and the pain was far more intense than anything I had ever experienced. As time passed, I got more and more out of control. I was afraid that my screams were echoing down the halls of the hospital but there was nothing I could do to stop them. Everyone knew my misery now. They tried giving me some nitrous but it had a paradoxical effect. I got crazy, and I became terrified that John and his spirits were trying to kill me. I started crying out, "John is trying to kill me. His spirits want me to die."

As I spiraled further and further out of control, Stacy leaned down putting her head close to mine. "This is between you and your god," she whispered. "John has no power to stand between you."

It was the perfect thing to say. Even in my distraught condition, I recognized it as a true statement. I was fighting for my life and for the life of my baby and at this point, John had nothing to do with whether or not we made it. Immediately after she had said it, I felt that we were going to be alright.

Not long after that, they loaded me and Boden, with Shannon still undelivered, into an ambulance and took us north to a bigger hospital where I had an emergency C-section. During the hour-long ambulance ride, my contractions relaxed a little and I was actually fairly comfortable but we weren't out of the woods yet. The big danger now was that as the uterus shrunk down, minus one baby, the placenta could sheer away from the uterine wall causing an uncontrollable hemorrhage that could be fatal to both unborn baby and mother in minutes. Nonetheless, we laughed and joked as we sped north to where there was an operating room and surgeons and pediatricians and everything we would need to bring Shannon safely into the world, if only we could make it there. The little ambulance was packed to overflowing. Of course there was the patient which, for a change, was me. Boden was at my head in a bulky, old-fashioned, baby warmer. I knew the ambulance crew well and they did all they could to make me feel safe and secure. Dr. Mark rode along with us as well, holding my hand for emotional support and at the last minute, one of the nurses squeezed in to keep an eye on the baby. We were a jolly group as we raced against time to save a couple of lives that hung in the balance. We were all relieved and thankful when we arrived uneventfully at the Emergency Room door. It was September 26th and as they pulled the stretcher out of the back of the ambulance and into the crisp morning air; a light rain had started to fall, blessing us like a baptism or was it tears for all the pain that John's' mental illness had thrust upon us. I wasn't sure which. Maybe it was both. As the anesthesia reached up to pull me out of my wracked body and into a deep sleep, I said a little prayer for my babies.

Shannon hadn't wanted to come out but we made him. He'd had a rough beginning but it looked like he was going to be alright. I was out of it for about 24 hours with a raging fever. IV antibiotics dripped steadily into my veins to fight the infection that had developed but by the following morning, I was awake and clear and ready to meet my sons. They were identical twins. They each weighed 5 ½ lbs. "You're so tiny and so perfect and I get to have two of you!" I crooned as I held each one in the crook of an arm. "I love you both so much!"

Chapter 32
Sue Clark

Sue Clark was a nurse extraordinary. She was practical, funny, steady and strong, and kind all at the same time. She was one of those special and lucky people who are never harshly criticized. Everything she did was beyond reproach because she did it well and with a tremendous amount of positive energy. I envied her energy. She seemed tireless. I used the past tense because Sue died of leukemia about 15 years ago. She must have been in her late 30s or early 40s. She was young and active and never sick. Then one day she started feeling ill, kind of like she had a mild case of the flu. A month went by and she hadn't managed to shake it. Finally, she asked the doctor she worked for, who ran a mobile clinic, to check her out. They drew some blood to send to the lab and she went on about her day. According to Sue, when she showed up for work the next day, there was a helicopter waiting to take her to UCSF, the big teaching hospital in San Francisco. I went to visit her there at UCSF just before her passing. I remember entering the room. I thought that I had the wrong room and mumbled my apologies as I turned to leave. "Juliet, it's me, Sue," Sue had said as I reached for the door handle.

I was embarrassed. I hadn't recognized her looking so worn out and completely bald. That's what cancer and its treatments did to you. She was such a brave soul. We laughed as we reminisced about the time John had brought Annie the goat to the hospital. It was when I was pregnant with the twins and I had left him there on the hill in Piercy. He had not wanted to milk the goat so it had become engorged with milk. The goat was in a lot of pain, and it was making a racket so John drove the goat into town, dropped her off in the hospital parking lot and left. It set up quite a stir. Fortunately, Sue was there on shift. She had goats of her own so she went right out into the parking lot, in her nursing uniform, and milked the goat. "You know," Sue was telling me as she lay there in the hospital bed, "one of my patients happened to be looking out of the window and he saw me out there in the parking lot milking the goat. Later he said to me, I knew that I was in a rural hospital but I never expected that it would be this rural." In spite of the cancer that ravaged her body, Sue and I couldn't help laughing, it was just so classic a story.

"I hadn't heard that part of the story," I told her. "It's precious."

After work, Sue had put the goat in her car and she took it home. It was the only thing to be done and she did it as if it was nothing unusual. That was Sue. She matter-of-factly did whatever needed to be done. Why would you do anything else?

After the twins were born, the four of us, Renee the two babies and myself, had nowhere to go. While I was still in the hospital recovering from the surgery, John came to visit me. He still seemed kind of out of it when he showed up with some strange guy from off of the streets. Apparently, the guy was living at the house with him. John didn't ask to see his babies. He just asked me for some money for food. Since I had about $20.00 dollars on hand, I gave it to him. He looked pleased and he said to the guy that was with him as they turned to go, "Didn't I tell you she always has money."

Needless to say, I didn't feel safe going, with my babies, back to that isolated living situation even if I could get John out. On the day of our discharge from the hospital, Sue came with Emily to pick us up and she took us all to her house where we were reunited with Annie the goat. She had a guest room off of the kitchen all set up and she took care of us until I had recovered enough to begin to take control of my life again. I will never forget her great kindness. To Sue, it was just something that needed to be done; why would you do anything different?

Sue died shortly after I had visited her in the hospital, leaving behind a devastated husband and couple of kids who were still in school. Again I remembered the teachings of Buddha. "Life is suffering."

Chapter 33
Forest of Arden

After we left Sue's, we rented a room in a house in Fortuna for a couple of months. The owner had recently been divorced and she needed the extra money to keep from losing her home. She stayed at her boyfriend's most of the time so we basically had the house to ourselves. We had a tiny little room with a giant bed that took up most of the space and we all slept, snuggled up together, in the family bed. I was breast-feeding my babies so there was no getting up in the middle of the night to make a bottle. I just put one on either side of me and rolled from side to side all night long, like a momma bear with her cubs, as they took turns waking up to nurse. Since their birth weight was a mere 51/2 lbs. in the first couple of months, they nursed every few of hours all through the night. But they were easy babies and they weren't fussy at all. During the time between feedings and diaper changes, we all slept well. I kept expecting that Emily would start acting difficult because we had not one but two new babies and our lives had changed so much in every way but she never did. She was always sweet and cooperative and she was happy just to be able to hold her little brothers once and a while.

That year we had an unusually stormy autumn. Many nights there were storm and flood warnings, and the electricity would go out for hours. A friend of mine had a tree fall right through the roof and into her living room just minutes after her daughter had gotten up and gone into the kitchen. Some nights, when it was raging outside and the electricity and heating were out, I would drag a big foam pad into the living room, pile it high with warm blankets, and make a big fire in the fireplace. Then we would all cuddle up by the fire, and I would read stories out loud mostly for Emily and my benefit, although I think that it was soothing to the babies as well.

Once Boden and Shannon were a couple of months old, I grew anxious to move back down, closer to the hospital, where I could get back to work and where I had friends. I felt very isolated where I was, and I needed money. After searching around for a few days, I found a quaint little, one-room, redwood cabin with big French windows that opened up to the redwood forest. There were several small cabins on the property and gift store that sold trinkets and redwood souvenirs. It was beautiful in a rustic sort of way and very cheap. I was happy to get it. We packed the wind up swing and our few belonging into the VW Bug and headed South on 101 to The Forest of Arden which was to be our new home for the next three years.

After we had been there a couple of days, I started feeling depressed. The place was charming but it was dirty. The large, beautiful old French windows were streaked with dirt so they didn't let in much light and the walls were the original old redwood which was beautiful but seemed dark and gloomy. The tiny kitchen was covered with old food stains and dust. I decided that I might feel better if I had some music and the house had a good cleaning so to that effect I went to town. I had a cheap tape player but no tapes so I bought a Crosby, Stills and Nash tape and Joni Mitchell's, *Clouds*. Then I went to the store to buy cleaning materials. It was difficult navigating in the store with two new babies. Right after going through the checkout, I ran into Maryanne and Bruce. I hadn't seen them in a couple of months. "Juliet, how are you?" Maryanne asked, giving me a big hug.

Immediately, I started to cry. I was under a lot of stress but I hadn't realized how the tears were waiting, just under the surface, to start spilling out with the first kind word from a friend. They took us all home with them and made us a bed in front of the fire. They fed us and entertained us through the weekend and so, by Monday, I felt stronger and not so isolated anymore. I was ready to get on with the task of building our new life.

When we got back home, I put on the music and washed the windows until they sparkled with the afternoon sun and the green forest reflected in the glass, mysterious and inviting. I scrubbed the entire house, all 600 square feet of it including the bathroom. I had managed to get hold of a white crib and I filled it with brightly colored baby blankets and two beautiful babies. That helped to cheer the room up as well. We were home.

Before long, I was working back at the hospital. I now worked the PM shift, 3–11. That way, I had mornings with Emily and the babies and, theoretically, I could sleep at night. It was hard though. The babies still woke up a few times each night and Emily woke up really early in the morning full of energy and raring to go. I was hardly getting any sleep and I was constantly on the go. It began to take its toll. For one thing, I was getting sick a lot. I was always exhausted and I developed a chronic cough and sore throat. I felt overwhelmed and I was lonely for someone to share in the joys and hardships of raising a family. It was too much for one person. I needed help. Then one day in early February, I ran across John in a restaurant in town. He was completely clear again, and he pleaded with me to let him come back and be with his family. I hardly hesitated. I needed him. We all needed him. He seemed stable now and I knew that, as long as he remained that way, he would love and care for his children in a way that only a father can. I had to let him back. It was the right thing to do. The house in Piercy had fallen into foreclosure so on a cold, blustery, February day John joined us at The Forest of Arden.

The first thing we did, as a family reunited, was to take a vacation to Baja Mexico. We fixed up the Volkswagen Van as a little home on wheels and headed south for Bajia De Los Angeles to spend three weeks living in our bus just bumming around on the beach. I was so exhausted that for the first three days on the drive, I slept in the back of the van about twenty hours a day. I remember waking up in Santa Barbra and going into a book store to get a couple of books to read aloud to the kids on our travels. It was nighttime but the weather was warm and balmy and the people were smiling and friendly. Music was playing in a sidewalk café and people laughed and chatted as they strolled along the tree lined boulevard. It was such an incredible contrast to the cold and isolation and to the tension of that winter.

We scouted around for a few days until we found a lovely secluded spot on the Sea Of Cortez and we set up our camp there. As the days passed, I felt the months of worry and weariness melting away. I was having the time of my life with my babies, playing in the sand, running in the surf and laughing in the sun. We were all happy and grateful to be together.

When we got back home, I went right back to work but it was so much easier now that their dad was around to be with them while I was at work and to hang with them if I needed a nap or just some time out. John, once again, had developed his own set of friends whom he spent much of his free time with. It was as if we didn't have that much in common any more, other than our children, but on a practical level, it was working out for both of us and things went smoothly for a couple of years.

One evening, I was standing in the Nurses' Station talking to Diane who was the Director of Nursing at the time. We were talking about what a special and interesting place our little hospital was. "I love the variety here," I was telling Diane, who had started working there around the same time that I had. "You get to do so many different things, OB, Cardiac, ER, and you never know what is going to happen next. There's never a dull moment but at the same time it can be overwhelming. Things can get crazy and dangerous in a heartbeat. That's the only thing I don't like about it, when it gets out of hand and you need help and there's no one to call."

Diane nodded; she had worked shifts there as a nurse. She knew exactly what I meant and she had to agree. "What if there was a nurse on call 24/7 and you could call her in to help deliver the babies and for other staffing needs. It would take a lot of the stress and anxiety out of working here, don't you think? We could pay the same on call rate that we pay the surgery crew, $2.00 an hour for being on call and time and a half when called in. Do you think anyone would want that job?"

"That's a fantastic idea, Diane. I want that job. Will you let me do it? I could do it 24/7 and John could be 'on call' for babysitting!"

We settled it right there and then and I became the first On Call OB Nurse that our little hospital ever had. We only had, on average, a delivery per week, but they called me in for any kind of staffing needs that couldn't be filled in other ways. Sometimes, I was called in to special patients who were really sick or to help in the ER if it was out of hand or just to work a shift if it couldn't be covered. I really only ended up working about three shifts a week though, on average, and I made almost twice as much money as I would have otherwise. I loved coming in for the births. Sometimes, I would head home after a particularly beautiful and high birthing and I would think to myself, *I really ought to be paying the hospital for letting me participate in this incredible experience.* Sometimes though the births were very stressful, like the time a mom was in labor for three days. By midnight on day three, she was fully dilated so we kept going. The poor, exhausted mother pushed with everything she had. With each contraction, a tiny bit of sticky scalp would appear at the opening of the vagina only to recede and disappear when the contraction passed. This went on for hours. My confidence was waning. The mom was exhausted but she hung in there. By 4 a.m., she had managed to push her healthy, nine-pound baby out but she had such a large vaginal tear that we had to take her into the delivery room to do a lengthy repair. It took a couple of hours. Then, after that, she kept bleeding from a small piece of retained placenta that prevented her uterus from closing down completely. She needed a D&C so we took her into surgery. In surgery, her blood pressure started to drop out and we had to scramble to get her stabilized. I found myself praying. "Please," I said to the universe in general. "She has a new baby. She needs to live." As I whispered this fervently under my breath, I was frantically pumping up a blood pressure cuff around a bag of IV solution so that the fluid would go into her veins faster. As her Blood Pressure picked up, she started to come around. She looked up at us from where she was lying on the surgery table under a mass of blue sterile drapes, not totally comprehending what all was happening. "Am I going to be alright?" she asked weakly.

We nodded, momentarily paralyzed by a flood of relief. We brought her back to her room in stable condition but to our great dismay, the slow and steady oozing of blood continued. Finally, we put her and her baby into an ambulance and sent them north to a bigger hospital where they had more resources. Everything was alright in the end but it had been a dangerous situation and it made us stop and think about what we should consider as a safe scope of practice in our little hospital. Even though we wanted to do everything, we had to admit that there were some things that we just weren't set up for.

As time went by, Diane made me the OB Nurse Manager as well as the on call nurse. I met regularly with the medical staff. We spent a lot of time looking at the issue of 'scope of practice' and I wrote policies and procedures based on our discussions. I taught classes to the nurses and gave OB hospital tours to the mothers in the prenatal classes. I oriented new staff and taught a yearly class on neonatal resuscitation with Dr. Bill. Over time, I became somewhat of an expert in the field of low risk obstetrics, and I loved every minute of it. I carried a beeper with me and, at all times of the day or night; if it went off, I would drop what I was doing and rush into the hospital.

One night when it was very stormy with flooding and mud slides, I was called in for a birth around 1 a.m. Outside, it was very dark and I could hear the torrential rain clattering down on the roof. Reluctantly, at first and still half asleep, I crawled out from under the warm covers and threw on a pair of scrubs, then I pulled on my rain gear and went out into the storm. Heavy winds pushed sheets of freezing rain under my hood and down my shirt and I was suddenly wide-awake. There were only two ways to get onto the freeway to get to the hospital and one way was already marked off and closed from a big slide. As I drove anxiously through the storm, I saw, illuminated as a blur in the headlights with the windshield wipers slapping wildly, a fresh slide ahead of me that went all the way across the road. I would have been totally justified in giving up and going home but instead I backed up and gave it a running start. Somehow, I managed to get across, slip sliding over the thick, heavy mud and debris that had just washed down off of the hillside. I thought of the post office slogan. *"Neither sleet nor snow nor driving rain,"* that was now my slogan as well. I thought about it with pride. I was Indiana Jones! I was a wild cowgirl! There was absolutely nothing that could keep me from attending my births!

My babies were growing into sweet and handsome little fellows. They were both easy-going and good-natured. They walked and talked and communicated with each other in the very close and intimate way that is classic for identical twins. I remember one time when they were sitting on the floor, hidden behind a big stuffed chair, with their heads close together. They were whispering to each other, naming the different items in their picture toy. "Red car," one of them whispered.

"Probably piece of cabio," the other one added, using the Spanish word that he had learned in Baja and pointing to the head of a horse.

The day that one of them stood up and took his first step, the other one watched in surprise. By that evening, they were both walking. And they were little troupers. One chilly evening, when we had been out late and our car had broken down on the freeway, we had to run along the side of the road so that we could get to a phone and call for help. I held a tiny little hand in each one of mine and hurried along, anxiously, in the dark. There was no way that I would have been able to carry them both but they hurried along with me as fast as their little legs would carry them and they never complained. "What tough little guys you are," I said when we were safely at home. I picked them up in my arms, one at a time, and gave them each a big kiss on their chubby cheek. "I love you so much!" They grinned back at me, identical little smiles.

Emily had just started school. We went shopping, mother and daughter, for some cute school dresses. She looked so sweet and lovely, all dressed up, toting her little school bag. School was easy for her and she got along well with the other kids. My children were, all three of them, growing so fast. Time seemed to be accelerating.

Once again, the cycle was repeating itself. Did signs of the beginning of another breakdown fuel my feeling of dissatisfaction in my relationship with John or did my feelings of dissatisfaction, subtly picked up by John, initiate the beginning of another breakdown? In those days, I didn't understand as much about mental illness as I do now. How a regular routine and steady support were essential to stabilization in mental illness. How much a person who suffered from mental illness could benefit from consistent therapy and from medication. How stress was an inevitable trigger for psychosis. All I knew was that I was becoming incredibly unhappy again. "You're turning into an old hag," John said to me one morning when I got home after being up all night at a birth. He was being, purposely, cruel and belittling. Another evening, John came home with the kids, and he was bragging about how he had been drinking and driving and how he had fooled the cops into letting him go without giving him a sobriety test. I felt then like taking the kids and running. At the same time, I felt confused. I was somewhat educated about the cycle of domestic violence, the episodes of abusive behavior followed by the honeymoon phase where the perpetrator showered the victim with love and promised that it would never happen again. It had never gotten to the point where John had been physically violent with me, and because of the mental illness factor, I felt that he had little or no control over his irrational behavior. I didn't really see it as domestic violence; however, some of the issues and cyclic patterns were definitely the same. I went to a counselor and poured out my life and my heart to her, as much as I could, in the course of an hour. When I was finished, I felt drained. She looked at me. I expected her to say something profound, and I hung on the silence. Finally, she said to me, "You need to eat three meals a day, get eight hours of sleep and plenty of exercise."

That was it. Years later, I can now appreciate the wisdom in that advice but at the time I felt betrayed. I was desperate for an answer. Her advice left me cold. Next I turned to the Buddhist teachings that I had been so inspired by when I first met John. During the last ten years, I had been busy and so caught up in charging ahead with my life that I had lost the thread of quiet contemplation and nonattachment that is so central to Buddhist philosophy. I began reading avidly again. In my readings, I came across a passage that said that if you study something too closely and too obsessively, then you lose the ability to see it. It recommended that one stop thinking, pondering and endlessly analyzing the problem with the mind. Instead, it recommended sitting with a quiet mind, letting oneself be open and expansive. In that state, the answer was more likely to rise to the surface with much of the confusion falling away. I took it to heart and I tried it. For the next couple of weeks, I went about my days quietly meditating, doing the daily things that needed to be done and attempting to be totally present in each moment as much as possible. John was starting to have delusional thoughts again, and he accused me of being a lesbian. He said that God was going to punish me for that. Then he started back up with the shakers at all hours of the day and night. The sound of them reminded me of war drums. They kept my nerves on edge. Should I stay or should I go. I didn't want my life to be like this. I'd had enough psychodrama to last me a lifetime, and I didn't want my children growing up with it either. I felt like some very important part of me was dying inside. Suddenly, it was very clear to me that I had to leave. I just couldn't decide whether to take the kids and totally relocate or to just go somewhere for a while with the kids to let things settle down and then come back to my town and to my job but not to John.

Once I realized that John was having another breakdown and that I had to get out before things got too bad, I went to the bank and put most of my money in travelers' checks. Then I went to the hospital and told Diane that I might be leaving suddenly, on short notice, because John was getting delusional again. She had seen him before, when he was really crazy and so she was supportive. She totally understood. She wanted me to be safe.

The next day, I decided to take the kids to the park and just sit quietly to see if some sort of plan would present itself to me. As I was leaving the store with the kids and our picnic lunch, I noticed a man on the sidewalk, standing there, smiling at me. "Are these all your children?" he asked.

"Why, yes," I answered. "The boys are twins."

He looked at us taking in the scene of my adorable, twin, three-year-old boys clutching at my skirt and Emily, who was seven, helping with the assortment of picnic stuff that we were carrying. I recognized him as someone I had seen around before, always with a different beautiful woman. He looked to be about ten years older than me, very handsome with a fine strong build. "Where are you going on this beautiful day?" he asked.

"I'm taking the kids for a picnic," I answered, already feeling a little charmed. "I have some important things that I have to think about."

"Do you mind if I join you?" he asked in a manner that was almost shy.

His smile was totally disarming and I could only shake my head. No, of course, I didn't mind. We met at the park and sat for a while talking while the kids ran around in the grass and played on the swings. He was so open and supportive that I ended up pouring out my entire sad and confusing tale of woe to him. "I'll help you with whatever you need," he told me. "I have a ranch in Modoc County if you need somewhere to go for a while, my horses are there. The kids would love it"

He seemed to be my 'knight in shining armor'. Here was the plan that I was looking for, being handed to me on a golden platter! Who could deny that I did indeed have a guardian angel?

Some might condemn me for leaving. Some might criticize me for staying for so long. In any case, it was cruel the way I did it. One day, when John was out, I stuffed all of his things into his beat-up little sedan. I padlocked the door to the house and left for three weeks, with the kids and a man that I had just met, leaving no more than a brief note, saying goodbye. I have had to make peace with my choices in life. I still sometimes wonder 'what if'. What if I had stayed and insisted that John get psychiatric help? What if John and I had broken up way back in San Cristobal, before kids? What if I had stayed with Lano up in Washington when I just had Emily? What if I had been strong enough to just deal with the mental illness? Sometimes, when

I'm feeling really lonely and thinking only about the good times that we had together, I think of that song that was popular back when I was breaking up with John for the final time, *"I may be crazy but it might just be a lunatic you're looking for."* He was so different from anyone that I have ever known and there were parts of that intensity of spirit that I was drawn to. John definitely had a side to him that was honorable, trustworthy and could be relied upon through thick and thin. That was the John that I wanted as a partner but the mental illness made a mockery of that other John and made life miserable for him and for everyone around him. Just like with my mother, I didn't hold him entirely responsible for his actions, but I couldn't live that way. He did in later years have a girlfriend that, I'm told, he was both physically and mentally abusive to. He had a daughter with her who would not even visit him on his deathbed because she could not forgive him for his abusive behavior as she was growing up. Would that have been my fate if I had stayed? A lifetime of craziness and abuse or would he have mellowed and stabilized, living in a loving and safe environment with his family? There's no way of knowing for sure. So many roads not traveled. But I have decided that I should not allow the things that I have chosen to do, or not chosen to do to for that matter, detract from the here and now or from the amazing miracle of life and the many wonderful things that I have seen and done along the way. One day I closed the door on the Forest of Arden and opened the door on another chapter in my life, only now my life was 'the four of us'.

Part Four
Homesteading

Chapter 34
China Creek

After we left him, John became very psychotic. He went up to his parents in Washington and completely terrorized them but eventually he settled down. He started a new family with a woman that he met and fell in love with, and I believe that his life stabilized for a while. We lost contact with him for several years.

I found a cute little house to rent that was close to work and school and set up housekeeping, and I continued to see Sunny, my knight in shining armor. One day, he flew into town in his 8484niner single engine airplane and surprised me with a new set of colorful porcelain dishes that I had admired, a few days before, when we were window shopping together. He had also bought an engagement ring. Sunny came into the kitchen where I was sitting at the table in a splash of sunlight, feeling happy to see him; he got down on one knee and took my hand in his. He looked into my eyes and he said, "I love you. I want to spend the rest of my life with you. Will you marry me?"

"There's nothing that I want more," was my sincere reply.

Sunny was eleven years older than me. I was 34. He was 45. He had made his money in some unclear manner. Most likely it had to do with the local economy. He had investments in property, and now he was in semi-retirement. Sunny was, what you would call, a free spirit. He liked to spend his free time either at one of his three remote country cabins or wandering around in the backcountry with Legs, his horse. The bar, I soon found out, was also a favorite pass time and he loved to go dancing which is something that I adored as well. Except for the drinking, we were perfect for each other. As time went by, the bar became more and more of a dominant attraction for Sunny and more and more of a stumbling block in our evolution as a loving, devoted couple. He was a sweet man though. I had never experienced such affection before, and I soaked up every bit of his love and attention, like a thirsty sponge.

"I am happier than a pig in mud!" he said to me one evening when we were out dancing. When he said this, he looked totally content and happy as he wrapped his arms around me and pulled me closer until I was resting, snuggly against his body, in the crook of his arm. We sat there like that listening to the music and feeling like nothing else mattered in the world except being together. Here was a love that I could feel. *So this is what it feels like to be loved unconditionally*, I thought. It is something so rich and fulfilling that everyone should experience it at least once in a lifetime. I gained a lot from that delicious feeling of being adored, even though it did not last.

One day, a few months later, we were sitting at a local café having breakfast. Suddenly, Sunny announced, "I'll be dammed if I'm going to let the government tell me who I can or can't live with!"

I looked at him. There had been no conversation leading up to this statement. "Does this mean that you don't want to get married?" I asked, having trouble fathoming what he was getting at.

"Exactly, I'm never getting married. Nothing has changed between us. It's just a piece of paper and we don't need it!" he said, sounding angry.

I turned my face away from him. I didn't want him to see that I was crying. To me, that piece of paper did represent something. It was a declaration to the world that said, "I am through looking. I have found the person that I want to spend my life with and I have no doubts." My unconditional love suddenly felt very conditional.

We still continued on with our courtship however. We had fun doing things together and the relationship might have worked out between Sunny and I if not for the fact that my main reason for living was my children and, to some extent, my work, and his main reason for living was to have fun and to get loaded. "We're on the fun trail," he was fond of saying. Sometimes, fun was just the thing that everyone needed and wanted but when the going got tough, Sunny would get in his plane and fly away. After we had been seeing each other for about six months, he told me one day, "I can't put my life on a schedule. If you want to hang out with me, you have to quit your job. You can give up your house in town and come live with me in China Creek, and we can get busy on the fun trail."

I had some money saved. Without having to pay rent, I could live on it for maybe a year. I wouldn't be totally dependent. The boys hadn't started school yet, and I wanted to spend more time with them. It was the perfect time to stay home with my kids and go on adventures with Sunny.

"Alright, I'll do it! We'll see where the fun trail takes us." I wanted things to work out with us although I had growing doubts.

China Creek Road went into the hills of Northern California for quite a ways as it snaked back into the golden rolling grasslands and connected with other roads that crisscrossed through the backcountry. It was a rutted out dirt road and slow going. Once we left the pavement, it took 45 minutes to get to his 40-acre parcel where he lived in a tiny, one-room cabin. The house that he was building stood a few hundred feet back from the cabin. It was almost completed but still lacked windows, insulation, sheetrock and the floors were bare plywood. Most of the hippy houses out in the hills started that way, a simple frame structure. Then families would move in and complete the work themselves as finances allowed. Some places were never completed, but they were often unique and had a special charm, reflecting an artistic touch and individual preferences. I had a couch, a table and a wood heat stove with a glass front so you could see the fire. We moved these things into the big open living room/kitchen area and began the work of closing the window openings up with hippy glass. We built simple wooden frames and stapled thick, clear plastic onto the frames and fitted them into the openings. There were a lot of windows so it took some time but we were really in no hurry. We were having fun with it. It was late fall and getting cold so we stayed in the little cabin, which was easy to heat, while we did the work to close the house up, put in stove pipe for the wood heat, gather firewood and other preparations. Meanwhile, we'd take little trips out of town on a regular basis. Sunny had a whole set of nearby destinations where a good time could be had.

We liked to go to Mendocino and go dancing. We would take Sunny's camper truck all set up as a little bedroom, park on the country road right outside of the tavern and go dancing while the kids slept in the camper. We danced almost every dance, slow dances and fast dances alike. I was always happy when Sunny held me in his arms. When the music stopped, we would go out to the camper and crawl into bed next to the kids. The next morning, we would all go out to breakfast and then spend the day together at the beach before driving home. Once, on a trip to Mendocino, we picked up a goose that had wandered away from its buddies and was stuck on the wrong side of the fence. It was a beautiful goose and I thought it would be happy living by the pond at the house so we picked it up and took it home. But the goose wasn't happy. I think it was lonely. It would wake us up at first light, honking and honking outside of our window until Sunny would get up, furious at having his sleep disturbed and chase the goose around and around the cabin in his birthday suit, trying to hit it with a big 2x4. I feared for the life of the goose so on the very next weekend we took it back to the same spot that we had found it and we put it back on the other side of the fence. It was a sight to behold. A large group of geese were standing in the field a few hundred feet away. When they saw our goose, they started honking all together and running, with their wings outstretched, as if they were planning to fold them around their buddy in an ecstatic group embrace. Our goose honked frantically as well and stretched out his wings as he rushed to meet the oncoming crowd. It was a joyful reunion. The other geese gathered around their friend who seemed to be wildly honking out the story of his goose-napping. Surrounded by the safety of the pack, they turned their backs on us and walked away. It was obvious that our goose was glad to be home.

By Christmas, the house was almost ready to move into. We decided to eat our first meal at the house on Christmas Eve and make our first fire in the stove. We cooked the holiday dinner in the cabin and then, when all the preparations were complete, we marched in line with our steaming dishes, though the frosty evening, through the frozen grass and across the little wooden bridge that was covered with sparkling ice crystals to the house where a warm cozy fire was waiting. We lit candles and placed them around the room and they glowed merrily, lighting up the darkness and casting flickering shadows across the room. The only window that was real glass was by the heat stove and it spanned an entire wall letting in the night sky which was filled with stars. It was a beautiful evening, one worthy of being thankful for. We had a few small presents that we opened after dinner and then we took turns reading aloud from the book *The Education of Little Tree.* When it was Sunny's turn to read, the boys snuggled up next to me and fell asleep. By the glow of the firelight, their rosy cheeks looked so healthy and their breathing was even and peaceful. Emily too, looked healthy and happy. She was enjoying the story and the moment of complete harmony in our family. It had been a perfect evening for which we were truly thankful.

There were a few other families with kids that lived a short walk away from us on China Creek Road. As the weather got warmer and spring flowers filled the hills with color, Emily, who was now 8, began to explore the countryside with her friends. She became very independent. She would walk a mile to see Jamie and then they would go to pick up Mook and the three of them, together, would hike over the hills to the swimming hole on China Creek. They traveled around in a little pack, and they were welcome and cared for wherever they went. The boys were still pretty young and they hung out with me most of the time. Now that Sunny had us set up looking after his home, he began to resume his independent, bachelor ways. He often spent his evenings in town at the bar, and I would be left alone, a mile away from any neighbor, with the kids. Sometimes, he would take off in his plane and be gone for several days. At first I didn't mind. I was enjoying my time with my children and the break from being on call at all hours, but I have always been a restless person, and after a while, I began to feel just that, restless. As my restlessness grew, I began to feel isolated and dissatisfied. I had gotten myself in a position where I was relying on Sunny for love, companionship, and entertainment. It was too much to ask of him. He couldn't be my 'everything'. He didn't want to be. We began to have little squabbles as our differences in expectations became more apparent. One day he got really upset with me for being too needy, and he left without saying goodbye and he didn't return for several nights. It was a hard time for me. A lot of my old feelings of abandonment and despair returned to haunt me. I couldn't sleep, and I lay there in the darkness feeling like nothing mattered anymore. I felt that I would never again find happiness, and that I was doomed to a life of isolation and heartbreak. Not even my children or the beauty of the surroundings could pull me out of the depression that I was sinking into. I felt like I was lost and I couldn't find my way. I felt vulnerable. What if Sunny decided that he didn't want us here? Where would I go with my children? As I thought about it, I realized something that I had realized many times before but for some reason I kept forgetting that I was the only person in my life that I could truly rely on. "So what did we need to feel secure and stable?" I asked myself. "We needed a home," was the answer that came to mind. "We needed a home to call our own where we could never be evicted or told to leave. We needed our own little spot in the world." The timing was right because I was just about to receive a check for all the money I had accrued in my retirement fund in the years that I had worked at the hospital. When I had quit, Diane had insisted that I close my retirement fund and take the money. "You might need it," she had said, looking at me seriously, as if she had foresight of these problems arising. She had been so wise. I now knew what I had to do. "I can't squander this money when I get it. I must invest it in a piece of land where I can live with my children. Where I can create a harmonious and safe space for us that we will always be able to return to no matter what else happens out there in the world." I sent out prayers to the universe to help us find the right spot that would be our home. Having finally found some peace of mind, I fell asleep.

Chapter 35
Evolution of the Homestead

When Sunny got back, I was no longer upset. Instead, I was excited because now I had a vision. Sunny was enthusiastic about my plans as well. It was such a long drive to get to town, to school and to and from the bar that it was clearly a great idea to have a piece of property where these things would be more accessible. My kids had at least 12 more years of school ahead of them. I didn't want to be right in town but I wanted to be close to the county road where they could walk to the school bus and then have just a short drive, where our days didn't revolve around getting to and from school.

I picked out a real estate office and talked to them about what I was looking for and my price range. Besides location, I was hoping to have a little bit of property and distance from neighbors. Land was still pretty cheap in those days. Even so, it was a lot to ask for a mere $20,000. They gave me a list of tiny lots to look at that were all in the $25,000 range. Systematically, I visited one after the other.

"This one is too small."

"Here the neighbors are too close."

"The road is too noisy."

"I don't like the location." Nothing pleased me.

Finally, the realtor said, "I have this one listing, I don't think you'll like it but it is all I have left to show you. There's no water, no electricity and no road and the people are asking $35,000. They recently dropped the price from $55,000 but they might come down a little more because they are anxious to sell and it's been on the market for several years. The good news is that it is 23 acres and it is right off of the county road. The school bus goes right by it."

"Alright, I'll check it out. I have nothing to lose." Secretly, I was a little bit excited about the 23-acre part. As it turned out, the parcel was on my very favorite road in the area, the road that led out to the coast. It was only a ten-minute drive to school and it was directly across from a big pullout where a school bus could easily stop to pick up the kids. When I got to the parcel that was for sale, I parked my car on the side of the road and hiked up the hill for a ways. The parcel climbed steeply uphill all the way. There wasn't much flat land for building. It would definitely need more of a road and it wouldn't be easy to build one or maintain one in such unstable, clay-like soil. I could see why it hadn't sold. But it was springtime and the usually golden hills were still verdant and wildflowers were everywhere springing up. Past the perimeter of the property, it climbed steeply up through hilly grassland for another ¼ of a mile until it reached the ridge top over which spilled the immense void of blue sky and streaks of brilliant sunlight. Skirting a section of the property, at the uppermost border, was a little forest composed of evergreens and tanoaks and fragrant buckeye. The forest separated the property from the view or sound of any neighbors which gave one the impression of being very remote, even though it was just off of the county road. There were a couple of seasonal creeks on the land. They were still flowing and they chuckled and gurgled as they flowed over the rocks and down the hill to a county maintained culvert where they flowed under the road and on down to the bottom of the canyon where they joined with Redwood Creek. Along the banks of the two creeks grew a perfusion of tan oaks and fir trees and other brush. I climbed under a bramble of vines and willows that lined one of the creeks and settled down in a shady patch of grass beside the water's edge. Way overhead, I could hear the cry of a hawk and the squawking of a crow. They seemed to be calling to me. Some little sparrows jumped around on the branches next to me and not far off a deer was grazing, unaware of my presence. The water sparkled as it cascaded downstream in the noonday sunshine and a slight breeze ruffled the leaves and the branches. I felt calm and peaceful. The land was speaking to me. "This is your home," it was saying. "You will be safe and happy here with your children." I knew that it was true. I knew that I had found my home. I said a little prayer of thanks and recognition to the land, climbed back down the hill, drove into town and put in my offer. Although I was only offering $20,000, most of it would be in cash when my check came and it was due any day. Within days we were in escrow. I was investing every penny I had. It was time to go back to work!

Escrow closed without a hitch. It was as if it was meant to be. The first thing we did was to put up the small teepee that Sunny had stored at his place out in China Creek. That was our new home now. Sunny was ready to have his space back. In fact, one night we drove all the way out to China Creek late in the evening for the sole reason that I thought that Sunny expected us and would be angry if we didn't show. Instead, he was irritated when we showed up because he really wanted to be alone and so he spoke rudely to Emily because she was afraid to go down into the basement by herself and he made her cry. It was totally uncalled for. Furious, I grabbed the kids and drove back to my land and the teepee, grateful that I now had a home to go to where no one could ever again treat me or my children like we didn't belong.

A few days later, Sunny showed up at the teepee. He was in a good mood and I was actually happy to see him. In truth, I had missed him. "Look," he was saying. "You're going to be much happier if you build at the top of your property instead of down by the county road where it will be noisy and where, when you walk out of your front door, you'll see cars driving by."

We had walked the perimeter of the property together and there was one nice, flat building spot at the uphill boundary. It was a good spot to build on with some beautiful views of the surrounding hills and it felt way up in the air, high above the canyon floor. The problem was that it would be a huge and expensive undertaking to get a road up the top of the property. I never would have been able to do it without the experience and confidence that Sunny brought to the project. Pretty soon I was $10,000 in debt but I had a great road and now I felt like we were living on top of the world. I liked it! In addition, during the process of building the road, they had pulled up a tree that was in the way but a little downhill from the road. Where the tree had been uprooted, they found an underground spring so now, at least part of the year, I had a place from which to pump water. Things were really coming together nicely. We took down the teepee and dragged Sunny's little 8ft travel trailer up our new road to the building site. I spent days drawing up plans and then changing them and trying to decide how next to proceed. Meanwhile, I was back working at the hospital and still attempting to make my life raising a family meld harmoniously with Sunny's life on the fun trail. There's no doubt about it. Life was good.

It was summer and we decided to take a little break from the intensity of developing a homestead to join Sunny on the trail. Sunny wanted to fly out to Modoc to spend a couple of weeks at his place and he wanted us, his riding crew, to go with him. We were going to take Legs and Rocket for a walk in the desert. The kids and I were all excited. We had never been packing with horses. It sounded like a great adventure. I had recently acquired several laying hens and a rooster and two angora rabbits that I had learned to pluck and then spin the fur into fine angora wool. "What should I do with the animals while we're gone?" I asked Sunny.

"Take them with us. They'll fit in the back of the plane."

So we loaded up the little plane with all our gear, three chickens, two rabbits, three children and Sunny and I. It felt like 'The Grapes of wrath' with wings. We laughed until our sides ached as we sped down the runway with the chickens balking, the rooster crowing, and the rabbits jumping nervously about in their cage. We were definitely on the fun trail now.

After we had been at the ranch for several days, we gathered up our gear, stuffed it all into the saddlebags, and loaded the horses. We took off on foot for the open desert that was just a short walk from Sunny's front door. We alternated walking and riding to give the horses a break. Sunny rode Legs who was tall and lean, and I rode Rocket who was short and chubby and the kids switched around depending on what was happening. Our first stop was a hot spring that came right out of a creek that sprung right up out of the desert clay. There was a little oasis around it of grass and a few willowy trees that marked the path taken by the ribbon of creek as it meandered out of sight. Our plan was to follow the creek as far as we could. After soaking in the pool of hot water that had been created with rocks and clay from the surrounding area, we were refreshed. We walked along, leading the horses, with wet hair and dripping wet tee shirts that we had soaked in the creek. Just before dusk, it started to cool off and so we stopped for the night and set up camp in the four-foot strip of greenery that bordered the stream which we were still following. It was kind of surreal being by the water camping on this little patch of greenery when everything else, as far as the eye could see, was barren desert except for an occasional scrub or cacti.

The next day we decided to leave our camp set up in this perfect spot by the water, and we set off on horseback to explore the canyon. The horses picked their way carefully down a rocky slope at the bottom of which we found an old abandoned cabin. It was intriguing. "Who would ever live here?" I wondered aloud. "It must have been so desolate and lonely. Where would they get food and water? I can't even imagine how hard it must have been."

"There's not a lot out here," Sunny agreed. "Maybe they were looking for gold."

As we meandered back to camp, I was struck by how truly remote it felt to be wandering in this place where all you could see was sand and sky in any direction. If not for Sunny and his compass, I would have had no idea in which direction to go to get back to our little oasis.

There's a thing about the night sky in the desert. It's like magic. The sky becomes much larger than the earth and not so very far away. It looks like if you walk far

169

enough, you will touch it and just tumble off into the stars. Perhaps that is why those folks lived in that cabin out in the middle of nowhere, because they wanted to experience the brilliance of the desert sky every night for an eternity. It is something that one would never grow tired of. Surrounded by such a breathtaking view of the universe, it seemed evident that there is a force out in the universe that is greater than any mind can fathom and that the energy of that force is cloaked in unsurpassable beauty. "The sky is so incredible. It's like living in a dream," I whispered to Sonny as I snuggled closer in his arms with my head resting on his chest. "Are we awake or are we asleep? Have we fallen into the sky?" I wasn't sure.

After a few nights out on the trail, we headed back to the ranch. It felt like time was standing still as we made our way slowly back. Emily and Shannon were riding up on Legs with Sunny. Rocket was trotting patiently along, behind Legs. I held on to the reins with both hands and my arms were wrapped securely around Boden. He leaned back against me and his soft curly head of hair rested just under my chin. The kids were silent as we rode along. There was nothing that needed to be said. It was a perfect moment in time.

When we got home, I felt rested and I felt a renewed intensity to develop the homestead. One evening, I was standing at the Nurses' Station talking with one of the nurses who was about to be out of work for a couple of months on a medical leave. We were talking about my property and how much I wanted to build a house. "I really don't want to spend the winter in that little trailer with the kids. I'd like to get a basic structure built that we could move into before the rains come but I don't have a lot of money." That same 'one track mind' trait that had helped to get me into nursing school was being awoken again, like a sleeping dragon. I had begun to think of nothing else day or night. I was becoming obsessed, anxious, and irritable. It was time for things to get moving. I had helped Sunny to make plastic windows, and we had moved into a house with just bare plywood walls and no plumbing or electricity. That was my plan now but I didn't know how to get going on it with my limited funds. I had tried my hand at building but after spending a grueling 8-hour day in the intense heat and having nothing to show for it other than a crooked little posthole carved painfully out of the hard clay soil, I had given up. I needed an experienced builder who was available now, during the busiest building season of the year and willing to work cheap. What were the chances of finding that! What was that expression? "Better chance of finding a snowball in hell."

"My husband built a small house for Judy not too long ago. It only took a few thousand dollars and less than six weeks. He didn't need a crew. He just did it himself. He could build something simple like that for you to move into before winter, and later you could fix it up and build on to it if you like. It would help us out too since I'll be out of work for a while. We could use the money." Maureen smiled at me as she leaned against the counter with her arms folded across her chest.

"Maureen, you're wonderful! Let's do it. Sunny and I talked about it a lot. The most practical and economical plan is to build a simple 16ft. x 24ft. two-story rectangle with lots of windows. Nothing fancy, all straight lines. We'll use peer and post foundation and it should go up quick and easy." I gave Maureen a big hug. I was so excited.

Sunny was a giant help. Every couple of days, we would go to the lumberyards and pick out what was needed for the next few days of building. They would load it into his little Toyota pickup and we would drive it up my road in 4-wheel drive with the back end dragging low to the ground from all the weight. We would unload the lumber into a pile and then, when the pile got low, we would go back to the lumberyard. Sometimes, we would make several trips in a day. Sunny also helped with the construction but he didn't have to be on the same tight schedule as Maureen's husband who was getting paid. Sunny could just meander in, help for a few hours with the parts that needed two people and then head out to the bar if he was so inclined. First the peers and post were cemented in. Not long after that, the plywood floor was laid. When the first walls went up, it was very exciting. The west wall and the north wall had very few windows in order to optimize useable space but the south wall had a large picture window that looked out across the canyon where the hillside rose sharply up from Redwood Creek and was covered, without a break, in a curtain of evergreens.

On the second floor, we used fur for the flooring so that the first story ceiling would be beautiful and would not need to be sheet rocked. When the second floor walls went up, it was time to open the bottle of champagne. I could not contain my excitement. The roof was all that was left to complete the basic structure. To save on plywood and weight one wall of the upstairs was 8 feet tall and the opposing wall was 4 feet high. The roof sloped from east to west, from 8ft. down to 4ft. On the eastern 8-foot wall, there was a giant opening for double doors through which you could see up the valley to the hills beyond and then the higher hills beyond them above which you could see the sunrise and the moonrise. I was ecstatic. After a lifetime of wandering, my children and I had finally come home. After we had filled the windows in with hippy glass and put in a wood cook stove that we would also use for heat, we moved in.

Over the winter, we made improvements around us, paycheck by paycheck, as money would allow. One month, we put in windows that we bought cheaply as seconds. The next month, we put an olive barrel up the hill, filled it with water and then ran PVC pipe from the barrel down to the house so that we could have running water. The next month we put in a sink and some counters. We took baths the way I had learned as a young child living in the tenement when the Herald Tribune Fresh Air Fund had sent me to a farm in West Virginia. We heated water on the wood cook stove and poured it over us as we sat in a small metal tub that we kept stored under the house. It worked better for the kids who were little than it did for me. Later, we bought a bathtub and a hot water heater. It was a huge pleasure to be able to have hot running water and a hot bath! After a time, we even built a little room close to the house for our tub and we called it the 'bath room'. Eventually, I got tired of living with plywood walls that had no insulation and so I bought a bunch of sheet rock and insulation and did the downstairs myself. It was an unpleasant job but it made a huge difference in keeping in the heat. Then I was able to paint the walls pretty colors and hang pictures. Our humble house was becoming a home. Over the years, the place has evolved until it has become a perfectly charming cottage with a small garden out back and a little brick patio in front with a park bench that looks out across the canyon and a statue of a laughing Buddha. Over the years, we have developed our solar system for electricity. We have a flush toilet, hardwood floors, a pantry with storage and a refrigerator as well as many other useful improvements. The many large windows let in a lot of light as well as the colors and moods of nature. Our home is cheerful and pleasing to the eye. It has been a place where, like a good marriage, in sickness and in health we have been able to find comfort and shelter from the world outside. It has been a place where the daily drama of our lives has unfolded and it has stood, like a rock, a stable port that has withstood the ravages of time. Once when Shannon was emerging from a particularly bad period, I had reminded him of how lucky he was to have a home. He looked at me with the bewilderment of someone who is not certain of how long he will be able to keep a thought, any thought, coherently in his mind. "I don't know what would have happened without it," he acknowledged. "Something really terrible I think." I felt grateful that our home had served to provide a buffer and safety zone from his demons that might have otherwise destroyed him. Through the years, our home has been our sanctuary.

Chapter 36
Registry Nursing

That fall when we moved into our new home, Emily was already in 5th grade. She was growing up so fast. The twins were starting 1st grade. My sweet little babies had just entered the age of conflict. I wondered if they had learned such aggressive behavior from their classmates, or was it just the natural evolution of identical twin boys who were bound to be competing and conflicting just trying to establish their individuality from one another. In any case, they began to quarrel amongst each other incessantly. I never knew who to scold. I couldn't keep track of the issues because it was everything. At any given moment, anything, no matter how absurd, irrelevant or farfetched, could be fodder for an argument. Boden always blamed it on Shannon, and Shannon always blamed it on Boden. It was often impossible to make sense out of the arguments, and I usually held them both to blame. Years later, when Shannon became ill, Boden insisted that it was Shannon's irrational behavior, as they were growing up, that was responsible for the majority of the fights. It's hard to know. Towards me, they were still sweet and loving, and I didn't see Shannon as a difficult child but to each other they were brutal. It seemed ironic that having based all my major choices in life on the search for harmony I would find myself in a position where my children, who were the most important thing in my life, brought nothing but discord to our peaceful country setting. Even Emily could not stand the constant bickering. Her best friend, Meadow, lived with her stepdad not too far from where we lived. As Emily got older and more independent, she began to spend more and more of her time at Meadows' house. At least, when Emily was at Meadows, it took some of the intensity out of the raging battles because when the three of them would get into it, things could get really out of hand. Out of sheer nervousness, I would sometimes find myself screaming too and acting like a two year old. Afterwards, I always felt guilty and ashamed. Wasn't I supposed to be the adult?

In an attempt to give everyone a little more space, I had an 8ftx16ft addition built on to the house, and I put up a wall dividing it into two 8x8 rooms. I went to an antique store and bought a few quaint pieces of furniture for Emily's room and set it up to surprise her. When she saw it, she said to me, gasping in amazement, "This is the nicest room that I have ever seen. Thank you, Mother."

Her appreciation and delight was the best present I could have gotten. The boys' room I set up with bunk beds and a place to store their toys and their clothes. Now we all had a place to go if we needed time out. The upstairs became my sanctuary. It was a large open space that was my bedroom, my office, and the place where I could go to get away from the world, and where I felt safe. It felt like being in a big tree house when I looked out of the windows and saw the tree tops swaying in the breeze below me. It's been an incredible place to escape to.

Sunny and I were still seeing each other but now I had my place and he had his three places so we didn't actually see that much of one another. Again I felt like a single mom but so many things were working out for us that I couldn't complain. One day, Sunny stopped by the house after having been in Chico for a few days. I was glad to see him until I saw how grumpy he was. "I always feel obligated to come see you when I get home. Sometimes, I don't want to stop by. Today, I really just wanted to go out to China Creek but I knew you'd be mad." He looked irritated as he sat down stiffly on the wooden bench that he had made to go with our homemade kitchen table.

I hadn't seen him in over a week and I had missed him. Now, suddenly, I was furious. "Don't do me any favors," I almost yelled. "If you don't want to see me, then stay away," I said, my voice sounding cold and distant even to my own ears, my arms folded tightly over my chest as if trying to protect my heart.

Without saying a word, he got up and left. I didn't want the kids to see me so upset so I ran out to the van that was parked in the driveway across from the house. I was sobbing violently, hardly able to take a breath. Rolling from side to side, I beat the mattress in the back of the van, repeatedly, with my fists. I felt like screaming. Finally, when I started to calm down a little bit, I took the engagement ring that I still wore as a symbol of our love, off my ring finger and threw it violently through the open door across the driveway to be forever lost in the thick gravel. Sunny had been a great and positive force in my life but things had changed, and it was time to be moving on.

After that, we had one of those on and off type of relationships for another couple of years but it was never the same starry-eyed love that we had in the beginning. One day, he showed up at the house with a metal detector and, searching through the rocks, he found the ring. I was really touched and impressed and I wore it for another couple of years even when we were having an off period. The day we said our final stormy goodbyes, he took the ring from me and he threw it off of the bridge at Tuby Park into the rushing waters of the Eel River. It was a dramatic gesture that symbolized how our love had become hopelessly tumbled and lost in the rapids along the way. It was no longer possible to retrieve it.

My idyllic vision of harmonious family life in the country was having some rough spots for sure, but on the whole, we were getting on and meeting the challenges with continued gratitude and enthusiasm. Emily was a thoughtful and fun companion. We liked to go shopping together, go to the movies, go to the beach, or just hang out. She was my daughter and my friend. The boys, when you could stop them from fighting, were good, enthusiastic companions as well. Finances became our next great hurdle. I needed more money. We still only had the wood cook stove for heat and it didn't put out enough to keep the house warm in the winter. Even though everyone had their own space, we were all sleeping together in my big bed for warmth. Sometimes, when it was particularly cold, we would all climb the stairs to my bedroom as soon as it got dark and get into bed without even taking our clothes off. There we would stay until morning, huddling together under a mountain of blankets. To help pass the time, I'd turn on a flashlight and read aloud from one of the many wonderful stories that we still enjoyed. Then all the bickering would stop. Everyone would get really quiet and we were content, all of us, just to be close together lost in a fantasy. In the mornings when I would get the kids up, they would push and shove to be the one closest to the stove. We were freezing. All the plants

174

upstairs died because the upstairs wasn't insulated yet and occasionally the temperature would drop below freezing in the house. I needed to get the upstairs insulated, we needed a good wood heating stove, and we needed a bigger car—just to name a few things. The list of expenses was growing. I had to get a second job. I decided to try and work registry. It paid really well and it was a short-term commitment that could be arranged, on a week-to-week basis, as conditions allowed. It could fit in with our life. As it was, every other week, I worked Wednesday and Friday 7 a.m. to 7 p.m. shift, and on the opposing weeks, I was on call 24 hours a day for 7 days. If I got called in during the middle of the night, I would carry the kids to the bed in the van and then leave them, sleeping in the van, parked in front of the big double doors of the hospital lobby. If I was still involved with the delivery in the morning, I would get them up and send them to the corner restaurant for breakfast and then they would catch the bus to school from town. It was an unusual arrangement but they thought it was fun, it was safe, and it saved me a fortune in babysitting fees. But if I was going to leave town to work registry, I would have to find a babysitter. I did find a wonderful woman whom the kids loved and so it was settled. Nurses were in big demand at the time and with my labor and delivery skills, it didn't take long to find a registry job.

The registry work was not as stressful as I had thought it would be. It was the same nursing just a different location. With my very first paycheck, the kids and I went shopping for an efficient wood heating stove. When it was all hooked up and its first fire crackled and danced behind the big glass window, we sat back on our homemade plywood and foam sofa and drank hot chocolate with whipped cream and reveled in the warmth.

I was scheduled to work a registry job on Christmas day. I was very pleased about it because it meant a lot of money. I was already making an excellent base salary for the first eight hours and then time and a half for the last four hours but on Christmas, I would be making time and a half for the first eight hours and double time for the last four. I could do a lot of useful things with that money. I decided to call Blanche. I had been going down to Berkeley to visit her, several times a year, with the kids, and she had come up a couple of times on the bus to visit but we hadn't spent a Christmas together since I was a teenager. "Hi, Mom, how are you doing?" I asked when she picked up the phone.

"Oh, Juliet, I'm fine. How are you? How are the kids?" She sounded well and like she was glad to hear from me.

"We're good. Listen, I have a job in a hospital around Clear Lake on Christmas Day and I thought that if you could catch the bus up, I'd get a hotel suite and we could all spend Christmas Eve together and then you could stay with the kids on Christmas Day while I worked. I know they'd love to spend some time with you. What do you think?" It seemed like a great way for me to make some money and yet still have a family Christmas. I was hoping that she would be up for it.

There was a pause. "Alright," she said finally. "When should I be there?"

"That's great, Mom. The kids will be thrilled when I tell them. Why don't you try to arrive sometime around noon? I'll pick you up at the bus stop."

On the morning of Christmas Eve, we loaded up the car with Christmas decorations, a small tree, presents and enough food for a feast. At the last minute, Sunny decided to join us because he didn't want to spend Christmas alone after all. We were a festive group as we headed down the highway, Sunny, Boden, Shannon,

Emily, and I, all singing Christmas Carols. *"On the first day of Christmas my true love gave to me, a partridge in a pear tree."* It was our favorite carol, and we all knew the words. There were lots of inexpensive little hotels around the lake and we were able to get a good deal on a little apartment with a kitchen for the holiday. We settled in and set things up for our family Christmas feast. It was good to see Blanche. She was in her mid-60s now, and she still looked very attractive with her red lipstick and high heels. It was amazing really. Her life had been so very hard and yet she didn't have any wrinkles. In fact, her face was smoother and more relaxed looking than mine. Perhaps it was all the responsibility and anxiety, not to mention the fair skin that gave me that knitted brow and perpetual look of worry.

"How is everything going for you?" I asked as we settled down in the kitchen with a cup of coffee and I began to cut up sweet potatoes and apples to cook for dinner. The kitchen got all warm and steamy as water boiled, coffee perked and the roast simmered in the oven.

"Everything is fine," my mother answered, smiling at Emily who was playing the hostess and offering her a cookie to go with the coffee. The boys wanted a cookie too so they all gathered around the table for cookies and milk.

"Don't spoil your appetite," I cautioned. "No more than two cookies each."

"Have you been writing any?" I asked, trying to draw my mother out a little.

At the thought of her poetry, she became animated. "Oh yes. I don't have that much time working five days a week at J. C. Penny, but I write on my days off. I might be getting some of my poetry published," she added proudly.

"That's wonderful, Mom. Do you have anything you've written with you?"

"I have something I just wrote. It's not very festive though. I wasn't feeling well when I wrote it." My mother looked sad for a moment. Although she was fairly stable, I could tell that life was still hard for her. "We'd love to hear your poem!" I said and the kids all agreed.

"Grandma, read your poem to us," Shannon said smiling his most irresistible, angelic smile.

"Alright, I will if you like."

"Yes, of course," we all said at once in chorus.

"I call it 'The Cast of Nature'." She paused for a minute before pulling a piece of paper out of her purse to read to us. Everyone was quiet.

"Beset with a doleful, dumb despair, grey as hoarfrost in the air, alas, I ache beyond compare.

The echoes that disturb my soul, that haunt and wound, exact a toll. Lord God of heaven cannot console.

The willful wiles of a troubled troll, who walks the world, dark as a raven, hardly crushed hardly craven.

Who knows no man but knows nature, no man can destroy this creature. I must muster courage and endure."

After she had finished, she was quiet. The kids had loved that their grandmother had read to them and that the words had rhymed. They were happy. I looked at my mother. She was dressed very festively in a red dress, and she was wearing red and green Christmas wreath earrings. There was a sparkle in her eye as she looked around at her appreciative audience. "It's a good poem, Mother. It really communicates a feeling of enduring despair. And you are a courageous woman. Life hasn't been easy for you."

"No, it hasn't," she agreed. "I have to be so careful. People are always taking things out of my apartment when I'm away and leaving me spiders or roaches. I don't know who would do such a thing but it makes it so hard sometimes to just get through the day."

"Oh, Grandma, we love you," Emily and the twins crooned as they gathered around and hugged their grandmother. She smiled and hugged them to her. Just then, a Christmas carol came on the radio. It was a well-known tune and we all started singing. *"Good tidings we bring to you and your kin. Good tidings for Christmas and a happy New Year."* After that, we moved into the living room where Sunny was busy setting up the little potted Christmas tree that we had brought from home. The kids were going to make decorations and string popcorn to put around the tree. I was glad that we were all together.

The next morning, I left early for the hospital while everyone still slept. When I arrived at the nursing station in labor and delivery, the night shift was happy to be going home. "We don't have anyone in labor and all our moms left with their babies to be home for the holiday, Merry Christmas." The nurse whom I was relieving waved, with a sleepy smile, as she turned and headed down the hall. I didn't have much time to wonder what I was going to do with all my free time because a young Mexican woman came in thinking that she might be in labor. She hadn't had any prenatal care, and she hadn't realized that she was so far along. She also didn't speak any English. Fortunately, I spoke enough Spanish to get by. I spent a pleasant morning with her filling out paper work and doing a thorough assessment. At one point, she told me that she was surprised that she was so big. She had thought that she was only six months' pregnant. I was pretty sure I had understood her correctly when she told me that and my ears perked up. "Mueve mucho el bebe?" I asked, hoping that I was using the right words to find out if there was a lot of fetal movement like you would get if there was an extra pair of arms and legs in there.

"Si, mucho movimiento todos los tiempo."

"Is this pregnancy different than your other pregnancy?" I managed to get across in broken Spanish.

"Si," she nodded. "Mucho mas dificile."

It was sounding so familiar, twins perhaps? I called the M.D. on call and told him what I was thinking. "Get an ultrasound right away and let me know the results," he said and hung up.

She was having mild, irregular contractions. She seemed to be in very early labor but if we were dealing with twins and prematurity, we would have to stop the labor right away in order to give the babies' lungs more time to mature before they were born. We needed to get that ultrasound STAT. As it turned out, it was twins and she was only about six months' pregnant so the rest of the shift was taken up with starting intravenous lines, getting a terbutaline drip going to stop her labor and getting a crew from Santa Rosa to come and get the mom to take her to a hospital with a higher level nursery in case we were unable to stop her labor for long enough. I waved as they hustled her onto a gurney and down the hallway, disappearing around a corner headed to the ER entrance and out into the night. They were in a hurry because a storm was headed our way and they were hoping to be safely back, in Santa Rosa, before it hit. "Well, that was exciting," the nursing supervisor said when they had left.

"It's a good thing we didn't have two little premature babies here without even a pediatrician on hand. Now that would have been exciting. That would have been a disaster!" I suddenly felt a flood of relief when I realized how crazy things could have gotten.

Soon after the ambulance left with the mom, the weather started to get blustery. Before long, it was snowing and the wind was picking up. By the end of my shift, we were in a full on storm. A power line went down somewhere and the lights went out for about five seconds before the backup generator kicked on. My replacement was a little bit late but I figured it was because she was driving slowly in the storm. I was anxious to get home to my family. Finally, the nursing supervisor stopped by. She looked apologetic. "There are some trees down and the night nurse can't get in to replace you. Can you stay? It's a policy that we have to have a qualified labor and delivery nurse in the house at all times and there's no one else to call. You'll get double time for the whole shift and you can rest if no one comes in." She looked at me hopefully and in truth it was a good deal. I was already there and there were no patients.

"Sure, of course. My kids will be going to bed in a couple of hours anyway." It was almost 8 p.m. as it was.

"Great, thank you so much." She looked relieved as she left for home to have Christmas dinner with her family.

After calling the hotel to let everyone know that I wouldn't be home until morning, I lay down to close my eyes for a few minutes but before long I heard it announced over the loud speaker "Labor and Delivery nurse to ER." I hurried down to the emergency room and was relieved to find that there was no crisis in progress. A mom had waited at home until the last minute because of the storm and she had come to the ER in advanced labor. The emergency room doctor didn't have a lot of labor and delivery experience, and he was hoping that I could assist and help things to go more smoothly. I checked the mom. "She's fully dilated," I reported. "It won't be long." They had all the basics needed for a precipitous delivery in the ER but I sent a runner back to the nursery to get the warmer and blankets and other things for the baby. By the time the warmer was all set up and standing, ready, at the foot of the bed, the mom was pushing with all of her might and the baby's head was starting to crown. With each contraction, she would grab her thighs and hunch forward baring down with such intensity that the veins on her temples popped up and beads of sweat stood out on her flushed, rosy cheeks. Strands of wet hair stuck to her forehead and the nape of her neck was damp. Her naked breasts heaved with the effort and the nipples stood erect, ready to begin their job of suckling the newborn. She was grunting and groaning with the strain of trying to push her baby out. We could see an enlarging circle of dark, sticky hair with each push. I didn't want her to tear so I helped her to pant and only push a little through the next couple of contractions. The head slid out with a little pop and the bag of waters gushed and spilled out over the sheets and plastic pads that covered the gurney. "Check around the neck for the cord before she pushes the baby out," I was reminding the doc, meanwhile helping the mother to pant her way through the next contraction instead of pushing. "Okay, one more push and you'll have your baby in your arms." The whole baby swished out with another big gush of water. We held the baby up for a minute, checking for color, tone, and breathing. It was vigorous and healthy, and we placed him in his mothers' arms just as he started to cry. "It's a boy!" she exclaimed with tears of joy in her eyes.

"It's a boy!" we all cried out, never ceasing to be amazed and humbled at the miracle of birth.

As soon as we could, we brought the mom and baby down to postpartum where I took care of them for the rest of the night, completing the pages of paperwork, taking footprints, giving Vitamin K to the baby, doing postpartum checks, and in general making sure that mother and child were safe and comfortable. In the morning, the storm had abated and my relief came. Everyone thanked me heartily for staying. The supervisor had my check ready for me as was the custom with this particular registry. "This cost us a lot of money," she was saying as she handed me an envelope with the check in it. "But you were worth it. You earned it!" she added warmly.

When I got out to my car, it was freezing cold. I started the engine to warm it up for a few minutes before driving. Then I took my check out of the envelope and peeked at the amount, hoping that the site of it would give me enough energy to safely drive back to the hotel. It was a little over a thousand dollars for the 24 hours. I was stoked. I could get some things that we needed badly for the house and I could take the kids for a week long winter vacation in sunny Mexico! It was a thought.

Chapter 37
New Developments

We did, in fact, end up going to Mexico for a week, just me and the kids. It was a little after the holidays, and flights were cheap. We went to a small, isolated village outside of Puerto Vallarta and rented a little hut with a dirt floor that sat high up on a hill, overlooking the ocean. In this fantastic setting, we read Robinson Crusoe out loud to the sound of the surf roaring in the background. We ate fresh mangoes and papayas and enchiladas with refried beans, and we did yoga in the warm sand and swam in the ocean. When we got back home, it was still the middle of winter, but we were tan and rested.

That spring, I was working one afternoon at the hospital when I was paged overhead for a phone call. It sounded like a personal call.

"Hospital, Juliet speaking," I said, searching for my pen in case I had to take down a message.

"Hello, Juliet," responded a familiar voice on the other end of the receiver.

"John, how are you?" I said, surprised to be hearing his voice after such a long silence. I hadn't heard from him in several years, and I had no idea where he was or what he was doing.

"I'm fine. I'm coming down to California next month, and I want to see the kids. I want to take them to Crab Tree Hot Springs for a week. Carolyn and Elizabeth really want to meet them."

"Who are they?" I asked, still not over the surprise of hearing his voice.

"Carolyn is my old lady, and Elizabeth is our daughter. She's two years old. She really wants to meet her sister and her brothers. I'm going to school in Klamath Falls, and I'll be getting some time off next month."

Had John been by himself, I would have been very hesitant about letting him take our children out of my sight but he sounded really good and with a stepmother and baby sister around, things probably wouldn't get out of hand. "Alright, I'll ask the kids what they want to do, but in any case, we'll have to meet everyone first to be sure that the kids and I feel comfortable."

"Fair enough, we'll see you next month. Take care and tell Emily and Boden and little Shannie that I love them very much. I miss them," he added before hanging up the receiver.

I had mixed feelings about the whole thing. Sunny hadn't really taken on the role of a father to my children. I knew that they needed a father, but at the same time I didn't want them to be like their dad. I didn't feel that it was right though, to keep them from their natural father if they wanted to see him. I would leave it up to them.

When I got home that evening and told them that their father wanted to take them camping and that they had a little sister, they went wild. They were so excited that there was absolutely no doubt about whether or not they wanted to see him. The sooner the better as far as they were concerned. I talked with John a couple more times over the phone and I talked with Carolyn. She seemed pretty solid and stable. She sounded like a trustworthy person and so it was arranged.

Sunny and I were still continuing with our stormy, on and off relationship. I blamed it on his drinking which seemed to make him moody and unpredictable. At any rate, we decided that some time to ourselves without the kids might be good for us and so we planned to spend a few days at his place outside of Chico and a few days on a motorcycle ride just cruising around in the Sierras. It looked like we were going to be heading out on the fun trail again. We were all looking forward to our little summer vacation.

In the meantime, I had gotten very involved in the care of one of my patients. I remember my first encounter with Andy. I had been nervous as I had pushed open the door to his room. They told me in report that he had recently been in a car accident which had left him paralyzed from his chest down. At first he had been on a ventilator but once he was off it, he had talked his buddies into taking him, against medical advice, from the large rehab center that he was in. Now, without proper care, he had developed deeply infected ulcers that went down to the bone and threatened his very survival. "He's angry," the nurses had said in report. "And he won't cooperate with his treatments." I had a lot of very personal care scheduled for him that morning. I hoped that it wasn't going to be a struggle. To make the situation less awkward, I went to his room prepared, not only with a variety of saline solutions, bandages, plastic pads, and the like, but I also brought the hospital tape player and a tape with the song *'Sailing Takes Me Away to Where I'm Going'*. I hoped that we could be friends.

As the door swung open, I was surprised to note that the ambiance in the room was very peaceful. I saw, at first glance, an extremely handsome man in his late 30s with a frozen body and a wonderful smile that lit up the room. As I arranged the supplies and plugged in the tape player, I explained to Andy what needed to be done. The music was just the thing. It put us both at ease. As I began the morning care, a pleasant stream of conversation developed, weaving a story that flowed in and around the notes of the music. I learned that he had broken up with his wife a while before the accident and that he had three beautiful young daughters. I also learned that he had been a singer in a popular local band. In the days that followed, I would often hear his rich melodic voice filtering down the hall.

Andy and I were both from back east. We had a lot of stories to share, and we quickly became friends. Sometimes I would get called in during the middle of the night to help at a birth or to work a 7 p.m.–7 a.m. shift. Then, in the wee hours of the night, I would go down to Andy's room to find him lying awake in the dark and stillness. I would pull up a chair and sit by his bed without talking. Inexplicably, at those times, I experienced a deep feeling of peace.

The infection had cleared and Andy's wounds had healed to the point that he was scheduled to be discharged from the hospital in another week. Although his wounds were healing, they were still open and with less than optimal home care. It would only be a matter of time before they were infected again. And then there was the matter of his arms, which were frozen to his sides. He would have been capable of a certain amount of independence had not his shoulder joints fused from lack of physical therapy. One after the other, I called every rehab center in California, trying to get someone willing to take his case on. Because of the amount of time since his accident, the fact that had left AMA, his insurance etc., no one would take him. Finally, I called a hospital in Chico that had a small rehab section. They surprised me by putting me through to the doctor who was in charge of the rehabilitation wing. A friendly female voice came on the line. "How can I help you?" she asked with sincere interest.

I told her Andy's story briefly being sure to emphasize the part about his arms and his infected wounds. After I was finished, an enthusiastic voice replied, "His accident has been recent enough. I think we can help him. How do we do we get him here?" I was very excited and I subsequently put a lot of energy into calling everyone involved so that we would all be on the same page and make this happen.

There were a couple of little stumbling blocks regarding method of transfer, reimbursement, availability of beds, and a few other vital details. It wasn't for sure that it would work out but I had high hopes. I had done my part, and now it was time for me to leave on my trip with Sunny. I had to put it in the hands of fate and my coworkers. When I left, I said farewell to Andy. "This has to happen," I said giving him a big hug. "It's your best shot."

I waved goodbye and ran off to meet John and his new family. Sunny was all packed and he was going to meet us as well, with the kids. Then, if everything looked good, we were going to head out to Chico, just Sunny and I, for our adventure. I was hoping that Andy would be transferred while I was still over in Chico so that I could visit him and see how he was adjusting.

It was a very sweet reunion as we all gathered together on the main street in front of the coffee shop. John took Boden, and then Shannon then Emily, one by one, up in his arms and hugged them tightly. The kids were jumping up and down with excitement while Little Elizabeth looked on shyly, holding on to her mother's skirt. Carolyn introduced herself. She looked to be five or even ten years younger than me. She had a thick southern accent, a pretty face, and short blonde hair. She was polite and soft spoken, and she sounded very reliable. I liked her. It felt like everything was going to be just fine as I waved goodbye and their Volkswagens Van, which was stuffed to overflowing, disappeared down the street and around the corner. The kids now had their dad and an extended family. I remembered reading in a psychology book how there were all types of families these days. There was the old-fashioned nuclear family, the single parent family, the gay marriage family, the family of friends living together, and the family consisting of step kids and step-parents. We were learning how to accept all of these new ways of being in the world.

Sunny and I headed over to Chico. It was really fun at first to have no responsibilities, no work, no kids, and no house to clean. We spent a couple of days riding bicycles in the park and hitting the dance spots at night. It was a college town and so there was a lot of night life but I had been up all night twice for births just before we left and I hadn't had time to rest so I found that I was tired and I didn't feel all that great. Then we took a motorcycle ride out into the hills that were to the west of Chico, but when we were about four hours out, a rainsquall hit. We got thoroughly soaked and cold before we could make it to any kind of shelter. The rain didn't show any sign of stopping so we cut the trip short and went back to where Sunny had his piece of property and the little trailer that we had lived in when I had first bought my land. We decided that we would just hang out there for a couple of days so that I could rest up but then the weather cleared and it became unbearably hot in the trailer so we had to give up that idea. We went out again on the motorcycle, headed this time up into the Northern Sierras. At first, it was really fun cruising around the back country roads with my arms wrapped tightly around Sunny's waist and my cheek resting against his back, but as the day wore on, I started to feel feverish. Finally, I was so sick that we had to turn around and go back to the trailer where I spent the rest of my vacation violently coughing and sneezing and feeling generally miserable. Needless to say, I was very disappointed and so was Sunny. A couple of days before we were to leave Chico and head for home, I called the hospital to see what had happened with Andy. When the person in admitting answered, they told me that he had gone home. That was that. I was so disappointed that I didn't even want to contemplate what might have gone wrong. Nothing had worked out in the last week or so. I hoped that the kids had had better luck.

When we got back home, John was there to meet us with the whole entourage. Everyone looked happy and healthy, rosy cheeked and tan. The kids said they had a great time. We all went together to get some pizza, and I got to know Carolyn a little better. I learned that she had brittle, type I diabetes. Her blood sugars were hard to control. More than once, John told me, he had found her passed out in a diabetic coma, and he had essentially saved her life. She needed him to look after her. I wasn't sure if she had discovered John's' vulnerable, crazy side as yet, but I knew that someday she would and I hoped that she would be able to handle it. I hoped that they would be able to take care of each other. As for me, I had no regrets. I had made the right decision to move on.

A few days after we got back from Chico, Sunny broke up with me again. This time, his reason was that he didn't agree with my food choices. Go figure! At least, I didn't spend every evening at the bar drinking until closing time, and at 5ft. 5in. and 120lbs. I wasn't fat by any stretch of the imagination, neither were my children. We didn't eat a lot of junk food. Perhaps it was the fact that I cooked a lot of spaghetti, and I didn't use organic ingredients. Who knows?

When I got back to work, I asked the nurses why Andy had ended up going home after all our plans. "Was it the insurance?" I wanted to know. "Did he change his mind? What went wrong?"

"Calm down. Nothing went wrong," they informed me. "A couple of days after you left on vacation, they sent an ambulance to pick him up. He's in Chico in Rehab right now."

That very day I called to see how he was doing. "Andy," I said when he picked up the phone. "How are you? How's rehab going?"

"Juliet, hello, I'm doing well. It's good to hear from you."

"How do you like it over there? Are they treating you right?"

"They're wonderful here. Some really good things are happening. My doctor's husband is paraplegic. She really understands the issues, and she's going to help me. Every day they get me up and take me down to physical therapy. They're working with me intensively."

I was thrilled that things were working out.

"One thing that's hard though is that I'm lonely here. It's too far for my friends and for my daughters to come very often so I don't get many visitors. I miss everyone."

"You'll be so much stronger and more independent after you're done there. I'm pretty close to Chico when I work over in Clear Lake. One of these days, I'll come over and visit you," I promised. "You can call me at home any time. If you get too lonely, we'll just talk." I was getting very personally involved but it felt like the right thing to do and somehow, talking to Andy always made me feel good.

I did visit him a couple times over the next few months. Andy was getting stronger, and he was able to be up in his wheel chair for increasingly longer periods of time. They had taken him to surgery twice for his shoulders and then done aggressive Physical Therapy. Now he could use his arms effectively to push himself around in the wheelchair, and he could eat using a special fork that wrapped around his fingers. He could even write short notes in a large undisciplined scrawl and on Christmas, he sent me a lovely little card to say thank you. He also sent a friend to deliver me a truckload of firewood. I realized then that we had gone far beyond the 'professional relationship'.

I was working in Clear Lake over the holidays again and this time the kids had gone up to Oregon to spend Christmas with their dad. Since we were both alone on this holiday, I decided to go over and pay Andy a visit. I got there in the evening of New Year's Day. There was a fancy hotel with a cocktail lounge just a couple of blocks away from the hospital, and the nurses suggested that we take a walk over there. We had permission to be out for several hours. It was going to be Andy's first time out of the hospital in over six months.

There was a frosty chill in the air as we stepped out into the night. Andy was happy to be out of the hospital where he had been captive for so many months now. I started feeling like I had not been out of doors in months either and had forgotten the feel of the crisp air on my cheek and the brilliance of the night sky. Because it was a holiday, the streets were empty. The world belonged to us. For me, the vicarious awaking of the senses to sensations and sounds that many of us take for granted, until they are withheld, was intoxicating. The night was filled with magic. We laughed and told each other silly jokes as we made our way down the dark street. "What do you call a brunette that's in between two blonds?" Andy had a serious look on his face as he said this.

"I don't know what?" I never could remember jokes.

"An interpreter," he said with a big smile.

Once seated in the lounge, we ordered drinks and talked about all the things that had happened over the last few months and all of the great people that Andy had met in rehab. The conversation was super charged. It was one of those times when nothing seemed ordinary. When our drinks arrived, we grinned at each other across the table. Andy reached over, picked up the glass and raised it for a toast. "To life and love and to our friendship," he said before tipping his glass to drink. It was a momentous occasion. After a while, we became worried about Andy's position in the chair. I got up and placed my knees against his and with a rocking motion, attempted to seat him further back in the chair the way that they had taught me in rehab. It was awkward and I was having a difficult time with it. I had to keep rocking him back and forth while crouched down with my arms around his back and our knees locked together. Andy sat there helpless, unable to fully participate. The lights were dim and our faces flushed from the effort. The juke box was playing *Baby don't worry about a thing cause every little thing is going to be all right* Reggae style. Suddenly, we realized that, except for the music, it had grown quiet in the lounge and everyone was watching us. We began to laugh and our laughter grew and grew until it echoed out of the building, tumbling out into the night and up into the heavens. Everything was going to be alright.

Chapter 38
An Epidemic

Over the next few months, Andy and I continued to talk over the phone with increasing frequency. In the spring, he was released from the hospital and he went back to his home where he lived next door to his ex-wife and his three beautiful young daughters. He was doing well, and he had a part time caregiver who could attend to most of his needs. We continued with our friendship and we began to spend a lot of time together. Eventually though, I became over extended and overwhelmed. I was constantly traveling back and forth between his home and mine, trying to keep up with the kids, the homestead, my 12-hour shifts and the on-call work that often kept me going for 24 hours at a time. In addition, I was still working registry, doing a lot of driving, and I was dealing with all the stresses of single parenting. It was too much for me. I began to get anxious and extremely depressed. I would be driving along and suddenly find myself sobbing for no apparent reason. What really scared me was that sometimes, when there was a sharp turn in the road with a steep drop off on my right, I would think, *Why not just keep going straight and fly off of the road? It would be so easy to do.* I was stretched way past my limit and I was losing it. I think that's why, when I finally fell ill, I fell hard. *'Ask not for whom the bell tolls, it tolls for thee.'* I was the one who was to do the suffering this time.

I remember clearly the petite blond in room 103. She wasn't my patient but I went into the room when she put on the call light and I brought her a pain pill. That was all the contact we had. Apparently, that was all that was needed. 'Fever of unknown origin' was her diagnosis. We didn't really know what was wrong with her. It was Friday and after my shift, I planned to spend a few days with the kids over at Andy's house. We were all going out to the coast for the weekend, Andy and myself and all six kids. The kids were all great and we had a lot of fun but it was also exhausting. When I got back to work on Wednesday, I was tired and I wasn't feeling well. They told me in report that they had been trying to get hold of me to see if I had had the measles as a kid. If not, they wanted to vaccinate me. It turned out that the woman in 103 with the fever had been sick with the measles. It was highly contagious. "No worries." I told them cheerfully. "I did have the measles when I was a kid."

By the end of that shift, I was very ill and feverish but I still didn't associate it with the measles. After all, I didn't have a rash. On Friday, I called in sick to work because I was too ill to get out of bed. I was supposed to go over to Andy's that weekend also, and when I called him to tell him that I was too sick to leave the house, he didn't believe me. He thought that I was going to be out with some other guy and he got angry. I hung up the phone and crawled back into bed. I was too weak to go up my stairs so I was sleeping on the futon couch that was in the living room by the fire. I had heard over the news that there was a statewide measles epidemic and that people were dying from it. *This can't be the measles*, I thought. *No spots!* By Monday, I was having very high fevers and I couldn't keep anything down, not even water. Never before had I been so ill that I couldn't take care of my children. Not until this. Emily was staying with Meadow while I was sick and her stepdad, John S., called to see if there was anything he could do to help. "Please take Boden. Shannon can stay with me. If they're not together, they will be very well behaved. Boden won't be any trouble." After that, it was just Shannon and me alone together. Finally, we went into the clinic just before closing and saw Dr. Bill. "You have the measles," he informed me. "Go home and go to bed. You're exposing people by leaving your house. There's an epidemic you know!"

I basically credit John S. with saving my life because he then came and got Shannon so that I could rest undisturbed. He also took all of the kids to Public Health to get them booster shots and every day he continued to check in on me. It was winter and there was a small broken pane in the window by the futon. The crumpled up piece of newspaper that was stuffed in the hole temporarily to keep out the cold and the wind had fallen out. I had gotten so weak that I couldn't even replace it and I couldn't make a fire. I lay there under layers of covers alternating between burning up and freezing cold while the wind whipped and whined through the jagged broken glass. I was no longer eating or drinking, I was still vomiting violently, and I had the runs. Day slipped into night and night back into day, and I lost track of the time. I woke up in the middle of the night and took my temperature. The mercury quickly soared up to the top of the thermometer, 106 it read. *Perhaps I am dying*, I thought and I didn't even care. I didn't care about anything. I was surprised that I wasn't delirious. I just wanted to sleep, and nothing else mattered. My face began to swell and distort until I was unrecognizable. It turned an angry, blotchy red and little red spots popped out all over my chest. I looked like a monster. *How long could one last with a 106 fever and no fluids?* I wondered, half asleep and in a fog. It had already been several days. One morning, John S. came to get me. "The Public Health Nurse told me to take you to the hospital," he announced. "They're waiting for you."

Once I was safely in bed with fluids drip, drip, dripping into my veins, I went to sleep and I slept for days. The nurses woke me up every few hours to give me something to try and keep the fever down and then I was back to sleep. I no longer had to worry. My friends were taking care of me. When I started to feel a little better and could think clearly and stay awake for an hour or two at a time, I started thinking about all the nurses who had died in various epidemics and wars throughout the ages caring for the sick and the wounded. Nursing, I realized, with a mixture of satisfaction, pride, and trepidation, could be a dangerous occupation.

After I had been in the hospital for a couple of weeks, I was ready to be discharged. John had come down from Oregon and taken the kids back home with him. I was still way too weak to take on the responsibilities of a household. I had lost almost 20 pounds and my hair had started to fall out from the high fevers. "Your hair follicles got burnt," Dr. Bill explained to me.

"Glad that my brain didn't fry," I responded, and I meant it seriously.

I decided to go to Berkeley to my mother's so that I could rest and recover somewhere where there was heat, electricity and someone to feed me until I was strong enough to make it on my own. I had left home when I was 16. Now, at almost

40 years old, in my hour of need, I was going back home to my mother. It felt like the right thing to do, and she was glad to have me.

Blanche had recently quit her job and gotten on social security. They also gave her SSI, I assumed, because of her mental illness. She was living in a small, one-bedroom apartment right on University Avenue in Berkeley. Twenty-four hours a day, the traffic whizzed by and bright lights glared and flashed in the windows. It reminded me of New York City. Perhaps that's why my mother was so comfortable there. I missed the quiet of the country. Her apartment was stuffed to overflowing. Tall stacks of books and old magazines crowded the small living room and the bedroom. I had to weave carefully around and through them like a maze to get to the far side of the living room where there was a couch that I could sleep on. The hallway, the living room, and the bedroom all had large walk in closets and they were all packed tightly with cloths. In addition, the hallway, the living room, and the bedroom had all been set up with little makeshift closets, the kind that you can buy at Wall Mart and are covered with plastic. These too were stuffed to overflowing with clothes. There were dresses and skirts the same blouse in six different colors, sweaters, pants, coats, and jackets, even cloths that still had the tags on them and had never been worn. Between the books, the magazines and the clothing, there was not much room to move about and one had to walk carefully in order to avoid knocking over one of the precariously high stacks or one of the heavily laden, leaning, freestanding closets. Clutter had always bothered me but I wasn't there to clean house. I was there to rest and recuperate. It proved to be really a good time for me to reconnect with my mother. She was very kind. She didn't make any of those little psychological digs that she was so good at. She let me rest, and she made me soft-boiled eggs and toast just as she had done when I was a kid. We read poetry out loud together, and we went for short walks, pushing the distance we would walk further and further each day until I could tolerate being up for as much as several hours at a time. I could understand now how someone who had been on bed rest for a long time could easily let themselves become an invalid. At first, just being up for 15 minutes was exhausting. I became light headed, my heart would begin to pound, I would feel like I couldn't get my breath and my legs would feel like they were collapsing under me. Still, I forced myself to walk longer and longer distances every day and my mother walked with me, quietly, lost in her own thoughts. By the end of ten days, I was much stronger and I felt ready to head back up north. "Mom, thank you so much for taking care of me. You are a good nurse and a good mother. I feel so much better. I feel well enough to go home now."

"Alright, if you're sure you're strong enough. Take care of yourself and don't overdo it," she cautioned me. She gave me a hug.

"I love you, Mom," I told her as I was heading out the door.

"That's nice," she said as she closed the door behind me.

I decided to stop at Harbin Hot Springs for a few days on my way back home. Years ago, it had actually been a sanatorium where people had gone for treatments and to recover from illness. They had some lovely, simple rooms for rent. The place was landscaped beautifully with little gardens and arbors and paths on which to take long quiet walks. There was a sauna and several outdoor hot pools surrounded by nature and beautiful stone work and there was a vegetarian health food restaurant and a bookstore that sold books whose pages were laden with healing spiritual messages. It was a perfect setting for rest and recovery. When I arrived, I was weary from the three-hour drive and so I rented a room and went straight to bed. The next morning, I got up just before sunrise and walked up the path to the sauna in the chill morning air. No one was around that early, and I enjoyed the peace and solitude. Something about the measles and the high fevers was causing my entire top layer of skin to slough off. My face still looked swollen and pasty and blotchy and not at all like my face. I hoped that the sauna would help. After that first invigorating sauna, I took a long shower. Layers of skin and fatigue and built up toxins seemed to be washing away. I could feel the life force rekindling in my weakened body and soul, and I was very grateful to be finally feeling like I was indeed on the way to recovery. I spent a week there, getting up at sunrise for a morning sauna, doing some light stretches and yoga, having fresh squeezed orange juice and oatmeal for breakfast and then resting until the afternoon. During the afternoon, while there was a lot of activity at the pools, I would meditate and read. I found a group of affirmations that spoke to me and I reflected on them every morning and afternoon and before I went to sleep. Sitting cross-legged on the bed with the lights off, I would repeat softly:

"I bring only warm love and light to myself and to others.
I see clearly through others to the love in their heart, that I may best guide and give loving support."
My intuition now guides me steadily and clearly.
I now easily see and choose the higher path in all my decisions.
I will fully enjoy the wonder and beauty of each instant and practice the presence of peace.
All difficulties I face now are perfect for my growth.
All misfortune will be transformed into the path of the Boddhi."

Repeating these affirmations that were a conglomeration of Yogananda, Buddhism, and 'New Age' brought me a feeling of peace. As my body was growing stronger, my spirit was growing stronger as well.

Although I was feeling so much better in every way, I still felt apprehensive about going home. It had been over a month since I had left my house feverish and deathly ill to go to the hospital. Because I had been home ill for so long, the house was a terrible mess and the water lines had all frozen and broken when the temperature had plummeted. There wouldn't even be water to clean with. I didn't feel ready to go back to work, and I had to get the kids home from Oregon so they wouldn't miss any more school. I also realized that things couldn't go back to the way they were. I had taken a big hit with this illness and I wasn't as strong or as young as I used to be. I had to start taking better care of myself. No more registry work for one thing and no more call. No more working all through the night on a minute's notice. As for Andy, he had called me while I was still in the hospital and said that he couldn't see me anymore. Relationship rollercoaster rides was another thing that I had to purge from my life. I remembered what that councilor had said to me several years before. I needed a good diet, lots of exercise and proper rest. Now, finally, I was able to see the simple wisdom in that advice. That's what the kids needed as well. As I started out on the three-hour drive home, part of me felt renewed and hopeful and part of me felt anxious and worried. Would I have the strength for the challenges ahead? I sure hoped so!

When I cautiously opened the front door to my house, the feeling of apprehension quickly turned to gratitude and joy. Some angel had gone in and cleaned up and had fixed all the water lines. But that wasn't all. I had wanted to learn piano for some time now but I didn't have one to practice on. There by the door was a beautiful little electric piano with a vase of roses on top and a beautiful card that said welcome home. It was from Andy. As I looked around and saw all of these things, my heart soared. I felt the love and caring that had gone into these thoughtful and really huge gifts and I knew now that I would be strong enough to rise to the challenges ahead because I was not alone. I had friends who cared. Several months later, Andy got mad at me again and he took the piano back and gave it to his daughter. I couldn't really blame him. I was too focused on my own path at that point to be of much use to anyone but myself and my children.

John brought the kids back down from Oregon a few days after I got home. They'd had a good time with their dad, but they were glad to be home. John was very sweet. He told me that he still loved me and the kids but that he also loved his new family and that he was happy in his new life. I was glad to hear it. Although I did go back to working shifts at my local hospital soon after the kids got home, it was several more months before I really felt well again.

Chapter 39
Grandma Blanche

About six months after my stay with Blanche and after many years of being stable, my mother went through another breakdown of sorts. She began to spend every minute, for weeks, obsessively writing poetry. Then she stopped paying her rent and she used the money to fly somewhere back east to stay at a fancy hotel and read her poetry at a poetry convention. She believed that she was about to become rich and famous. It was basically a scam, taking advantage of an older woman who was out of touch with reality and had big dreams, but it made her feel good. It would have been harmless enough had it not left her homeless again. She hadn't put in a phone call to me in years but now she called me to say that she had nowhere to live.

The kids and I drove down to Berkeley and got Blanche and some of her things, and we brought her up to our home. She was understandably very unhappy and anguished about how everything had turned out. She said to me accusingly. "My life has been a complete and terrible waste and, Juliet, so has yours."

Excuse me, I thought to myself. *I have three beautiful children, a profession that I love, and a home in the country that is right out of a fairytale. My life has certainly not been a waste.* I didn't say anything though, and it did hurt me to hear her talking like that. Again, I had to remind myself that my life, although it certainly had its ups and downs, had been an incredible adventure. I had to have compassion for my mother whom I knew suffered greatly.

If even for one deluded moment I had entertained the thought that she could simply live with us, after the first five minutes at our house, I realized that it was out of the question. She was irritable and depressed, and she criticized everything about my home and everything I did. The kids annoyed her and the spider webs scared her. And, of course, she couldn't go to the bathroom in our outhouse the way we did. That was unthinkable. We had to find her a place in town as soon as possible.

We actually found her a cute little apartment the very next day, and within a few days she was settled in and adjusting to her new life as Grandma Blanche living in a small town. At least now she would be able to have some interaction with her grandchildren and I would be able to check in on her regularly and see how she was doing. Although she told me, in no uncertain terms every time she saw me, that she hated living in this small town and that she was going back to New York City as soon as possible, I felt confident that it was a good arrangement for her and that she would adjust over time.

At first I tried to visit her every week and take her out to lunch or for a walk by the river or some other entertaining distraction, but soon the thin façade of congeniality and pleasant conversation began to wear through. I began to see that although she hid her delusional thoughts from the general public, there was always some degree of paranoid and delusional ideation going on in her head. Sometimes, someone would stop us on the street and say, "Hello, Blanche. How are you?" Later they would say to me, "Your mother is so sweet. She's such a lovely woman." Little did they know that after they were out of earshot, my mother would whisper, "I hate them, I know they're stealing my checks from my poetry. I wish they'd leave me alone!" At first, people reached out to her and tried to become friends and establish a support system for her but little by little, she pushed everyone away and isolated herself in her own little world. Often, when I would knock on her door, she wouldn't answer, and when she did, she would often exclaim upon opening the door and seeing me, "Oh! If I had known it was you, I would never have answered the door. Don't bother me." These episodes upset me and at first I was tempted to believe that I was unlovable and not a good person, especially since I didn't have a man in my life that loved me either. But I tried to look at it objectively and not like an emotionally crippled child. *'What doesn't kill you makes you stronger.'* Isn't that what they say? When I studied the situation objectively, I realized that I wasn't a saint or a perfect person but neither was I evil or intolerable. I was just an ordinary, well-intentioned woman, perhaps slightly selfish, who didn't always know what the best path to take was, but kept on trying to find it. There was a song out at the time about being and ordinary, average person and I adopted it as my personal theme song. Although I didn't feel that my life was entirely ordinary, I did feel that I was alright, nothing more, nothing less, than your average Joe. What could be so bad about that! Furthermore, if I believed that cultivation of compassion to my fellow travelers through life was one of my major goals, then surely I must have compassion for my imperfect self. These thoughts helped me greatly to accept myself with my strong points and my limitations. It also allowed me to forgive my mother and to love her. It allowed me to process and let go of feelings of bitterness and inadequacy. Because I could still love my mother and love myself, I was a happier, healthier person.

It was almost harder for me to accept my mother's rejection of her grandchildren. The boys didn't seem to notice or they didn't care, and I could understand how they could aggravate her with all their energy. But Emily was so sweet and really loved her grandmother and it hurt me when Blanche was mean to her. One time, Emily and I were going to take my mother to a fancy restaurant for lunch. I was excited because Emily, who was now becoming a teenager and was rarely at home, was going to spend the entire afternoon with us. When we stopped to pick up Blanche, Emily politely got out of the front seat to let her grandmother sit in the front. "I don't want to go if you're taking her!" Blanche exclaimed angrily, when she saw her granddaughter.

Emily didn't seem upset. Perhaps she didn't hear. "That's alright, Mom, you don't have to go. Emily and I will go without you," I said, trying to sound calm. I felt very angry.

Without another word, Blanche got into the car and the three of us went to lunch. My mother cleared up after that, and we had a nice afternoon. Another time I found a Christmas card that Emily had written to her grandmother. It began, "Dear Grandmother, I love you very much and I hope that you have a wonderful Christmas." It went on in that vein for a while then suddenly she wrote, "I don't know why you hate me so much. I've never done anything to hurt you and I love you." After that emotional outburst, it picked back up again in the tone of, "I hope you are well and having a nice holiday, Love Emily."

Despite of all this, my mother could be, at times, very genuine, easygoing, and fun to be with. It made me feel, all the more deeply, her pain for I realized that her mental illness made her behave in ways that went against her true nature. I think she would have been a very lovely and successful person if not for her illness. Once, when she was particularly rude to me she cried out in anguish, "Oh, Juliet, I don't know why you even stay with me when I am feeling like this. I can't help myself. You should just leave me alone." It turned out to be very solid advice and after that I visited her less and less. We both seemed happier with that arrangement.

Blanche always got angry at the slightest suggestion that she might suffer from mental illness so she never received any psychiatric care, and we never even discussed the matter. I had no idea what she herself understood about her condition. When Shannon started to get sick, I went to visit my mother one day. It was late afternoon but she was still in her pajamas. All the lights in the apartment were turned off and the curtains were closed tightly against the daylight. We sat next to each other on a bench in the dark kitchen. "Shannon isn't well," I said to my mother who was sitting hunched forward with her arms around her knees, staring blankly into space. This got her attention and she looked up at me with a concerned expression.

"What's the matter with him?" she had asked, sounding worried and surprised.

"It's mental," I answered, feeling like I was about to cry. "He's having mental problems."

"You mean schizophrenia?" she whispered, as if she were revealing a dark secret.

So there it was. She did know. "Yes, Mother," I studied her to see her reaction. "He is suffering from schizophrenia."

"Can you get him some help?" she surprised me by asking.

"He won't let me take him to see anyone. He gets angry if I talk about it. He says that nothing's wrong."

"Oh," she said and then looked away, staring off into space again. I had no idea what she was thinking.

We sat there together in the darkness, not saying anything. After a while, I got up to go. Blanche walked me to the door and as we parted, she broke the silence by saying, "I'm sorry about Shannon." I realized then that, between the two of us, only she could really appreciate what a dire sentence that was, to be suffering from schizophrenia.

Chapter 40
The Three Trips

I continued to look in on my mother at least once a month. I never knew who would be answering the door, Dr. Jekyll or Mr. Hyde. I was glad that I had moved her near to me though. It seemed like the right thing to do; she needed my help. Once, when she was told that she had to move on short notice, she became very upset and didn't know what to do but we all swooped down and got her relocated and settled in a nicer apartment all in one long, daylight savings time day. I'm sure she realized then that there were times when having a family could really come in handy.

During that time period when the boys were in 4th grade, Emily was in Junior High and my mother was newly relocated to Humboldt County, I kind of dated on and off for a while, nothing serious. There was one man, Brian, with whom it almost got serious. It started to look like he might be the one but then one day, he walked out of my life as decisively and abruptly as he had walked into it. I didn't go after him. I felt that it was hard enough keeping a relationship together if both people were communicating well and both were trying. One-sided relationships were not of interest to me.

Emily was entering her teen years, and she suddenly became very head strong and rebellious. Once or twice the school called me to say, "Your daughter is not in school today. Is she at home? Do you know where your daughter is?"

A couple of people at work mentioned that they had seen her in town with her friends looking very attractive and grown up and smoking cigarettes. When I tried to talk with her about these things, she became defensive and angry and she put up a wall that I could not break through. I felt like I was losing touch with my daughter, and I didn't know what to do about it. I wanted her to have happier, more stable teen years than I had experienced. I wanted her companionship. Most of all, I wanted her to be safe. A couple of times, she didn't come home or call for several days. I became frantic and I called the sheriff. "Unless you actually know where she is and that she is in imminent danger, there's nothing we can do," they told me. I spent my days off, driving desperately through the hills on lonely backcountry roads, following one lead after another. "Yes, Emily was here. She's fine but she left. I think she was going back to town."

When I finally caught up with her, I could only put my arms around her and hold her close to me, grateful that she was just being a rebellious teenager and that nothing worse had happened. "Look, Emily," I told her. "I love you very much and I think that you need a mother, but you don't seem to want one so will you let me at least be your friend? I want you to know that you can come to me at any time if you are not comfortable with what's going on around you or if you need me for anything at all. I just want you to be safe and happy and to make good choices." I think that she heard me because things smoothed out a bit after that and she started communicating more about what was going on in her life.

The boys too were having a hard time. The sweet, innocent, easygoing years were a thing of the past. They were beginning to get into trouble at school for being too rowdy and their fights were escalating to the point where it was often unbearable to be around the two of them when they were together. I tried to separate them a bit by having one of them, usually Shannon, go to Blanche's after school one day a week but she didn't have the patience for high energy boys and so we had to give that up. Boden sometimes went and hung out at Brian's office, and they'd eat Ramen soup for dinner and do schoolwork together which they both seemed to enjoy. I felt, once again, like I was in over my head. What could I possibly do to influence my children in a positive way and yet, not alienate them? Grasping at straws, so to speak, I decided that perhaps they each needed some individual, undivided attention and some quality bonding time. I came up with an idea to take each one, separately, on a trip as time and money would allow. They liked that idea, and to my amazement, they didn't fight about who would get to go first. We came up with a plan to go in birth order. Emily first, then Boden and then Shannon; we were all excited about it. We would start right away. It was summer vacation.

Town was unusually crowded. I leaned against the hood of my car, waiting for Emily and watching all the hip young visitors to our little town walking in and out of the stores in small groups or just standing around like me, watching the goings on. It was the first weekend in August, the weekend of Reggae on the River. Every year, thousands of people poured in from all over the north coast and points beyond to hear three days of reggae greats playing their favorite tunes. We'd spend the weekend dancing, kicking back in the sun, swimming in the river, enjoying good food and, for many, indulging in recreational drugs in a fairly safe environment. It was a three-day party on a gigantic scale, and for those of us who lived right there on the Eel River and liked Reggae music, it was a blast. I planned to work one day in the Rock Med tent for our tickets and then just hang out and enjoy the show.

John and his family had already come and picked up the boys to take them camping for the three weeks that Emily and I would be traveling in Guatemala. After the show, my daughter and I planned to catch a flight to Guatemala City. We had put our heads together to plan out the trip and Emily had even gotten a job through the first part of the summer, cleaning hotel rooms, so that she would have lots of spending money. We were ready to rock and roll! As I waited for Emily to show up, I felt a keen sense of anticipation. The boys were safe with their dad, and I was free to spend uninterrupted time with my daughter. We were going to have a mother-and-daughter adventure. Nothing could have been finer!

When Emily walked up to greet me, I was pleased to see her. She looked happy and healthy and lovely. "Ready?" I asked.

She nodded. "I'm all packed," she told me. "We can leave right after the show."

The music was fantastic. I hung out for a while with a man who was very beautiful and a great dancer. He told me tales of his adventures traveling in exotic countries. I told him that I was on my way to explore Guatemala with my 14-year-old daughter. We danced to the music with wild abandon, and I was happy in the knowledge that my daughter and I were soon to be traveling companions. Emily and I were about to step through the looking glass and into wonderland just like Alice did.

When we arrived in Guatemala City, it was nighttime. We caught a cab and went to a nearby hotel. Only the year before, I had taken a trip to Ecuador by myself. I had felt so vulnerable and alone in strange hotel rooms with strange noises in the night. After that trip, I had decided that I would never travel alone again. Now with Emily for company, I felt strong and safe and happy. She wasn't afraid of anything, ever!

The next day, we got out early and walked around the city but it was so crowded and noisy and hectic that I started to feel anxious. "I want to get out of the city," I told Emily. "I remember, from years ago when I was here with your dad, that the highlands are very beautiful. I think we should head out of town today."

"Sure, let's go," Emily said, not yet having any particular opinion of what it was that she wanted to do.

We went to the bank and exchanged some of our cash for Guatemalan money, then packed up and headed down the street to where we were told we could catch a bus to Lake Atitlan. We were directed to the wrong bus station. Frustrated, we found ourselves pushing through crowds of people with our backpacks, searching for the place where we could catch our bus. After wandering around in circles for a while, unable to find the right street, we finally found the right bus stop. Gratefully, we boarded the 3rd class bus which was crowded. We couldn't get two seats together so Emily sat in the back and I sat in the front. As we pulled away from the city, I began to relax a little. The green rolling hills and pine forests were as I had remembered them. We were entering the Guatemalan highlands. We passed a stop that reminded me vaguely of the turnoff to Lake Atitlan but it had been over twenty years since I had been there so when the driver grumbled in Spanish that it wasn't the turnoff, I believed him. Sometime later, he stopped in a small town and some people got off. When he announced the name of the town that would be the next stop, I panicked. I knew that there was some political unrest in Guatemala and so, before we left, I had called the consulate and asked if it was safe to travel there. They had said that it was perfectly safe in most places but to stay away from the town that the bus driver had just announced was our next stop. I jumped up from where I was sitting next to an old man who looked like he worked in the fields, with tattered and worn clothing, and called out in what must have been an anxious voice, "Emily! We have to get off the bus this very minute." I was terrified that the bus driver would just take off and not let us leave. After all, he had not cooperated with any of my requests thus far. I now realized that we had long ago passed the turnoff to Lake Atitlan. Emily, who was sometimes slow moving when you wanted her to do something, grabbed her pack down from the overhead rack and was at the front of the bus in seconds flat. She must have heard the urgency in my voice. We jumped down and immediately the bus pulled away, leaving us standing in a cloud of dust. When the dust settled, we stood there, looking around and then looking at each other, trying to figure out what to do next. I had the feeling that we had just escaped some terrible fate. I was happy to be standing there, on the side of the road, with my darling daughter.

It turned out that we were in Chichicastenango, and the very next day was market day. I learned all of this from the elderly woman who ran the small pension where we rented a room with a couple of cots. It was tiny and sparse but very clean, and it felt safe. When she found out that I was a nurse, she was pleased. "Enfermera," she said, and she told me that her hip was hurting her. I gave her a Celebrex to take. "Where can I get this medicine?" she wanted to know. "No mass me duele," she exclaimed happily when I saw her, a few of hours after she had taken it. I didn't know if it was available in the local pharmacy, but if it was, she wouldn't need a prescription like you would back in the States. I wrote down the name of the medicine for her. I could see that medical care was a rare luxury to many of the people in these highland towns and villages.

The pension was only a few blocks from the town square where market was held every Sunday. Emily was not feeling well. She was developing a huge, angry cold sore on her bottom lip, and her stomach was upset. On top of that, she was exhausted from the busy schedule we had been following. She needed some rest. We decided to head over to the square to find something light to eat and then go to bed early. The square was deserted. There was only one little café on a side street that was open. We had some chicken soup and bottled water and then we left to have a look around. On one side of the plaza, there was a beautiful old cathedral with narrow steps that climbed up steeply to the huge wooden doors that were the entranceway to the church. It reminded me of the ancient Mayan temples that I had visited with John. The south side of the plaza had a couple of cute cafés that were closed. In the center of the square, there were a few benches but it was mostly bare, open space. In a sudden gust of wind, a few pieces of trash were swept up and blew about the empty plaza before settling back down in the stillness. No one was around and it was hard to imagine that there would be a market there the next day. Perhaps the woman had been mistaken.

After a good night's sleep, Emily said that she felt better but she was unusually quiet and I could tell that she wasn't back to her old self just yet. We decided to walk back to the square for breakfast. I was hoping that one of the cute cafés would be open and serving fresh-brewed Guatemalan coffee. We walked, arm in arm, down the narrow cobblestone streets. The hustle and noise of the market getting into full swing could be heard from a few blocks away. As we approached, the sights and sounds and delicious smells of the market grew stronger. When we reached the square, we did not even recognize it as the small, deserted, empty space that we had seen the night before. We looked around in wonderment. Indians from villages far and away had walked for miles carrying their wares to be sold. They had come laden down with bundles in their arms and babies on their backs. Where the square had seemed small and lonely the night before, as if by magic there were now dozens of stalls hung with beautiful hand woven fabrics, people selling colorful pottery and tables laden with fresh fruits and vegetables. Many different languages and Indian dialects could be heard as people bartered and haggled over prices. I bought a lovely long string of purple beads that had silver bangles strung decoratively every few inches. Emily got a pretty hand-woven shawl, and she wrapped it around her shoulders to protect her against the chill morning mist that had settled in the plaza.

We sat down at one of the tables in front of the cafe to watch the festivities and to get a bite to eat. The plaza seemed huge, at least four times as big as it had seemed the night before. There were so many people and so much going on. Candles and burning incense lined the steps of the church, giving the entire scene an ethereal atmosphere. Chuchkajaues (indigenous prayer leaders) in their ethnic dress were gathered in small groups, swinging tin cans from which poured the smoke of smoldering copal resin. The fragrant incense filled the air as they chanted magical incantations in honor of their ancestors, their strong voices echoing mystically throughout the plaza above the noisy market chatter. Across the plaza from the impressive Iglesia de Santo Tomas was a smaller church. A few carts were positioned there, selling fresh tacos and chicken to hungry people passing by who could not resist the delicious smells as the meat sizzled over the coals.

By late afternoon, we had explored every square inch of the plaza. Emily was looking tired again and she wanted to rest so we went back to our room and napped. It was dark when we finally got motivated to return to the square. Like magic, most of everything had disappeared again, but several pots of smoldering incense still lined the church steps and a few vendors still lingered selling their food by candle light. A couple of weary families lingered on, gathering up their wares and preparing to head back to some mysterious destination in the hills that was their home. We bought some deliciously spiced pieces of barbequed chicken and sat on the church steps in the dark looking around us. There was something magical in the air. Maybe it was the incantations. We felt blissful and serene. The night had a timeless feeling to it. "This is incredible, Mom. Thank you for bringing me here. I love it." I could tell that Emily was starting to feel better.

The next day we caught a bus back to Lake Atitlan. I was really trying to travel on a tight budget so when we got there, we rented a very inexpensive cabin with only enough room for two little beds in a compound with other cabins where the bathroom was outside. That evening, smoke from some continuous smoky fire nearby filtered under the eaves of our cabin. I kept waking up coughing from the fumes. Around midnight, I was woken up by the sound of little mice scurrying around the floor and in the rafters, and I got really scared. "Emily, are you awake? I hear mice. I'm afraid of mice." Irrationally, I felt like I was going to panic.

"It's okay, Mom, they won't hurt you. Go back to sleep," Emily answered, not even concerned enough to fully wake up.

"Emily, do you mind if I get into bed with you?" I asked timidly, feeling really silly but frightened nevertheless.

"I don't mind," she said, moving over as far as she could in the tiny little bed to make room for her mother.

Laying there next to my daughter with her soft, even breathing, I felt content and safe and before long I fell asleep. As soon as I woke up, I started coughing again from breathing smoke all night.

I grumbled to Emily as we were brushing our teeth at the very public outdoor sink, "We have to find another place to stay. It's not worth it to save money if we're going to be miserable. I don't want to spend another night here."

Emily had to agree and so we set off to find new lodgings. We found a very nice little place on the edge of town that was affordable and comfortable. Without delay, we moved in. Then we spent a very pleasant day going from café to café, checking out the vendors and exploring the Indian village where I had lived with her father many years before. Things looked different but the same. Change came slowly to rural Guatemala.

The cafés were hip and fun to hang out in. They had great ambiance and great food. "We're going to get fat if we stay here for very long," I said to Emily. "The food here is way too good."

"I know. I can't wait for breakfast so we can have waffles with fresh fruit and yogurt again. That was so delicious. Yum," Emily and I were laughing. We had been eating all day long and all we could think about was eating again.

"Any ideas about what you would like to do tomorrow?" I asked Emily when we were snuggled in our beds for the night. I was looking through the travel guidebook. The lamp that stood on the bedside stand separating our beds cast a soft puddle of light where I was reading and on my daughter's sweet face.

"What are our choices?" Emily asked, sounding sleepy.

"Well, we could just hang out in the cafés and eat all day, or we could take a boat across the lake and visit the town of Santiago Atitlan."

"Oh, let's definitely go to Santiago Atitlan."

The lake was huge and the boat ride took us a couple of hours. When we arrived, we walked up the steep stone path that led from the dock to the main part of town. The streets were ancient and quiet, lined with a row of neat little one-story stone houses and a few cafés for the tourists that arrived daily on the boats. Usually, the tourists returned to the other side of the lake at the end of the day. There weren't many overnight accommodations. The cafés seemed like the hangout spot for the few hip young castaways from other countries who had taken up residence in this out of the way Indian village. It was intriguing really, and I wished I could spend a few days, or maybe even weeks, but there was so much more we wanted to see. We had to keep moving. Before getting back on the boat, I stopped to look at some paintings by a local artist, depicting the life of the local people. The paintings were really good, and I wanted to buy several but I couldn't afford it. I did, however, settle on buying a small painting of three Indians sitting next to a campfire by the lake at sunset with the volcano San Pedro in the background. It was entitled 'Descansando'. I am looking at that picture as I write this. Looking at that picture, I can still feel the magical power of Lake Atitlan even now separated as I am by time and space.

I was beginning to feel very comfortable and at home on Lake Atitlan, and I was thinking that I never wanted to leave. I was actually starting to consider staying at the lake until it was time to go back to California. When I told Emily what I was thinking, she wouldn't hear of it. "It is really wonderful here but we have to go to Livingston and we have to see Tikal. Come on, Mom, you'll regret it if we don't go. You'll be glad when we get there."

"You're right, of course. I've never been to Livingston, and they've been working to restore Tikal for years. It's probably really changed since I was there with your dad. In that case, we'll have to go head back to Guatemala City in a day or two."

"Let's do it. We can be in Livingston in a couple of days!" Emily was an enthusiastic travel companion. There was no one that I would rather have been traveling with.

I hadn't realized that we actually had to take a boat to Livingston. It was on the eastern coast just south of Belize. There was no way to get there by land. That made the trip all the more exciting as we raced along the coastline in the small launch with the salt spray in our faces. When we arrived, it was late in the day. We found a sweet little one-room cabin in a compound of small cabins that was owned and run by a very nice, older American woman. Our cabin was right on the edge of the water were the Rio Dulce emptied out into the Caribbean Sea. As we lay in bed that night, we were lulled to sleep by the sound of the water lapping gently against the steep banks that marked the perimeter of our compound. Emily had been right. I was glad to be there.

The next day, we got to know Jean, our landlady, a bit. She had come to Livingstone years before with her sweetheart. They had exciting and romantic plans to make a life for themselves in this isolated little village far away from anywhere that was familiar to them. She had spent all her money developing the cottages and then, after little more than a year, her lover had left and he never returned. She told us that she loved her life and yet, at the same time, she felt trapped. In spite of the many years that she had lived there, she still felt like an outsider. "The government here is very corrupt, and the people here are poor. The government doesn't care," Jean told us. I had heard this from other Guatemalans as well and I believed it to be true, but Jean sounded so paranoid, talking about the politics of Guatemala. She gave the impression that she was always looking over her shoulder to see if someone was after her. Perhaps she wasn't telling us everything. In many ways, she seemed to have a peaceful easy rhythm to her life and she did appear to have friends. She didn't sound happy though. Things had not turned out the way she had expected. Probably the nights were hard for her. They could be long and lonely. I suggested that she go back to live in the United States, but she felt that she had been away for too long. She didn't belong there either any more. She was a woman without a country. The very first day we had met, her she had seemed so cheerful and content with her life but as we got to know her, there was an air of quiet desperation and a hint of madness about her that made me feel afraid for her.

We had dinner that night at the local hang out and an Australian man, who was sitting alone, walked up and asked if he could join us at our table. He sounded just like Crocodile Dundee. He talked a blue streak going on and on about economics. Emily looked bored but I was happy just to listen to his accent. After he had finished with his spiel on economics, he told us that he had written a movie script. "In the script, a man and a woman meet in the jungle under dangerous and romantic circumstances. They fall in love," he paused here and his eyes widened in a look of expectation, "but somehow they get separated," he continued in his fabulous Aussie accent. "Neither of them has any idea of what has happened to the other and so, sadly, they go on about their lives. Several years later, however, back in the city, they meet again under unlikely circumstances. They're still in love and they get married and sail back to the jungle together. In the end, they walk off into the setting sun holding hands. What do you think? Does it have potential?" the Australian guy wanted my opinion.

"Just my kind of movie," I told him.

We were meeting a lot of interesting people. On our walk home, along the dirt path, that night we met a woman who stopped to talk with us. She told us, "I watch everyone. I see everything." Then she told me that I should move to Guatemala. "It's not for everyone," she said, "But you would be happy here. You would be good for the people."

"I did have an idea to open up a clinic," I replied. "There is such a need for health care here in the rural areas."

She shook her head knowingly. "Follow your heart," she told me as we parted.

We continued walking down the path in the direction of our little hacienda. As we got further from the main street, it got darker and more isolated. I would have been frightened had I not been with my fearless daughter. There was little dog yapping frantically. Emily wanted to see what kind of dog it was that barked so much. We searched around for a moment, curious, not quite sure where the noise was coming from. When we finally caught sight of our little yapping puppy, we burst out laughing; it was so hilarious. It wasn't a dog at all. It was a parrot that sounded just like a dog, and it was sitting in an open window furiously barking. It continued to bark until we were out of earshot.

That night there was a terrific thunderstorm. I had never heard thunder like that before. It gathered and rumbled and grew until the sound of it was deafening, and then it would explode in a loud piercing crack that shook the building and felt like the sky was being ripped open. The storm was awe-inspiring. It was exquisite. The rain pelted down in giant drops that seemed like they were going to pound right through the roof and waves crashed over the riverbanks, dashing up against the house. I did love the wildness of it, but after several more deafening claps of thunder, I began to feel anxious. "Emily," I called out as a jagged flash of lightening momentarily flooded the room with bright light. "Can I get into bed with you?"

"Sure, Mom. But there's nothing to be scared of. I love this storm!"

Guatemala is such a diverse country with so many exotic, exciting, and extreme faces of nature. It seemed like the land could never totally be tamed here. We took a launch up the Rio Dulce as it meandered through the jungle which grew right down to the water's edge. From within that mysterious wall of green, with its hanging vines and climbing vegetation scrambling and grasping, intertwining and choking, clambering towards the light, there emanated the sounds of teeming jungle life, of exotic birds and insects and monkey screeches. If there was no visual at all and you only heard the sounds, you would still feel the tremendous power of its life force. It was the sound of millions of years of evolution expressing itself in symbiotic survival. It was the sound of the jungle. We traveled down a thin tributary deeper into the heart of the jungle where we swam in the clear water beneath a thick canopy of vegetation. A kaleidoscope of greens reflected off of the cool waters enveloping us in its secret hidden world. Every once and a great while, we would see a curious little hut perched right down at the water's edge. *Who could be living there, and what must it be like to live there always?* I could not help but wonder. I think I would have made a good cultural anthropologist, so fascinated was I with isolated and extremely remote cultures.

The next day, we took an excursion up the coast towards Belize where we spent the morning at a beautiful white sand beach and we swam in the warm, clear, blue water. Emily loved to swim. She was in her element. There was no shade so to get out of the heat, we sat for a while, with our hats on, in the water up to our necks and I told Emily stories of when her dad and I had traveled in Guatemala. I had not been much more than a girl then myself.

In the afternoon, we went to La siete alteres, a stair stepping series of seven pools that led back into the jungle. Emily was fast and adventurous, and she scrambled up the little waterfalls like gazelle. The guide and a few other tourists were with her. I could not keep up so I settled down in the shade to meditate. It had been a long time since I could remember feeling so alive and well. I sat there following the breath and letting my mind open. Gradually, I was overcome by a feeling of deep peace and contentment, and it translated into a kind of euphoria. Emily bounded down the hill to greet me. "It's so beautiful, Mom, you really ought to climb up to the top pool. It's unbelievable."

We timed our leaving Livingston so that we would get back to Guatemala City in time to catch our plane to Flores, the picturesque town on Lake Peten Itza. There we would be able to find lodging and make the daily commute to explore the ruins of Tikal. We stayed at the Hotel El Peten. It seemed luxurious with a balcony that overlooked the lake for only $30.00 a night.

The next morning, we gathered with other tourists to catch the 5 a.m. mini bus that would take us to nearby Tikal. Things had changed dramatically since I had been there nearly 20 years ago when it was little more than some piles of broken rocks buried beneath the jungle. I remembered feeling a little like Indiana Jones one evening after exploring the temples as John and I hung out, the only foreigners in the isolated little cantina, with wild Mexican music playing on the jukebox and everyone a little drunk on tequila and Mexican Cervesa. Now, it seemed almost elegant and there was a $6.00 entrance fee. The grounds at the entrance were kept totally spotless and trimmed. The restoration of the park was an amazing and impressive feat. We started up the rocky path to the 'Great Plaza'. Temple#1 was still undergoing reconstruction. It was a towering stone temple approximately 135 feet high. It was said that it was built to honor the great King Ah-Cacau by his son in 700 A.D. One of the workers told me that a couple of tourists had ignored the 'keep out' sign and had slipped and fallen to their death the year before. Directly across the plaza was located temple#2 in better repair. Narrow stone steps climbed steeply, almost 100 feet high, up to the temple's entrance. Along with a few other tourists, Emily and I climbed this temple. At the top was simply a small stone room, the colorful hieroglyphics that had once decorated the walls had been mostly warn away through the centuries. At that tremendous height, one could see all around for miles, above the jungle canopy. With no guard rails or anything to hold on to, I began to feel light headed and anxious. Emily was prancing about on her tippy toes at the edge of the stone platform and skipping lightly down the narrow stone steps. "Emily, stop that," I pleaded. "It's making me feel sick!" She tried to ignore me but I insisted. "You have to be careful up here. If you fall, you will probably die."

"I'm not going to fall. Don't worry so much." At least she had stopped jumping around on her tiptoes.

I found that I could not walk down the narrow steps, looking down from that tremendous height, as easily as I had walked up. I sat down on my butt and inched my way down, always either having my butt or two feet solidly planted. In this embarrassing manner I scooted my way down the temple steps while a group of Guatemala men looked on with amusement. Emily waited patiently at the bottom for her mother to catch up. When I finally made it back down to the sweet earth, I felt relieved. The congenial onlookers nodded their approval and applauded. For an adventurous woman, I certainly had a lot of fears!

As we walked along the dark, overgrown trails, the air vibrating with sounds of the jungle, I imagined I could feel naked dark shadows slipping silently between the dripping vines. In the stone pavilions I imagined the colorful markets bustling with vendors who had traveled from far off places to trade their wares. I imagined that I could still feel their spirits in another dimension, occupying their lost city. Once or twice, when everything was perfectly still, a single branch would start waving wildly up and down as if shaken by some invisible presence. As the tourists began to filter out and leave, the magic of the 'Ruinas Mayas' became stronger. I took a picture of Emily who was crouched beneath some large leafy fronds. The expression on her face was one of thoughtfulness and wonder. She looked peaceful, and I could tell that she was tuning in to something greater than the small and sometimes petty everyday material world. I knew that we would be returning home soon, but I didn't think that either of us would ever be quite the same.

Sitting comfortably on the plane bound for home, I reflected on the trip. Guatemala was an incredibly diverse and beautiful country with wonderful people but it also had a dark side, a face of violence and of poverty. That could also be said of the history of much of the planet. I hoped that, as a species, we would be able to survive and evolve beyond that. Learning to live and work together peacefully in the stewardship of the planet was our only hope.

The trip had been a huge success. The time my daughter and I had spent together was precious, and she definitely seemed to have matured since we had left California a mere three weeks before. It seemed like a lifetime ago. I was looking forward to seeing my boys and being home but in my mind's eye, a part of me was still out there on the Rio Dulce, peacefully navigating its waters in the early morning mist.

After we got back home, Emily became very focused. She wanted to get through high school, which she did not particularly like, and she wanted to get on with the task of finding a meaningful and interesting path to follow. Teenage kid stuff was not of interest to her anymore. She had returned home with a much broader view of life.

That winter, I decided to take Boden to Puerto Vellarta for our one-on-one trip together. It was a perfect destination because the weather would be great and it was still an affordable place to travel to. We only had a little over a week but I was sure that we would have a great time.

The town of Puerto Vallarta was kind of expensive so we only stayed a couple of days, walking around and seeing the sights. It was no longer recognizable as the quaint little seaside fishing village that it had been when I was there with Gary, back when I was 18, but even though it was much larger and rather touristy now, it still retained some of its old world charm. Boden and I were enjoying the break from the daily routine and the rigors of the rainy season. He had some 5th grade homework that he needed to do so we tried to get as much of it out of the way as we could. We sat in the hacienda courtyard that was dripping with bright tropical flowers pouring over the pages of grade school exercises, and when we tired of that, we went out to walk on the beach or sit at some sidewalk café and watch as people went on about their day talking to each other in Spanish. It was fun to be in a foreign country, and we were enjoying the novelty of just the two of us, tripping around together, with no deadlines to meet and no schedule to follow. After a couple of days though, we were ready to get out of the city. We took the ferry down the coast to Yalapa and rented a room overlooking the bay at the mouth of a small river that flowed out of the hills and down to the ocean. At the high tide, the river would rise up under the pier blocks, flooding the cement underside of the building. Fishermen could navigate their small boats from the bay right up to the hacienda steps. It was charming. The front of our room was wide open to the ocean and to the sky and we could sit out on the balcony and watch the goings on at the beach and in the little cove. We were happy with our spot. Our Landlord, Jose, was a very nice Mexican man and he took a liking to Boden and me. After we had been there a couple of days, he invited us to dinner at his little beachside stand. It was a moonless night, and it was exciting to be ferried in his little canoe, from the steps of our hacienda, across the river to the part of the beach where his restaurant was. No one was around. The beach was completely deserted and quiet. Our host opened up the front of the restaurant to the sand and the sky and the ocean. It was so beautiful that I felt like I was falling under some sort of spell. I was mesmerized. The tide was carpeted in sparkling phosphorescence. It gave the impression that some of the stars had fallen out of the sky and were floating around in the water and up on the damp, sandy beach. Gentle, foaming waves washed in, bringing with them more sparkling jewels. Jose prepared for us a delicious meal with cilantro chicken and rice, and we sat there by candle light, enjoying the meal and sharing experiences about living in California. He had lived in San Francisco for several years doing restaurant work and his English was excellent. Boden really took a liking to Jose, and they talked about boats and cars and fishing and the like. It was fun for me to watch Boden having such a good time talking guy talk. Jose had a small boat that tourists chartered with him to be taken out ocean fishing, and he had a trip arranged. He promised to take Boden along if it was all right with me. I didn't really want him to go, but Boden was very excited. It was going to be his big manly adventure. One-on-one with Mom was nice, but he really wanted to have some guy time.

It was wonderful, separating the twins for a while. Without his brother to bounce off of and fight with, Boden was actually quite calm and a good companion. "Let's play a game," I said the next day when we were sitting down to a lunch that was much less exotic than our meal the night before.

"What game?" Boden wanted to know.

"Let's take turns saying something that we like about this trip. I'll start."

"Alright, we can do that." Boden didn't seem thrilled about the idea, but he was willing to go along with it.

"I like the fact that I'm here with you and you're so much fun to be with," I said as he sat there sucking down his soda and looking very cute with his new haircut and his suntan, his light blue eyes and his dark brown hair, his baggy shorts and his new Mexican sandals.

"I like the fact that I'm going fishing with Jose tomorrow," Boden offered, looking extremely satisfied as he said it.

"I like that it's so warm and that our room looks out at the ocean." I was very happy to be getting a break from cold rainy Northern California and the view was incredible.

"I like missing school. We should do this more often," Boden said as he smiled his adorable, crooked little smile.

We went on like that for a time, and then we decided to explore up the river a ways and see if we could find a good swimming spot. It was dry and rocky without much vegetation along the riverbanks. We hiked back into the hills for quite a ways watching out, as we went, for rattlesnakes and scorpions. We were feeling hot and sweaty when we found a small, clear pool of water, and we splashed around in it for a while to cool off. Afterwards, we walked back to our hacienda refreshed with our hair dripping wet and hungry for dinner. That night, Jose stopped by and he invited me to come to his room down the hall and visit after Boden was asleep but I never went. I was too content snuggling up with my son and drifting off to sleep to the sound of the surf.

The next morning, true to his word, Jose came to get Boden and they headed off on their fishing voyage. "You have a life vest for him, don't you?" I wanted to know, feeling anxious and still feeling like I didn't really want him to go. "Of course, I do.

Don't worry; he's a big boy. He will be fine. We will have fun. We will be back before dark." Jose was so sweet and reassuring. I knew that I was just being paranoid.

I made one last, worried mother pitch. "Boden, I don't know if you should go. It's dangerous out there on the ocean." But there was no stopping him now. Nothing I could have said would have influenced him in the least. All of his mighty, 11 year old boy energy was focused on this fishing trip. I let him go.

As I settled down in the shade of the balcony with a good book under a brilliantly blue sky and a salty breeze, I felt content and happy. I read all morning with the warm ocean breeze keeping the flies and mosquitoes away. Towards mid-afternoon, the sky became overcast and thunderclouds started to gather. I felt a little concerned. I hoped that they would take note of the weather change and come in early. Besides, now I was tired of reading and tired of being by myself. I had started to miss my son. By late afternoon, the wind began to howl and the surf could be heard, with growing intensity, breaking on the shore. It began to rain, first in little tentative drops and then in a giant cloud burst that darkened the sky and turned the ocean into a churning, crashing tempest. My heart came up into my throat. I felt like I was choking. I hadn't actually seen the life vest and what good would it do him anyhow if he was swept overboard or if the boat had capsized in what seemed to me to be gale winds. I tried to remain calm but I was cursing my judgment now for letting him go. As it got later in the day and it started to grow dark, my fear grew to panic. I felt like I was losing my hold on reality. I felt like I was losing my mind. I watched with baited breath as several small boats, one after the other, cut their engines at the mouth of the river and silently paddled upstream to dock along the riverbank. You could follow their little light that they used for navigation on the moonless, starless night. It looked like a firefly making its way up stream. By then the storm had abated but it was still quite overcast and dark. After total darkness had fallen and no more boats could be heard, I totally lost it. I started ranting, totally distraught and screaming, "I want my son, I want my son, I want my son," over and over again as if the sheer power of my will could bring him home. Anyone listening must have thought 'gringa loca'. But no one knocked on my door to see what was going on as I grabbed up a little wooden chair in the room and slammed it repeated against the wall until it shattered into pieces. Suddenly, I heard, out of the dark and silence, the sound of another boat engine idling at the mouth of the river. I went over to the balcony and looked out. The engine was cut and I could see a little light moving silently through the dark. It was coming closer. I held my breath not even daring to breathe. Finally, I called out in a small, scared voice, "Boden!"

"Hi, Mom, can you see us? We're almost there. It was really fun!"

All I could think of was how grateful I was that he was safe and that I didn't have to spend an agonizing night not knowing that he was safe.

"Yes, it was very stormy," Jose was grinning. "We docked in Puerto Vallarta to get out of the storm. I wanted to spend the night but then I thought that if we didn't come back tonight, you would lose your mind."

"Yea, Mom, Jose and I wanted to spend the night. It would have been fun."

I was weak with relief. Jose was my new hero for bringing my son home to me safe and sound. "There is music tonight at the local cantina, and we're very hungry. Let's all go out to dinner," Jose suggested.

It sounded like a great idea. "Let's go!" Boden and I both agreed enthusiastically.

We were all in high spirits now. When we got to the restaurant, there was good dancing music and good food. The place was crowded. "It's too bad that you have to leave tomorrow," Jose was saying.

I know but I have to get back to my other kids and work and Boden has school, I was thinking to myself, *I could live here. Life would be sweet.*

"Why don't you let me take you back to Puerto Vallarta in my boat? I know this beautiful little isolated beach that no one ever goes to. I'd like to show it to you."

"Let's go with Jose; Mom, please," Boden wanted some more time boating with his friend.

"Sure, thank you. It sounds like fun." The ferry was leaving early in the morning but we would wait and go in with Jose. It sounded like a nice little, family type adventure.

"You should come to my room tonight," Jose said when Boden had walked away for a minute. "I'll leave a light on for you."

I was feeling really happy and adventurous now that Boden was out of danger. I wanted to make the most of the last couple of days of our vacation, and I was glad that my son was having fun. The music was good so Jose and I went out on the dance floor while Boden sat and looked on. It was crowded and somehow, people got in between us. I couldn't see Jose for a minute. A young American woman came over and danced next to me. "Don't trust him," she said in a whisper. "He seems like a nice guy but he's really dangerous. He beat up his girlfriend and now she's hiding in the hills because she's so afraid of him. And watch your purse." The next minute, she was gone.

"What did that girl say to you?" Jose wanted to know. He sounded annoyed as if he knew that it was something bad.

"Nothing really, it was too noisy. I couldn't hear." My antennas were up now. I didn't know for sure what was going on but I did know that we were in a foreign country where we could just disappear and no one would ask any questions. I couldn't afford to give Jose the benefit of the doubt. I had to keep my son and myself safe. The next morning, in spite of angry protestations by Boden, we packed up before dawn. Early in the morning, we left our room to go and sit at the dock to wait for the ferry. Boden was very upset with me. He wanted us to go with Jose, and he badgered me something awful until finally I turned to him and I said, "Look, Boden, you're too young to understand but it's not safe. You have to trust me on this one."

Boden shrugged. He didn't understand but he was willing to trust me, and I loved him all the more for that.

A crowd had gathered waiting for the ferry and now I felt perfectly safe. Jose came by with a group of guys. "Why didn't you come to my room last night? Why aren't you going with me to Puerto Vallarta?" he demanded. He sounded angry.

"I'm sorry, we need to get back. I'd rather just take the ferry."

He muttered something angrily to his friends in Spanish and then turned abruptly on his heels and walked off. I hadn't seen that side of him before.

On the plane ride home, the noise of the engine was bothering Boden so he stuffed some tissue in his ears to block out the sound. It was late at night as we were driving home from the airport, and I noticed that Boden was sitting next to me quietly with a look of pain on his handsome face. "What's wrong, Boden? You look like you don't feel so good."

206

He explained to me that the tissue had gotten shoved deeply into his left ear and he couldn't get it out. He was in a lot of pain. We were nearing Santa Rosa and we still had another 3 hours of driving after that. "Let's stop in Santa Rosa and go to the ER. They'll get it out."

"No, don't stop. I can wait until we get home. You can take me to your ER and get it out."

"We should go now. You look miserable." I had worked at Santa Rosa Community Hospital. I knew that the ER could be hectic and noisy and expensive. I wasn't anxious to go there but I didn't want Boden to be in pain.

"It's alright. Just keep going. I can handle it. You can get it out when we get home." His voice was strained and he was holding his hand cupped protectively over his ear. I didn't know what to do.

"Don't stop," he insisted when he saw my hesitation.

There he was, trusting me again, trusting that I would be able to make it better when we got home. It was more precious than anything money could buy. When we drove into town, it was around 1 a.m. and we went by our little hometown ER. It was peaceful and quiet and we were among friends. I had a look in his ear with the otoscope and I could see, pushed up against his eardrum, the ragged end of a piece of tissue. I grasped it with a thin forceps and carefully pulled out the offending material. Immediately, he felt relief. We were road weary and ready to call it a day so I thanked the nurses and headed for home with my son. All in all, it had been an interesting trip. 'All's well that ends well' was my new, favorite motto.

Not long after Boden and I got back from Mexico, I met a man at a local dance who seemed to be a truly nice man. He was a carpenter and he lived in an isolated area called windy nip on the edge of a canyon where the wind howled through on a daily bases. Recently, I had decided to turn our 8x16 back-porch into another 8x8 bedroom so that I could separate the boys and also an 8x8 bathroom so that we didn't have to go out in the rain to take a bath. I also had it in mind that it would be a welcome luxury to have an indoor toilet if at all possible. I hired a local carpenter to do the work, and he got going on the project enthusiastically. But as the work progressed, he got slower and slower and his workdays began to be fewer and further apart until he was hardly ever showing up. The rainy season would be arriving soon and that was a bad time to build. When Dan told me that he was a carpenter, I told him my story of frustration with my half-finished project. "No worries," he had said. "I can finish that in a few days. I'll be over this weekend." True to his word, he showed up and he danced around the rooftop making carpentry work look like a walk in the park. My knight in shining armor had rescued me, and then he refused to take money for it. He was cheerful and good-natured and a most honorable man. The kids all liked him right away.

It was almost time for another winter break, and Shannon and I were about to go on the third trip. Shannon had waited patiently for his turn and now we were planning to go to Cancun and Isla de Mujeres in Southern Mexico. "Shannon," I asked one day after Dan had left to go back to Windy Nip. "Would you mind if I invited Dan on our trip? I won't invite him if you don't want him to go." I thought that Shannon might like having a guy along and I knew that we would be safe with Dan.

"I'd like Dan to go with us. That would be great. Ask him." Shannon seemed pleased at the idea.

I was glad that Shannon wanted Dan to go along. I liked Dan a lot, and I trusted him. I was hoping that we could spend some quality time together and get to know one another better. One morning, late in the fall, we all set off for the Yucatan Peninsula on yet another adventure. It was fun having Dan with us. He had a knack for finding all of the right places to go. I wasn't used to feeling so safe and so looked after. It was a nice feeling; one that I thought I could get used to.

I sometimes look back at that trip searching for any signs of the trouble that Shannon was to have later. He seemed like a normal kid. He had some problems with concentration. It was a bit of a struggle to get him to read or do schoolwork but that, in itself, wasn't so unusual. Usually, he was pretty easy going and that was a delight, but if he wanted something a certain way, he could be very stubborn and then there was no reasoning with him. In that respect, he was a little like my mother. Recently, he told me that he had heard voices occasionally when he was a kid. I never saw any indication of it. Like his brother, he was well behaved while separated from his identical twin and he seemed to be having a great time.

The three of us palled around the island. We swam in the ocean and rode motor bikes down twisting dirt paths. We took a little excursion to some mainland beaches and we went once to the bullfights. It was a quick trip but a welcome break from the routine, and I believe that Shannon had a better time because Dan was with us.

I had kept my word and taken all three of my children on an individual adventure. After that, I felt that I knew them a little better, more intimately, as individuals. And I felt like they knew me a little better too. I also think that the experience matured them some. Emily and I continued to love traveling together but neither of my sons, ever again, was interested in taking a trip with just me. However, the three of us together, Boden, Shannon and I, did have a couple more memorable travel adventures as a response to some big problems that came up. It seemed like when things went wrong, taking a trip was one of my ways of easing the tension. It was like getting to run away but only temporarily. I got to step back from the problem and look at it from a safe distance and then drop back into the situation with renewed energy and new tools with which to deal with the issues. Another positive aspect of travel for me was that whenever I was in some faraway place, I would be reminded that there were an infinite number of interesting variations on the theme of life and that most of them had appeal and value in one way or another. In short, when I traveled, I could let go of the feeling that if things weren't a certain way something was terribly wrong. I would see that there were actually millions of fascinating variations on how things could be. That realization helped me to let go of the 'grasping' which according to Buddhist doctrine is the source of much suffering. As the kids like to say these days; 'it's all good.'

Chapter 41

A Family of Five

After our trip to Mexico, Dan and I started getting serious about our relationship. He started spending every Friday, Saturday, and Sunday with me and the kids. Early Monday morning, he would make the long drive back to Windy Nip where he lived and worked with his friends. One morning, we were lazing around in bed talking about our childhood and growing up. "How old are you?" he asked.

I realized then that I had been avoiding the subject. In the past, all of my relationships had been with men who were older than me. In our culture, it seemed like it was the norm for the woman to be younger but not so much the other way around. I knew that Dan was 34, and although I didn't think that it was a big deal, I hadn't really wanted to tell him my age. We'd been seeing each other for over six months now. The time had arrived to tell him.

"I'm 41," I said, feeling apologetic, like I had just informed him that I was suffering from gonorrhea or some other contagious disease.

The poor man could not hide his shock. "You're how old!" he said with a look of amazement.

I was flattered that he had thought that I was younger. People always did. But his response didn't sit well with me. Forever after, I always felt self-conscious about the age difference. The awkward moment quickly passed and Dan never brought it up again but I never forgot it.

That spring, Boden and Shannon were in different 5th grade classes. Boden was doing fairly well and his teacher liked him, but Shannon was having a lot of trouble in his class. His teacher said that he wouldn't listen to her and that he was constantly disruptive to the classroom. He started getting a lot of 'time out' in the office. A young councilor called me in to school for a meeting and she told me that Shannon was a young man with a lot of anger. "If he doesn't get some help now, he's going to have a lot of problems with it in the future." There it was. I have never been able to forget what she said, but at the time I just didn't see it. Still, I wanted to send him for counseling but he wouldn't hear of it and he called his dad. "Counseling is for idiots," John told him. "Don't you go; you don't need it."

Later the teacher called me to come to school for a parent teacher conference. She must have been in an especially bad mood that day because she was angry and she painted a picture of Shannon as being a little monster. She said that he was disrespectful and that he would not stay in his seat. "He stirs up the other students with his antics. He's making it impossible for me to control my classroom. You've got to do something with him or he's going to end up spending the rest of the year in detention." It wasn't so much what she said but the angry and demeaning way she said it. I left her classroom in tears. Later that day, when I had regained my composure, I wondered, *If she can do that to me, what kind of effect must she have on the kids?* I had to get Shannon out of there.

There was a sweet little one-room schoolhouse for grades 1–6 out in the hills near where Dan lived. I wasn't sure that I was being textbook appropriate but it seemed like a good solution to ask Dan if, for the last two months of that school year, Shannon could live with him and go to school out by Windy Nip. "Sure, if you want," Dan replied, wanting to be helpful. I think Dan was a little surprised by my request but he didn't seem to mind. It was perfect because the school only held classes Monday through Thursday and the rest of the week Dan always spent at my house anyway so Shannon would still be spending three days a week at home. It would also give the twins some time apart from each other, which would be good for everyone. It seemed like a win-win situation. And Shannon did do well in this new setting. For a couple of months, he had a new life with new friends that he liked and got along with. It was a growing experience for him, I think, to be in a situation where he couldn't blame everything that went wrong on his brother. At the end of the semester, his new teacher gave him the book 'Tom Sawyer and Huckleberry Finn' and passed him on to 6th grade. When he came back home for the summer, Dan gave up his place in Windy Nip and came home with him. We were now a family of five.

I look back on those times with fond memories. In many ways, it was a very fun time and what I consider as one of the most 'normal' times of my life. We always had a full house. Emily was turning 16, and she was dating a guy who was twenty but he was very sweet and thoughtful. Sometimes, they would hang out at the house when I had to work. I'd come home tired after a 12-hour shift and dinner would be cooking, there would be a blazing fire in the stove, the house would be warm and cozy and everyone would be happily watching movies or just hanging out together. I loved coming home to a house full of happy people. The boys had started Junior High and they had several sets of friends who lived nearby. Some group or another was always in and out of the house.

In those early days of our relationship, Dan was a very positive force in our life. He was a hard worker and completely trustworthy. It was a new thing for me to feel that I could really trust someone. I recognized, from the start, that Dan was a good man, and I made a clear commitment to myself to do what I could to keep us together as a strong and loving family. Years have gone by and I still trust Dan completely, in all situations, to do the honorable thing. What I no longer trust are his moods. His moods, in the end, were our undoing.

It was the last day of school and we decided that we would leave that very day, when school got out, on a family summer vacation at Big Bend Hot Springs. We had a lot of gear so we needed to take both my car and Dan's truck. Besides, we could separate the boys that way. We stopped at the Junior High school. Dan picked Boden up and they took off. Emily and I waited around for Shannon to get out of class. When he finally showed up, he refused to get into the car. "I don't want to go to Big Bend. You said that you weren't going to make me go on trips anymore." I think I had said that, in frustration, after some other trip we had taken. I regretted saying it now. I liked to keep my word to my kids whenever possible.

"Look, it's a family vacation. Of course you have to go. Did you think that I would let you just sit at home alone for the next ten days."

"I'll be fine," he insisted. "I'm not going with you!"

"You are going. I'm not leaving you here. There's no food at the house and no one to look in on you and the school bus just left. You don't even have a way to get home," I said this, trying to reason with him. Looking back, I can say that was, perhaps, an early sign of Shannon's illness. When he had his mind set on something, there was no reasoning with him. They say that there is, approximately, a 30 percent chance that if one identical twin has schizophrenia, the second one will develop it also. That is one way they know that there is a genetic component to the illness. Boden, although every bit as stubborn as his brother, could usually be swayed with a strong and reasonable argument; how I held on, years later, to that precious thread of evidence that Boden was going to stay healthy.

"I'm not going. You can just leave me here," he insisted again. As he said this he stood there, like a rock, not budging.

How could he even think that I would just drive off and leave him standing there on the side of the road like that? He was only 13 years old. Dan was getting further and further down the highway and I was losing my patience.

"You said that I wouldn't have to go on any more trips," he kept repeating stubbornly.

Finally, after going back and forth like that for another four or five minutes, I totally lost it. "I don't care what I said," I screamed at the top of my lungs. "Just get in the car!"

Still, he just stood there looking at me defiantly. A man passing by at that moment looked at Shannon and he said, "I think she means it, son, better get in the car!" I had the sense that my guardian angel had just dropped by again. Shannon looked at the man for a moment and then, without saying a word, he got into the back seat of the car and we took off.

By the time we caught up with Dan, we had all recovered from the drama, the sun was shining, and we were ready for a good time. I looked at Shannon. It was hard for me to figure him out sometimes, but he didn't have any of the early signs of schizophrenia, and I really wasn't looking for it. He wasn't socially withdrawn. In fact, he had lots of friends and everyone liked him. He was physically very coordinated. He rode motorcycles up and down our steep, bumpy hills and he didn't get hurt. He was having some problems in reading, and he was in a special education class for that, but in other subjects like math and science, he was doing very well. No, he was mostly a normal kid and I look back on those years and I feel grateful. It is not well understood why the average age for developing schizophrenia is between 17 and 25 years old but there are some who develop schizophrenia as a child. I count my blessings that we had Shannon, relatively intact, until he turned 23.

When we got to big Bend and we were soaking in the natural hot pools beside the rushing Pit River, riding inner tubes down the rapids, having barbeques or just laying around in our hammocks, I watched Shannon for signs that he was not happy to be there with his family. There were none. He was having as good a time as the rest of us were. When the boys started up with their bickering and fighting and driving everyone mad, Dan pulled out a pair of brand new bright-red boxing gloves that he had recently bought. He showed the boys how to put them on and lace them up, and he gave them some instruction; then we all sat around the campsite and watched as they started a boxing match. In this way, they got out some of their wound up energy and aggression without anyone getting hurt and peace was again restored.

Later on that summer, when John had picked the kids up for his couple of weeks with them, Dan and I went back to Big Bend. We were looking forward to spending some time alone together. We had the place to ourselves, and we decided to set up our camp, in a secluded spot, close to where the trail narrowed down just a short walk to the river. There in the broad and Rocky River valley, where the rocks were bleached white by the sun and surrounded by pine forests, were several small stone pools at the edge of the river. Hot crystal-clear spring water welled up and flooded the little pools and cold river water spilled in at the edges creating the perfect temperature. We soaked in the pools and talked about the kids. We lay in the sun and swam in the cool water. At the very height of the heat of the day, we walked the mile or so along the path that was cut through thick vegetation to where there was a developed pool. This pool was shaded, artfully, by cement and stonework. It looked out upon a mass of rapids with foam that sprayed high into the air and that pounded, like a herd of wild stampeding stallions, down the river to quieter waters. The days passed lazily in quiet companionship. We read our books and took long walks and sat around a campfire at night telling our stories. On our last afternoon, I was feeling high and euphoric from the flow and sheer beauty of the days. I got down on my knees in the white and grey, sun-bleached rocks with the river flowing swiftly by and the sun shining down and I gave thanks to the Gods for all the blessings in my life. I said a prayer of thanks for all of the love and light that I had been shown, for my children, for Dan, for my home and for the work that I was allowed to do in nursing the sick. I held my hands up to the heavens in acknowledgement and gratitude for all the wonder and blessings of the universe. I was totally and completely happy. Not more than thirty minutes after that, Dan asked me to marry him. "Yes, of course. I want to marry you with all of my heart." In the beginning, Dan and I had made mention of marriage several times, but after a while, he never brought it up. But that was what I wanted. I wanted to get married to Dan, and now he had finally asked me. I was ecstatic.

That evening, we shared a bottle of wine to celebrate. We stayed in the hot pools by our campsite until late, kissing and talking and being sweet and sexy. When we got back to our campsite, we put some music on. I was very high on life and on the wine, and I danced around in the warm night air under the stars in ecstasy for over an hour. Dan retreated into the tent almost immediately, but in my euphoric trance, I could not break away from the starry night and dancing under the open sky. By the time I crawled into the tent, Dan was falling asleep. Perhaps that is why, two days later, he told me that he was taking it back. He didn't want to get married. It had been a mistake, a mood, nothing more. It hurt me very deeply when he said that but he didn't seem to care. It was the first in a long, drawn out series of Dan pulling away from me and from our family.

Chapter 42
Emily's Coming of Age

At the beginning of the following summer, we went back to Big Bend Hot Springs. We were all going to spend a few days together, and then Emily and I were going to drive up to Canada for a road trip, and Dan was going to head back home with the boys. This time Shannon was a willing participant.

That school year, Emily had decided that she didn't like going to the local High School. I gave her a lot of leeway to make her own choices, partly because that was our agreement but more so because I knew that she could handle it. She was coming of age, and she made thoughtful choices which she followed through with, when it was appropriate. First she tried out the alternative public school for the kids that didn't do well with the school routine. At Osprey, you only had to attend school a couple of days a week and then you did the rest of the work at home. The boys had wanted to go there also but I wouldn't let them because they were too undisciplined. Emily was a different matter though. If that's what she wanted to do, I knew that she could pull it off. She attended the Osprey Learning Center for a few months, but she didn't like that either. Then she tried going out to Petrolia which was an alternative private school out by the coast. It was expensive and a long drive to get there. I picked her up every Friday and brought her home for the weekend, and every Monday morning Dan would drive her back on his way to work in Windy Nip. I think it was a good experience for her but she grew tired of that as well. Finally, she studied to take her GED and she passed it. In the fall, she planned to be looking for a place to rent with her girlfriend, Shante. They would both be attending the local Jr. College.

After a few fun-filled days at Big Bend, Dan and the boys headed home and Emily and I headed north to the town of Shasta. The weather was unseasonably cool and cloudy. That first night, camping at a higher altitude in our cheap little tent, we were so freezing that we hardly slept. "How can we head north to Canada when it's too cold for us here?" I wanted to know. We were walking around town trying to decide what do next when a big dark cloud suddenly appeared out of nowhere, right above our heads, blocking out the sun and all of its warmth. We were shivering. Glancing, at that precise moment, to our left we noticed that we were standing in front of a travel agency with a large poster of a sunny beach in Hawaii displayed, invitingly, in the window. Emily and I looked at the picture and then we looked at each other as we stood there shivering. "Let's go in and check it out," I suggested casually.

"Good idea," Emily agreed. She didn't like cold weather much more than I did, and she loved beaches. The only place that there was a cheap flight that we could book for the next day on such short notice, the travel agent informed us, was a flight leaving from LA.

"Let's do it," we agreed. We bought the tickets, rushed out to our car, and started on the 900-mile drive to LA. Our plane would be leaving in less than 24 hours.

The next day, we were warm and happy standing at a payphone by the beach. We called Dan. "Guess where we are?" I said hardly able to contain my delight.

"I don't know. Oregon," was his guess. He didn't sound pleased to be playing this little guessing game with me.

"We're in Maui," I blurted out, feeling wildly spontaneous and enjoying every minute of it.

"You're where? Hawaii, how did you end up there?" He actually sounded impressed. It was very good natured of him to take it so well when he was stuck at home working every day and hanging out with the boys who were undoubtedly driving him crazy with their fighting. He probably wasn't having nearly as much fun as we were.

"Well, have a great time. We're fine, don't worry." I knew that I needn't worry. Dan was holding down the fort.

That first night we couldn't find anywhere to stay. As far as I could tell, there weren't any hotels on that particular island, and I couldn't find any campgrounds either. After driving around until after dark, we ended up frustrated, parked on the side of the road, sleeping in our compact rental car. It was very uncomfortable, and the next morning I was in a terrible mood. To make matters worse, I had started my period in the middle of the night. Here I was in a tropical paradise with my favorite traveling companion, and all I could think about was how miserable I was feeling and how I needed a shower. When I stopped at a gas station to gas up and the middle aged Hawaiian attendant came up to the window and asked me how my day was going, I burst into tears. "What's wrong?" he asked in surprise. He sounded very kind and concerned. I cried all the harder. I blurted out my story about how we had arrived in Maui the day before but we couldn't find anywhere to stay. There didn't appear to be hotels or campgrounds. I didn't know what we were going to do. He smiled at me, a very sweet and patient smile. He said gently, "I have a house but I never stay in it. I don't like to be indoors. Here, on this island, it is so beautiful and warm. I just sleep wherever I am. There's no need to worry."

I started laughing through my tears. Of course he was right. I felt so silly. Somehow, I had forgotten how to stay open to the beauty around me, and I had gotten stuck in my small world where things had to be a certain way or something was very wrong.

"I just sleep wherever I am," he repeated. "There are wonderful beaches everywhere." I felt like I had just had another visit from my guardian angel. "And there are campgrounds too!" he added. He gave me the address of the office that had listings of places to camp and their availability. It was nearby. As we drove away, Emily, who had been happy and enjoying our adventure the entire time, was relieved to see that my mood had improved. "That man was like some sort of Guru," I said to Emily who had been in the restroom and had missed the whole interaction. "He was so peaceful and content, and he just went with the flow of things. He taught me a lesson to be more in the moment and to stop trying to create a disaster when, in reality, all is well." From that moment on, our trip was fantastic!

The next morning, we woke up, all snuggled in our sleeping bags, in a nice campground that was close to the beach. It had rained heavily that night and water had poured in at the loose seems of our cheap tent. It felt like we were in a bathtub with our sleeping bags floating in a large puddle of warm water. We lay there for a while, in no hurry to get up, talking about our plans for the day. When we did finally emerge from the tent, we took an outdoor shower to freshen up but it was all the same really. The weather was so warm and humid that it was all a pleasant, embryonic dampness, and it really didn't make that much difference whether one was wet or dry, showered or not showered.

There was a very exotic, outdoor café a short walk away, and we went there for breakfast. We sat there by the coy pond, enjoying ourselves in the tropical setting and reminiscing about the first time we had come to Maui together. Emily had been almost two. She didn't remember the trip at all but she did remember Lano. He had visited us a few times over the years when he was driving through on hwy. 101 to San Francisco, and we still talked on the phone quite frequently. "We met here on this island," I told her. "But we were on the other side of the island. This side is less developed and this is where the bamboo forests are." We were really looking forward to exploring a bamboo forest.

On our explorations, we passed through a small town with a hospital and we stopped to check it out. The nurses were very friendly as they showed me around. "It's not that different from my hospital," I told them. "Where I work is kind of isolated and we have to transfer out all our really sick patients as well."

"If you decide to move here, you have a job," they told me as they waved goodbye. Many a time over the years, when it has been cold and rainy for weeks in Northern California, I have thought of that little hospital where it is always warm and it is surrounded by palm trees.

Over the next week, we managed to get a delicious sampling of the many pleasures of island life. One day, we rented a kayak and explored a large beautiful bay where we swam in the warm water in and amongst schools of colorful tropical fish. The next day, we went out on a bigger boat and watched in awe and delight as dolphins frolicked around us arcing gracefully out of the water, high into the air. We wandered, for hours, through a thick bamboo forest and then hiked up to a sacred waterfall where rainbows gathered. We sat mesmerized, certain that we could feel the spirits of the mountain. On our last day, we explored art galleries and fine restaurants, and we danced to live reggae music to a band that turned out to be from back home in Humboldt County. They knew us and dedicated their first song of the evening to us. It was a very fine time down to the very last minute. I had visited Maui with Emily, 14 years earlier, and since then she had grown into a beautiful young woman and a delightful companion. I felt very fortunate indeed to have been able to spend that magical week with Emily in Hawaii before she got busy in the pursuit of her own dreams.

That summer, Emily moved, an hour drive north of home, to a town close to the Junior College that she and her friend Shante would be attending. They set up a meditation alter in their little apartment, and they began to include periods of meditation in their daily routine.

Then in the beginning of summer, Shante invited Emily to go with her down to Southern California to attend a large spiritual gathering. It was attended by people from all over the world. Emily was very moved by the message of inner peace and love that was the central theme of this Eastern religion, and she requested a private meeting with the Nuns. They had a long talk during which she became even more inspired. She had a feeling of recognition, she told me later. She felt, beyond a shadow of a doubt, as if it was what she was meant to do in this lifetime. The Nuns told her that she was too young to come and live with them but that if she was still interested when she turned 18, she could return to the ashram and they would ease her into the monastic life. She could live outside in the community but work with them during the day and see if it really was her calling. Emily was just turning 17. The following year in early September, the day that she turned 18, she packed her belongings into her little golden Nissan compact convertible and drove to Southern California to see if she was really meant to be a Yogic Nun. She felt certain that she was.

Chapter 43
Boys, Boys, Boys

With Emily living out of the area, my life became overrun with boys and boy stuff. The guys had gotten into cars and motorcycles and engine work. They were good at it too. There were cars everywhere. They each had their own car and friends brought cars to be worked on. If a car was a hopeless, mechanical mess, it was sometimes abandoned on my property, but instead of towing it away, the boys would insist on keeping these eyesores around for extra parts. Once, when I had gone to the time, aggravation and great expense of having a broken down car with no paper work towed away, I was shocked to find it sitting in my front yard when I came home from work. *It's like a bad penny that keeps turning up*, I thought to myself in dismay. I wasn't a drinker but I needed a drink! The boys had towed it back, and they were furious with me. That was the thing. It was very hard on me when they were angry with me. It made me miserable so, instead, I put up with having my beautiful, wild property turned into a wrecking yard. I did, however, draw the line at rebuilding engines in my living room on the coffee table. The house was my domain and anything they left lying around that didn't belong would quickly disappear. So we came to a compromise of sorts that allowed us to coexist. I leave your car parts outside alone but no car parts in the house. Their room was kind of a grey area though. They had car parts stashed in all corners of their rooms, on the desk, under the desk, under the bed, spilling off of the shelves, but nothing that put off fumes was allowed. If we could keep the house clean, I figured that I could put up with the car stuff until they grew up and left home. Then I would clear it all away and put little Buddha statues all around instead.

The next couple of years were very nice, normal years. I worked, Dan worked, and the boys went to High School. We were a family, but we each had responsibilities and a schedule that we needed to follow. Boden and Shannon had their friends to hang out with, and Dan and I had a little more time to do things together. There were frustrations to be sure, teenage boys and speeding tickets, teenage boys wanting to drink alcohol, teenage boys being pushed to do their schoolwork, but, in general, life had a good flow to it and everyone was healthy and safe and happy, or so I thought.

When we first got together, Dan had wanted to experience family life. His older sisters had both left home by the time he was starting school, and his father had left his mother as well so, like me, he had been brought up as a single child living with mom. Dan resented his mother for a lot of reasons. After he knew my mom for a while, he started appreciating his mother more I think. At any rate, he was curious as to what it would be like to be in a family so he took us on. It turned out to be more than he had bargained for. The frustration of parenting two headstrong, teenage boys was more than he could handle, but the problems went deeper than that. One morning I heard him crashing around downstairs. I went down to see what he was doing. It looked like he was packing his things. "I'm moving out," he told me when I asked him what was going on. We tried to talk about it, but Dan was never very good at expressing his feelings, and he wasn't able to make me understand what it was all about for him, why he was leaving us. We both cried but in the end, he got into his truck and he drove away. It was so sudden and unexpected. I didn't understand it, and I blamed it on my age. "He wants a younger woman," I told myself, "a woman without so many responsibilities, someone more carefree." I could understand that. I was a bore. My job, the kids, our very home were all high impact responsibilities that needed constant attention. Why would anyone sign up for that if they didn't have to? We would manage. We always did.

Dan dropped out of my life for almost a year. I didn't go after him. What would have been the point? If he didn't want to be with us, then he shouldn't. I got very depressed though, for a while, but I'd been through worse. I knew I'd snap out of it eventually. The boys had a friend who didn't have a stable home to go to and he ended up moving in with us for that school year. It was kind of fun living with my three sons. We made a list of things that needed to get done and a schedule. Following our schedule, the guys took turns taking care of the day-to-day chores of living in the country, such as bringing in firewood and pumping water and taking the garbage to the dump. The three of them, together, seemed to be a good balance and there was relative peace and harmony in our home. Peace and harmony in our home was what mattered most to me.

I dated a little bit for a while, but it wasn't that much fun. It was almost a chore. There was no one I really felt comfortable with. I liked to be with my old friends and with my family. It was hard for me to establish new connections. Lano came down from Washington a couple of times and spent a few days helping us out with some projects that needed a man's hand, but he wasn't ready to move down to California, and I wasn't ready to move up to Washington and anyway he had a girlfriend or two or maybe even three and so we kept it at just friends.

The following summer, Dan walked back into my life, or should I say he kayaked back into my life. He came, one Sunday afternoon, bringing gifts and he asked me if I wanted to go kayaking. The area where we live is rich with rivers. Getting out on the river on a sunny day is a marvelous thing to do. "Alright, that sounds like fun. Let's do it." I didn't intend to get emotionally involved again but before long we were once again a couple except that now he had his house and I had mine. Now he could leave whenever he felt like it.

During this time period, Shannon was doing well and it was Boden who ended up getting into some serious trouble. He was hanging out with some long time boyhood friends who broke into their neighbor's house and took some things. I don't believe that he took an active part in the theft, but he went along for the ride and he was spotted leaving with his friends. He was in big trouble. I hired a lawyer and it took a year and a few thousand dollars to be resolved, but I sort of fell apart while we were going through it. I was very shook up by the whole thing. I found myself obsessing over it and becoming very depressed. I cried easily over nothing. Perhaps my exaggerated reaction had something to do with the trauma of my mother's arrests when I was a child. I don't know but I ended up going to counseling over it, and I could not shake the depression. That was when I decided to take Boden and Shannon to Nepal. I had wanted to go to Nepal for years. This was my chance to fulfill a lifetime dream, cure myself of obsessing about the court stuff, and expose my two young men to another view of life. I hoped that the trip would give them a broader view and that it would be a maturing experience for them.

Chapter 44
The Jomsom Trek

I invited Dan to go to Nepal with us but he wasn't interested. He did, however, drive us to the airport where we all spent the night together in a hotel. The plane would be leaving early the next morning. I have always found getting out of town to be stressful, and this day was no exception. Early in the morning, John had called me about Boden and his court case. He was lecturing me and yelling at me about legal issues and disciplining Boden, and then Dan started lecturing me about Boden as well. Everyone was getting on my case while Boden slept peacefully in his bed. I was suddenly really glad that I was going to be leaving town for a while. Work had been very stressful of late also. I had recently become the nurse manager of ER, OB, and Acute Care, and everyone had something to complain about. The entire hospital was on my case. I wasn't sure how much longer I could take it. Even with meditation and my positive affirmations, although I'm sure that they helped, I was having a difficult time getting control over my rising anxiety. I needed to get away. Once we were out of town and down the road a ways, things began to lighten up a bit and it turned out to be a great evening. Dan was in a good mood, I was getting excited about our trip, and the boys were ready for another travel adventure. We were on a roll.

It was a long journey to Kathmandu, and it seemed like we lost a day in there somewhere. We stopped in Thailand for a few hours to change planes. It was hot and humid at 1 a.m. but we had a delicious Thai dinner before driving through the crowded streets back to the airport. When we finally arrived, tired and disheveled, in Kathmandu, I arranged with one of the many taxi drivers who were competing for fairs to be taken to The Kathmandu Guest House. I had read about it in the Lonely Planet Travel Guide, and I was very set on that particular hotel. "Yes, I know it well. I will take you there," the driver assured me. He took us instead to a dumpy looking place with a similar name.

"This can't be it," I kept saying. When we got up to our room, it was so dingy and disappointing that I finally realized that we had definitely been conned.

"It's alright, let's just stay here," Shannon said, taking off his pack and sitting on the bed. He was tired of traveling but I was very upset.

"I want to be at the Kathmandu Guest House and this isn't it." I hadn't taken my pack off.

Boden surprised me by saying assertively, "If this isn't where you want to be, then let's go." I was relieved that he was being assertive in my favor. We marched back downstairs and the driver, not wanting to lose his customers, assured us that he could take us to the right place this time. When we got to the real guesthouse, we were all happy that we hadn't settled. It was very lovely with gardens and an outdoor café and many international tourists. It felt very cheerful and safe, and it was reasonably priced.

I knew that we needed a trekking pass to go up into the mountains so our same driver, who was still hanging around, took me to a nearby travel agency while the boys showered and freshened up. My plan had been to go without a guide and just follow the book but the man at the agency convinced me to hire a guide to show us the way, the best places to stay, and to be our interpreter. It was actually an excellent deal, price wise and really, it was a good idea to have a guide. However, when I got back to the hotel, jet lag started catching up with me, and I suddenly felt exhausted. I lay down for a nap while the guys went to the hotel's outdoor café for dinner. Outside, it had grown dark. As I lay there in the sleeping bag, trying to rest, my thoughts started going crazy. I got really paranoid and I thought that the guide, who I hadn't met yet, was going to push me off of a cliff and steal my, what? I didn't really have that much. I was sounding like my mother now. Unable to rest and getting more and more anxious with every passing minute, I went out to the restaurant to find Boden and Shannon. I sat down with them and told them what I was thinking. I couldn't hold it in. My thoughts were getting out of control, and I was starting to feel terrified. They both looked at me. They were so calm, and they were obviously enjoying themselves.

"That's ridiculous," Boden said, giving me that 'whatever' look. "Nothing like that is going to happen."

"Here, Mom, you need a drink. You're sounding just like Grandma now," Shannon said as he shoved his rum and coke, across the table, over towards me. There was no restriction on the drinking age in Katmandu where boys were men at a very young age. I sat there sipping at the rum and coke, trying to calm my nerves. Boden and Shannon were talking about a movie that they had seen on the flight over and the somewhat normal tone of the conversation was starting to ground me. Mercifully, the insane paranoia left me as suddenly as it had come. We hung out for a couple of hours, and I had dinner and a couple of drinks with my two young men. We laughed and talked about the traffic and how it didn't seem to matter what side of the road people drove on. The cars were all over the place.

"It's worse than in Mexico," Boden observed.

"How do people survive?" Shannon wondered. He was amazed that there were people in the world that drove more wildly than he did and that here, in Nepal, it was actually acceptable.

The next day, we were introduced to Gokarna, the man who was to be our guide. He was a very nice, easy going, and capable man who spoke fluent English. He appeared to be in his late 30s or maybe a bit older. I felt immediately comfortable with him, and I was extremely glad that he would be accompanying us on our trek. Gokarna took us to the airport where we caught a plane into Pokara. We stayed there overnight, resting up, waiting for Gokarna to arrive on the bus. The next day, we continued on to Jomsom, together with our guide, in a small plane with 10 or 12 seats. When I stepped off the plane at the tiny landing strip in Jomsom, the site of the surrounding, glacial covered mountains, took my breath away. We were obviously entering a very remote and spectacularly beautiful country. This is what I had come for. Not the food, not the cities or the crowds, not local crafts but for these snow covered mountains that loomed so impressively in the background. I had read in the guidebook that the Jomsom trek is the final third of the Annapurna circuit. It follows the Kali Gandaki Valley which is surrounded by the Annapurna and Dhaulagiri Mountains with the Himalayas towering, majestically, in the distance. That is what I had come for, and I could see, as I stepped down from the plane, that I was not going to be disappointed. As I watched Gokarna talking with the ground crew, directing Boden and Shannon where to pick up our things and herding us all, protectively, over to a little café for a delicious cup of Yak milk tea, I began to wonder how I had ever imagined that I could make this trip without him.

As we made our way through the town of Jomsom with its cobble stone streets and rock walls and little stone houses surrounded by the stark but spectacular beauty of rocks and mountains against slate blue sky, I felt like I had stepped into a fairy tale. The main street led out of town and on to the Jomsom trail which had been the pathway of all traveling and commerce for centuries. There were no roads and no motorized vehicles. They could not have made it along the steep and narrow and often inhospitable footpaths. Once away from the village, all that remained was rock and sky with breathtaking glimpses of glacial mountain peaks. We were walking through an area that was known for its high velocity winds, but thankfully, it was pretty calm that day. After walking for a couple of hours, we came to another little village and we stopped at a teahouse for some lunch. The teahouse was very lovely with big picture windows that looked out on the spectacular mountain scenery. I was finding that the Nepalese people were very beautiful as well with classic features, high cheekbones, broad faces, lovely large eyes and beautiful welcoming smiles. My guys didn't seem to be as taken by the culture and surroundings as I was. They sat down, ordered a coke and hard-boiled eggs, and took out their playing cards. While I sat and looked around me in wonderment and delight, they played poker. They seemed to be in their own, identical twin world.

When we got to Kagbeni, at around 10,000 foot elevation, we were tired and we were beginning to feel the altitude a bit also. I had a slight headache. According to the guidebook, Kagbeni was as close as one can get, in Nepal, to Lo Monthang, the capitol of Mustang in Tibet. It did have a very Tibetan feel to it. We stopped for the night in a teahouse appropriately called Shangrila where we got a room with three little wooden cots, one for each of us. Gokarna made his own arrangements. We were the only guests and that intensified the feeling of remoteness. I loved it. After resting for a bit, Gokarna came to see if we wanted dinner so the four of us went into the dining room. We sat down at the long wooden table. It was the only furniture in the chilly, stone room which was dimly lit by a single lantern. The lamplight flickered across the faces of my companions and reflected off the light in their eyes. Everyone seemed content and happy. The starkness and the simplicity of these mountain villages and the people that inhabited them resonated with some part of me. I felt very at home. The woman of the house brought a large ceramic bowl that was filled with glowing coals and placed it under the table for warmth. As the welcome heat spread upwards from our feet to our chins, we were very aware of the fact that we were indeed in a faraway land. Gokarna and I had rice and dahl, the food of the local people, but Boden and Shannon had coke and eggs again. They pretty much lived on that diet for most of the trip. Back in our room, we threw out our sleeping bags on the hard wooden cots that lacked a mattress and turned in for the night.

The next day started with an extreme climb of almost a three thousand foot elevation gain in only a couple of miles. The going was very steep and arduous, and I quickly fell behind. Gokarna stayed with the guys, and I was glad for that. I didn't

222

have to worry about them. At one point, I caught a glimpse of Gokarna walking along with a big smile on his face. He was listening to Shannon's Walkman. When I finally made it to where the trail began to level off, the boys were sitting on the ground looking totally wiped out and talking to a traveling monk in saffron robes who sat cross-legged in the rocks looking peaceful and at home. A herd of tiny cows were passing by and they fascinated Boden. It was the first time that I had seen him take interest in our surroundings since we had left Kathmandu, where he had been fascinated by the crazy traffic. Then a herd of tiny goats passed by while we were still sitting there resting. The tinkling of all the bells they wore, in different tones, seemed like the music of the mountains.

We stopped that night at a teahouse in Jharkot, too tired to walk another step. The next day, feeling rested, we took a day hike up to Muktinath. I felt like we had gone somewhere in a time machine. I no longer had any idea what century we were in, perhaps medieval times. Gokarna, Shannon, and I stopped in the village just before the final climb up to Muktinath to have lunch. Boden had stayed back in Jharkot because he was having trouble with the altitude, and he said his lungs hurt. I suspected that they hurt because of the hashish he had managed to buy from a stranger, somewhere along the path, in one of the remote villages. It just went to show that there was nowhere on earth one could go to escape such temptations. We sat outside on the roof top café and watched the activity in the streets below us with interest. Small stone houses lined either side of the broad, open street. In the middle of the roadway, several women sat weaving on floor looms roughly cut out of large beams, and off to one side of the street a group of women were laughing and chatting as they washed their dishes and clothes at a communal faucet. "It's so incredible here," I said to Gokarna, feeling, once again, like I had fallen under some sort of magic spell.

"You should come back to Nepal soon, and I could show you my village. You would really like it. Tourists never go there. You could stay with me and my wife and my children." Gokarna and I liked each other. It felt like we were old friends. Maybe we were, from some other lifetime. We sat for a while longer, contentedly watching village life. A beautiful young mother was sitting on her doorstep spinning wool while her child sat quietly watching and towards the edge of town a couple of men were herding their miniature goats down the street. You could hear their bells tinkling in the distance as they hurried along. The village appeared to be only a few blocks long, and it looked like a good percentage of the population was out of doors doing daily chores in the noonday sun. I tried to imagine what life was like in the winter here in Muktinath. It would be cold, I imagined. Very cold and everything would be covered in snow. It would probably be dark much of the time. You would be truly isolated. There were no stores to speak of, no entertainment, no fuel to keep the homes heated. I suddenly had a longing to experience life here in the winter but I also knew that it was, at least partly, a romantic illusion. In reality, it would be very hard and lonely and I wouldn't last long. Still, the people seemed to be happy and I felt certain that within the outward appearance of hardship there was also a deep richness and a great beauty.

Shannon decided to walk the couple of miles back to Jharkot to hang out with his brother while Gokarna and I continued on to the monastery. Here, already at over 12,000 feet, we had a view of Himalayan peaks towering high above us. The monastery of Muktinath was a study in color. The sky was a brilliant blue streaked with grey clouds. The mountains were white in their shrouding of snow. The ravens that rested in the silver, leafless trees were a silky jet-black and monks, dressed in their saffron and ocher gowns, glided silently between the ancient, weathered stone temples. At the request of Gokarna, one of the monks pressed a dab of powdered incense to my third eye and uttered an incantation. His finger was icy cold and yet I felt its mysterious blessing burning deeply into my mind. It was a mystical experience.

Gokarna led me to where there was an open structure built in a semi-circle. Every few feet, at about six feet high, there was a beautiful ornate faucet in the form of a deity. "Each morning at dawn, these faucets are opened up and icy glacial water pours through them. The monks go from faucet to faucet, standing naked under the water, in order to free their body of the desire for worldly comforts."

"It's definitely a calling to choose this life," I was saying to Kokarna and thinking about how I didn't like to be cold. Still, this way of life, I felt certain, held a great beauty that outsiders had no concept of. Muktinath was considered a sacred destination for many travelers. Both Buddhists and Hindus made the Pilgrimage to Muktinath to worship at the temple in which, miraculously, there burnt the fire of an eternal flame. Gokarna took me to see this eternal flame and we knelt down to say prayers, pay homage, and to make our offering. I knew that I had received a great blessing just to be able to experience such a sacred and timeless way of life. Perhaps the blessings that I received that day were even more far reaching than I imagined.

That night, as I lay awake in my sleeping bag, I thought about my life back home. I was basically still a single woman. Dan wasn't interested in any permanent commitments, and it wasn't too long before my sons would be leaving home. I would be alone again. Traveling always brought on a bout of introspection. It was another benefit of travel as far as I was concerned. I loved it here, and I was incredibly curious about these beautiful people and their way of life. But I probably was not going to be moving to the mountains of Nepal any time soon. I realized that where we lived was very beautiful as well and even somewhat remote. "What did I want to do with my life?" I asked myself. That was the first time that I really began to think seriously about becoming a Nurse Practitioner. I wanted to see another side of medicine. I loved being a nurse but I wanted to do something that was a little different; something that still utilized and built upon the skills that I had developed over the years; something interesting and challenging that would bring me satisfaction. I had read somewhere that people often went into medicine to heal themselves. Perhaps that was part of it too. My sons would be graduating High School in a couple of years. Perhaps then, I should go back to school. I wasn't too old yet. I wondered how long it would take. It was something to consider.

Because I was getting some painful blisters on my feet, I had to walk even slower than before. I left Jharkot early in the morning while the boys still slept. Gokarna stayed behind to see that they got packed up and headed in the right direction. We were going back down to Jomsom. Since it was mostly downhill, we were hoping to make it to Jomsom by late afternoon. This time, the area known for its heavy winds lived up to its reputation. I had to cover my face with my scarf peering through the thin gauze to avoid getting sand and dirt blown, at high speed, into my eyes. With nothing to stand in its way, the wind howled up through the Kali Gandaki Valley. It was a great strain to push my way, step by step, forward against the gale winds. The noise was deafening. I could not hear anything outside of the moaning of the wind.

I was still walking by myself, and now I wished that Gokarna and the boys were with me. Alone and pushing my way against the wind, in and amongst a valley of nothing but rocks for as far as the eye could see, I started to feel very vulnerable and a little frightened. It was with a sense of relief that I finally arrived in Jomsom. The wind had died down and the boys and Gokarna, who had gotten ahead of me at some point, were waiting for me in a little café. To see their smiling happy faces made my moment of fearfulness dissolve and fade away without leaving a trace. I sat down and ordered a cup of their delicious milky coffee and some home-baked bread. It was exactly what I wanted. The boys took out their deck of cards and played some poker. There was definitely something to be said for routines. They could be so comforting at times.

That night, again, there was no one else staying in the teahouse where we were. We had the place to ourselves. It was just our little family, me, the guys and Gokarna, by candle light. I was able to take a hot bath for the first time in days. It made me feel really refreshed and festive, and I put on some clean clothes that I had been saving. Then we had a sweet dinner together, the four of us. I wrote in my journal "Gokarna, funny and unusually talkative, after two glasses of apple brandy."

The next day, we hiked to another small village that was very picturesque. To escape the winds, which could be brutal, the town had constructed tunnels that went from one side of the street to the other using as their main building material, nothing other than rocks. In these rock tunnels, one could walk, for short distances, protected from the wind. I sat on the porch of our tea house and watched as mules and cows wandered through the narrow stone streets. Across the street, some little kids were playing and chickens kept running into this ladies' house. She would run the chickens back out into the street shaking her broom at them. The kids would chase the chickens, laughing with delight, as the chickens would run back into the house to get away from them. Then the woman would chase the chickens out of her house again and the game would go round and round. I had started reading the book *Seven Years in Tibet*, and I took out my book to read some now. As I looked around me, I felt like I was there, in the book, in Tibet.

When we got to lower elevations, the scenery began to change. I missed the stark contrasts of high elevation but this country was beautiful as well. The lower we got, the greener it became. We stopped at a waterfall in the middle of nowhere where there was a sweet little tea house that had giant picture windows that let in the light and the surrounding spectacular views. It was perched precipitously on the side of the mountain. Far below, the Kali Gondaki River rushed through the canyon. The café was filled with foreigners all speaking different languages. I was happy to be there with my crew as the boys pulled out their cards and started playing yet another game of poker, seemingly oblivious to the fact that we were hanging on the side of a mountain in a place that was every bit as strange and fascinating as anything out of the Star Wars Movies. I was sorry that Emily wasn't able to come with us. But instead she was adjusting to her new life as a monastic, and she was loving it. The timing was not right for her to be leaving on a trip. She was on a journey right where she was. It was a soul and spirit journey, an inner journey.

We had fallen into a routine where each day I left early in the morning and walked alone until the early afternoon when the guys would catch up and we'd all stop for lunch. Then towards the end of the day, I'd fall behind again and Gocarna would send the boys ahead with a specific destination and walk with me for a while.

One morning, I was walking alone when I came to a long, flimsy-looking swinging bridge that was made of wood. That had been my great fear when planning our trek in Nepal, the rickety swinging bridges that were strung across great and deep chasms. I had crossed some smaller ones and not had too much trouble. I was alright if I didn't look down, and they didn't swing too much. But this one was long. Maybe 40 or more feet to the other side, and it was a long ways down to the Kali Gandaki River far below. I wished that Gokarna was with me but it seemed silly to wait. I didn't know how far behind they were. I gathered up my courage and started out. It wasn't too bad, and I was making good progress. In fact, I was almost to the other side, maybe 15 feet or less to go, when a young Nepalese boy started herding his train of mules on to the bridge. They were loaded with packs and they took up almost the entire width of the bridge. I wasn't sure if I could get by them but neither did I want to turn around and start running back to the other side with a herd of mules on my tail. I found myself, suddenly, right in the middle of a Nepalese swinging bridge nightmare. I didn't have much time to think about it, and I made the decision to stand my ground and try and push pass the mules to the other side which seemed so very close. Wrong decision, for I quickly found myself trapped between the lead mule and the second mule. My feet were the only part of me that was still on the bridge. The rest of me was pushed out over the chasm and the metal cable, that was used as a handrail, was the only thing keeping me from losing my footing and falling to my certain death. At this terrifying vantage point, I could see that there were still a dozen or so mules to come, and the boy was apparently on a time schedule. Even though I was screaming and crying, he wouldn't pull his mules back to let me pass. Just when I thought that I wasn't going to make it, a Nepalese man came along and got the boy to call the mules off of the bridge. I was incredibly grateful to him for that. I was also very shaken up. Minutes later, we all met up at the border checkpoint just on the far side of the bridge, and, still shaking, I told my story. Everyone started to laugh, maybe not Gokarna. When I mentioned it to my sons later, they said they were laughing not at me but at the border patrol guy who had been laughing so hard that he fell over backwards in his chair just as I was leaving the building. I have read that, culturally, the Tibetans feel that it is very important to be able to laugh at oneself and not take oneself too seriously. In that case, I probably should not have been so offended when everyone laughed at my frightful experience. I guess in some ways it was kind of funny, especially since I lived to tell the tale. All's well that ends well!

On one of the last days of our trek, we saw an elderly man hobbling along the rocky trail carrying his wife on his back. "Where are they going?" I asked Gokarna.

"Most likely his wife was ill and he took her to the hospital. Now they are going home. For many there is no other way but to walk."

It was a sobering thought as I realized how much we, in the West, take things for granted.

As we got closer to where there were roads and we would be able to catch a bus back to Pokhara, the little villages seemed to get more populated and busier. We were easing back into modern civilization. Boden and Shannon were tired of walking, and they were looking forward to being in Kathmandu where there was more American type food in the restaurants. I had completely forgotten about all the troubles back home. The hardships that I had seen here in the Annapurna certainly put things in a different perspective. I had absolutely nothing to complain about. I would have been happy to stay longer but I was also happy at the thought of getting back to my own, sweet home in the country. I was even kind of looking forward to getting back to work. And now I had a new dream to work on. I planned to at least look into what would be involved in becoming a Nurse Practitioner.

On our last evening on the trek, we all had a sweet dinner together. After we finished eating, the boys went back up to the room but Gokarna and I remained in the dining hall drinking rum and coke by candle light and talking about our trip. "I think this trip was good for your sons," Gokarna was saying. "In the last few days, they have seemed more mature. They have been concerned about your feet. We all were actually. I wasn't sure you would be able to make it."

My boots, which had been fine and comfortable at home for doing work around the house and walking on the beach, were a total disaster here in the mountains with its extremes of up and down. All ten of my toes were covered in giant blisters and there were several blood blisters underneath my toenails. It had become very painful to walk.

"Well, I'll be glad to give my feet a rest but I am going to miss you and your beautiful country. I'm really glad that you were with us, Gokarna. It wouldn't have been the same without you."

I was starting to miss him already, and I found myself wondering what life was like for married women in this country. We were feeling relaxed and a little euphoric after the long day's hike and a couple of drinks. I felt very content. We had been allowed a glimpse into another world and another way of life, and it had changed us all for the better and it had given me an even deeper appreciation for the amazing diversity of this planet that we live on. I hoped that I would be able to return to Nepal someday.

"You'll be back. Everyone says they'll come back but they don't, but I think that you will be back, and I will take you to see my home and meet my family." Just then we were joined by a Sherpa whom we had seen a while ago carrying a heavy load by a strap that went around his forehead. He told us that he was 72 years old. He was energetic, and in the candlelight he looked much younger than his years. The most amazing thing about him was the light in his eyes that danced and sparkled as he spoke to us about his life as a Sherpa. Gokarna translated for him. "I walk up and down these mountains every day of my life," he told us. "It is what I live for."

Gokarna visited us in Kathmandu the day we left, and he took us to the airport, as our friend, not as our guide. He gave us each a present of a Nepalese scarf that is supposed to bring good fortune. He had been a good friend, and we were going to miss him. When we got back home, we were all happy to see Dan. Spring had arrived in the three of weeks that we had been gone. The front porch was spilling over with fragrant lavender and purple wisteria blossoms. Life was good. Sometimes you have to go far away to see what's right in front of you. Not that long after our trip, Nepal went through a terrible political upheaval. Young communists rose up in the countryside, terrorizing and killing some of the mountain peoples and the entire royal family was murdered. Travel there was no longer considered safe. I wondered what had become of Gokarna. I hoped that he was adjusting and doing alright. Now that things have stabilized politically, I still long to return but there are only a limited number of paths that one can travel at one time and my path has, as yet, not led me back to Nepal and to the Annapurna. It's in my heart though and perhaps one day I still may manage to return. After we got back from Nepal, Boden finished his community service and we went back to court. "You did well, son," the judge announced amiably after reviewing Boden's extensive community service logs. "I see no reason not to close the case."

Chapter 45
Tragedy Strikes

That autumn, a horrific tragedy befell one of our staff at the hospital. Everyone was shaken to the core and the memory of it added to my feeling of alarm when, a few years later, Shannon became ill. Those seeking help, either for themselves or for a loved one who is suffering from mental illness, quickly become dismayed by the difficulty in accessing services. Furthermore, even if the person is very ill, if they don't want help, there is nothing that can be done for them. And of course most people who are suffering from severe mental illness don't want help because they don't see that there is a problem. That is part of their illness. It often takes a terrible tragedy to get them the help that they so desperately need. Often it comes too late. When I left work one evening after a 12-hour shift, Sue was all excited about her cross training to the ER so she could help out when it was busy. She had been worrying, for over six months, about her 19 year old son whom she felt had some sort of mental illness. Although she had contacted numerous agencies, she hadn't been able to get him any help, partly because he refused help, partly because he was no longer a minor, and partly because there wasn't much help available. It was a failure of the system. He made her nervous. He was kind of crazy and really angry sometimes. His moods were unpredictable. She didn't really want him living with her and his younger brother who was still in H.S., but he had nowhere else to go and she didn't want to abandon him. She didn't know what to do. Everyone had different advice for her. Having been through something similar with John, my advice to her had been: "If you're really afraid, leave town and don't leave a forwarding address. You shouldn't have to live in fear." Economically, she didn't feel that it was an option and she loved him. He was her son. Sue had a small build and she was very sweet and quiet and nervous. She was worried all the time. She seemed so frail. But that evening, after helping in the Emergency Room all day, she was in an unusually good mood. Here was something new and interesting for her to do, and she was excited about it. The next morning, she didn't show up for work and she didn't call. That was not like her at all. She was extremely reliable. One of the other nursing assistants walked over to her house to see what was up but the place was locked and there was no answer to her persistent knocking. Worried, she had called the sheriff. Piecing things together later, after reading the coroner's report, we figured that when Sue got home after her shift, her younger son was probably already dead. Sue was found beaten to death with a baseball bat. One can only imagine the nightmare of her son's tormented mind that night, after what he had just done, as he streaked through the dark empty streets like a madman to the bridge on the outskirts of town where he jumped to his death.

On January 10, 2001, three people were shot and killed by a psychiatric patient. One of the victims was Laura Wilcox, a 19-year-old college student. In response to this tragedy, in 2002, Laura's law was passed in the California State Legislature that would allow for court ordered, mandated treatment for psychiatric patients who were deemed to be a danger to self or others.[2]

Laura's law was modeled after 'Kendra's Law' which was passed in N.Y. where a five year study showed that mandated Assisted Outpatient Treatments resulted in a significant decrease in many of the most severe consequences of untreated mental illness, e.g. decrease in homelessness, incarcerations, suicide, and violent crimes. Laura's law is supported by NAMI. Even so, the 'danger to self or others' is often difficult to establish, and the system is so overburdened and underfunded that even when it is proven, usually nothing is done. Often a person will struggle along, with no help whatsoever, until something terrible happens. The suffering and tragedy experienced by Sue and her family is unthinkable. It is very likely that with timely intervention, this tragedy could have been prevented. It was a system failure and we, as a society, suffer when such things are allowed to happen out of neglect.

[2] http://www.theunion.com/article/20061003/NEWS/110030124/-1/THEMES05

Chapter 46
The Om Watch

That autumn, Boden and Shannon had just turned 18. It was their last year of High school. Blanche was doing fairly well. She had her good days and her bad days, but she had finally adjusted to life in a small town and she had gone back to writing poetry. She pushed away anyone who tried to get to know her but in her isolated little world she was comfortable and somewhat content. As a gift, I got her a TV and I paid her monthly cable bill. Her favorite programs became her friends. Sometimes when I would stop by early in the day, I would find her sitting comfortably in her pajamas in front of the TV enjoying an old movie with her morning toast and coffee on a little tray in front of her. She had her routine and within it she felt safe. She was growing old gracefully in spite of her troubled mind.

The hospital had recently gone through many changes in response to the rapidly changing economics of medicine. We had turned eight of our sixteen acute beds into long-term skilled nursing beds. That way, we would always have at least eight beds filled. We also lost our surgery capabilities and our labor and delivery as well. Small rural hospitals everywhere were closing down. Those that were managing to keep their doors open had to make huge and innovative adjustments in an effort to stay afloat. It was a sign of the changing times. I resisted all of the changes but to no avail. There was no turning back the hands of time. Many of our community doctors had left the area. Of the regulars, only Dr. Mark remained. Unable to recruit new doctors to our little community, we contracted with Valley Emergency Physicians to cover our emergency room. At first, I was against that too but then it turned out to be really valuable and inspiring as many competent and interesting physicians came, for short periods of time, to be part of our medical team. I got to know some really cool people, and it made working in the ER an adventure in personalities as well as a challenging adventure in medicine. One of our Valley Docs, Dr. Steinbach taught medical students at U. C. Berkeley and another one, Dr. Starr, spent much of his free time traveling in third world countries working to bring ecologically sustainable solutions to various problems. Our little hospital attracted some remarkable and well-liked physicians.

Both Doctor Steinbach and Doctor Starr encouraged me when I told them that I was thinking about going back to school to become a nurse practitioner. "That's what I would do if I was in your place," Dr. Starr told me.

"Go for it. Give yourself a time frame and try to stay within it," Doctor Steinbach advised.

I looked around at my options. If I were even going to consider becoming a Nurse Practitioner, I would first have to get a Bachelor of Science degree in Nursing and then I would have to get into an NP program and get a Master's Degree. It would take anywhere from a five to ten years, depending on my pace. That seemed like a long time. I decided to take a 'just one step at a time' approach and see how things went. I would start by looking into long distance, correspondence courses and I would check out the University in Southern California where I could be closer to Emily for a few years. I would just have to see what was out there. I would also need to start gathering together all my college transcripts from over twenty years ago. That alone seemed like a monumental project. "One step at a time," I had to remind myself.

I hadn't been down to see Emily since she had moved into the ashram. I missed her a lot. It was time to pay her a visit. After having lived for years in a small town with no stop lights, the L.A. freeway was frightening with cars whizzing by every which way but once off the freeway, as I drove up the quaint, narrow, winding streets with lots of greenery to where The ashram was located, I started to feel more at home. The temple was beautifully landscaped with well-kept lawns and flowers, little ponds and quiet, meditative spots. As I drove through the gates, I was suddenly aware of a peaceful feeling as though I had just entered onto sacred ground. Between the recent tragic events at the hospital, my stressful job, Boden and Shannon constantly getting into trouble at school for disruptive behavior and Dan's unpredictable moodiness, I was a bit of a wreck when I entered the temple to look for Emily.

"Can I help you?" the kindly Nun in saffron robes asked as I walked up. The entrance room was spacious and hushed, emanating a feeling of sanctity and grace. As I stood there in the stillness, my jangled nerves from a morning of LA airport and LA freeway and life in general began to settle. The tension in my shoulders began to relax, and I felt happy in the knowledge that I would soon be face to face with my daughter.

"Yes, I'm looking for Emily. She's expecting me," I added

"Can I tell her who is calling?" the Nun asked in a kindly voice.

"I'm her mother," I said with a feeling of pride.

"Oh, Emily's mother, welcome, she's so looking forward to seeing you! You look like sisters." She made a phone call and minutes later Emily came down the broad, polished, winding staircase that went up to where the Nuns dining room and some of their offices were located. She was gracious and lovely, happy and in glowingly good health, and she was still my Emily, only a bit older and more mature. She hadn't turned into somebody else that I didn't recognize. We hugged and looked at each other at arm's length and got all excited about spending some time together.

"Are you hungry? The postulants have invited us for lunch."

We left the gated grounds and went across the street to a charming older house where Emily lived with the other postulants. The postulants lived the life of a monastic but would not be taking vows until they moved on to the next step which was Novice. Then they would take their first set of vows. After that came Brahmachurini and then Sister. The Nuns moved along at different paces depending on their dedication and spiritual development, and at each step of the way, new and deeper vows were taken. Emily was just beginning her journey. We were met at the door by a group of charming and enthusiastic young women. They reminded me of the book *Little Women* that I had loved so much as a girl. They were sweet, unpretentious, polite, and kind. They were lovely young women in their 20s and 30s, and I could see how Emily could be drawn to walking the spiritual path with them. I felt relieved. These were good people, and I was glad that my daughter was with them.

The long dining table was beautifully set, and the food was wonderful. The Nuns did not eat meat and they had a very healthy, well-planned diet. A lot of their food came from their own organic gardens that were tended by Monks who lived in a separate area. Care was put into making the dishes as nutritious and enjoyable as possible. As we sat around the table talking about the monastic life, the monastery and some personal stories, I felt very privileged to be spending time with such a gracious and sincere group of young women.

"We are so happy that Emily is here with us," the senior Sister, who was dining with us, was saying. "She is a delight to be around."

"I really miss her," I said. As I looked around the table, I could see all the bright and smiling faces looking at me. I imagined that they wanted to hear some personal and revealing story about their sister. "Emily was very sweet and easygoing as a child. She never threw temper tantrums, and if I said that she couldn't have something that she wanted, she was fine with it," I told them. Looking around and seeing that I had a captive audience, I continued. "But she did have a short but difficult period when she was 13," I added. "She was very rebellious for about a year. It was a tough time for both of us but, as you can see, we worked it out." In order to give a humorous example of Emily's period of rebellion, I started to recount the story of when she wanted to wear my lace stockings. "A friend of hers had just spent the weekend, and I left to drive her friend home.

Emily stayed behind at the house. I felt pleased because I had gone out of my way to make sure that they both had a very nice weekend and I thought that it had been a success, but when I got back home, Emily met me at the front door." I paused here in my story. Everyone was listening intently, curious for a little insight into the early life of their fellow Nun.

"'Where are your lace stockings?' she had demanded. 'I want to wear them.'"

The Nuns all gasped and looked at Emily with a merry sparkle in their eyes.

"They're very delicate and you're too hard on clothes. You can't wear them, I had told her. I was still standing on the threshold of the door." I paused again and looked around before continuing.

"Well, if you don't tell me where they are, I'm going up to your room and I'm going to tear it apart, and when I find them, I'm wearing them." The peals of laughter from the Nuns made it worth the telling. I hoped that I had not embarrassed my daughter too much but even she was laughing.

"I didn't know how to respond so I just backed out of the door got into my car and drove away. I went directly to the local bar and had a couple of drinks. When I got home, Emily met me at the door again."

The Nuns weren't laughing now. Their look of amusement was mixed with concern and filled with compassion for human frailty.

"'Where did you go?' Emily had wanted to know; she had been worried. 'Oh, Mom,' she had told me. 'I'm so sorry. I don't want you to drink. I'll never do it again.'"

I looked over at Emily who was smiling. "Now she's my best friend."

After lunch, we sat in the living room talking for a bit. The Postulants were from all over the world. There was one from South America, one from Italy, someone from Germany. There was a lovely young woman from California who had been a lawyer but the corporate world had seemed empty and unsatisfying to her. She had left it behind to follow the spiritual path. What all of these young women had in common was that they were all seeking love and light in their lives and they were seeking it by following the spiritual path. "Change your life and you will change thousands," one spiritual teacher had said. As I sat with these young women, I could feel that their path was a good one. Everything they said made perfect sense. Through their striving for goodness and harmony, they were making the world a better place to live in. It occurred to me then that we actually had similar callings. I was a nurse of the body and sometimes of the mind, and they were nurses to help with healing of the soul. If any part of either the body, the mind or the soul were not well, life could be miserable. All three needed to be cared for and nurtured.

We spent the rest of the weekend walking on the beach, meditating and reading inspirational, spiritual passages from the many books in the ashram. A recurrent theme was "Fully enjoy the wonder and beauty of each instant. Practice the presence of peace. The more you do that, the more you will feel the presence of that power in your life." These words were becoming a way of life for my daughter. During our few days together, I tried to stay fully present in the moment, becoming centered and gathering all the strength that I could from our time together. By the end of the weekend, it was time to go home but in just a few short days I had found such an incredible sense of peace and wellbeing that I felt like I had been gone for weeks.

Once back home, I wondered how I could hold on to that feeling of centeredness and contentment that I had experienced over the weekend. I got this idea that if I had a watch that would chime every hour, then I could constantly be reminded to stop in the business of the world and tune into the infinite, at hourly intervals, every day. I did have a watch with an alarm on it so for a few days, I kept setting the alarm to ring every couple of hours. I called them 'Om Moments' when my alarm would go off. On one of my Om Moments, I was helping a dying patient to get comfortable in bed. When the alarm went off, it shifted the focus of my awareness from the mere mechanics of the task, done more or less automatically, to encompass the fuller deeper reality of the gracious and peaceful aura that emanated from my patient as she adjusted to the idea of her imminent death. She had already begun her transition from this life into the next, and she had an 'other worldly' glow about her that was beautiful. Suddenly, in the midst of the Om Moment, I saw things in so much greater depth. I realized, too, that I was still just touching the surface. There was so much more there that I couldn't see. At other Om Moments, I would say an affirmation or an inspirational phrase to remind myself of how I wanted to walk in the world. "Every step is a prayer," a friend of mine once said.

Part Five
Stay the Course

Chapter 47
The Evasion Charge

The intense feeling of happiness and calm lasted for a few weeks but then, after a while, the daily stresses began to wear me down once again. I was undisciplined and I could never seem to stay with the requisite regular daily practice. Boden was having a hard time with one of his teachers, and it was looking like he might not graduate with his brother. As far as I was concerned, that was totally unacceptable. We arranged for Boden to make up his history class after school at the Osprey Learning Center. He did really well, and he amazed his teacher by taking a test on an entire section of the book on his first day and getting every question correct. He was so proud, and I loved to hear him tell the story. He told it well. That first day when Boden had handed in his answers to the entire first section, the teacher had been surprised. She got out the answer template and began to check every single answer as wrong. "They can't all be wrong," Boden had protested with a sinking heart.

"I'm the teacher. Don't tell me how to do my job," the teacher had responded, feeling annoyed by Boden's attitude.

Finally, in desperation, he said, "Look, here's an easy one. This one can't be wrong!"

At that point, the teacher realized that she had grabbed the wrong template. He had gotten every single question correct. But he still lacked confidence and he told me, "I'm not interested in graduation. Don't order me a cap and gown. I'm not going."

I would not hear of it, however, and so, a few weeks before graduation, I put in my order for a cap and gown for both Boden and his brother. I don't think there was a happier, more glowing student than Boden on graduation day when he walked up to receive his diploma. Dan and I were in the bleachers, and we clapped and cheered so loud that you could hear us all through the stadium. I was a proud mom that day, proud of my two young men who had just received their High School Diplomas.

With my sons graduated from High School, I imagined that some of the day-to-day stress of raising children would start to ease up. Little did I know that the real heartaches were about to begin. At the end of summer, in August, Boden and Shannon started taking classes at the local Junior college. I felt that a good education was important for young people. It had, in a way, saved my life. I was pleased that they were going to school.

I started looking around at my own options for continuing my education. I tried my hand at the long distance schooling, but it didn't feel solid enough to me. I felt that I needed to attend classes. Moving down to Southern California to go to school would be very expensive. I couldn't afford it. I considered applying to Humboldt State University, which was less than a two-hour commute from my house. When I met with the councilor there, I was discouraged to learn how many classes I would need to get my Bachelor of Science in Nursing Degree. I felt overwhelmed. I had to think about it. While I was mulling it over, I came upon my horoscope in a magazine. It read: "Go ahead and pursue that seemingly distant possibility. Nothing will come of it unless you pursue it now with determination and patience. Its fruition will benefit all those around you." Call me crazy if you will, but it spoke so directly to my question that I took it as a sign. I put in my application to the nursing bridge program, and I was immediately accepted. I had taken that first, big step.

That September, Shannon, who had a problem with driving too fast, was traveling North on the freeway when a highway Patrol car that was traveling South did a U-turn on the freeway to stop Shannon and give him yet another speeding ticket. Shannon, seeing what was happening, tried to get away, taking the next freeway exit. A little chase ensued but then Shannon, realizing that it was of no use, finally pulled over on the river bar. He was given a ticket for reckless driving but the DA charged him with evasion. Those were the early days when his mental instability first began to show. Whether the traumatic events that followed served to destabilize his sensitive and impressionable young mind or whether an underlying mental instability made the events more traumatic than they would have otherwise been is hard to say with absolute certainty. I think that things would not have happened the way they did if Shannon had not already been germinating the seeds of mental illness.

That entire next year was very stressful for all of us including Dan. John became fascinated by the court proceedings. He called Shannon several times a week and they would talk on the phone for hours planning a court case. Although he never came down from Washington, it felt like John and all his craziness was back in my life. Shannon began to obsess over the legal proceedings and he fired his court appointed lawyer and went along with John's manic proposals and instructions. He failed all of his classes that semester. He basically spent the entire semester at the law library researching the things that his father assigned him. That spring semester, he quit school and got a job locally. I was glad that he was at least working. People were always coming up to me in those days telling me how much they liked Shannon, what a nice young man he was, and how much he had helped them to find the parts that they needed at the local wrecking yard where he was working. I knew he was a good guy. If he had been mean spirited or dishonest, I don't think this whole thing would have upset me as much as it did.

I tried going to his court appearances to give him some emotional support but it was too painful for me. He couldn't see that he was being an arrogant young fool and that he was headed for disaster. Everything he said was the voice of John. He wouldn't listen to me at all. I finally stopped going. On the advice of his dad, he took it to a jury trial and he acted as his own defense lawyer. Everyone said to him, "He who represents himself in court has a fool for a lawyer." Everyone but John that is; John egged him on. "You can do those people," John told him. Part of what made the whole thing so heartbreaking, to me, was that Shannon was doing all of this to prove himself to his dad. He lost face when he was convicted and sentenced to six months in the county jail. The look on his face, when he told me the outcome of the trial, broke my heart. I looked at him and somehow I saw him as if through a mirror that had shattered, reflecting back many fractured and mismatched pieces. He was never quite the same after that.

He and his dad then worked up an appeal and it took another full year before the proceedings came to an end. At every step of the way, the court tried to let him out of his sentence through plea bargains and legal advice but he and his dad had an agenda, and they wouldn't rest until they had their demands met to have the charges completely dropped. In the end, he got an additional 90 days added on to the original sentence which could be dropped for good behavior. The day I took him to be interned in the county jail to serve his sentence, I was a nervous wreck. Shannon, thankfully, was calm and resigned. He would make the best of bad situation. I was grateful to him for trying to ease my anxiety. They led him away in handcuffs, and I went home to sob into my pillow all that night. Some of his behavior in those days had seemed obsessive and irrational. I called the jail and asked if they could do a psychiatric evaluation on him. "He's fine," they told me.

During that time period, I had started classes at HSU. In a way, it was a Godsend. I didn't have time to dwell too much on what was going on with Shannon while he was in jail. I too had the tendency to obsess about things, and if I hadn't been caught up in my studies, I think that it would have been much harder on me. As it was, I visited him once a week. It took them a couple of weeks to set up visitation, and the first time that I went to see him, he didn't look good. He had lost weight. He was very thin and very pale. We had to talk on a little telephone with a glass window between us. I wanted to put my arms around him but he was unavailable, not only because of the glass window between us but because of a certain aloofness in the way he held himself, as if he were already hardening himself and pulling away from the world. Who was this person? I wasn't certain that it was the Shannon I knew. Something had broken.

After a couple of months, Shannon started going out with the road crews to work. His mood seemed to improve with the activity and being able to get out of doors. He also got into playing cards and this, more than anything, eased the tension of being incarcerated for him. He loved playing cards.

That spring semester, Boden moved into the dorms at school. For the first time in my entire life, I was living alone. I didn't really like it. Sometimes, going home after work or after a late day of classes to a dark, cold and empty house would be all that was needed to make me start crying. Sometimes, too, I would feel afraid in the night if I heard strange noises. Dan moved to a little cabin on his friend's land that was a short hike to my house, uphill and through the woods. That was definitely comforting, knowing that he was close by, but he was busy a lot of the time, and I really didn't see all that much of him. Even though I was incredibly busy, with school and shift work, I still felt lonely living alone. I worried about Shannon all the time and my house that had once been so full of life, now felt like an empty nest. I invited a couple of the Valley Docs who I worked with regularly and who came from a long ways a way to work a few days at a time at our hospital to stay at my house if they needed to come the night before and had nowhere to go. They took me up on it and so, at least a couple of times a month, I had their company in the evening. It was fun and I looked forward to their visits. Dan, of course, still came by and spent time with me. Usually on the weekends he would visit and we would have dinner and a glass of wine and watch a video. I really appreciated those times.

"These six months sure went by quickly," I was telling Shannon on one of my last visits to see him in jail. He would be getting out in a week or so.

"Maybe to you it went by quickly," Shannon responded with justifiable sarcasm.

Of course I had been busy working and pursuing my dreams while he had been stuck in the county jail and working on the chain gang. How could I even think that the six months had felt the same to him as it had to me? I was glad that he would soon be coming home.

Shannon was released on mothers' day. It was a mixed blessing really because I was so happy to see him, but he brought me another inmate who had also been released that day. A group of Shannon's friends came by the house to celebrate his release and the other kid got so loaded that he fell out of the truck, face first, hitting his head on the rocks. He then vomited all over my kitchen floor, and we had to rush him into town to the emergency room. In the end, he was alright, but I didn't want him back at the house so I had to rent him a hotel room in town. Happy Mothers' Day! The next day, his brother came to town and took him back up north. I was relieved that he wasn't going to be hanging around. Things began to fall back into order. Shannon was glad to be home.

Chapter 48
Peru

Shannon floundered around, after his release from jail, trying to get back into the swing of things but things were different now. Although it had only been six months, it was six months at a time when all his friends had just graduated High School and they were starting jobs, leaving the area, starting families or going away to college. He tried a few different things but he couldn't quiet find his place and he started to get depressed. He talked a lot about his time in jail and playing cards. He sounded as if he actually missed it. I felt like Shannon needed some engaging and positive of experience to break the spell of his last six months of being institutionalized. Although he was no longer in jail, he still did not seem free. At that same time, Boden's semester at the Junior College was coming to an end and one day he asked me, out of the blue, "Where are we going to travel to next, Mom?"

"Peru actually," was my immediate response.

Only days later, Boden and Shannon picked me up from work after a 12-hour shift and we drove to San Francisco. Early the next morning, we caught a flight to Lima. Hours after settling into our little hotel room, there was a 4.1 magnitude earthquake. The rickety floor shook, rattled and rolled our welcome to Peru. It was a startling event. Before the day was out, the congested, noisy city was too much for me and so after only one night in Lima, we went back to the airport and flew to the small airport outside of a little town called Puno. Hours after we were settled in our room in Puno, a revolution broke out in Peru. A state of emergency was declared and the road to our little town was blocked off. No one could enter and no one could leave. Welcome to Puno!

In a couple of hours, we had gone from Lima which is at sea level to Puno which is on the shores of Lake Titicaca at close to 13,000 feet elevation. That evening, as we sat in the dimly lit dining room at our hotel, I began to feel ill. We were the only people in the restaurant and once again, I had that exciting feeling that we were somewhere very different and very far away from home. That rush of having the senses bombarded by unfamiliar sights and sounds was addicting. I craved it and the fulfillment of that craving was what kept me traveling despite my many misadventures. Even though my head was throbbing, breathing was difficult and I felt very weak, I was still really glad that we were there. The health issues I could deal with. I wasn't as sure about the revolution.

Our waiter was explaining to us that all over Peru, underpaid workers were striking and marching for better wages and benefits. "In Peru's economy, even the teachers cannot afford to feed and house their families," he told us, shrugging his shoulders in a sign of resignation. "The army is marching also, with their guns, to control the strikers. Just the other week the army shot and killed five students here in Puno." Our waiter shook his head. "The workers have closed the town off because they are protesting the death of the students. Don't worry. You will probably be able to leave in a couple of days," he added. "But right now you can't get to the airport. They are smashing the windows of all the vehicles that try to leave or enter Puno."

As we climbed the stairs up to our room after dinner, the guys were surprised to find that they were weak and winded after just a few steps. "It's the altitude," I told them. "You'll adjust in a day or two."

I was starting to get a fever, and I felt very weak. I wasn't sure if it was the altitude or if I had picked up some bug or maybe a combination. If it was all altitude sickness, then it was very severe. I would have to be careful. The cure for altitude sickness is to go back down to a lower elevation but just at this time, no one was going anywhere. The city was on lockdown. That evening, the guys sat contentedly in the room playing poker. I tried to join them but it took too much effort to sit up. I spent the next day in bed, feverish and miserable and once again worrying about the safety of my sons. Outside my window, all day, I could hear voices over loud speakers proclaiming solidarity and freedom. People were marching in the streets and making speeches in Spanish on the church steps. The military was marching also, with their guns in order to 'keep the peace'. Our hotel had a sliding gate that they had constructed, for safety, to cover their big plate glass window and the front door in case the crowds got out of control. All day long, the hotel manager stood guard, opening the gate a crack to let Boden and Shannon slip out into the street, locking the gate behind them and then opening it a crack again when they returned. The guys were fascinated by this firsthand experience of political unrest in a third world country. Boden had his camera, and he went around enthusiastically taking pictures. No one tried to stop him. He got one excellent picture of dozens of soldiers marching in uniform holding their rifles across their chests. In the background, painted in giant red letters on the wall of the building, is 'Buscamos la Paz para un mundo sin Guerra', roughly translated as: 'We look to peace for a world without war'.

The day of demonstrations passed without incident and the next day was a relatively normal workday for the people of Puno. I was starting to feel better as well. Things were looking up. We took a boat to visit the floating islands of Lake Titicaca. "These amazing islands are made by harvesting reeds that grow in the shallow parts of the lake and then laying many layers of these reeds to create a floating island. The islands are maintained by continually adding new layers of reeds. Originally, this was a survival tactic to escape from attack but now it is a way of life for a few Aymara and Uros Indians who live here on these islands and make a living on tourism and fishing," the young, charismatic boat guide was informing us in Spanish and then again in English as we stepped gingerly from the boat on to the solid mass of land that was like a large, woven floor mat floating in the middle of the lake.

"Wow; creating your own island really is creating your own reality!" I remarked to the guys who had their eyes on the pretty young girl sitting across from us. The lake was so large that once we had traveled for a couple of hours, we could no longer see the shore. We had wanted to stay the night on the more remote island of Taquile but it hadn't worked out, and I regret it. I still have a longing to know more about what their life is like on silent starry nights, removed as they are from the rest of the world. Perhaps, some day, I will return.

When we got back to Puno late that afternoon, we got on a bus headed to Cuzco. We had it in mind to visit the ruins of the great Inca Empire in the heart of the Andean Mountains that were located not far from the city of Cuzco. My 'Lonely Planet' guidebook made the comment that 'going to Peru and missing Cuzco is like visiting Egypt and skipping the pyramids'. We did go to Cuzco but we did skip Machu Picchu, another experience that I regret missing out on. However, at the time I still wasn't feeling well. The crowded, freezing and uncomfortable 3rd class bus ride through the night had left me feeling chilled to the bone and feverish again. On top of that, I had been conned out of almost $200 by a guide in Puno. I was usually very cautious about such things but, perhaps because of the altitude, I wasn't thinking clearly and had given money to a man who had promised to set some things up for us and had then disappeared. Now I was short on cash. We went to a travel agency off of the plaza which was crowded with more soldiers carrying rifles and more protesters marching. We were debating whether or not to sign up for the tour and train ride to Machu Picchu. It was expensive, and there didn't seem to be any way around going without taking the expensive first class tour. Feeling indecisive, I turned to Boden and Shannon for their input on what to do. There was a beautiful large poster on the wall of the ruins at Machu Picchu. Boden pointed to the picture saying, "There's Machu Picchu. We've seen it now." I guess he wasn't that interested in going.

The rest of the day, we walked around the beautiful ancient city that was founded in the 12th century by the early Inca. At almost 11,000 feet above sea level, the air was crisp and pure. Quechua speaking Indians crowded the narrow, stone streets, selling their wares and going on about their day dressed in colorful native dress. That night we had a wonderful dinner, our best since arriving in Peru. By candle light we were serenaded by local musicians who played panpipes and other indigenous instruments. The atmosphere was magical. As I sat comfortably resting in the dim light, listening to the ancient music and sipping wine, I felt that intoxicating sense of timelessness that was, for me, one of the most compelling aspects of travel.

The next morning, we had breakfast on the town plaza in a quaint little café. It was there that the guys discovered coca leaf tea. The unprocessed coca leaf is legal in Peru and it is used by the Andean Indians to combat fatigue. It is also recommended for problems with the altitude and is sold freely in the markets. Both Boden and Shannon considered this discovery much more interesting and of greater value than seeing the ancient Inca Ruins. After breakfast, we went to the airport where we boarded a small plane to fly to Iquitos. One of the largest cities on the Amazon, Iquitos can only be reached by air. Since grade school, when I was first fascinated by the wild jungle pictures, I had dreamed of visiting the Amazon. It was a lifelong desire that was about to be fulfilled.

We arrived at the small airport late in the afternoon. The place was full of activity, people traveling, locals selling their wares and guides, hotel employees and drivers all trying to get a customer. We were barraged by people who wanted to take our packs, drive us somewhere, sell us something or provide some type of service for which they could then charge us. I was very wary because of my recent experience in Puno; however, somehow one Peruvian man stood out from all the rest. He sounded reliable, had a nice vibe, and said the right thing. I don't know but we let him take us under his wing and he led us through the crowd and out the door to a waiting taxi where he instructed the driver to take us to a particular hotel overlooking the Plaza de Armas. We liked it. The place was decent and the price was reasonable so we checked in. From our balcony, we had a good view of the goings on of the city. Round and round the plaza motorcycles that were set up with back seats that could hold several passengers and resembled little rickshaws droned like swarming mosquitoes as they picked up fares and drove them to different destinations in the jungle and river locked city. Being back at sea level, my energy seemed to pick up and I was glad for the warmer weather.

After we were settled in our room, Lewis, who was to be our guide and companion while in Amazonia, picked us up and took us to see some of the sites that were in walking distance from the hotel. Just a few blocks from where we were staying was a promenade that was lined on one side with cafés and shops, and on the other side coursed a broad band of water that emptied into the Amazon. The weather was balmy and warm. As evening fell, the promenade filled with local people who walked with their families or hung out in small groups talking. Children ran around playing and laughing. There were food stands and musicians and other artists selling their wares. The feeling was very festive but there was no special occasion. Instead, this was just a typical evening here in Iquitos where the evening breeze coming up from the Amazon made it a fine time to be out of doors and socializing. It was the way of life for these people who seemed to be very gregarious. We had a nice dinner there by the promenade, and Lewis, who spoke excellent English, told us about the lodge in the Amazon jungle that belonged to the man he worked for. We could hire a boat that would take us there where we could stay for a few days. He would show us around and we could get an idea of the daily life of the peoples that lived in the isolated areas on the banks of the Amazon. He quoted us a price that was very affordable. My anthropological tendencies were being excited again.

The next day, Lewis picked us up early and took us for breakfast on the plaza in an iron building that was designed by Eiffel of the Eiffel Tower. The building had been brought, piece by piece, from Paris in the 1890s during the rubber boom when Iquitos was a wealthy city and flourishing. Although it was an interesting story, the building itself didn't impress me much. I didn't find it beautiful like some of the old colonial architecture or the simple stone houses that were everywhere. After breakfast, we took a motorcycle taxi to the Belen market which did impress me. There were blocks and blocks of tacky, makeshift stalls, each with its own blue plastic awning to keep out the sun. It was like a makeshift shantytown for selling wares and it seemed to go on for miles. It had the look of poverty. Nevertheless, people seemed happy as they walked about chatting and bartering and purchasing the items that they would need for the day. One of the sellers had a tame little monkey that was no bigger than of the palm of my hand. I was fascinated by that little monkey. It had such a sweet and trusting nature that I wished I could keep it with me always but of course it would never have survived the traveling and the climate of Northern California. Sometimes, I still think about the little monkey and I miss it as if it were an old friend from a past life or had some other mysterious, deeper connection. The shantytown extended out onto the water where people lived in little huts that were built on stilts and on floating rafts. We were there at the time of the year when the water is high and the huts were only accessible by boat. We rented a small rowboat and rowed around the houses where children sat playing on their small front porches surrounded by water. "At the time of the year when the water is low," Lewis explained to us, "it is not so nice. It's very muddy and dirty."

That evening, for entertainment, Lewis took us to a disco. He brought with him a couple of girls. They looked to be in their late teens or early 20s, and they also worked for his boss at the travel agency. Boden was really enjoying their company but Shannon, for the first time since we had left California, got into a really bad mood. He sat there at the table with a scowl on his handsome face, and I could not get him to tell me what was wrong. The place was small and crowded and noisy with blaring Latin music and people yelling to be heard over the music. On the dance floor, people were scantily dressed and dancing the hot, sexy moves of the Maringa and salsa dances. "Would you like to dance?" Lewis asked me. I couldn't resist. I had wanted to learn some of these very dance moves and here was my chance. Sweat poured down our faces and our wet shirts stuck to our bodies as we twirled around and shook our hips, hugging and spinning, rolling our butts and sticking out our damp chests in a wild frenzy. It was a blast, but when I returned to my seat, Shannon looked even more cross and he wanted to leave.

"Let's go back to the hotel," he said. "I'm done with this." Back at the hotel, he hung out in the lobby with the people at the desk listening to CD's until late at night.

Boden didn't come back until it was almost morning, and he was in a great mood. "Why did you leave so early?" he asked his brother. "It was really fun."

Shannon said nothing. He still looked a bit grumpy. Later that afternoon, I can see it even now, like a snapshot in my mind's eye, Shannon sitting on the plastic covered couch in the hall outside of our room. He looked weary and distant, lost in his own world. I thought perhaps he was just tired.

As we boarded the small launch with a couple of other tourists to head up the Amazon and into the jungle, I felt very happy. Of all of our experiences while in Peru, this was the one that I had most enthusiastically anticipated. The farther away we got from Iquitos, leaving the sights and the sounds of the city behind, the more incredible the sights and sounds of nature became. The sky was so vast and it transitioned so seamlessly into the equally vast water that we seemed to be awash in blue grey ether amidst which our tiny boat was the only solid object interrupting the perfection of this melting, merging, gently undulating world. We traveled like that for several hours lost in a world of watercolors. Did the sky reflect the water or was it the other way around. Were we up or upside down in this strikingly muted wash of colors? The setting was surreal. Then, when we finally took off on a side tributary called the MoMo River, our world narrowed and dripping fronds of green began to close in on us. We docked at a small boat ramp smack in the middle of nowhere. We had arrived.

The lodge consisted of a ring of cabins the largest of which was the dining room where meals were served. We got settled into our little wooden cabin and then went to the dining room for dinner. There were several other groups of tourists, perhaps eight of us in all, and then there were the guides. The boss was also there. He was actually an English man but he had lived for many years in the jungle making a living off of the tourist trade. I was a little disappointed when I was introduced to him. From the start, I didn't entirely trust him. He was middle aged. Around 40, I would say, and he was constantly shadowed by what can only be described as a harem of young Peruvian girls. One of them was just flesh and bones; she was so thin. She seemed very weak, and the other girls seemed to be looking after her. I wondered what was wrong with her but I didn't ask. Instead, I assumed the worst. I didn't, in fact, know what was going on with their secretive little group but it didn't feel right and it made me uncomfortable. The owner, learning that I was a nurse, asked me to join him at his table with his girls for dinner. I did so out of curiosity and we actually had a very interesting conversation about the medicinal properties of many of the still undiscovered plants of the Amazon Jungle. Had I trusted him, I probably would have kept in contact with him, over the internet as he had suggested, in order to learn more about the business in medicinal plants that he was developing. Towards the end of our conversation, he offered to introduce me to a medicine man who gave guided, hallucinogenic tours of the mind. I thought about my friend from Reggae on the River who had told me that there was a marvelous hallucinogen in the Amazon Jungle that, when you took it, was akin to seeing through a clear windshield as opposed to one covered with dirt. The covered with dirt windshield being the everyday state of our limited, cloudy, consciousness. I was interested and wanted to hear more but Lewis, who had joined us, looked at me gravely and shook his head. "You wouldn't like it," he whispered. "It will make you vomit and defecate and you won't know where you are." I was touched that he was so concerned about my wellbeing even at the great risk of displeasing his boss. When he said this, I realized that my curiosity was about to get me in trouble again. I did, however, settle on having the Great Shaman from the Amazon jungle come to my cabin and perform a sacred water ceremony. It sounded interesting and what could be the harm?

That evening, Shannon got very ill. He had a fever, and he just wanted to sleep. The night sounds of the jungle were coming alive around us. They were almost deafening. Crickets and frogs and other critters announced their presence in a crescendo of sound that seemed to fade in and out in waves. Boden was hanging out in the dining room playing pool and talking with the girls who had gone dancing with us in Iquitos. Shannon slept fitfully in his bed in a corner of the cabin. There was no electricity, and the candle light and the sounds of the jungle added to the mystery and remoteness of the setting. I was not displeased. Lewis knocked on the door announcing the arrival of the Shaman. I had put on my bathing suit as instructed, and the Shaman and I got into the bath tub. Lewis stood by the door watching with curiosity. They had brought into the bathroom, a big metal tub of 'sacred water' for the ceremony and the Shaman dipped a ladle into the sacred water and poured it over me while he sang incantations in his native dialect that I could not understand. He lit a cigarette, and periodically he vigorously blew smoke into my face, causing me to sputter and cough while he sang and chanted the magic words that were meant to increase my health, vitality, and good fortune in this lifetime. A slight breeze made the candle flame dance, throwing shadows across the walls. It all seemed mysterious and interesting at first, but after a while, I started to get chilled. As I stood there shivering, the elderly Shaman became obsessed with pouring the sacred water over my breasts and watching as it dripped down through the narrow channel of cleavage. Shivering and shaking from being soaked for so long with cold water, I watched with detached interest, unable to break away, as if I were indeed under a spell. Finally, unable to take any longer, Lewis stepped in and said, "Enough!" He led the Shaman out of the bathroom carrying the tub which still contained a large amount of the sacred water. I was glad when they left. From the corner of my eye, I caught a glimpse, out the window, as he dumped the rest of the sacred water out into the bushes. I was relieved to see that Shannon slept on, apparently unaware that I had just participated in such an embarrassing display.

The next day, Shannon was feeling a little better and he was able to join us when we took a boat ride to an animal reserve situated on the edge of the water upstream a short ways. They had colorful parrots and monkeys and huge pythons that the men in the group strung around their shoulders like a giant vine. This was a big hit with the guys. Two huge colorful parrots settled one on each of my shoulders, and Boden caught it in a picture. It was a funny picture, and you could tell, looking at it, that I was afraid that at any moment they might start pecking at my head. Nothing like that happened. We also visited some jungle Indians who lived primitively in a bare hut with no walls under a palm roof dressed in loincloths and paint. I wondered if, after we left, they put on blue jeans and hiked back to their cabin. There was no telling. In any case, there was no denying the remoteness of the setting. That evening, Lewis took us on a canoe ride down through narrow, twisty waterways to see caiman. The jungle closed in on our little boat as we paddled silently through the water underneath a covering of leaves so thick that we could only catch brief glimpses of the brilliant night sky. Lewis shone a flashlight into the murky depths to attract the slithering green creatures. We held our breath. Breathing itself seemed to be too intrusive a sound into this secret nightlife of plants and animals. We were in a world now that was totally foreign to us. We were out of our element, living a dream that was very beautiful but didn't belong to us. With a start, a caiman flipped its great tail slapping it down onto the water with a cracking, splashing sound. Lewis was swift as he grabbed the caiman around the mouth and the tail, easily gaining control of the large and intimidating animal. He let Boden and Shannon each take a turn at holding its squirming, scaling body with its gleaming, needle sharp teeth, and then he turned to me. "You must also hold it," he said to me. "It will make you stronger to be able to hold a caiman in your hands, and it will help you with your fears." Under his careful direction, I enclosed the snout within my grasp while Lewis continued to hold the long powerful tail that was wriggling desperately as it struggled to be free of its captors. The whole episode only took a few minutes. Lewis flung the creature back into the water and it swam away, and we retraced our way through the dark waters back to the dock. I had been afraid that we would forever be lost in the labyrinth of shallow water pathways that snaked their way under and through the trees, but before long we were back at the lodge with the friendly welcoming lanterns that lit up our little compound. I felt at that moment that the true sacred path that I was seeking lay in experiencing and honoring the incredible diversity of life on this amazing and wonderful planet.

Shannon seemed like he had recovered from his brief illness and had been enjoying our jungle adventures, but when we got back to Iquitos, he fell into a deep gloom. We still had a couple of days before our flight back to Lima and then home but Shannon asked me if I could change the tickets so that we could leave right away. It wasn't possible. Boden had a great time exploring the city and its outlying areas on motorcycle and taking his Peruvian young ladies out on the town, but Shannon settled into his bed and he refused to leave the room. He said later that it was because he was sick but it seemed to me like the illness was more in his head than in his body. I was upset at first that we had traveled all the way to the Amazon for him to sit in a hotel room, but then I thought about the six months that he had been in jail and how much I would have given at that time to be able to spend even a single day just hanging out with him at home. I rifled through my pack and got out the book I had brought with me to read. So far, I hadn't had the opportunity. Now I settled into my bed that was next to Shannon's and read while he retreated into his thoughts. I was content to be there with my son. I only hoped that, wherever he was in his head, he could feel my love and that, on some level, he found it helpful.

Chapter 49
Fire on the Mountain

When we got back home, it seemed like Shannon was able to throw off the reflections and thoughts that had kept him down, and he fell back into step with a productive and easygoing life. He hooked up with a couple of his friends who were starting a construction company, and he worked as a mechanic for them, helping to keep their large equipment in good working order. If they didn't have enough equipment maintenance to keep him busy, they would employ him working on the roads or constructing houses. He was busy working with friends and earning a good salary. He seemed pretty content. That is when I decided that I could stop worrying about him. It looked like he was going to be alright.

Meanwhile, I was pushing ahead with my schooling. I had started out tentatively only taking one class and I added more classes on to my schedule each semester as I gained confidence. Now, it had been two years and I was taking as many classes as I could squeeze into a two-day schedule. By my calculations, I could be graduating with a BSN in one more year if I kept it together. "After that, who knows," I said to one of the faculty who had asked me about my future plans. "Maybe I'll get into Public Health." My last semester I would be required to make a rotation through public health and I would be receiving a Public Health Certificate in Nursing as well. I didn't know that much about Public Health Nursing but it sounded interesting. Some very famous and inspiring nurses had been Public Health Nurses, such as Jane Delano. She developed an arm of the Red Cross to care for the health needs of the poor and underserved which eventually evolved into Public Health Nursing in 1918.

It was a fun summer starting out with our trip to Peru. Later in the summer, Dan and I went on several backpacking trips. I had a personal goal of 60–70 miles per summer divided up into different trips, and that summer I definitely met that goal. I loved being out in nature and it kept me strong and healthy and, also, it was something really fun that I could do with my friends. Backpacking was one of those win-win situations. I had a little garden going too. It was a pleasure to go out to work in the garden on a warm day. I would put music on in the house really loud and leave the doors open and then go down to the garden surrounded by the hills and trees and sky. The sweet notes of the music drifting in the air would calm my restlessness and I would become absorbed, working in the soil with flowers and vegetables. I could feel the healing power of the earth at such times. The tomatoes were the best I had ever tasted. Store-bought tomatoes were, forever after, such a disappointment after having eaten homegrown tomatoes. Zinnias grew in a perfusion of reds and pinks and wildflower orange, delighting the eye. Lavender was a treat with its delicate stalks and purple blooms that could be dried and kept for its fragrance. Zucchini grew easily like a weed and was delicious in many dishes, and Boden planted some grapes that had yielded their first tiny but delicious purple fruit.

Towards the end of July, Dan headed out to the Sierras for a couple of weeks on the trail. I couldn't get that much time off from work or I would have loved to have joined him. Instead, I took a long weekend and paid a visit to Harbin Hot Springs where I had gone to recuperate from my bout with the measles. In addition to the lovely rooms that they had for rent, they had several hundred acres where one could pitch a tent and camp with the added luxury of daily saunas and hot springs. I went there to relax and meditate and try out my brand new, lightweight, easy to put up backpacking tent that I had never used. Before I left, I had a long talk with Shannon. He had recently bought an old, broken down motor boat and in his spare time he was working to restore it. He wanted to work on it on the flat above the house but that was the highest site on the property with beautiful views to the east and west and I didn't want it cluttered up with junk. In addition, it was all tall dry grass and the potential for a fire was very high. I had, several times, told him that he couldn't work on his boat up there but I thought to remind him one more time before I left. "Don't bring your boat up to the flat above the house while I'm gone. I know that you want to work on it up there but you can't. Besides, it's a huge fire hazard. I don't want to have to worry. I'll be back in a couple of days."

"Don't worry, be happy," he told me as I drove off for a weekend of physical and spiritual renewal. The trip was even more fun than I had thought it would be. Usually, I didn't like camping alone because I would get scared in the night but here there was enough room that one didn't feel crowded but enough mellow happy people around that it felt perfectly safe. For the couple of days that I was there, I kept a schedule of quiet meditation and saunas and really light healthy meals. It was very renewing and so, happy and at peace and in the spirit of light and love, I returned home. It was late in the day when I got back and I was disappointed to find that Shannon had disregarded my wishes and was working on his boat on the flat above the house. Still, I was in a mellow, peaceful mood and I just shrugged it off and settled in to cook us a nice dinner. It was a warm balmy night, and I had all the doors open. Crickets chirped and frogs croaked and soft music played as I worked peacefully in the kitchen, attentive to the process of cooking as a meditation and in the spirit of love. Suddenly, the spell was broken by Shannon, who rarely got excited, running into the house in a panic yelling, "Where's the fire extinguisher?"

"What's going on?" I demanded to know.

"Fire," he proclaimed with agitation. "I was working on the engine and it shot a stream of gasoline into the tall grass and now there's a big fire!" As he said this, he grabbed our tiny fire extinguisher and raced out the door and up the hill.

Terrified by what this might mean for the whole neighborhood, I called 911. "My son just told me that there is a fire in the grass at the top of our property. I haven't seen it yet but I wanted to alert you in case it's bad."

The man at the other end of the phone was wonderful. His helpful, take-charge attitude helped calm my freshly shattered nerves. "We're going to start rolling," he said decisively. "You go up the hill and check it out. If it's nothing, just call and cancel. No harm done. Otherwise, we'll be there in a few minutes."

When I got to the top of the hill, what I saw made me almost pass out. A solid wall of flames, five or six feet high, danced in the light breeze, licking upwards towards the sky. I stood there, momentarily stunned. The dark night was lit up by the several acres of tall grass that was on fire. Sparks were flying through the air, like the 4th of July, and igniting more grass. I was grateful that help was on the way! We had a big 3000-gallon swimming pool that we used for our outdoor water and thankfully, it was almost full. As the fire engines labored up my steep, narrow road, Shannon and I were carrying buckets of water and pouring them on the flames with minimal success. The flames were actually getting lower as the grass burned down but the size of the area kept growing and the flames were dangerously close to a big rock that had a small grove of trees just below it. If the fire got into the trees, it could get much worse. It wasn't that far from the house either. The fire trucks got situated and firemen piled out, dragging the big fire hoses over to the source of the flames. Guys with axes and shovels fanned out around the perimeter, doing what they could to keep it from spreading. Shannon worked with the team of volunteer firemen and I continued with my buckets of water that I doused on areas where the flames had been put out but where coals were starting to ignite again.

We all worked feverishly until almost midnight. At that point, the fire appeared to be out and the entire group of firefighters dropped out of site below the big rock to be sure that there was no danger of the trees catching fire. Alone, I continued to work now with a shovel because every few minutes an area that appeared charred and cold would begin to glow with live coals being rekindled by the wind that had just come up. Suddenly, the perimeter closest to my house and furthest from the firefighters sprung up in a thin line of flame. The fire was expanding over towards the house. I ran down the hill and began to frantically stamp out the flames using the shovel. With a sinking heart, I began to feel like I was losing the battle. I was too far away for anyone to hear my yells. I didn't want to stop what I was doing to go and get help and risk the flames getting out of hand while no one was there, but I wasn't sure that I could keep it under control by myself. I was in a predicament. The wind was whipping up the flames into fresh tall grass and the flames were blowing towards me. Things started to heat up and I began to suspect that I personally might be in danger. "What should I do?" I couldn't decide. Just at that moment, a dark figure, silhouetted against the night sky, appeared at the top of the hill.

"Do you need some help?" he yelled. It was Dan. He had come home early from his hiking trip because of storms in the sierras and his neighbor had informed him that there was a fire raging below her house.

I almost wept for joy. "Get more help!" I yelled to him. "They're all down below the rock. Tell them the fire is breaking out again." Dan left me but quickly returned with a handful of guys with axes and shovels. This time the fire was quickly subdued. The neighborhood and my house had been saved! I was very grateful. As we all stood around at the top of the hill surveying the damage and talking about the fire, the fire chief came up to me. It was after midnight; there were ashes and charred grass all around us, and I was soaking wet from head to toe but I was as happy as I could be. Everyone had worked hard and we had been saved. It was a beautiful moment. I thanked the fire chief profusely. "Your son told me what happened. He was very open and honest about it. I like him. Accidents happen and I want you to know that we're not going to send you a bill."

I tried not to show my amazement. I hadn't known that they could send me a bill. I thought it was a free public service. "I'm so grateful for your help. I don't know what we would have done without you," I answered, feeling doubly grateful now that I knew that they could have charged me and that they weren't going to.

That was two disasters that had just been averted. As for Dan, he was truly my knight in shining armor. "Who was that masked man?" I said to myself with a smile.

Chapter 50
The Gathering Storm

Almost exactly a year after the fire, in June, I graduated from Humboldt State University with a Bachelor of Science degree in Nursing. Dan and a couple of my friends attended the graduation, and Boden and Shannon came up onto the stage to pin me. It was a proud moment. I can't say if I was prouder of my scholastic achievement or of my handsome twin boys who were up on stage with me trying to get the pin into the lapel of my jacket. They were certainly the greater of the two accomplishments. Going back to school had been a lot of work, but it had been fun. I had enjoyed breaking out of my routine and learning new things. Even if I didn't take it any further, it had certainly been a worthwhile experience.

After I graduated, one of the nurses suggested that I apply for the Director of Nursing job which had come available recently at the hospital. With a BSN, you can get into administration, but that wasn't for me. I liked patients, not paperwork. Public health had not interested me either. It was just not my cup of tea. What next then? I'd have to think about it. I was still contemplating going on to a Nurse Practitioner program but I didn't talk about it. I was afraid that no one would take me seriously. I think I still carried with me that High School dropout mentality. I didn't have confidence in myself so how could anyone else have confidence in me?

One of the classes that I had taken to get my BSN had talked about the stages of development throughout the life span. According to lifespan development theory, I was at the age where one considers what is left to accomplish that wasn't accomplished in younger years and gets on with it before it's too late. My biological clock was ticking away. *What are my goals?* I wondered. I was not in that blissful, loving, and devoted relationship that I imagined I wanted. That wasn't something that I seemed to be able to make happen and as for continuing on with school, like my astrological reading had predicted, "Nothing will happen unless you pursue it now with determination and patience." I had to make a decision. I had to go now or it wasn't going to happen. After much deliberation, I decided to apply to Sonoma State University, to their Family Nurse Practitioner program. In a last minute decision, I got my application, my transcripts, and my essay on why I wanted to be a Nurse Practitioner into the mail, special delivery, just a few days before the application deadline. When I got my acceptance letter, I was excited. It felt like a path that I was meant to take. It seemed as if I was doing exactly what I was meant to do.

That spring, once I had decided to go for it, I became caught up in the process of hastily gathering what was needed for my application and preparing for an exam to challenge a prerequisite physiology class. Once I was accepted into the program, as a present and a way of congratulations, Dan worked on my bedroom so that I would have an uncluttered, cheerful place to study. In the process of developing the homestead, which had spanned over many years, my bedroom was the last area of the house to be addressed. The floor needed to be sanded and stained, the windows needed trim around them and a good storage area need to be built so that I could keep things more organized. I also cut back from five 12-hour shifts every two weeks to four. That extra day would give me the added edge I needed to begin working at the clinic as a student nurse practitioner. Even as preparations were being made to position myself so that I could focus with an undisturbed mind on the program and the tremendous commitment that it entailed, I began to notice the gathering of storm clouds in the distance. Shannon, whose easy-going nature had always been so endearing and such a delight, began to be moody and uncooperative and he began to have angry outbursts. All through his teen years, he had seldom been rude to me, but now this change in attitude with his hostile and often rude comments began to upset me, and if I tried to talk with him about it, he would either laugh at me or fly into a rage. I became really concerned about him. I hoped that it was just a phase he was going through and that it would pass.

That first day of orientation to the program, the room was filled with confident students all of whom had been nurses for varying numbers of years. They all seemed to have no doubts about their capabilities and their rightful place in the program. I was very discouraged. It was a little like my first day of High School. I sat on the periphery and I felt almost ill with a neurotic conviction that I did not belong. "What am I doing here?" I asked myself. "I don't fit in. I'll never make it." Not even the 98th percentile grade on the Physiology test that I took to challenge the class could convince me that I was intelligent and could carry my weight. Another burden from my past, I eventually realized. Still, I pushed persistently ahead, as was my habit, which was perhaps one of the gifts I had received as a result of the adversities of the past!

After I had gotten through the first few weeks of classes, made some friends and started working with my preceptor at the local clinic, I began to feel more comfortable. Suddenly, my goal began to feel like it was within my reach. It was around this time that I realized, with heart wrenching dismay, that my son was very ill.

Chapter 51
5150

The day after I discovered my son, alone in his room talking to unseen visitors, I happened to glance out of an upstairs window. I saw him walking around in circles in front of the house, alternating between beating his tightly clenched fists against his head and pulling out his hair in helpless anguish and confusion. I wept to see him suffering so. He refused to let me take him to see a doctor so I sent for his sister to see if she could manage to persuade him to get medical care. She too wept tears of dismay to see him; one minute so brave and stoic making jokes and pretending that everything was normal while the next minute the curtain would fall over his gaze and he would stare vacantly into space tending to the clamoring mob of voices that were rendering his thoughts scrambled and undecipherable, even to himself. "Tell me about your voices," I would ask, wanting to get a better understanding of what was going on in his mind.

"I don't hear voices," he would insist on the defensive. Another time he told me with a big smile on his face, "My voices aren't saying anything that I don't want to hear." One night he told me with a chuckle as I said good night on my way up to bed, "I'll tell my voices to speak quietly so they don't keep you awake." Eventually, he admitted to me that the voices said terrible things about him and that it was killing him.

Shannon wasn't eating much and he was losing weight. He looked like he was ill. "Try giving him Zyprexa," Larry, the Physicians' Assistant at the hospital had advised. "It'll make him feel better," he generously offered to give me some samples. In those days, I myself was still wary of antipsychotic medication but I wanted very much to give it a try. Of course, Shannon would not have any part of it. One day, Shannon came into the house looking ghostly pale and fragile; my heart was breaking to see him that way.

"Everything is going to be alright, Shannon," I said to him, hoping desperately that it was so.

He drew his breath in deeply, "I like the sound of that," he said in a quiet voice. His faint, wistful smile was sweet and yet unbearably sad.

Schizophrenia, it seemed, was another legacy from my past. Although I'd had lots of personal experience with it, I was actually not that well informed. I started reading now, searching desperately for any information that might help me to help my son. I found, in a couple of alternative medicine sources, that Niacin and vitamin B12 and also Vitamin C could be extremely helpful to the brain's chemistry in schizophrenia so I started making smoothies and all sorts of healthy drinks with these vitamins in them. At the time, I felt that it helped a little but I could not really say how helpful it would have been if he had been taking it regularly. Most sources agree that the main treatment for schizophrenia is antipsychotic medication. Most sources also agree that strong family support is one of the predictors of a good outcome. I've also read that families that are too emotionally charged can actually be harmful to the person who suffers from schizophrenia. I took that piece of information seriously and I tried to act as calm and as matter of fact as I could when I was around Shannon.

Another thing I decided was to try and remove the stigma from the diagnosis by talking freely and casually about it as if I was talking about diabetes or the flu. I read in the book *Surviving Schizophrenia* by E. Fuller Torrey M.D. that having the right attitude was an essential part of dealing with the illness. The author felt that acceptance of the illness and realistic expectations were important aspects of having the right attitude. It's like that with any illness really. I knew a young woman who had a sudden onset of severe diabetes. For several years, she wouldn't accept that diagnosis. She almost died a couple of times, with ragingly high blood sugars, before she finally came to terms with it. Once she learned to accept and cope with her diabetes, she began to have a meaningful and full life. It seemed helpful to think of Schizophrenia like a chronic illness, something you live with and work with in order to minimize its impact on the quality of everyday life.

A sense of humor is always a helpful part of any strategy for developing good coping mechanisms. Shannon has a good sense of humor, and I tried to take advantage of that whenever I could when discussing his illness. "You may be crazy but you're not stupid," I told him once in what I hoped was a light-hearted tone, when he was recounting the story about how someone had tried to sell him the wrong car part. At first I wasn't sure if I was doing the right thing, making jokes and talking about it so openly. I didn't want to make him painfully self-conscious either, but as time passed, I was glad that I had taken that approach from the very beginning because eventually it got to the point where we could talk about it openly among friends and family and laugh together at some of the absurdities. But it took a while to get there.

We were all just sort of hanging in there, trying to maintain a secure, supportive environment, feed him healthy food, educate him about his illness and approaching him frequently with the offer of medical care. We hoped that at some point he would accept the offer. It seemed at first like we might be making some progress. He had times when he seemed more together and then times when he seemed really ill. A few times he got catatonic. I would catch him, frozen, with his foot suspended in midair, partially through the act of pulling on his boot. He would stay suspended like that for several minutes with a blank look on his face before seeming to wake up and finish the job.

After a little over a week, Emily went back home to the Ashram. Boden had, long ago, moved out and now he kept his distance. I know that it was hard on him to see his brother that way. At times, Boden seemed a little angry and aloof but later his girlfriend told me that one day, when they were talking about Shannon, he had broken down and cried as if his heart were breaking. No doubt it was. Dan lived up the hill and he was busy with his own schedule of work and friends. Shannon and I were left to ourselves. I continued with work and school, grateful for the positive, constructive distraction that they provided. Shannon was still able to work, some, with his friends but things were changing rapidly. His angry outbursts were becoming more frequent. Even though I understood that it was his illness talking, it hurt me deeply to be yelled at by my son and often the things that made him angry did not make any sense.

On Thanksgiving Day, Dan's neighbor and good friend had a holiday get-together. Shannon knew and liked most of the people but he wouldn't come up and join us. He preferred to sit alone in his room working on a model airplane. Towards the end of the evening, some of us went down the hill to say hello and to bring him a plate of food. We found him in his room with his doors and windows tightly shut. His room was like a sauna, and he was sitting in front of a small propane space heater, pale as a ghost with streams of sweat running down his face. He looked distracted. He held a half-finished model in his outstretched hands, and he was staring at it. When we opened his door, he looked up at us blankly but suddenly the curtain lifted and he smiled to see us all standing there in the doorway in a cluster bringing good food, good vibes, and lots of love.

We continued on with our lives, just trying to make it from day to day, trying to make the best of things, attempting to keep on an even keel. Then, one terrible night, a couple of weeks after thanksgiving, Shannon got into a fight with his brother. Boden had come over to give me some advice about my computer. Suddenly, Shannon had started yelling at Boden and he was shoving at him with both hands. It looked like Shannon was trying to get Boden off balance and push him onto the floor. I saw that he had slipped a knife into his back pocket and remembering the hospital tragedy, I became alarmed. "I'm calling 911, and I'm going to ask them to send the sheriff to 5150 you, Shannon, if you don't stop fighting right this minute," I said, heading over to the phone, my heart pounding in my ears.

He ignored me. I knew I had to be decisive. Things had gone way too far already. I called 911 and they said that they would dispatch the sheriff right away. When I hung up, I announced that the sheriff was on his way.

"You're lying," Shannon said accusingly, disbelieving.

"I called them, and they're on their way."

The effect of this news was that both of them left the house, got into their separate cars, and drove off. Minutes later, when the two sheriff cars pulled into my driveway, I was the only one at home. As I was explaining the situation to the police, Shannon drove up. He seemed to have cleared, and he talked very reasonably and calmly to the police. He was being his sweet and charming self. After talking to him for a while, they said to me, "You can press charges, we can take him to jail, and we can issue a restraining order so that he's not allowed to come near the house but we can't 5150 him. We can't put him on a 72-hour psychiatric hold because from what we're seeing, he does not appear to be a danger to himself or to others."

The familiar yard felt like a strange and alien land. It was brightly lit up from the headlights of the two sheriff cars, and there were four sheriffs standing around with their hand on their hips, talking amongst themselves and assessing the situation. Everything else receded into the darkness. I looked over at Shannon. He looked relaxed and in a good mood. He was leaning casually against the hood of his truck, and he had a smile on his face. It was almost like he was enjoying the attention.

"I don't want to press charges," I said. "I don't want him in jail. I want him to get a psychiatric evaluation and I want him to get on medication."

"I'm sorry, we believe what you are telling us but there's nothing we can do."

They got in their cars and drove back down the hill, leaving Shannon and me standing there together, in the dark and stillness. I was suddenly aware of the cold, and I shivered as I pulled my coat tightly around me. As we walked back in the house, I told him, "Violence is not an acceptable way to settle things. You're not a child anymore. Don't do that again."

We each went to our separate rooms and that was that for the evening, but through my half-opened window, I could hear him talking and laughing crazily in his loft bed that was just below my room, and it made me feel so alone and so frightened for him.

Over the next couple of weeks, Shannon started obsessing over the fact that I had called the police on him. He got angrier and angrier with me and with his brother. He became increasingly rude and difficult to be around. I began to feel like my own fragile mind was at the breaking point, and I worried constantly that he might try and hurt his brother. If I tried to talk with him about medication, he would scream at me, "I don't need medication, you need medication. You're the crazy one!"

One night, Shannon didn't come home, and I felt sad, worried, and relieved all at the same time. The situation was deteriorating. Shannon seemed to be lost in some dark and stormy place. More than anything in the world, I wanted to reach out to him and pull him to safety but I couldn't. He was trapped where no one could reach him. Something had to be done.

On Christmas Eve, I had a small dinner planned with Shannon and Boden and Dan, but Shannon got really hostile and started talking about sinners and evil spirits. He got kind of scary, and the evening ended poorly with Boden leaving abruptly. Shortly after Boden left, Dan was preparing to leave as well. I didn't feel comfortable being left alone with Shannon in the angry mood that he was in so I went with Dan up to his house, leaving Shannon alone with his voices and his angry, delusional thoughts. He was not someone that I knew anymore, and I had begun to feel like I wasn't safe in my own home. I could no longer stand to live with him, but I didn't want him to leave either. I still hoped for a positive outcome and I was afraid that if he had nowhere to go, that he would join the millions of mentally ill homeless and I would lose him forever. Dan's house was a great solution. It was near enough that I could check in on Shannon every day, but I wouldn't have to subject myself to his rude and crazy outbursts that were becoming a daily occurrence. Dan was happy to be of help, and so I took a few of my favorite clothes, my computer and printer and all of my school books, and once again, as I had done many times before in my life, I left my home because of mental illness in a loved one.

Shannon had an old-fashioned gun that used gunpowder. One afternoon, I went to see how he was doing and bring him a sandwich. He was parked in such a way that I could not pull into the driveway or turn my car around to drive safely back down the long, steep, narrow, and winding road. I left my car where it was and, with trepidation, went inside the house to see what was going on. Shannon was sitting at his work table, cleaning his gun. He was angry and he started waving the gun around in the air. I didn't know if it was loaded or not. "Get out of here," he started screaming.

"Can I get a few things from my room first?" I asked, foolishly thinking that I could talk him down.

"No, you can't," he yelled. "Just get out."

"Will you move your car so that I can turn around?" I asked, trying to sound relaxed and nonthreatening.

"No," he shouted again. "Just get out," he followed me onto the porch. "Get out! Get out! Get out!" he shouted repeatedly. I got into my car and backed down the long driveway carefully and slowly so as not to cause my own death by driving off of the steep road in my consternation. I scrawled in my journal that night: "Shannon reaches new levels of insanity." I was grateful that I had a safe shelter with Dan.

The next evening, because they were short staffed, I had agreed to work the first half of the night shift from 7 p.m. to midnight. I was so distraught that I could hardly do my work. I was basically useless. Someone suggested that I send a sheriff over to the house to do a safety check on Shannon. I had my doubts about the efficacy of such a plan. I told the ER Doc, "If you ever see my son in this Emergency Room, you must put him on a 72-hour psychiatric hold. He has to have a psychiatric evaluation! He needs help!" I was standing at the nursing station, staring distractedly at a dark stain on the rug, telling the ER Doc and the other nurses, who were trying to console me, that somehow I had to get help for my son. Suddenly, I looked up. I had been so distracted that I hadn't heard anyone come in. There at the counter stood a young man, his face ashen and ghostly. He was asking for help. It was Shannon.

We hastened to get a wheel chair, and we wheeled him down to the ER. Shannon's story was certainly not threatening. Under different circumstances, it might have seemed almost comical. He had been watching a Clint Eastwood movie and he was trying to twirl his gun the way his cowboy hero did when he accidentally shot himself in the leg. In a panic, Shannon had tried to drive to town and he had gone off our steep road. He would have rolled down the 500 foot hill to his certain death if not for the small, flat knoll that his car landed on. Then he had crawled, scared and in pain, back up the hill, through the mud and pouring rain, where he got into the old car that we kept around for emergencies and drove himself to the hospital. He was looking to us for help. I took the ER Doc aside. "He shot himself. You have to 5150 him." The Doctor agreed.

After the IV had been started and Shannon was recovered a little from the shock of it all, he said to me, "I just want to have a normal life." He looked sad and sincere and innocent as he said this. My heart went out to him. A normal life was exactly what I wanted for Shannon. He still didn't know that we were planning to send him to the county mental hospital. I felt confused for a minute. Maybe we could work this out without using force and confinement to a mental hospital. I didn't want to betray his trust but I felt a bigger responsibility to get him medical help and to assure the safety of his brother. "It's tough, love," I told myself. We might never get this chance again, not until after something terrible had happened. "They're going to 5150 you and send you to the Psych hospital," I informed him, trying to hide the fact that the idea of it was frightening to me and that I wasn't so sure of myself anymore. "You have to get help, Shannon."

Upon hearing this news, he became very upset, and he tried to leave so we had to call the sheriff to detain him in the Emergency Room and to accompany him up north. They would be sending him first to a bigger ER to assess his leg for surgery. At St. Joes ER, when they saw that it was scattered, small shrapnel, they said it would do more damage to try and retrieve the fragments than to leave them. They bandaged him up and sent him on, after midnight, to the locked mental facility.

The quiet street was dark and empty at 3 a.m. as Dan and I stood there without speaking, ringing the bell at the gated door of Semper Virens. We were both exhausted but we powered through with the massive adrenalin rush that followed on the wake of the evening events. "Can I help you?" a very much awake and business-like, disembodied voice queried over the intercom.

"We're here for Shannon. He was just admitted. I'm his mother." I was glad that he would finally be getting a professional evaluation but heartbroken that he had to go through this much misery to get it. There was a loud buzz that alerted us that we could push open the heavy iron door. We entered and walked up a narrow flight of stairs to the first floor landing where we were met by a friendly man in a white coat. He unlocked another heavy door so that we could enter and lead us to a small, dismal lounge where there was an old plastic covered couch, a straight-backed chair, and a small lamp. The room gave the feeling of institutional poverty. It reminded me of the welfare office that I had spent several days in when I was a little girl, and it made me feel sad. So this is where one goes when one becomes a danger to themselves or to others, when the mind can no longer even pretend to function in the world, when one has lost all hope. They come here to a cold, drab, empty, prison-like place, devoid of any warmth. Such was my first impression of the County Mental Health locked facility. It was reassuring, however, to find that the staff was not without human kindness. They were very supportive and understanding, and their sincere concern helped ease the anxiety of the situation. It was too late to see Shannon but they took a history and asked us questions that would make it easier for them to help him. Tomorrow, we could come back and see him.

We did go back the next day. He was angry with me, and his anger was like that of a caged lion that will rip you apart should he escape. In a way, I could understand it. I had betrayed him. He had come to me for protection, and I had allowed them to lock him up. With his ailing mind, there was no way that he could understand that this 72-hour hold was for his benefit so that he could get the help that he so desperately needed. Shannon had already called his dad, and John had advised him that he shouldn't take any medication and that they couldn't force him to take it. Shannon was now further lost in the labyrinths of his disorganized nightmarish thoughts than ever. The stress of the situation had robbed him of what little clarity he had left. When we entered the room, he was pacing around and around in tight circles, posturing, with his body stiff and his arms held high over his head uplifted to the sky. When he saw me, he started shouting and he looked like he might attack me. "You'd better leave," the nurses told me as they tried to restrain him. "You're upsetting him." After that, just Dan went up to visit.

That night was New Year's Eve, and although I wasn't in a party mood, I certainly didn't want to be alone. Dan, Boden, and I and a couple of my nursing friends met for a late night dinner. It was comforting to be with everyone. "I can't believe his dad told him not to take the medication. It's like a nightmare; mentally ill father giving crazy advice to his mentally ill son. Could things get any worse, any more bizarre?" My nerves were shattered. As we had left Semper Virens that night, I had seen Shannon watching me out of a barred upstairs window. The crazed and evil look of hatred in his dark eyes when he saw me is something that, as much as I would like to, I will never be able to forget. I honestly didn't know how much more stress and heartbreak I could take. I felt as though I was very close to the breaking point. "They have to find the right medication for Shannon, and he has to take it. There's no other way," I said, knowing that I'd probably have to abandon Shannon to the streets and under the bridge and leave the area with no forwarding address, if we couldn't get him at least somewhat stabilized. The noisemakers started to go off and there was cheering and fireworks in the distance. "Happy New Year!" everyone was saying, raising their glasses for a toast. Again, I visualized Shannon having a sweet and simple life with a family who loved him. "Happy New Year," I said, raising my glass for a toast, with giant teardrops falling, like rain, into my champagne.

If I thought that things were as bad as they could get, I was wrong. The 72-hour hold was almost up and nothing had been accomplished other than to make my son more psychotic and consumed with hatred towards me. To keep him for any longer, we would actually have to go to court and request a 14-day hold. Lea was the NAMI representative for the area, and she advised me that we would have a better case if I took the stand and testified. We were introduced to Lea at Semper Virens where she visited regularly to give classes and to advocate for patients and their families. She was there for Shannon, and she was there for me as well. "It's never an easy process. You're doing what needs to be done. You just have to hang in there. Things will improve, you'll see," Lea reassured Dan and me as we floundered in the system. Everyone seemed to be well-meaning, but resources were so limited and the laws only served to tie their hands. It just didn't seem like they were helping Shannon at all. If anything, matters were getting worse. Lea also had a son who suffered from mental illness. She knew how traumatic it was for the families and loved ones. She reassured us as much as she could and she went to court with us when I had to take the stand and explain to the judge why I thought that my son was a danger and needed to be hospitalized and forced to take medication against his will.

I hadn't seen Shannon in a few days because he always got so angry when he saw me that they wouldn't let me visit, but I missed him. I was anxious to get a look at him so I could see for myself how he was doing. From across the courtroom, Shannon glared at me as I took the stand. "Raise your right hand. Do you solemnly swear to tell the truth, the whole truth and nothing but the truth, so help you God?"

Suddenly, I was overcome with emotion and I couldn't speak. I was afraid for a minute that I was going to start crying hysterically. The courtroom was silent. Everyone looked at me. As I struggled with my emotions, I realized that there was no backing down now. I had to go forward with this. As briefly as possible, I recounted the circumstances of the last couple of months and we got our 14-day hold but we still did not know if we could force medication. The following week, we went back to court again to address the medication issue. We were requesting court-mandated medication compliance. Two days after that, we got a call from Semper Virens informing us that the judge had finally given the okay to give him medication. They were going to give him an injection that would stay working in his system for one month and then they would be letting him go at 7 p.m. That very evening, Shannon was given a depo injection of Haldol and put out on the street. Dan and I were there to meet him. The night was dark and cold and it was raining lightly. Shannon seemed kind of dazed and he carried with him a sheet of printed discharge instructions and a handful of prescriptions which, if he were to buy them all, would have cost him well over $1,000. "How," I wondered, somewhat shocked, "could anyone with mental illness and no family to take care of them possibly navigate this kind of a system?"

With the Haldol on board, the promise of a good hot dinner and a night in his own bed, Shannon seemed much improved. He actually seemed better than he had been in months. I knew it was the medicine that was adjusting his brain chemistry so that his thoughts were becoming organized again and I was very grateful.

As soon as we left Semper Virens, we went to the pharmacy to pick up medication for him. They had put him on four different antipsychotic drugs at medium to high doses and one drug to combat side effects. To get one month worth of all his prescriptions, I would have needed over $1,500. Now that seemed crazy! Most psychotic people put out of the county institution in the rain after dark do not even have the money for a hot cup of coffee or a much-prized cigarette. Whatever would they do with $1,500 worth of prescriptions that they didn't even think were needed. It made no sense. Luckily, as a nurse, I had some background in medication management and I could sort it out for Shannon. For one thing, he didn't need four different psych. meds. I figured that Haldol was one of the older antipsychotic medications, and as such ran the risk of having more side effects. Depakote was a mood stabilizer and more for bipolar than schizophrenia. It didn't seem like it would be that helpful. Of the two newer antipsychotics that they also prescribed, Zyprexa and Risperdal, I wasn't sure which would be better but I had a friend whose daughter suffered from schizophrenia and she did well on Zyprexa so that was what I decided to go with. They had prescribed for him three times the recommended dosage. I would cut that in half. "Whatever were they thinking?" I wondered to myself.

While I was in the pharmacy working all that out and spending several hundred dollars on a couple of weeks' worth of medication, Shannon's public defender happened to be passing by, and she recognized him and Dan sitting in the car in front of the pharmacy. She stopped to see how he was doing, and she told him, "You know you don't have to take that medicine if you don't want to."

After all that we had just been through to get Shannon on medication, it was so bizarre to be thus thwarted, first by John and then by the public defender who obviously didn't know a thing about mental illness. Many people who suffer from schizophrenia have what they term anosognosia, which is an impaired awareness of their illness. Because of that, it is common for them to refuse to take the medicine which is the only thing that will really help them. Shannon clearly did not realize how ill he was. He thanked her kindly for her advice and when I got out to the car, he informed me that he was not planning on taking any medications. He didn't need it. He had thought that the judge's ruling meant that he had to take it but his lawyer had explained that the ruling only covered his stay in Semper Virens. I was beside myself with consternation. I could not believe my own ears. "You have to take it," I replied with a calmness that did not reflect how I was feeling. "Or you can't live at the house." We discussed this at length over our meal. I had read in several books that it was important to set realistic boundaries and that one of the most important boundaries to establish was that without strict medication compliance the person with schizophrenia would not be allowed to live at home with the family. After much discussion, seeing that I wasn't going to back down, Shannon finally agreed that as long as he was living under my roof, he would take his medication. After dinner, we took him home.

Chapter 52
Through the Woods

With all the storms and heavy rains that we had been having, part of my road washed out. Shannon's large 4-wheel drive truck could make it up the driveway but my little car could not. Cut off so from the world outside, the eroded, washed-out road seemed to reflect the mood of Shannon's inner isolation. Things were coming apart but I was determined to do what I could to keep it all together. We could not work on the road until the spring when the rains let off, but we could work on getting Shannon back now that we had a few tools, mainly medication and a connection with mental health workers. I had been thinking of staying up at Dan's and letting Shannon have the house for a while. Now that I couldn't get up the road, it became obvious that it was the most practical way to proceed.

Dan lived in a little redwood cabin. The large main room had a kitchen area, a table and a couple of chairs, a small couch, and a wood stove with a glass window so that you could sit and watch the fire. The bed was off to the side in a little sleeping alcove. It was small and simple and very cozy. I thanked him for letting me stay and he replied, "I am glad that I can help. You're welcome to stay as long as you need to."

Although it was a most generous and helpful offer and I so appreciated it and planned to take him up on it, I was sorry that it didn't include a warmer, more personal clause such as, "I really like having your company."

I stayed with Dan for the next year and a half while I continued with the NP Program. I felt safe and sheltered in the refuge he offered. I was always either at my computer working on school papers or at the hospital working a shift or at the clinic as a student. The days were busy, and I had to be obsessively organized to get everything accomplished. Within this framework, I tried to see Shannon as much as I could. Since my car wouldn't get up the driveway, I started walking down from Dan's. It took me ten minutes down through the dark, thick woods and underbrush to get to the house. The return uphill trip took a few minutes longer. At first, I was nervous about going down to the house. I never knew what to expect. Although he was much clearer, he was still angry with me. Since he had been home, he had been mostly keeping to himself, alone and brooding. He took the medication when I went down and gave it to him but on the days that I couldn't make it down to see him, he usually didn't remember or didn't care to take it. I was cooking for him when I could and I would buy him groceries and put them in my little day pack and carry them down to the house so he would have some easy-to-prepare meals. Usually, I would find him still in bed fully dressed with his coat and his heavy Danner boots on or lying on the couch where he had spent the night and much of the day. I could tell at a glance if he was angry or in a dark mood. Then I would put away the groceries, give him his medicine, and leave him to his thoughts. If he seemed in a friendly mood, I would stay and visit. He rarely made a fire and the house was always cold, so if I was staying for a while, I'd make a fire to warm things up. I'd make us some tea and hot cereal, and we'd sit together warming ourselves by the fire. Sometimes, he'd start to get angry again and he'd tell me, "It's time for you to leave." I always listened when he said that. I'd get up, gather my things, and head for the door. "I love you," I'd tell him as I was walking out the door. I hoped that he understood that. Around four times a week, I made it down there. I couldn't go down on my shift days or if I had to go down to the school. I didn't go down after dark either. I was still afraid of the dark.

One afternoon, about a month after his release, Shannon came up to the cabin. Dan had left for the day, and I was there by myself. I was surprised to see him. He still looked weary but the expression on his face was more relaxed and he didn't seem angry. "I'd like to go into town," he told me. "But I have a flat tire."

I was glad that here was something that I could help him with that he would appreciate. "Let's go into town and get your tire fixed," I told him without hesitation.

We ended up spending the day together, driving around town and doing little errands to help him get some things together. We went and got him a haircut, and he looked great. He seemed fragile and you could tell that something was not right when you talked with him but compared with where he had been just a few weeks ago, he seemed light years better. While we were waiting to get his tire fixed, I observed Shannon from across the parking lot. The people at the tire place were friends of his, and I think that it was stressful for him to have the social interaction for he started walking around the parking lot in circles with his head down and his hands held high up in the air, fingers pointing towards the sky. It made him look very strange indeed. I went over to him and grabbed his arm. "Let's go get something to eat while we're waiting," I said as I pulled him away to a nearby café. It felt good to be able to touch him. He hadn't let me that close in months.

That evening, when we got back to the cabin, Dan was still out. I had a good movie that I had planned to watch on my computer so I invited Shannon for dinner and a movie. He accepted, and we sat companionably together watching the movie and eating burritos. It was dark outside but in the flickering firelight, I could see that Shannon looked relaxed and comfortable. I felt like it was a turning point. We were friends once again, and it made me so happy that I wanted to jump up and down and laugh and cry for joy. After the movie, he thanked me for my help and he headed down through the woods to the house using a flashlight to illuminate the way. After that, I started spending more time with Shannon. I set up a work space for my laptop by the fire and I would go down to the house, make a cozy fire and something for us to eat, then I would do my schoolwork while Shannon sat around and watched a video or just hung out. One day, we watched a really funny movie together and we laughed and laughed, and we beamed at each other in appreciation

Early one morning, on my way down to school for a class that I could not miss, I got a flat tire. It was 5 a.m. and the flat happened conveniently at a good pull-off spot about five miles from the house. Dan was out of town for a few days so I tried calling Shannon. I was relieved when he answered the phone. "I'll be right there," he told me in a sleepy voice.

When he arrived, he looked paranoid, but once he swung into action, he seemed fine. I noticed that he had a big knife lying on the passenger seat of his truck. *He was frightened*, I thought. *He was afraid that it might be a trap*. I was used to the paranoia of my mother so it didn't alarm me that much. When I mentioned it to him, he grabbed the knife and tossed it behind the seat without comment. My spare tire was one of those little tires and it couldn't withstand the 3-hour drive to Sonoma State University, so I asked Shannon if he would drive me down in his truck and hang out while I was in class. I promised to take him out for a great dinner. He protested at first, but he saw that it was important so he agreed to do it, and he did incredibly well, but when I came to get him at the library after a full day of classes, he looked pale and shaken. It had been too much for him to sit there all day with so much sensory input, amongst a steady stream of animated and happy students going on, with purpose, about their busy day. Anxiety was written all over his face and in his body language as he sat there tensely staring straight ahead with his arms folded tightly across his chest. The contrast between his convoluted, frightened, inner world and the relaxed happy world of the students was painful to see. "Are you ready to go?" I asked, feeling sorry that I had put him through the stress of it but it did show me that in a pinch, even with his illness, he was there for me, and it made me love him all the more.

Chapter 53
The Art of Medicine

One of the Valley Docs that I was friends with was working, east of Redding, at a clinic that had a small hospital and emergency room attached. I had always liked working with Dr. L, and he was good at teaching. I called him and asked if I could spend a few days at his clinic as a student. It seemed like getting a different perspective on things might be good for me and I thought that it would be fun. "I don't see why not," he told me. "I'll have to talk it over with the clinic administrator, but I'll get back to you."

We set it all up, and early one morning I set out, driving through a snowstorm, to join Dr. L. at his daily practice. He saw clinic patients there and covered the emergency room and the in-house patients as well. His days were very full.

It was a long drive and slow going in the snow, but it was beautiful. All around me, the hills and valleys were blanketed in white. It didn't snow that often in these parts, and everything looked so different that I was completely caught up in the moment as if I had to concentrate with all my being in order to find my way through a lost world. Now this was a worthy adventure. I arrived at the clinic after dark and went into the little ER to get a key to the house that was used by visiting physicians. ML had not arrived as yet. I opened up the door with stiff cold hands and went in. I had to search around for the light for a moment. When I switched on the light, I was pleased to find that I was in a very pleasant and comfortable sitting room. Some thoughtful person had turned on the heater in preparation for our arrival and it was warm. I was extremely tired from hours of driving in the snow so I lay down on the couch and covered myself with my sleeping bag to await the arrival of my friend. I must have fallen into a deep sleep for when I awoke, it was morning and he was putting on a pot of coffee. "Shall we go out to breakfast?" my friend asked cheerfully. "We have another couple of hours before we have to start."

"Yes, that sounds great. It was dark when I arrived, and I didn't really see much of the town."

"Well, there's not much to see but we can see what there is." ML poured out some coffee for us and we sat and chatted about various events in our lives and then we set out for some breakfast. It looked like a western style town, but it was all covered in snow and it was hard to get around. We slithered and skidded through the streets and parked in front of a busy roadside café. Over eggs and toast, he told me about the clinic and the hospital and we decided that I would first see the clinic patients by myself and then we would talk about the encounter. I would tell him my plan and then he would check in on the patient with me to finish up the visit. The ER we would do together.

After introductions around the clinic were made, we went to work. It was a busy day spent running, through the snow, back and forth from the clinic over to the little ER. After clinic, we visited the two inpatients in the little hospital and then we stopped by the building that held the skilled nursing patients. By the end of the day, I was wiped out. We made a simple dinner and talked about the day's work. I felt like I had already learned a lot in just one day. One very useful thing that he taught me is that there are often many different options for how to treat any given problem. So many of the other docs that I had worked with gave me the impression that their way was the right way and that anything else was wrong, but as I worked with ML, he showed me, at each patient encounter, the variety of options that were available for treating each illness or complaint. Usually, the option chosen was positively impacted by patient preference and, more disturbingly, by method of payment. That was part of the art of medicine, creating an individualized plan that took many different factors into consideration. That night, I heard ML get up several times to walk over to the ER when a patient came in. Although I was interested, I found sleep more inviting and so I let him go on without me. 8 a.m. to 8 p.m. was quite enough fun for one day.

The next day, I entered the clinic room with two charts. We were seeing identical twin brothers who were in for their immunizations. Their mom was telling me about their past medical history. "They both suffer from schizophrenia," she said in a matter-of-fact tone. "They're on medication now but before the medication, they were having a really hard time. They both heard voices that told them to do bad things. They couldn't get along in school and they were always in trouble. Things are so much better now."

"Do they take their medication willingly?" I asked, suddenly feeling like the luckiest person in the world because my story was not nearly so heartbreaking.

"Oh yes," their mother assured me. "They don't like the way they feel without it."

The boys seemed very sweet, and I imagined that their life was a hard one and that it wasn't, in fact, going to get that much easier. ML joined us, and in his comforting way, he made the mother and her sons feel at home and cared for. That too was part and parcel of the art of medicine.

For every patient that I saw that day, I would give my report and plan to ML. He would then council me on the value of my plan and show me some of the other options I could have chosen. In this way, I began to see medicine not so much as a rigid, inflexible discipline but more as an adaptable and unfolding story that had at it's very core the individual needs and preferences of the patient. This evolving model of medicine, with the patient as an integral part of the medical team, was much more appealing to me than the older, paternalistic model.

The next day, we were called over to the ER for a woman in labor. They didn't do deliveries at that hospital, so if delivery seemed imminent, we were going to have to send her quickly over the mountain to another town. I was the only person there really familiar with labor and delivery. After checking, ML wasn't sure whether or not she was dilating so I was, in a way, able to save the day by ascertaining that she was six centimeters dilated and should be heading over the mountain right away. I was pleased too that I spoke enough Spanish to be able to reassure the mother and let her know what was going on. I felt useful, like I had really helped out the situation. It was those very satisfying moments in medicine that kept me hooked.

At the end of the week, I drove back home feeling much more confident about my role as a Nurse Practitioner and about life in general. As I drove through the mountainous back roads with the full moon shining down and my favorite music playing, I was so high on life that I didn't even feel tired. *Medicine is an art*, I was thinking. *Living is an art for that matter. The more love and the more beauty that one can bring to one's life, the greater and more precious a work of art it becomes.* I was continually working to bring greater beauty and love into my life. I knew that, already, I had many treasures and much to be thankful for. For one glorious moment, I felt as I were one with the music and the sky and the tree-covered hills that were lit up all around me by the bright, silvery light of the full moon.

Chapter 54
Isolation and Suffering

The second year of FNP program started out a bit a bumpy also. Towards the end of the summer, Shannon went through a period where he stopped taking his medicine. He stayed away from the house in the daytime so I wasn't able to connect with him and pressure him into compliance, and he started to get crazy again. He told Dan that Boden and I were making a machine to steal peoples souls and that we needed to be eliminated. By mid-September, I had managed to get him going back on his medicine and by September 26, his and Boden's 24th birthday, he was thankfully starting to come around again. After spending a couple of days giving the house a much needed cleaning, I had a little birthday get-together for them. Surrounded by friends and loved ones, Shannon was able to smile and join the party, although he sat off to the side and didn't interact much unless someone went out of their way to draw him out. Once again, I was thankful to see that he was coming back. Always when he was unrecognizable, lost in the storm of his psychosis, I would tell myself that the Shannon that I knew and loved was still in there somewhere, trapped, and once again I was seeing the proof of it.

Blanche was not doing so well. She had high blood pressure but she would not see a doctor and she refused to take medicine to control her hypertension. I think she was having some very tiny strokes because she seemed more distant, delusional, and confused than ever. She wasn't paying all of her bills and she wasn't getting out much to buy groceries. Boden and I agreed to take turns visiting her weekly to check on her and Shannon helped when he could. One evening, Shannon and I took Blanche out to dinner and afterwards we went to her house and Shannon fixed the light in her kitchen. My mother was very appreciative. Somehow, there was something very touching about that. Shannon shared the same genetic burden as his grandmother and it was sweet to see that he was concerned enough to help her even though he wasn't doing so well himself.

That October, we got word that John was in the Intensive Care Unit up in Washington. He had some sort of intestinal blockage that had gone on for weeks. Apparently, instead of going to see a doctor, he had just stayed at home and stopped eating. John had been living alone for quite some time since Carolyn had left him. Without anyone looking in on him, there had been no one to notice how much he was suffering from his illness. Carolyn told Boden that she had become worried because she hadn't heard from John in a long time. When she went over to his house to check on him, she was shocked by what she found. He was emaciated and jaundiced and he looked like he was about to die. She insisted on taking him to the Emergency Room, and they took him right into surgery, but in his weakened condition, the surgery had been hard on him and he went into adult respiratory distress syndrome. "He's unconscious and he's on a ventilator. He's not expected to live," Carolyn had told Boden over the phone.

"I'm coming right up," Boden responded without hesitation. "I'll be there in the morning."

Shannon wanted to go too. We couldn't stop him. It was his father also but the news had sent him into a relapse. I looked on anxiously as they drove off into the night with Shannon looking wild eyed and crazed and Boden already exhausted from a long and stressful day but planning to drive through the night so that he could see his father one more time before he passed away.

Miraculously, after spending a month in Intensive Care, John recovered enough to be put out on the medical unit and my sons came home. Shannon hadn't taken his meds while he was up there, and the stories that Boden told me made me shake my head sadly. "Day after day Shannon stood at the bedside," Boden told me. "With his arms crossed over his chest, muttering and laughing to himself."

"What's he on?" the woman doctor had asked.

"Nothing, that's just the way he is," Boden had replied with a shrug.

When he regained consciousness, John had apparently been kind of out there too and had said some pretty crazy things.

Emily had also gone up to see her dad, thinking that he was about to die. I was relieved that they had Emily's grounding presence to help balance out the difficult situation. I believed that with all of his family surrounding him, against all odds, their love must have given him the strength to pull through. It was a long, hard road to recovery for John, and it was several months, well after the New Year, before he was finally able to return to his home.

When Shannon got home from Washington in the beginning of November, I immediately got him back on his medication, and by Thanksgiving he was starting to do better again. This year, once again, Dan's neighbors had a big Thanksgiving celebration. This time Shannon was well enough to attend but his hands were so stiff and uncoordinated that Dan had to serve him his food, and he stood off in the corner by himself without talking to anyone and looking very strained. It was hard on my heart to see him like that, but I was also grateful that he was so much better than he had been the year before. It was definitely something to be thankful for but it didn't last long. Around Christmas, Shannon started disappearing for several days at a time. When I did see him, he looked as bad as he had ever looked. When he was really psychotic, his pupils would dilate and his beautiful blue eyes would actually turn black. He was going through another dark period, and when I would see him, his eyes would look dark and angry. He was scary when he looked at me like that, and at those times I avoided him. If his eyes were blue and he was smiling, I knew that I was seeing my son Shannon and that all was well.

We had fixed the road over the summer and so I was able to drive up to see him. I would park the car in such a way as to be able to make a quick escape if I needed to. It gave me the courage to keep checking in on him even though he was out of touch with reality again. Finally, he ran into some trouble with some new 'friends' that he had made. I believed that they were giving him speed and that was making him even more psychotic. When his new 'friends' stole his truck, Shannon fell apart. I drove up the road to check on him one day, and I found that he had been lying in bed for several days without taking off his coat or his heavy boots and he wasn't eating. I succeeded in getting him to take his boots off and the stench of it was horrible. His feet were literally rotting away. Then I got him to eat and take one of his pills and afterwards he fell into a deep sleep. He slept for three days, only waking up when I roused him to take another pill and have something to eat and drink. I was on the winter break from school so I spent a lot of time down at the house working on my computer and looking after my son who mostly slept. The last couple of years had been such an unstable and chaotic time. *Would we ever recover from this? I* wondered. *Would we ever regain our equilibrium?* After the third day, he started coming around again. His eyes were a sky blue as he gazed at me. "I have been suffering," he told me sadly. "For the last year, I have been doing nothing but lying on the couch. I have been alone, and I have been suffering."

"I know, Shannon. I've been trying to help you. I gave you the house so at least you would have somewhere familiar and safe to stay."

He looked at me now, for the first time with appreciation. "I don't know what would have happened to me without it. Something terrible I think."

I knew that there was a high rate of suicide among those who suffered from schizophrenia, and I was thankful that I had been able to offer my son a refuge.

"Will you help me find my truck?" he asked. "I think I know where it is."

We drove into town and looked at several different locations. We found it on a side alley in the local trailer park. The keys were in it so he just got in his truck and drove it home. The next day, when I went down to see him a couple of hours before sunset, he asked me if I would go down to the flat spot at the bottom of the property and help him fly his remote controlled airplane.

"Sure, let's do it," I replied glad for the opportunity to spend some quality time with him.

As we walked down the road together in quiet companionship with the crickets buzzing and the sun going down behind the hills and soft shades of pink and yellow starting to spread across the sky, I began to think, for the first time since he'd had his first break that perhaps things actually were going to be alright.

A couple of weeks later, in a sudden change of circumstances, I put Shannon on a plane headed up to Washington. His father had recently gotten home from the hospital. He was very weak, and he needed help from his sons. Boden couldn't go because he was just starting the school semester, but Shannon wanted to go. John promised me that he would make sure that Shannon took his medication. "I take lots of different pills now myself. We'll take our medicine together," he assured me with a chuckle.

It was risky but I hoped that it would prove to be a positive thing for both father and son to spend some time together, and it would get Shannon away, if only temporarily, from the temptation of street drugs. Self-medicating with recreational drugs was a common thing for those suffering from mental illness but in the end, it only served to further destabilize them.

I called that night to see if Shannon had made the trip alright and he told me that he had gotten lost in Seattle and had to take a taxi to the small town of Everett where John lived. He seemed a little shaken, but he was glad to be there with his dad.

"I'm going to call you every day to remind you to take your medicine," I told him.

"That's alright. I'll talk with you tomorrow," he said, sounding clear and in a good mood.

"I love you," I said to him before hanging up.

"Love you too," he told me.

That was something that he rarely said and it made me feel good to hear it.

It was the end of the final semester in the NP program, and there were lots of papers to be written, tests to be taken, and plans to be made. I called Shannon every day, and he seemed to be doing well enough. He was enjoying his dad's company, watching TV, and taking his medication. At that point, it was the best that I could hope for.

Chapter 55
Graduation

I wasn't interested in driving for four hours, getting all dressed up, and spending a lot of money staying in a hotel and eating in restaurants just to attend my graduation. The ceremony at HSU had been enough. Instead, I decided to have a party at the house on the same day as the Sonoma State ceremony. I would invite my closest friends and I would fly Emily up to be with me on my special day. I was very excited and glad that the school push was coming to an end.

The year and a half that I had lived with Dan, I had tried to keep up on my house where Shannon was living, making sure that the dishes were done and the floors swept and that garbage had not accumulated. But I hadn't really gotten in there and deep cleaned. Now that I was planning a big party, I walked down through the woods to the house and really took stock. Over the last six months, mice had moved in and there were mouse droppings and nests everywhere. The place was neglected and filthy. It was going to be some job to clean it up. Now that my schooling was over and Shannon was up in Washington for a while, I was thinking of moving back to my house. I had never even gotten to enjoy the room that Dan had fixed up for me, and I thought that if I was able to keep Shannon on his medication, it might be a good thing to be at home where I could keep a closer eye on him. I wanted Dan to move back with me, but he told me that there was no possibility. I was on my own.

I spent the better part of the next two weeks cleaning and painting and taking large loads of trash to the dump. Dan worked with me and it was fun. We threw open the doors and windows and let in the fresh air. We performed a ceremony saying prayers and smudging all of the rooms with the smoke of fresh sage to clear the house of bad energy. Then we watched movies and cooked dinner and drank wine in the evening in an effort to reclaim the feeling that I was in my home. The last few days before the celebration, Emily arrived and she helped with the finishing touches.

On the big party day, I counted 28 guests. The sun was shining and the whole house was opened up. People gathered in small groups on the porch or out on the patio or in the living room that I had painted terracotta orange. It had a pleasant southwestern feeling and its big glass double doors opened wide to let in the greens and blues of the hills and the sky. The food was plentiful and delicious and the wine flowed freely. I had placed bunches of flowers everywhere and they brightened the house with their colors and fragrance. Out on the porch, Dan was barbequing shrimp and chicken, and Karl, a nurse that I had worked with for many years, was playing his Bali pipes. The beautiful music floated out over the meadows and hills. Billi, a good friend of mine and a nurse, was there with her family for the celebration. She had often supported and advised me in my struggles with Shannon. As a gift, she had brought a beautiful statue of the female deity, Kwan Yin Goddess of

Compassion, and she was directing her friend to hang it on the wall next to the front door where, she pointed out, the Goddess could watch over me. Boden was there with his girlfriend, Ruby. She was a sweetheart and a very lovely young woman. It was a pleasure to see them together looking like star struck young lovers.

My buddy, Pete, had flown in from N.Y.C. to come to my graduation celebration. Pete had known Dan for many years, and for the last few years he had been joining us on our yearly summer hiking trip in the sierras. He was a funny guy and very charismatic. Everyone loved him and I felt honored that he had flown out to share this special time with me. He definitely contributed to the good vibes of the day. Our newest addition to the three Sierra trailblazers, or the three musketeers as we affectionately called ourselves, was Dan G. He too was a very cool guy who owned his own airplane. He would always fly out to the east sierras to meet us when we would gather together in Mammoth Lakes for our trips. Of course my daughter, whose presence always made any event a special event for me and who had encouraged me from the very first time that I had shyly mentioned the idea of becoming a Family Nurse Practitioner, was there to support and celebrate the coming to fruition of a the vision that I had worked so hard to obtain. I was sorry that Shannon could not be there, but I was also glad to be taking a break from the daily up and down dramas that plague the lives of the mentally ill and their families and from the constant worrying about him. This was my special day and I flitted about the house and talked with my guests and ate shrimp and drank wine and thought briefly about where I'd come from and where I had arrived. Although we had talked about it a lot in our classes, I didn't think that I would be going on for my Doctorate in Nursing. I'd had enough of school for a long while. I was ready to get out there on the front lines. I was ready to be a practicing family nurse practitioner and join the ranks of healthcare providers.

After the party, I moved back into my house. I was happy to be home again. I wished that Dan would come and live with me and be my partner, but I had to accept that he wasn't interested and love him for the great guy that he was and for being my very best friend ever and part of the family. In order to have plenty of time to job-hunt and enjoy the summer, I dropped to per diem at the hospital. The next challenge was that I needed to find employment and also, I had to begin studying to take my National Certification test. Unfortunately, there were no provider openings in my own little community so I started to look elsewhere. I didn't really want to leave my home and relocate but after all that schooling, I was determined to work as an FNP no matter where I had to go. Really, I was prepared to go anywhere. I was even willing, if need be, to go to the Arctic Circle, although I hated to be cold. I went on a couple of interviews that for one reason or another didn't work out and then I got a break. I got a temporary part-time job for the summer working in a little clinic about three hours' drive from my home. I had told them that I absolutely needed the end of June off to go hiking in the Sierras with my trail buddies. "No problem," they told me. "We're just happy that you're available for the next three months for our Hispanic women who want to see a female provider. Until September, it's only us guys here." It was lucky that I happened to speak some Spanish. The job was perfect for me. I'd get some experience to add to my resume, get my feet a little wet and still have lots of free time to enjoy the summer. Meanwhile, I would continue to look around for work.

That first job turned out to be quite a challenge. I took too long. I asked too many questions. I was too unsure of myself. My Medical director was very charismatic and a cool guy. Everyone liked him. I liked him, but he was impatient with me. He said that I acted too much like a student and not enough like a practitioner. His partner was nicer to me, and when I told him that I felt stupid, he said reassuringly, "I'm sorry that you feel that way because I think that you're doing a great job."

He saved me from feeling completely worthless when he said that. Another time, I saw a young Mexican woman who was pregnant and I took a cervical sample for a pap which turned out to be abnormal. My medical director, who I looked up to, said to me, "We're glad that you're here. If you hadn't been here, we wouldn't have caught that." I sighed, a big sigh of relief when he said that, finally a word of approval. I tried to be quicker, more professional and ask less questions but the truth of the matter was that I was scared stiff of making a mistake. I hadn't realized what a tremendous responsibility it was to be a medical provider. I took my certification test and passed with a good grade which provided me with some assurance that at least I wasn't a complete idiot.

At the end of June, Dan and I set out for the east side of the Sierras. It was a beautiful summer day, and I suddenly felt lighthearted and free and glad to be on the road again. That evening, we met up with Pete and Dan G who had brought a friend along to join us by the name of Pete. It was too funny. I was going hiking with Dan and Dan and Pete and Pete. All we needed was another Juliet. We made endless jokes about it like, "Well, this way you don't have to remember so many names." Or "If you want to hike with us, your name has to be Dan or Pete." It was silly but fun. Now every time I meet a Dan or a Pete, I can't help thinking to myself that they should go hiking with us. We had a festive dinner out that evening and afterwards we pulled out the maps and talked about the logistics of the hike.

The next day, after breakfast, we drove to Mosquito Flat and set up camp by the river at 10,000 feet elevation. The altitude was making everyone feel tired, and we hoped that by the next day, we would have acclimated a bit. I always loved it in the tent where it was so comfortable and cozy. No sooner had I set it up then I was in it, opening up a good book that I had brought along, content with the sounds of the gurgling river and my happy companions in the background. The last couple of years had been very stressful, and I was looking forward to a few days where I could forget who I was and where I came from and just be with the beauty of nature.

The first part of the hike was a steep climb up to Mono Pass at 12,000 feet elevation. It was the second time that I had been there and it was a favorite spot of mine. After the steep, uphill hike, we stopped at Mono Pass for lunch. We were well above tree line and all there was to see were the grey rocks and blue sky, and way down below us, a small, crystal clear lake that sparkled like a jewel in the afternoon sun. It was not that unlike the scenery of the Himalayas, and it was incredibly beautiful, stark, and magnificent in its simplicity. When we set out again, the guys wanted to go on a little detour along a higher ridge top to check out another lake. Being a much slower hiker than the rest of the group, I kept to the trail and walked along by myself in the vast expanse of wilderness high country. The wind picked up a little, and I pushed along against it for a couple of hours passing through a canyon of granite boulders and then up along a ridge with steep switch backs and a view of a sheer granite cliff in the distance, silhouetted against the sky. By the time we all met up again, it was late in the day and everyone was happy to set up camp. It didn't take too long before I was in my cozy little cocoon, warm and happy in the tent.

The next day, one of the Petes was cutting some salami and sliced his finger badly. He was very upset and couldn't decide whether or not to abort the trip and hike out. "Let the Nurse Practitioner look at it," one of the Dans advised.

I checked it out. It definitely could have used a few stitches, but there didn't appear to be any nerve or tendon involvement. "We have steri-strips with us. If you think that you can keep it clean and dry for a few days, we could close it up with steri-strips and wrap it good. It will leave more of a scar that way but it will probably heal without a problem."

"I can do that," Pete decided. "I'm staying!"

We were all glad that he had decided to stick it out.

"We might have to help you put your pack on, but other than that you'll be fine. No washing dishes for you either," I added, hoping to cheer him up.

We were camped beside a beautiful lake and we decided to stay there for a couple of days and do some day hikes. The next day after a leisurely breakfast we hiked up to a ridge-top a few miles away. We passed through several fields of wild flowers where the ground was carpeted in a perfusion of bright colors, a dozen shades of lavender and purple, and here and there a bright flash of red or orange.

Barley, our trail dog and Dan's very faithful companion, ran up ahead of us and raced back and forth chasing ground squirrels and birds that would flap away, squawking their displeasure. She would stand there, panting and looking after them with her tail wagging as if to thank them for the chase, then she would race off, searching for her next conquest. She never caught any of these mountain critters. They were too wild and fast, but she never tired of the game. At the top of the ridge, we hung out and had lunch and lay around in the rocks feeling as comfortable and at home as if we were in a four-star hotel. We all loved the high mountains and this, to us, was far more inviting than any luxury hotel room. The guys had endless discussions about the geology and history and the cosmic meaning of everything, but I just looked around me enraptured by the profound beauty and happy to be there, at the top of the world, with my good companions.

The following day, the guys took another hike and I stayed back at camp. I read and took pictures of the trees and the mountains and of our little tent, and I just hung out enjoying the luxury of spending the day surrounded by the purity and timelessness of the Sierras. By the end of the day, however, I was happy to hear the welcome sound of the guys coming down the trail talking and laughing and bringing freshly caught fish for dinner.

On our way out, we stopped at Mono pass again. We found a patch of snow, and Dan took out a small flask and made us all tequila and lemonade margaritas. At that high altitude and with all the exercise and the sparse trail food rations that we had been on, we all easily got loaded. We hung out there for a good part of the afternoon, posing philosophical questions that could not easily be answered and feeling high in the spirit of the journey. I was with my troop, yeah, and I couldn't imagine a finer group of trail companions or more exquisite surroundings. At that very moment, there was nowhere else on the planet that I would rather have been.

We had another festive dinner together that night to celebrate our trip, and the next day we all went our separate ways back to family and jobs and the busy everyday world while the timeless mountains continued on without us as they had for millenniums. Dan and I stopped for lunch in a little café in the small town of Chester. While we were waiting for our food, we were talking about our trip and we were already thinking about the next trip when my cell phone went off. "Hello," I said, not recognizing the number that came up on the tiny screen.

"Is this Juliet Hegdal?" the voice on the other end sounded business like.

"Yes, that's me." Part of me was still walking in the mountains. Talking on the cell phone seemed foreign and strange. My mind was kind of blank, and it caught me completely off guard when the voice on the other end told me that the sheriff had been called to my mother's house because her neighbors hadn't seen her in over a week. When they found her, she had already been dead for several days. It was a heart attack, the coroner informed me. I started crying and then I couldn't stop. I cried not so much for her death, which I realized had finally brought her peace, but for her life that had been so hard and so full of suffering because of her mental illness. When I regained control, I realized with gratitude that I had not had to put her in a nursing home. She had lived on her own until her last breath. That, at least, was something to be grateful for.

"We'd better get back home," Dan said in his steady, practical way. "We have some work to do," he gave me a big hug. I felt very lucky to have his support and friendship.

The next week or two was taken up with the chore of cleaning up Blanche's small apartment, notifying relatives, and preparing for her cremation. I had not talked with her sisters or their children since I was a young girl, but I called them now to let them know of Blanche's passing. They were all very sweet. My mother had actually maintained contact with them over the last ten years, and so they were not surprised to hear from me. They were grateful that I had called. I wanted to have some sort of ceremony to commemorate her passing, and since she didn't have any friends, I wanted her family to be there. It occurred to me that we should take part of her ashes back to N.Y.C., where she always said her heart was, and scatter them over her mother's grave. Her brother and sisters loved my mother and they too mourned over the difficulties that she had experienced in her life. If I went back to New York, they could all be there to send her off with their love, into the next world. In addition, I would be taking my children, and they could see where I grew up. Everyone approved of the idea and plans were made.

During this time period, I had begun to fear that Shannon was having another relapse. Just recently, he had started refusing to talk with me when I would call. I had to talk to him through John who also sounded a bit out of touch with reality. When I called to tell Shannon that his grandmother had died, John passed the message along to him. When I told Shannon, through John, about our plans to go back east for her funeral ceremony, Shannon said that he wouldn't go. I repeated the invitation to include him a couple of times but I didn't press it. We were going to be staying with Pete and his lady friend while in New York, and I didn't want to bring them a hostile, crazy house guest.

I began to feel like a fractured personality; there were so many stressful things going on at once. I started worrying about Shannon obsessively again. As time went by, his dad began to be verbally abusive to him while we were on the phone. "You're an idiot, Shannon," he would scream. "Shut up and listen. You don't know anything!" he would yell at him, like some sort of abusive drill sergeant. It was unforgivable except for the fact that John, too, suffered from mental illness. When I protested, John explained to me in an agitated tone that Shannon did not need medication, that his voices were demons that needed to be purged. "And that can only happen," he informed me, sounding very angry and controlling, "when Shannon sinks as low as possible and then, when he can't sink any lower, he has to do battle with his demons and banish them forever from his consciousness. It's a moral battle and it has to be fought on moral ground," he proclaimed emphatically, sounding as crazy as he ever had in the past.

My only consolation was that this was all happening a thousand miles away from me. I asked Shannon, through John, if he was ready to come home and he said no. I knew that he needed to get out of there and into a healthier environment, but there was a lot going on just then. I was afraid that if I took the time to go up to Washington, he would still refuse to go with me. I didn't know what to do. I finally decided that I would go up and see if I could convince him to come home, just as soon as I got back from N.Y.

Meanwhile, I continued on with my part-time job, making slow progress and finding the work very stressful. I went on a couple of job interviews and put my application in at a community clinic that was about an hour and fifteen minutes' drive from the house. "We'll keep it on file," they assured me, "But right now we have no openings."

There was a small community clinic in Arizona that was very interested, and they offered to fly me out to Arizona and put me up in a hotel so that I could come out for an interview. We set it up for the beginning of September, after I got back from N.Y. and my mother's funeral service and after my trip to Washington, to try and get Shannon. If I had to move to Arizona, then perhaps I could convince Shannon to go with me. Everything was up in the air. The future was very unclear. I was very glad that I had graduated, but it seemed like I had traded the stress of school for a whole new set of stresses.

Chapter 56
Return to NYC

Boden picked me up from work, and we drove to a hotel in Santa Rosa where we spent the night. I was really tired, and I went right to bed, but Boden went out to find a store where he could buy a few things for the trip. I found myself worrying about him, out all alone at night in a big city and I had to remind myself that he wasn't a kid anymore. He was a young man. Early the next morning, we took a shuttle to the airport in San Francisco and there we met up with Emily who had just flown in from LA. We were all happy to be together, and we felt good that we were going to honor my mother in this manner. I was thinking that she would have approved. Together we boarded the plane for New York. In my day pack were my mother's ashes. I had not been back to N. Y. since I had left when I was 18. My memories there seemed very remote, almost as if I'd seen a movie about some poor, lost, homeless girl and her troubled mother. It didn't seem to have anything to do with me. In a way, I was glad. Most of my early memories had not been happy ones. It was almost midnight when we landed at JFK airport. Pete was there to meet us, and by way of welcome, he took us for a midnight walk at the beach in Coney Island. I hadn't been there since I was 14, and I didn't recognize it. For one thing, it looked much cleaner.

The next day, Pete had to leave early for work. He was the main architect on the new United Nations building that was under construction in New York City. "Yeah, I got to go and set them all straight," my party animal, backpacking buddy was saying about the other people that worked with him. "I'd love to take the day with you but duty calls. Dinner on Friday and I've got you all day Saturday," he said over his shoulder as he was heading out the door. His girlfriend Deanna was busy as well but she spent the morning with us, fussing over my very grown-up kids and making us all feel at home and welcome.

We had arranged to meet my aunt Liz and a couple of my cousins at Tavern on the Green in Central Park late that afternoon for dinner so we decided to spend the day in the park. Many of my best memories growing up had involved Central Park, but everything had changed so much that I didn't really feel a connection anymore. California was my home now. Blanche, however, had talked wistfully about N.Y. and the park even weeks before her death so we had decided to have a little ceremony, just the three of us, in the park as well. We gathered in a circle, holding hands while Emily said a few words of blessing and prayer. I imagined that if my mother were astral traveling to join us at that moment that she was happy to be back in her old stomping grounds. Afterwards, we stopped for some lunch at the Boat House. It was fancy now. No more of the bare plastic table tops with the wind whipping through. It was upscale and crowded. Central Park had become Yuppified.

In a way, I liked it. It felt safer and much cleaner, but I wondered, *where did all the poor people go?*

Dinner was fun, and it was sweet to reconnect with all my long lost relatives. I felt comfortable with them, and I wondered if the pleasant sense of familiarity that I had was actually because we were genetically related. I really liked my mother's sister Liz, and I thought that my mother would have been a lot like her if not for her illness. Boden and Emily felt comfortable with everyone as well, and it really was as if we were all family although my children had never even met them. We made arrangements to be picked up by my cousin Audrey and her husband on Sunday and from there everyone would meet at the grave site of my mother's mother. It seemed fitting.

The next couple of days, we continued our site seeing. We went to the Museum of Natural History and that was pretty cool. Boden and Emily really liked it. Unfortunately, I felt a little bored. I would much rather have been on some rocky outcropping surrounded by sky in the high Sierras. I tried to show my children some of the places I had lived as a kid, but everything looked so different that I couldn't find anything. We were just walking around some big anywhere USA city. I didn't really like cities and felt that I hadn't missed anything in staying away for so long. The next day, when Pete took us to see Times Square, it was so crowded that I felt overwhelmed by all the people rushing around. I was distracted for a moment because I saw a poor person begging on the street, and I wondered where the rest of them were, those masses of starving homeless that I knew had once inhabited these streets. Someone had once given me an article about an underground homeless encampment in N.Y.C. that was in a defunct subway station. *Where are those people now?* I wondered. It wasn't too far from here that my mother and I had spent part of the night sitting out on the subway steps, shivering and hungry, in the snow.

It seemed like only seconds that I had been lost in my thoughts but when I looked up, I found that my group had disappeared. I was standing in the middle of the block with swarms of people pushing past me and going every which way and none of them were Pete or Emily or Boden. Just then, my cell phone went off. Thank goodness for cell phone technology. "Where are you?" was Peter's somewhat annoyed and worried question.

"I have no idea," I answered, relieved that at least we had voice contact. "I looked up and you were all gone. I've definitely lost all my city smarts over the years. If there are more than two stoplights, I'm out of my element." I felt a little like a child lost in a great big department store.

"Well, just stay where you are. We'll find you. Walk to the corner and then wait," were Peters instructions. Later, Pete told me that Boden had looked very worried when I had disappeared and we both smiled because it was so sweet; son worried about mother.

My Grandmother's grave was in New Jersey. It all looked the same to me; freeways, big buildings, and concrete—where was my little winding river? Where were the hills and the towering Redwood Trees? When we got to the grave site, we gathered around in a large circle. Emily led us in a ceremonial prayer that was simple and very nondenominational. Blanche's sister Liz, then her brother Jake, and then my cousins all took turns recounting memories of my mother when she was a young girl. How bright she was, how smart she was, how, as a teenager, she had suddenly withdrawn and was never quite the same again. I read a synopsis of her life that I had prepared in advance. It briefly recounted some of her aspirations and her heartaches. It spoke, too, about her years in Berkeley when she was fairly happy. I read a poem that she had written, and then we ended by sprinkling her ashes over her mother's grave. It was comforting to think of her spirit as reunited with her mother. My own mother had always seemed, to me, like someone who really needed a mother to look after her.

"Now at last she has returned to the eternal mother," Emily said softly as she sprinkled the last of the ashes at the base of the tree that grew by my Grandmother's grave.

After the ceremony, we all went out to a cozy little Italian restaurant that was nearby. There were about ten of us all-together and we completely took up one, very long, table. It amazed me to know that I was related to every single person there, and I wondered what it would have been like to grow up with such a large extended family. Things certainly would have been different. But now I had my children and they were my family. Although I really liked all of these relatives of mine and I would love to have been able to see them on a regular basis, I didn't think that I would be moving back to N.Y. anytime soon.

Once back in San Francisco, Emily headed back to LA and Boden drove me to the clinic where I had left my car. "It was fun seeing you and your sister together. You're both so grown up now. I love spending time with you."

"It was good," Boden said, and he gave me a hug.

As he drove off, I thought about how lucky I was to have such great children. Shannon was a wonderful person as well but his illness made his life difficult. It wasn't his fault. He suffered because of it just like my mother had and John also.

After I had driven for a couple of hours, I decided to stop for something light to eat. I went into a little café that I knew had fantastic chicken soup. That was just what I wanted. While I was sitting there, waiting for my soup and thinking about the trip to New York, my phone rang. The ring was a mellow little classical piece. I always liked to hear it when it went off. I didn't recognize the number. "Hello," I answered, a little distracted as the waiter was just bringing me my soup.

"Juliet," I didn't at first recognize the voice. It was a woman, and she sounded like she was very upset about something. I could feel my stomach muscles tighten with the rush of adrenalin. From all my years of crazy, traumatic experiences, I had developed an exaggerated startle reflex. It was hard on my body. "Shannon just tried to kill John. He's crazy and he's dangerous. He's in jail, and I hope he stays there for a long time."

"What happened? Is John alright?" I blamed myself. I should never have let Shannon go up there.

"Shannon attacked John with a knife, and John had to fight him off. John broke away and ran to a neighbor and they called the police. Shannon is in jail now and the DA wants to put him away for ten years. Juliet, we're afraid of him," she told me. "We don't want him back here."

Ten years, I thought to myself. *That would kill him.* I was dismayed and frightened by the idea that Shannon would try to hurt his father, but at the same time I felt that John had pushed him to it with his taunting and insults and by taking him off of his medication. In some ways, I felt that Shannon was as much a victim as John had been. And they were both victims of their mental illness. I found out a few days later that the scene of the crime had looked grizzly with blood everywhere and the bedroom door broken down. As it turned out, the blood was Shannon's blood. He had cut his hand badly when he had stabbed at the door. John had a broken finger. I was shocked by the whole thing, but I also felt that it wouldn't be justice if Shannon went to jail for the next ten years. I was going to have to hire a lawyer.

The Washington State prison system seemed much more humane and efficient than anything I had seen in Northern California as far as mental illness is concerned. When the police had arrested Shannon, they had recognized immediately that he was mentally ill and they put him in a separate part of the jail for people with mental health issues. He was seen, in jail, by a psychiatrist that first day and put immediately on *Abilify,* one of the newer antipsychotics. Once I was able to talk with him, a few days after his arrest, he was already sounding more in touch with reality. His treatment in jail in Washington had been much more effective and timely than his treatment had been in California when he was in a mental hospital. Nurses came around twice a day to give the patients their medication, and everyone had their own cell so that they had a place where they could 'chill out' if the stimulation got too intense. "No one ever got into fights there," Shannon later told me, and although he didn't want to be in prison, it was not as traumatic for him as it would have been if he had not been treated humanely and like someone who was mentally ill. He called me almost every day. I was his contact with the outside world. That's when I contacted the NAMI office in Washington to see what they could do to help and they sent me an email saying, "Right now you are an advocate for your son and you must stay the course." The whole situation was making me crazy but I knew that if I were to fall apart, I would not be able to help him. Shannon signed a release and I was able to talk with the prison nurses about what was happening with him, and after a few weeks, I stopped feeling so anxious and frightened. For the moment anyway, he was safe.

Chapter 57
Long Valley Health Center

I flew into Albuquerque New Mexico and drove through the red and brown desert to the little clinic in Arizona for my job interview. The people at the clinic were wonderful, down to earth, and friendly. I liked them a lot. That first night, they had me over for a big dinner party with all the clinic staff and their families. Everyone that is except for the doctor that I would be working with in a smaller satellite clinic a few miles out of town; he was notably missing. I got the impression that they had liked me because they could tell, over the phone, that I was a kind person and nonthreatening and that I would probably do well working with a shy and reclusive medical director in an isolated satellite clinic. I was up for it. I was up for anything that would give me the experience I needed to get a foothold in the profession. I did feel some concern about moving to where I didn't know anyone, and I wasn't crazy about living in the dry, high desert where there were no trees. Most of all, I didn't know what was happening with Shannon or how he would fit into this new equation but it was a job and I was willing to give it a try if they would have me. Perhaps the area would grow on me. "We have to talk things over but we'll get back to you by the end of the week," they told me. "We're really interested in hiring you and we're probably going to make you an offer," the medical director of the main clinic assured me. "We just have to check references and that sort of thing."

When I got back home, I took 48 hours of call at the hospital. I ended up working two busy and stressful night shifts. It was a good reminder of how much I was looking forward to getting out of shift work. True to their word, at the end of the week, they emailed me an offer. It was a decent offer and it included a $5,000 dollar relocation bonus. It looked like I was going to be moving. As fate would have it, however, that same day I got a call from the clinic that was a little over an hour drive from my house saying that they were in the process of creating a new position and was I interested. "Very much so," I answered. "But I just received a job offer in Arizona and I have to let them know by the end of next week. I don't really want to move," I told them honestly. The following week, they brought me in for an interview and the very next day they called me and offered me a job. I wasn't going to have to move after all!

The Long Valley Health Center is designated as a Federally Qualified Health Clinic. As such, it has a sliding scale and other programs that make it possible to be able to see most people regardless of finances. That was very suited to my political and moral beliefs. The clinic already had four providers, all women, and they listened to my concerns and insecurities without judgment. "You should feel scared," my new medical director reassured me. "It's a lot of responsibility. It would scare me if you weren't scared." They arranged that for the first month I would report to the provider of the day on each and every patient encounter. I could ask as many questions as I wanted. It was a perfect situation for me, and I was excited to start working. Once again, I thanked my guardian angel for being 'on it'!

Even with all the fantastic support, I still found the work stressful. I was nervous and I worried over almost every diagnosis and treatment plan, no matter how simple. I'd wake up in the middle of the night worrying about my patients and on the weekends I would find myself calling people at home to make sure that they had not suddenly taken a turn for the worse. "No, I'm fine, thank you," they would usually tell me, surprised that I had called. Then I would hang up the phone, breathe a sigh of relief, and go on to worry about the next person on my long list of worries. The long drive on narrow twisty roads, although beautiful, was stressful as well and every morning as I turned the corner and drove into the clinic parking lot, I could feel my blood pressure rising. I took to repeating over and over again my spiritual mantra on the drive into work and this I found extremely helpful. "I am filled with loving kindness. I am well. I am peaceful and at ease. I am happy." It helped to calm my nerves and it reminded me that, although it was essential to know my trade, unless I kept in mind the deeper meaning of the concept of 'healing', it was just another job and, as such, not very satisfying.

Chapter 58
Western State Hospital

"How long will it be till you're returning?" Shannon was reciting to me the words of the Kate Wolf song that he was memorizing in jail to try and keep his mind focused. "I went to court today. The DA charged me with 'assault 1', and that's a ten-year sentence. It's all a terrible mistake. I never would have hurt that old man," he told me. "I can't believe this is happening."

I couldn't believe it either. The county jail was a safe place for him right now but federal prison was quite another story. "It won't be so easy on a pretty boy like your son," a couple of people had warned me, "when he gets into federal prison."

It made me ill to think about it. At all cost, I had to get him home. I looked up lawyers on the internet and called around to talk with a few of them. I left a message for a Karen H. attorney at law, and she called me back almost immediately. I could hear her high heels clicking along as she walked quickly down the street on her way to court. "The public defenders almost never speak with family but I trained this new one and I could talk with her and get her to listen to what you have to say. You don't need to pay me for that. I'll do it this afternoon after court."

I explained to her that I was hoping to get a plea of 'not guilty due to reason of insanity' (NGRI). I was also hoping to get Shannon a more intensive psychological evaluation.

"I've had a lot of experience with that sort of thing," she assured me. "It's complicated but I can talk with you more about it later; right now I'm due in court. If you want me to take the case, I have a secretary who always answers the phone and who knows everything that's going on. You and your son will always have someone that you can talk with."

I liked her and I felt like she was the right person for the job. "I want you to take the case," I said without hesitation.

"Alright, I'll send you a contract in a couple of days. Meanwhile, I'll go over to the jail and meet with your son. Feel free to call if you have any questions."

I hung up feeling like a huge burden had been lifted off of me. We had another advocate now and she sounded extremely capable.

I tried to put aside my personal concerns when I was at work but it was hard. I found myself thinking about Shannon all of the time. I was glad that I could talk with him as often as I did. Sometimes, we would be talking on the phone and he would suddenly tell me, "I have to hang up right now. We're going into lock down." Sometimes, I almost felt like I was there in jail with him. Our phone calls automatically cut off at 20 minutes, and when he was really feeling down, he'd say to me, "Can I please call you back?" I had found a way to get the phone calls cheaper by getting a cell phone with a Washington phone number. That way, it was a local call and I could afford to talk with him as much as he wanted. Over the months, I felt like we were growing closer. At the end of every call, I would have him repeat a mantra with me, "I am filled with loving kindness. I am well. I am peaceful and at ease. I am happy." He had a little trouble with the 'I am happy' part, but otherwise he seemed to appreciate the thought and he told me that there was another guy in jail who really liked it.

"When you feel anxious, Shannon, say that over and over to yourself. It will help you to feel more relaxed," I advised him.

Sometimes, he'd ask me to sing one of the Kate Wolf songs and he'd join me where he knew the words. "I'm trying to play cards," he told me one day, "but most people won't play with me because I can't think any more. My brain just doesn't work."

I wondered, with the right care, what his potential for a normal happy life would be. At that point, it wasn't looking that hopeful.

Just in case I didn't feel like I was under enough pressure, Dan decided to move to a bigger town about an hour's drive north of where I lived and over two hours north of where I worked. Without Dan as my next-door neighbor, I found myself spending most of my evenings alone. My fear of the dark became somewhat of a problem. For entertainment, I bought the entire series of Friends, and once it was dark outside, I would retire upstairs to my cozy bedroom where I did feel safe and I would watch an episode of Friends on my computer or read a book or research medical questions until it was time to go to sleep. It was not exactly an unhappy time, but I was lonely and anxious, and I felt uncertain and fearful over the future. "The situation will improve," I had to tell myself. "But right now, I must stay the course."

Around Christmas, our attorney called me to let me know that Shannon was going to Western State Hospital for his NGRI (not guilty due to reason of insanity) evaluation and he would be there over Christmas. I would be able to visit him at the hospital if I wanted. I hadn't visited him in jail because their visits were over a TV screen, not even in the same room but at the hospital we would be in the same room and I could even bring him a meal and a Christmas present. It was good news. Dan and I planned to make the trip up there over the holiday.

We planned to take a leisurely three days' driving up the coast to make it to WSH in time for our Christmas Eve visit. The first two days of our trip were stormy. We drove along slowly, with the windshield wipers slapping madly back and forth, as the wind whipped the torrential rain in sheets, angled against the windshield. Visibility was very poor. At times, the rain would turn into thick slushy drops, making it almost impossible to see where we were going. The ocean, when we could see it, was a raging, churning mass of white water. I watched as the path, on the way to see my son, became strewn with fragments of dripping, torn-apart, evergreen branches. The trees lining the road flung their branches wildly back and forth in a chaotic dance. "How fitting," I said to Dan who was concentrating way too hard on driving to appreciate the irony of the storm. Actually, I was enjoying the turbulence and wild energy of the stormy weather and I was happy for Dan's company. It was also good to be getting a break from the stresses of the clinic, and, of course, I was very excited about seeing Shannon. It had been almost a year since I had seen him last.

The spacious grounds of Western State Hospital housed many different buildings. The campus had that drab institutional feeling, but it was bordered on one side by a forest which afforded some relief. The building that Shannon was in was a locked facility. We had to show our ID to an armed guard, and then a thick iron gate slid open electronically to let us through, sliding shut and locking, with a loud metallic thud, behind us. The room that we were to meet him in was very drab and the lights were too bright. There were already a few other inmates and family visitors sitting around the long metal tables in plastic chairs. It looked like a mental institution more than a jail. The inmates were dressed in sweats and casual clothing rather than the bright orange jump suit that Shannon had worn when I had visited him in jail in California, and they shuffled their feet and spoke of mundane matters in a way that conveyed a feeling of hopelessness. A very nice, amiable guard sat watching over everyone. He was playing Christmas music softly on a little tape player that he had brought in from his own home. The familiar Christmas Carols did wonders to improve the atmosphere. Finally, another guard brought Shannon in. He was very thin and pale and I noted with some concern that his hair was falling out. His bushy head of hair was getting really thin. It had been months since he had been out of doors, and he looked like he wasn't eating much. He probably was suffering from some sort of vitamin deficiency, I thought. His face lit up when he saw us. I put my arms around him and just held on to him for a long time. He seemed so fragile to me, but he was happy to see us and he laughed, a weak little laugh, in a valiant attempt to be companionable and lighthearted. He asked about everyone back home and wolfed down the steak and mashed potatoes that we had been allowed to bring him. "They started me on a new medication," he told me. "I like it. It gives me a little energy."

Schizophrenia was considered to have two separate sets of symptoms; negative symptoms and positive symptoms. The negative symptoms were things that you were supposed to have but weren't there such as energy and concentration and enjoyment of life. The positive symptoms were symptoms that you weren't supposed to have but did, such as hearing voices or delusional thinking. The medications were actually supposed to be fairly effective against the positive symptoms but not so much against the negative symptoms. Because of that the negative symptoms, although not as dramatic, actually impacted quality of life as severely as the bizarre positive symptoms. Energy was a big problem for Shannon. He was always tired. People accused him of being lazy but a lot of it was the negative symptoms of the schizophrenia. "They told me that the Risperdal should make the voices stop, and I hope that it does, but I don't think it will be able to stop them," he said this as if he were resigned to living the rest of his life in misery.

"Have you made any friends here?" I asked Shannon, hoping that the answer would be a yes. He really liked people, and I knew that having a friend would make this whole ordeal easier on him.

"I do have a friend," he told us. "Her name is Shannon also. She doesn't have anyone to send her stuff so I share my commissary with her."

"Isn't this much better than jail?" I asked him, again hoping that the answer would be a yes. "You seem to have a lot more freedom here."

"I like jail better. Nobody plays cards here. Even if they say that I can plead NGRI, I don't think I'll go for it. I'd rather be in jail."

This statement surprised me and made me feel frustrated. In order to use the defense of not guilty due to insanity, the person who was ill had to actually request it and then a psychological evaluation had to substantiate it, but if Shannon didn't want to plead NGRI, then he didn't have to. If he didn't want to use the insanity defense, then he would be treated just like any other criminal. I wanted him to be where he could get full therapeutic treatment and that wasn't in prison. If he was found not guilty due to insanity, he'd do his time in the mental hospital. Without it, he could do as much as ten years in the federal prison. He'd be almost 40 when he got out, basically spending some of the best years of his life incarcerated because of his illness. It would not be justice. I couldn't bear to think about it and so I changed the subject.

"Do you talk to your dad at all?" I asked.

"He lets me call him once a week. He says that he won't testify against me but because it's considered domestic violence; the DA doesn't need him to testify. He said that the DA wants to put me away because I'm a danger to society."

That was not new information to me, but I was glad that he and his dad were at least talking. John had finally admitted to me that he had been wrong about the medication. "I see now that Shannon really does need that medication," he had said to me when we were talking about the incident. "But it's in the hands of the DA now. There's nothing I can do." John had also finally admitted to me that he himself suffered from severe mental illness. We had been on the phone one day discussing Shannon and I was saying what a curse mental illness was and how it caused so much suffering. "Juliet," John had said to me, grasping at this small opportunity to be understood. "I suffer from mental illness." But the moment of opportunity suddenly shifted and we never spoke of the matter again.

Dan and Shannon chatted about car stuff and guy things that weren't of much interest to me, but I sat next to my son quietly and soaked in the fact that he was safe, in good spirits, clear thinking and relatively intact at the moment. All too soon, visiting hours were over. Through the big glass window that separated our little meeting room from the main corridor I could see a nurse hurrying by, on her way to her workstation I imagined. She smiled and waved to Shannon with a nod of encouragement. There seemed to be some very nice people here, and for that I was grateful.

The next day was Christmas day, and since we had driven from out of State, they were allowing us to visit for two hours on Christmas day as well. Dan and I checked out of the hotel and drove around the quiet, empty town for an hour or so before it was time for our visit. It was snowing and I was pleased to be having a 'White Christmas'. We found a little drive up stand that was open where we could get a steaming hot cup of coffee, and we sat there in the car, with the snow piling up around us and on the windshield, feeling warm and cozy in our white world with our delicious hot morning java. Although some might have found the situation a bit depressing, I had to look on the positive side. Shannon was getting a good psychological evaluation, and they had found a medication that he liked. I was not sitting in my house by myself but instead greatly enjoying Dan's company. I was getting to spend some time with my son. It was snowing and we were toasty warm. Perhaps that was another gift of hard times; once you had experienced really far down, one was quicker to appreciate anything up.

Shannon was initially found unfit to stand trial so they kept him there at WSH for another four months. One day, when we were talking on the phone, he told me, "I didn't think the voices would stop but they have. I'm really glad they stopped because they were killing me."

Shortly after that, they sent him back to jail. Except for a brief two-hour visit in the early spring back at WSH, it was almost another full year before I saw him again, in the court room, this time shackled and in his bright orange jump suit.

Chapter 59
Mothers' Day Retreat

As I was becoming more confident and comfortable with my work, the new challenge became to see greater numbers of patients in shorter amounts of time. Sometimes, I would have two patients in a 15-minute slot for my first patient of the day. Then my medical assistant would assure me, "Oh, this will be quick and easy. This person is just here for a blood draw."

I would go into the room and introduce myself to a patient that, often times, I didn't know. I'd ask them a little about their history and then I would quickly review the chart trying to decide what labs to order. By the time I'd have filled out the paper work and said goodbye, the allotted 15 minutes would have elapsed but I still had another patient in that same time slot. Then, as I was ready to leave the room and go on to see my next patient, the person would often tell me something like "Oh, by the way, I've been having chest pain for the last 24 hours," or "I have this new rash that's really bothering me, and I don't know what it is. Will you look at it?"

Then I would spend another 15 or 20 minutes evaluating the problem, falling hopelessly behind for the rest of the day. Some days were fun and pleasantly paced, but other days I would run frantically from one major problem to the next, trying to really connect with the person, fully evaluate them, and provide them with competent and compassionate care and still get out of the room in 15 minutes or less. It was quite a challenge for me, and I began to develop this love/hate relationship with my work. If the day had a good flow to it and I had the luxury of spending some quality time with my patients, then I loved it. To hear the phrase, "I am feeling better," after I had seen someone and made a diagnosis and treatment plan, became my raison d'être. I thrived on it. As one of the docs that I used to work with had once said to me, "I don't work to live; I live to work!" On the days where I was booked solid and saw complex problems that took me more time, I would try to hurry along, eventually and inevitably falling behind. Patients would become irritable towards me because they had to wait. My anxiety level and blood pressure would begin to rise and my blood sugar fall. I would start cutting corners to get back on schedule, and then I would worry that I wasn't doing a good enough job or that I might miss something really important. Then I would get more anxious. It was a vicious cycle. On those days I found myself wondering if I was really cut out for the work. Take ten hours at that pace and then add on the total of two and a half hours of driving that I had to do for my round trip commute, my days left me totally spent. As I got more exhausted, I got more anxious. Then I would go home to a dark, lonely, cold house and worry about my son.

One day Emily called to tell me that she was leading a Mothers' Day retreat. There were still some openings, and she thought that it would do me good to get away and to experience the healing power of a spiritual retreat. I had to do something. I was starting to feel like a rubber band that was stretched too tight. I felt like, at any minute, I might snap.

When I arrived at LAX airport, I was tired but looking forward to seeing my daughter. I started to get lost in the busyness of the large international airport. I found myself swept up in throngs of people but I didn't know where they were headed. Eventually, I made my way to the correct level and out the door and down the street to the car rental building. There were many different crowded lines of people there as well, and it wasn't well marked. I didn't know which line I should be in, and no one seemed to be able to advise me. I stood in one line for a long time only to be directed to another line. Finally, it was my turn to go up to the counter. The woman ahead of me had apparently finished her business and had stepped aside to put things away in her purse so I stepped up. The man behind the counter started yelling at me, "Why are you so rude? Don't you see that the lady is still at the counter? Get back in the line."

It was bad timing for a greeting like that. I struggled with all of my might to keep my composure. When I stepped back up to the counter, I tried to conduct my business in a casual manner but it felt like the rubber band was starting to snap. Just then my daughter walked up. I shoved my wallet and ID at her muttering something about having pee and rushed off to the bathroom where I locked myself in a stall and sobbed uncontrollably for about five minutes. It was not even that I was that depressed. It was more that my nerves were so on edge and that was the way my body chose to relieve the pressure. When I got back up to the counter, Emily and the guy looked at me questioningly. I'm sure it was obvious that I had been crying and the man went out of his way to be more gentle and considerate. When we finally got settled into our rental car, my daughter asked me, "What was that all about, Mom?"

"I don't know, Emily, I'm just so tense. I'm under so much pressure with my work, I'm so worried about your brother, and I'm alone so much of the time." As I said this, I started crying with huge wrenching sobs.

Emily put her arms around me. She said softly and tenderly, "Go ahead and cry, Mom. Just let it all out. Everything is going to be alright."

I'm sure that I had many deep wounds, from both the past and present, that had never totally healed and that was part of the pain that I was feeling that day, but I believed that with the right perspective, all wounds could be healed. The love and concern I received from my daughter that afternoon was a step in that direction.

The next day, I continued to be very emotional. Early in the morning, we sat in the chapel in meditation. Amidst the chanting and prayers for deeper understanding and compassion, I found myself sobbing again and I had to leave. With head bent, I hurried out of the little chapel trying to stifle my sobs until I was safely back in my room. By the time the gong rang to go down to breakfast, I was feeling more at peace. Everyone was very sweet and gracious. We went about serving ourselves in complete silence and finding a place to sit, with our breakfast plate, at one of the long, elegantly set, tables. I was glad that it was a silent retreat. I found it very soothing to be amongst all the women on the retreat and the nuns. Their loving energy seemed so much more apparent in the silence. Emily took the seat across from me at the table. Although we couldn't talk, I felt very connected with her. Every once in a while, we would look up from our meal and gaze across the table, smiling at each other. Her peaceful, loving gaze was like a healing salve to my wounded heart.

We continued, mostly in silence, through the next two days. We meditated, listened to inspiring spiritual talks and sat quietly, looking out over the ocean. Before long, the layers of tension, anxiety, and loneliness started to fall away, and I found myself feeling tranquil and content. My dampened spirit light was being rekindled, nurtured, and supported by the peace and love that surrounded me. On the last day of the retreat, as we were leaving, one of the other women asked me, "Do you know Brahmachurini, Emily? The two of you seem to have some special energy between you."

"Yes, she's my daughter," I answered. We all laughed happily in appreciation, all of us mothers, here on the mothers' day retreat.

After the retreat, Emily and I had a day that we could spend together before she had to take me back to the airport. We walked, for a couple of miles, shuffling barefoot though the warm sand, and we swam in the warm Southern California Ocean. Later, we got to talk with Shannon when he called my cell phone from jail. We put the call on speakerphone, and it almost felt like he was there with us on the beach in the bright sunshine. In the evening, we went to a local restaurant where we had a long, leisurely dinner of fresh sushi. It was fun and relaxing, and by the time Emily was dropping me off at the airport, I was no longer the same nervous wreck that I had been when she picked me up.

When I was thinking about it on the flight home, I remembered a poster I had seen some years ago that said, "You are never going to be able to control the waves but you can learn to surf." As in the dance of martial arts, where one stays fluid and uses positive energy to deflect the blows of ones opponent while at the same time staying balanced and centered, I needed to learn to dance with the chaos and uncertainty that so often accompanied the trials and tribulations of life. I was doing it a little bit I think, but I needed to learn to do it better.

Chapter 60
Harmony Quest

It had been a long, hard winter. Many a night, I had lain awake in bed listening to the trees thrashing about in the wind and the rain hammering down on the roof just above my head. The sound of the creek, just outside the door, raging down the hill to join Redwood Creek was so loud during the storms and such a constant roar that it was overwhelming at times. It sounded like the road and the house might, at any minute, wash away. It was strange because while I loved the sounds of the tempest and the raging waters, it also made me feel very alone, insignificant, and vulnerable. I struggled through many a night caught between the duality of fear and enchantment. But the loneliness and isolation that I experienced over the dark and stormy winter did serve to enhance my enjoyment and appreciation of the companionship of my family and friends at those special times when my little house was once again filled with conversation and laughter.

With the weather turning warmer and days getting long again, I started to feel less isolated. The time spent with Emily on the retreat had helped me to feel centered and I was ready, once again, to face the challenges that lay ahead. I really liked Ruby, Boden's girlfriend. Sometimes, the two of them would come over and we'd all have dinner together or just hang out and visit. I imagined that it would be fun to have a little grandchild to read stories to and take walks with, some day. Once or twice a month, Dan would come down for part of the weekend, and we'd have dinner and a glass of wine and watch a movie. It was a real treat just to sit by the fire together in the morning, sharing breakfast and the companionship of a dear friend, and he was the only person to whom I could just go on and on venting my obsessive worrying about Shannon, and he understood. He was worried about Shannon too. It had been a long hard winter, but as the winter progressed into spring and then into the bright days of summer, I felt like I was learning to appreciate the calm and quiet flow of the days spent alone and to cherish the times when I had the sweet companionship of a friend or loved one. I was adjusting to the changes of life and to growing older. I was learning new ways of being in the world.

I was very grateful for my children who were a powerful source of love and companionship. Cherished friends created a sense of community and support, and all around me the beauty in nature sustained my soul. My spiritual practice, although never disciplined, was always present in the rustle of leaves as the wind blew or the slow, graceful movement of the fog as it drifted up the canyon or a rainbow arching across the sky on a cloudy day or a million other expressions of the infinite and the sublime. I felt that life was good, and all in all I had to admit that where I'd been was definitely worth the things I'd been through.

At the clinic, as the weeks and then the months passed, I got faster and more confident with my work, and I started to feel like I really was a Practitioner and not just pretending. Now that I had an established practice, many times each day I would enter a room to find a patient that I had gotten to know quite well and it gave me a tremendous feeling of satisfaction. I really enjoyed getting to see the same person again and again over a long period of time, getting to understand their issues and gain their trust. Many times, a patient would thank me profusely and tell me how much my assistance had improved the quality of their life. I felt fulfilled in my work that was actually helping people to be healthier and happier. Recently, I was talking with a patient who had been homeless when I first saw her in the clinic. I had been seeing her regularly for a little over a year. She was looking and sounding so much better than she had in the past, and she was telling me that she now had a home. She thanked me for my part in helping her to get her life together, and we talked about the importance of having a place to go to where one could feel safe and comfortable and sheltered from the world. As we talked, we both got all tearful and choked up. I knew what it was like to not have a home, and I too was grateful that I had a place to call my own; a place that had long been a source of strength and solace.

That summer was fun with lots of hiking and kayaking and being outdoors as much as possible. In the fall, when the days began to get cooler again and it started getting dark earlier and earlier, I got busy buying firewood, stacking it, setting up the water collector to catch the winter rains for household use and generally winterizing the house. I felt a little anxious as I prepared for spending another winter alone but at the same time, I was looking forward to the wild sounds of the stormy winter nights.

For Shannon, the wheels of justice were turning slowly. He was still in jail, and although it had been a year and a half since his arrest, he still hadn't gone to trial. At the end of January, I got a call from his attorney. "The psychiatrists have finally agreed that Shannon does meet the criteria for an NGRI plea. Shannon doesn't want to plead NGRI now but I think it's helped us anyway because now the DA has agreed to a deal. Shannon will plead guilty to a lesser charge. He's already done the time. The Prosecutor is asking for ten years on probation with certain stipulations, like he has to take medication, but we're going to court on February 11th, and I think that Shannon is going to be released on that day. You should be here to take him home."

Just a few days before my birthday, Dan and I drove up to Washington to go to court with Shannon, and after a brief review of the records, he was released into my custody. It had been a year and a half now since he had been out of doors, and his face was pasty white and drawn. There were dark circles under his eyes, and he appeared to be malnourished. Shannon walked stiffly out to greet us, and he looked like someone who suffered from mental illness, but he smiled happily as the guard handed him over to me. I threw my arms around his thin, bent shoulders. I was so relieved to have him back and all my mother's instinct cried out to protect him. We took him to a hotel where he took a long, hot bath, and he put on the new clothes that we had brought for him. Then we took him out for a steak dinner. He loved steak, and he looked like he could use the iron and the protein. We were calm and matter of fact as we talked about his jail experiences, about court, and about going home, but inside I was rejoicing. It was good to be with him. He seemed very fragile, but he was thinking clearly and the fact that we were holding a normal conversation seemed almost too good to be true. The next day, we drove all day through snow flurries arriving at the house late in the evening just before the storm broke. After making a fire in the wood stove and putting on some soft music, I made something light for us all to eat. We were safe and sheltered from the storm, and Shannon was home.

Over the next year, I watched with satisfaction as Shannon grew stronger, healthier, and more relaxed. There were times when he seemed like a perfectly normal young man. The clear, blue-eyed, smiling gaze of Shannon when he was feeling well was a treasure beyond compare, and at those times I was as happy as I could be. He took his medication daily and stayed away from recreational street drugs, and he saw a psychologist on a regular basis. He spoke with her about issues that he couldn't talk with anyone else about. After a while, he was able to take on small responsibilities, and eventually he started taking a few classes at the local Junior College again. There were still a lot of crazy, confusing things going on in his mind at times that tortured him and motivation was still a huge problem. There were times when he would stop taking his medication for a few days and the only indication would be the wild stare that would start to creep back into his eyes as he strained to follow the mysterious dialog of his voices. I had to be vigilant for those ominous signs and catch him before he fell too far. He told me that it was often a struggle just to make it through the day. Shannon had his good days and his bad days. He wasn't going to live a completely full and independent life, but he was finding small pleasures in day-to-day activities, and he was learning to live with his illness. The other day, we were having a conversation. Shannon was telling me about how 'messed up' his brain had been. "It seems like you're doing really well now but it must still be hard on you," I said, feeling love and compassion for how his young life had been ravaged by his illness.

"You don't even know," he said to me, and I realized that there was a whole dimension of hell that he personally experienced, that others had no idea of. Still, with that said, Shannon was doing better than I had dared to hope for, and I still held out hope that things would continue to improve. Maybe, some day, he would even be able to live independently and realize that vision of a loving family that he so much wanted.

Recently, I found a homemade greeting card that had on it a quote from Vincent Van Gogh. It read, "Even though I'm often in a mess, inside me there's still a calm, clear, harmony of music." I had read somewhere that we could neither escape nor ignore conditions but that the cessation of suffering meant that we should all do our best to create better conditions from moment to moment. It was a practical approach to the concept that Buddha had talked so much about and I felt that, to some extent, my life was actually an example of the success of that approach. In the day-to-day struggle to make things better, I had found a large measure of peace and happiness in my own life, and I felt that those benefits had spilled over enough to touch those in my life that I have loved and that are vulnerable. I do believe that in spite of all the pain and suffering in the world, the essence of the universe is a bright and loving vibration. A patient of mine recently said that he was amazed by how even the most brutal and painful situations for him still held a fathomless beauty that could be seen in the natural rhythms, the ebb and flow of life, when he was open enough to tune into it. Through the years, in the quest for harmony, my experiences with all of the heartache and the mental illness in my family, with medicine, spirituality, nature, and even travel have lead me to this conclusion: Stay the course, do our best to make each moment better. But even though I have learned, over the years, that promoting harmony and balance in one's life requires hard work, dedication, and vigilance, I still like to imagine that, to quote Alan Watts, "The inmost and ultimate self of us all is dancing on nothing and having a ball."

Addendum: AANP SmartBrief (American Academy of Nurse Practitioners)
Researchers found that 20% of American adults, equivalent to more than 45 million individuals, suffered from mental illness in 2009.

Resources
www.nami.org
www.schizophrenia.com
www.psychlaws.org
E. Fuller Torrey, M.D. *Surviving Schizophrenia: A Manual for Families, Consumers and Provider,* 4th edition. New York: Harper Collins Books, 2001.

9 781528 926904